FREE RIDER

FREE RIDER

How a Bay Street Whiz Kid Stole and Spent $20 Million

JOHN LAWRENCE REYNOLDS

McArthur & Company

Toronto

Published in Canada in 2001 by
McArthur & Company
322 King Street West, Suite 402
Toronto, ON M5V 1J2

National Library of Canada Cataloguing in Publication Data

Reynolds, John Lawrence
Free rider : how a Bay Street Whiz kid stole and spent $20 million

ISBN 1-55278-235-2

1. Holoday, Michael 2. Securities fraud—Canada.
3. Stockbrokers—Canada—Biography. I. Title.

HV6248.H64R49 2001   364.16'8'092 C2001-901665-4

Design & Composition: *Mad Dog Design*
Cover & f/x: *Mad Dog Design*
Printed in Canada by *Transcontinental Printing Inc.*

The publisher would like to acknowledge the financial support of
the Government of Canada through the Book Publishing Industry
Development Program (BPIDP) and the Canada Council for our publishing
activities. The publisher further wishes to acknowledge the financial
support of the Ontario Arts Council for our publishing program.

10 9 8 7 6 5 4 3 2 1

For Kylie Wolfenden

CONTENTS

ACKNOWLEDGEMENTS

Tracing the story of Michael Holoday and all of its consequences required more than five years' work and the assistance of dozens of people. Among the most valuable were Toronto fraud squad detectives Gary Logan and Jeffrey Thompson. Both men brought professionalism and dedication to their work in equally large measures. In a similar fashion, Crown Attorneys Brian McNeely and Greg Tweney afforded me access to important documents while maintaining the sanctity of the court. The energy and attitudes of all four are reassuring to anyone who might question our law enforcement and justice systems.

Doug Cunningham provided key insights into the internal operations of the brokerage industry while Brad Doney contributed his important point of view on the same topic. Paul McLaughlin of Lindquist Avey was helpful on the forensic accounting side. Jack Geller of the Ontario Securities Commission and Greg Clark of the Investment Dealers Association were more than generous with their time and observations. Steve Kee and Tom Atkinson of the Toronto Stock Exchange provided their perspective. I am also indebted to lawyers Neil Gross, Jeffrey Hoffman, and David Kent for their assistance. Deborah Thompson and Paul Palango were considerate of my queries, and Kevin Bousquet knows how important his contribution was, in ways that must remain unspecified.

Katherine Macklem of the *National Post,* John Lancaster of CFTO-TV, and especially Tony Van Alphan of the *Toronto Star* provided valued support. Doug Bunker permitted me to interrupt his busy schedule for photographs. Without losing either his charm or temper, Albert Robinson spoke with candour about his experience. Tanya Sargent deserves special mention; I wish her only good luck and success in her life.

Most of Michael Holoday's clients understood the nature of this book and the important message it strives to deliver. Those who were especially helpful and supportive include Gary Davidson, Ted Gittings, Roger and Debbie Gordon, Anthony Honeywood, Ray Kundinger, Paul Legere, Mona O'Hearn, Roy O'Hearn, Helen Rentis, Brian Rocks, and Kurt Schleith. Ervin Schleith helped in more ways than he may know, as did Maureen Conn. My special thanks as well to Jacques Soucie, George Gunn, Ronald Holoday, and David Walters.

The opportunity to follow the criminal trial proceedings was much enhanced by the kindnesses (and in some cases indulgence) of court staff Karen Roche, Holly Tang, Mila Morales, and Gabreal Weldemikaeal, and especially Madam Justice Patricia German, whose concern and understanding were deeply appreciated. Once again, thanks to them all.

Kim McArthur again proved that she is the most passionate publisher in the business, and Catherine Marjoribanks demonstrated her celebrated professionalism as an editor. I am grateful to both.

Finally, the usual inadequate thanks to my agents, Jan Whitford and Jackie Kaiser; and to my wife Judy Reynolds who, in addition to researching and recording thousands of facts and documents, performed her customary duties of prodding, cajoling, encouraging, and laughing when each was needed most.

John Lawrence Reynolds
August 15, 2001

ONE

There is no calamity greater than lavish desires.
There is no greater guilt than discontentment.
And there is no greater disaster than greed.
— THE WAY OF LAO-TZU

At 2:00 p.m. on July 11, 1994, a young man stepped off the elevator at 181 University Avenue in Toronto and shuffled to Suite 1204. He wore a bespoke double-breasted suit by Armani, Italian-made tasselled loafers, a perfectly knotted silk tie, and an Egyptian cotton, French-cuffed shirt that was damp with perspiration.

He paused for a moment at the door of Suite 1204, whose neat lettering identified the tenant as Fahnestock Viner Holdings Incorporated. Investors and stock market observers familiar with Fahnestock Viner might have expected a hubbub of activity behind that door, perhaps a maelstrom of meetings and conferences, or at least a hierarchy of staff working at banks of computer monitors. Fahnestock Viner controlled over 80 brokerage offices in the US, and more in Brazil and Argentina. The firm, listed on the Toronto Stock Exchange, was seeking a similar listing on the New York Stock Exchange, and it boasted total assets of over US$600 million. Not bad for a company that began life in 1933 as Sheep Creek Gold Mines Limited.

In reality, the tiny office area behind the windowless door of Suite 1204 was the workplace of just one man and two women, and the perspiring young man dreaded what he was about to reveal to them. The man, whose reaction he feared most, was an avuncular 84-year-old former allergist who had abandoned an exceptional medical career in mid-life to become a real estate developer. His name was Kenneth "Doc" Roberts, and he was among the wealthiest men in Canada. At an age when most men were content to reminisce about the past and clip their bond coupons, Doc Roberts was directing the operations of international investment firms generating annual revenues exceeding $200 million in US funds.

The prominent exception to Doc Roberts' legendary insight and investment skills was his association with the nervous young man who lingered outside the office that July afternoon, a man who, for almost three years, had played the dual role of surrogate son and investment advisor to Doc Roberts. His name was Michael Holoday.

Drawing upon an eroding reservoir of determination, Holoday finally turned the doorknob to Suite 1204 and entered. He nodded to the secretary as he passed and walked into the inner office shared by Doc Roberts and his daughter Elaine.

Elaine Roberts, a plain-spoken woman of 42, looked up at Holoday and said, "This is a surprise."

Michael Holoday usually visited the Fahnestock Viner offices at noon to invite Doc Roberts to lunch, walking from his office at First Marathon Securities. His unexpected arrival in mid-afternoon was unusual. Besides, Doc and Elaine Roberts had already heard from Holoday earlier that day, when he called to chat at mid-morning, boasting of the commissions he had earned so far that month.

He would be receiving about $200,000 for July, he had told Elaine Roberts, down from his normal monthly commissions of about $500,000. Mind you, he had expenses to cover out of that, including rent on his large corner suite in the First Marathon facility, plus personal staff salaries and the usual niggling things. But six million a year wasn't a bad gross annual income for a guy who, upon arriving in Toronto from a small BC lumber town a few years earlier, had walked up and down Bay Street practically begging an investment firm to take him on as a trainee, a gopher, a floor sweeper, anything. Now Holoday's July commissions were nudging $200,000, and it wasn't even the middle of the month yet. But what else would you expect from a guy who was called a Whiz Kid, a Future Genius, and The Brightest Trader on Bay Street by most of his clients and many of his colleagues? Michael Holoday was successful. All his clients were growing wealthy. Life was good. Finishing his telephone chat, Holoday had hung up without saying anything about dropping in after lunch.

Now here he was, closing the door behind him and taking off his jacket, his face pale and the armpits of his shirt soaked. Doc Roberts looked up from his desk next to Elaine's and smiled at Holoday. But the older man's smile vanished at the sight of the young man's obvious distress.

Holoday couldn't stop pacing. He walked in one direction across the enclosed office area, and then turned and walked in the other direction, his mouth moving as though he were speaking, or trying to, while Doc and Elaine Roberts watched in silence. Then he collapsed in a chair, placed his head in his hands and burst into tears. He wanted it to end, he said. He couldn't stand the pressure. He just couldn't take it anymore.

Couldn't take what? The pressure of being a commodities trader? The stress of earning millions of dollars a year in commissions to maintain his lifestyle? Kenneth and Elaine Roberts were confused. Was Holoday having a nervous breakdown? If so, why was he choosing their offices to have it?

"I made a terrible, terrible mistake," Holoday said. "It's

gone. It's all gone." He was out of control, wrapping himself in his arms, his body shaking in spasms of sobs.

What, Elaine and Doc Roberts wanted to know, was "it"? What was gone?

The money. Their money. It was gone, vanished. Ten, twelve, thirteen million dollars in US funds, whatever. Holoday didn't have it. He had none of it. He had never invested it for them. It wasn't at Eastbridge or Southbridge, it wasn't in New York or in the Cayman Islands. It wasn't in the trades; it wasn't anywhere. It was just gone.

Doc Roberts and his daughter were stunned into silence. This wasn't just a bond trader, some hustling-for-a-buck stockbroker, confessing to them. This was someone who had ingratiated himself into the Roberts family. He was a neighbour of theirs in three locations — here in Toronto on Forest Hill Road, at a summer cottage north of the city, and in the exclusive Sandy Lane area of Barbados. At Holoday's extravagant wedding reception less than three years earlier, he had introduced Doc Roberts to the guests as his mentor, his father figure, the man he admired more than anyone else in the world. He had even begun to win over Elaine Roberts, who hadn't liked Michael Holoday at all, couldn't stand the sight of him, but conceded admiration for his investment skills when he began generating substantial profits for her and her father.

Elaine spoke first. "What happened to the money?" she said. "Be honest with us, Michael."

The story emerged between sobs. He had lied about investing their money. There had been no investments and no profits, as he had promised. There had been no pool of funds in the New York–based investment fund called Eastbridge, or its spin-off Southbridge, or its Canadian version Northbridge. Northbridge didn't exist. The entire two-year experience had been a sham. Holoday had used their money, millions upon millions of it, to cover his own trading losses. He was tired of it, tired of trying to keep all the balls in the air at once. He couldn't do it anymore. He wasn't sleeping, he wasn't eating, he couldn't take it another day.

There was more. Many of Holoday's clients, those he had tried to help, people he had entertained and socialized with, people he had befriended and tried to make wealthy, these same people were blackmailing him now. The ungrateful bastards were threatening that, unless Holoday repaid their trading losses out of his own pocket, they would spread evil stories about him, ruining his career and reputation. Even his in-laws were abandoning him, demanding answers and explanations he couldn't give. And he had been so good to them, so generous. He had tried to improve their lot in life, and now they were turning on him. What could he do? *What could he do?*

He continued for an hour, sobbing in despair one moment, promising to replace the Roberts' money the next, always protesting at the unfairness of it all, the ingratitude of people he tried to help, the back-stabbing of clients to whom he had been so generous. They were out to destroy him. They were mad, they were greedy, they were voracious. He had done so much for them, all of them, and they were turning on him like hyenas. And First Marathon, they made profits from all his trades, but they wouldn't help him. He was still earning commissions, though, and he was going to keep working until this was straightened out. Most of his earnings would go directly to the Roberts, he'd see to that.

He forced himself to calm down. This was not his nature, after all. The most commonly used adjective to describe Michael Holoday was "cool," and blubbering like a baby in front of his largest client was decidedly uncool.

He would make every effort to repay the Roberts, Holoday repeated. His voice grew steady. He became the composed, convincing Michael Holoday. He had assets to transfer and income to earn. He would make monthly remittances to them, paying back the millions over time. He would come out of this with his head held high. The Roberts would not rue the day they had first entrusted their money to him. They had his word on that.

Then, gathering himself together, he slipped back into his Armani jacket and left the office, closing the door behind him and leaving Kenneth and Elaine Roberts at their desks trying to fathom all they had heard, all the implications and the amazing revelations.

Michael Holoday returned to his suite of offices at First Marathon Securities, the one his wife Maureen had decorated to resemble that of the fictional Gordon Gecko in the movie *Wall Street,* and conducted business as usual for the rest of the afternoon. He smiled at his secretary, Tracy Ellis. He gave orders to his options trader, Chuck Oliver. He nodded to the senior vice-president of First Marathon Securities, David Wood, when they passed in the hall. He issued statements to clients, reassured them of the wealth they were accumulating, and basked in their gratitude.

In reality, the investment portfolios of many of Holoday's clients were as empty as Holoday's own, and had been for a year or more. But they did not know this. Nor would they for another three months.

T W O

In 1885, Donald Smith drove The Last Spike into the CPR mainline track at a riverside site named Craigellachie. That same year, 60 miles to the east, CPR management chose a settlement on the flatlands of the Columbia River as the location of a major railroad repair and maintenance facility. Applying a common practice for the time, CPR management named the settlement for Lord Revelstoke, a British banker who had advanced substantial funds to the railroad to maintain its liquidity at a critical point in its construction.[1] The railroad continues to rumble through the town today, its main line running parallel with, and two blocks north of, the community's main street.

With a population nudging 10,000, Revelstoke could be the quintessential Rocky Mountain town, except for a distinct absence of horses. This may be the West, but it is not ranch country. Pickup trucks and 4WD utility vehicles dominate the traffic, driven by men and women in faded denim and plaid cotton, while the music of Garth Brooks and Shania Twain pours from the vehicles' tape decks and radios. The melodies are heavy with fiddles and guitars, spinning tales of dingy bars and cheatin' spouses. The pre-

ferred vehicle is a Ford F-150 or a GMC Jimmy; the preferred uniform is a plaid woollen shirt and a faded pair of
Wranglers. In Revelstoke, Hugo Boss is as rare as Hondas.

Revelstoke must have been a fine place for a young,
active boy to grow up in the 1970s. The hunting and fishing were good year round, you could white-water raft in
the summer and ski the mountains in winter, and on
Saturday nights there was always a little hell to raise over
at McGregor's Pub. A boy could choose worse places to
grow up in than Revelstoke, and parents far worse than
Ronald and Mary Lou Holoday.

The Holodays returned from Vancouver one day in the
mid-1960s with two-month-old Michael Edward, born May
7, 1964, the first of four children to be adopted by the couple. Ronald Holoday operated the town's largest accountancy firm, providing a stable middle-class life for Michael,
and later his younger adopted brother, David, and two
adopted sisters, Terri and Iris. Prominent in the community, thanks to his accountancy business and his dedication to ice hockey, Ron Holoday also pursued a career in
politics, sitting on town council and running as the local
Liberal candidate in one federal election. Even into his
mid-50s, Ronald Holoday continued to play hockey on
organized teams, standing in goal where his bulldoglike
presence belied the stereotypical image of an accountant.
The Holoday home was as normal as any middle-class
Canadian's, and more comfortable and appealing than
many could strive for. "It was like living in Pleasantville,"
Michael Holoday would later recall.

Raised a Roman Catholic, young Michael played hockey in local rinks from September to April. He worked out
with weights, participated in track and field events, joined
pickup baseball teams, and drifted through puberty and
young adolescence with all the curiosity and discoveries of
a normal middle-class boyhood. When summer vacation

arrived, the local streams and rivers beckoned him and his friends to hike across grassy meadows, fishing poles over their shoulders and timothy grass in their mouths, Huck Finns all, while the railroad trains roared by on tracks that follow the river through nearby Eagle Pass to and from Vancouver.

The addition of three more adopted children to the Holoday family following Michael's arrival may have threatened the eldest boy's sense of security, but he seemed to take it in stride. The family was more comfortable than wealthy, but as Ronald Holoday, who managed money for several local Revelstoke citizens, often preached to his adopted children: "Don't overestimate the importance of money. Family, friends, neighbours and enjoying life — those are the things that really matter."[2]

Holoday's closest childhood buddy was Ervin Schleith, whose father owned Revelstoke's largest lumber mill. Holoday, Ervin recalled years later, "was just an average kid. A good student at school and a not-bad athlete, especially when it came to hockey."

The exception to this near-idyllic boyhood, the traumatic turning point in Michael Holoday's life as he later described it, occurred in late August 1975 when Holoday was 11 years old and deemed capable of caring for his younger brother David, age 5. Riding their bicycles, Michael was herding David along Orton Avenue to visit neighbours. The younger boy, eager and impetuous, suddenly broke from the path and steered his way through the intersection, deaf to his elder brother's warnings and unaware of a heavy truck approaching at high speed.

Michael froze a few feet away, little more than an arm's length really, as the truck, unable to stop or swerve, struck the boy and Michael watched open-mouthed as its heavy wheels and multiple axles, one by one, passed over his young brother's small body.

This was, as Ronald Holoday would remind his surviving son 22 years later, the worst thing that ever happened to him.

After the accident, Michael developed a nervous tick that persisted through his adolescence, and his parents, concerned that he needed help in overcoming the emotional trauma, arranged for him to see a psychiatrist. The two or three sessions Michael spent with the therapist appeared to have no effect. The Holodays decided that keeping their son busy and active might be the best treatment. They encouraged him to participate in sports, and Ronald Holoday, who was part owner of a local hotel, obtained work for his son first as a pool cleaner and later as a kitchen helper. He would be earning his own money, learning something about financial responsibility.

At Revelstoke Secondary School, Michael Holoday left few memories with the teaching staff beyond his painful efforts in public speaking class. "Giving a speech embarrassed him," one of his teachers recalled 15 years later. "When he sat down after speaking, he would be as red as a beet. He was very shy, and public speaking seemed painful to him. But he kept at it anyway." Otherwise, his profile was so low that no one noticed his name was misspelled on his graduation photo.

Completing high school, Holoday wasn't certain what he wanted to do. He knew only that he would not become an accountant like his father and, whatever profession he chose, he would not pursue it in Revelstoke.

A career as an architect appealed to him, because he had enjoyed drafting class in high school. The University of Victoria offered courses in architecture, and his application was accepted. Michael Holoday followed the rail line west through Eagle Pass to the coast and the mild, soft climate of the BC capital. But from the beginning, things did not go well. Later, Holoday suggested that he

lost enthusiasm for the idea of sitting at a drafting table
day after day, drawing straight lines and sketching build-
ings. His father had another theory. "In his first year at
U Vic," Ronald Holoday said later, "Michael tended to
major in female anatomy."[3]

Whatever the cause, Michael failed his first year at
university and changed his goal. He would return to U Vic,
this time to work on a straight BA, and then complete his
studies in Vancouver at UBC. His father suggested
Economics and Commerce, which sounded like a good way
to make money, more appealing and less strenuous than
architecture.

Having satisfied his hormonal urges at U Vic, Holoday
discovered a new inclination being fostered during his two
years at UBC Commerce.

"I'd always understood things like interest rates, even
in high school," he said years later.[4] "And I knew about the
stock market, through my father, I guess. Bonds appealed
to me more than stocks, because I appreciated the impact
of interest rates. Once I got to UBC, I didn't want to spend
a lot of time there. I just wanted to get out and make
money. I wasn't one of those guys who wanted to go to grad
school. I wanted to get my degree in Economics, then figure out a way to make money." UBC Commerce in the
mid-80s was an excellent place to learn how to do exactly
that.

Holoday studied with, among others, John Forbes
Helliwell, the head of the Economics Department and one
of the country's leading lecturers in macroeconomics.
During Holoday's two years at UBC, John Helliwell was
completing his work on an article titled "Supply-Side
Macroeconomics" to appear in the *Canadian Journal of
Economics,* and Holoday absorbed Helliwell's teachings
with fascination.

But it was another man, off campus, who provided the

student with something more practical than economic theory.

During Michael Holoday's final year at UBC, he joined the Economics Students' Association and represented the school at the Vancouver Board of Trade. He also joined the Association of International Students of Economics & Commerce, and was appointed an assistant campus recruiter for Price Waterhouse. All of this qualified Michael as the ideal candidate to organize career opportunity forums on campus. For one of these sessions, Holoday managed to entice Clark Gilmore of Pepperton Hughson Willoughby, a stockbrokerage on the west coast, to host a session. Gilmore connected with Michael in the manner that older, successful men often do with bright, ambitious men a generation or two behind them, and he eventually invited his young protégé to join him for lunch near the broker's offices in downtown Vancouver.

Holoday arrived at Clark Gilmore's office one afternoon to find the older man on the telephone. Gilmore waved him in, spoke a few unintelligible words into the receiver, and then hung up and smiled broadly at the UBC Commerce student.

"Just made three thousand dollars on that deal," he said.

"You sold some stock?" Michael asked.

The other man nodded and rose from his desk.

"How long were you holding it?" Michael asked, following the broker out of his office.

"About two minutes," Gilmore said.

Holoday stopped in his tracks. "You're not serious," he said.

"Of course I am," the broker replied. "Do the right deal and you don't have to wait months for the profits. Let's go." He punched the elevator button. "You like Chinese food?"[5]

During lunch that day, and over several lunches during the ensuing weeks, Holoday abandoned the world of his Revelstoke childhood, where work was rewarded on an hourly basis, and entered another. In this new world, value needn't be enhanced and rewarded by labour at all — at least not the kind of labour a kid from Revelstoke might understand.

Professor Helliwell's Macroeconomics had opened Holoday's eyes to the concept of risk and reward through the application of labour and assets, moving each to where it was most needed and thus most valued. But his discussions with Clark Gilmore went far beyond that.

Holoday grasped the concept that it wasn't necessary to set a long-term horizon in pursuit of impressive returns. Be in the right place at the right time with the right idea, show you have more balls than the other guy, and the rewards could be instantaneous. With the right tools and the right opportunities, you could double your money in time frames measured not by months or years but by keystrokes on a computer.

Soon after that initial lunch, Holoday knew what he wanted to do. "Hire me," he practically begged Clark Gilmore, but the older man shook his head and smiled. "No room here," he said. "Besides, if your ambition is that big, you shouldn't stay in Vancouver anyway. You should go to Toronto. That's where the big money is made in this business."

Holoday took the advice. As he tells it, he wrote a thesis on RRSP life-cycle savings behaviour and the impact of raising contribution levels over time, and the research led to studies of data and interest rate analysis, where he immersed himself in rate cycles, and the complexity of 30-year curves.

"I understood the volatility of rates inside that curve," he recalled later.[6] "On the trading side, the markets are all about reaction to a change in the underlying index or commodity. The index can be bonds or stocks, the commodity could be coffee, beans, anything at all. I understood this stuff, and I also learned I had a natural sales talent. The key is just being a likable person, just being yourself. I've never been intimidated by anybody. I can talk to anybody I want. I don't use a sales approach. I just be myself."

It was around this time when, his eyes focused on an economics text in the UBC library one afternoon, he heard a voice softly call his name. "Mike?" the young man standing next to him almost whispered. "Mike Holoday?" Holoday looked up to see his high school buddy Ervin Schleith grinning down at him.

Ervin and Michael had played hockey together and attended the same school until Grade 11. In that year, Ervin's father Karl sold the family sawmill for a substantial sum and fulfilled his dream of becoming a gentleman farmer. With proceeds from the sale, the Schleith family headed west through Eagle Pass to Kelowna, where Karl purchased an idyllic Tudor-style farmhouse and apple orchard set in the hills above the town, the waters of Okanagan Lake shimmering in the distance.

The two school chums hadn't seen each other in years. Ervin, still living in Kelowna and visiting a UBC friend, remained determined to become a commercial airline pilot, and they held a brief *sotto voce* conversation there in the study room. Ervin suggested they go for a coffee or a beer, but Michael said he couldn't spare the time.

"He had changed by then," Ervin Schleith said. "He had become very focused on his schooling, his business training, and he was very goal-oriented, wanting to work very hard and get to be number one. That's what he said. He was going to be Number One, which I took to mean very wealthy and successful. That's what he told me. 'I'm planning to get wealthy and successful,' and I had the feeling nothing was going to stop him."[7]

On the day of his class graduation, Michael called his

father from a pay telephone in the Hotel Vancouver and asked for a loan of $750 to cover his airfare to Toronto. When the money arrived by wire, Michael hopped the first jet headed east.

In Toronto, Holoday began literally knocking on doors along Bay Street, walking in like Willie Loman with nothing but a smile and a shoeshine. Wood Gundy was sufficiently impressed to offer the new grad a position as a junior researcher, but UBC wasn't entirely co-operative in granting his degree. During his final year at university, Michael had devoted so much time to studying interest rate curves and their macroeconomic impact that he failed to complete his French studies. No second-language marks, no degree, said UBC. "Come back when you've got your degree," Wood Gundy advised him.

Michael Holoday returned home to complete his studies and qualify for the sheepskin that, in turn, would open the doors at Wood Gundy. But the firm wasn't ready for him when September rolled around; acquisition talks had begun with one of the banks (according to Holoday), and Wood Gundy asked him to delay the start of his employment. For more than a month, Michael remained in Revelstoke, playing golf with his father, reading the *Financial Post* and *Report On Business,* and watching the markets back east.

It was painful, this waiting around. People were making big money on the street in Toronto. Some were turning multi-thousand-dollar profits in mere minutes, just like Clark Gilmore. What on earth was he doing in Revelstoke, watching the trains rumble by?

The hell with it. In early October, 1987, Michael borrowed more money from his father and caught another flight east to Toronto. He couldn't wait around for Wood Gundy to make up its mind. He was here, he was ready, and he was ambitious. Who wanted him?

Midland Doherty did. They offered the new grad an entry-level position in the accounting department, paying $18,000 a year. He was instructed to "start work next Monday."

"Next Monday" was October 19, 1987. On the day Michael Holoday began his career as a major force in the Canadian securities industry, prices on the Toronto Stock Exchange suffered their biggest single-day loss in history.

THREE

Some day I want to be rich.
Some people get so rich they lose all respect for humanity.
That's how rich I want to be.
— RITA RUDNER

If success depends as much on good timing as hard work, Michael Holoday's date of entry into the fast-paced world of investment could not have been more fortuitous. The panic of that day, and the events that unfolded as the aftershocks died away, shaped Holoday's view in a manner that an introduction in more relaxing times could never have achieved.

All through October 19, 1987, or "Black Monday" as it became known, the twin engines of Greed and Fear that drive Bay Street roared while investors and their advisors watched open-mouthed. During introductions to other employees in Midland Doherty's "back room" where the routine paperwork was conducted, Holoday saw panic on the faces of many who watched the TSE sink hundreds of points in a matter of hours.

Holoday also noticed that a number of detached professionals carried out the trades, soothed their clients' fear, crunched numbers on their calculators, and took advantage of investment bargains. "It's going to be all right," they would say. "Everything's going to be fine." The more cynical among them might even have pointed out that, among the many things that had changed since 1929, central air-conditioning meant that skyscraper windows no longer opened. "They'll have to jump in front of subway trains."

The cool traders, Holoday noted, were proved correct. What's more, they didn't just sit back and wait for the market to recover. They took action. Michael Holoday liked that. He preferred aloofness to emotion. Stay cool. Don't panic. Lie if you have to. Never let them see you sweat.

Holoday's timing proved exquisite in other ways. During the late 1980s, Midland Doherty began to shrug off its old-school cloak, its low-key method of building business through personal and family relationships, and it launched an aggressive expansion program. By mid-1988, it had become the largest independent brokerage in Canada as a result of hiring ambitious neophytes like Michael Holoday and via the more immediate method of acquiring its competitors. Soon after Holoday joined the brokerage, Midland Doherty purchased the remains of Osler Inc., a failed Toronto brokerage firm, adding 60 qualified securities brokers to the roster and raising the total number of its retail salespeople to 767.[1]

Through 1988, Midland continued to pursue growth, both internally and via other acquisitions. By September of that year, Davidson Partners Ltd., a Toronto-based brokerage firm whose Calgary office was accused of providing many clients with disastrous investment advice, became part of Midland, adding more salespeople and more investor files to the mix. One of the transplanted Davidson brokers was a man with a celebrated last name in Canada: Jack Labatt.[2]

Midland's motivation for continued growth was based on sound business principles and foresight, not just growth for its own sake. In many ways, Midland management saw expansion as a keystone of its strategy to remain independent amid a topsy-turvy environment driven by — of all people — Canada's chartered banks.

Until the last quarter of the twentieth century, the liquidable assets of most Canadians were firmly rooted in safe, secure, and low-yielding bank deposits and life insurance. Traditional wisdom says this was the natural legacy of the Scots highlanders who had established the country's business culture. Shrewd, suspicious, frugal, and conservative, the Scots defined much of Canadian fiscal philosophy — especially the nation's banking system — for generations.

Added to the conservative Scots-based banking habits was the psychological impact of residing in a northern climate. Even during the soft sweet days of a Canadian spring and the warm richness of summer, Canadians know in their hearts that winter is biding its time somewhere beyond Baffin Island. The awareness lends a sober reality to Canadian life, one that many in southern temperate zones and tropical climates find either dull or amusing. Canadians were once the most-insured people in the Western Hemisphere, building their life insurance companies into colossal entities that exercised enormous financial clout and demonstrated unquestioned stability. They were among the most savings-conscious people, as well. Generations of young Canadians, when handed a dime by a relative, were advised to "put it in the bank" immediately, lest the temptation to exchange it for candy or a toy became overwhelming.

Even during the mid-1990s, when North American stock markets were generating 30 percent annual yields in the face of virtually zero percent inflation, Canadians remained conservative. At the beginning of 1998, 53 percent of investible assets owned by Canadian households were in the form of cash deposits, even though the money was earning interest at a rate so slow — typically 2.5 to 4 percent annually — it almost seemed insulting. In comparison, more than half the value of all US household investments were in equity stocks and only 28 percent in bank deposits.[3]

The majority of Canadians once took great comfort in examining their bank savings passbook and watching the balance build, however slowly, from month to month. For much of the twentieth century, life insurance salesmen were actually welcomed into Canadian homes, where they brandished investment growth charts like proud grand-parents displaying their latest grandchild, earning nods of approval and signatures at the bottom of long-term insur-ance contracts. "Money in the bank" became synonymous with "a sure thing," and most Canadians chose the reality of liquid cash in a bank over the illusion of quick profits and future promises from stock and bond markets.

But on the cusp of the 1990s, things began to change, and the nation's financial attitude underwent a quiet rev-olution. The impact of economic globalization, the ability to make instantaneous transfers of money and securities via computer linkages, the emergence of financial com-mentators as media celebrities, the growing popularity of self-directed RRSPs, and the mass media reportage of financial and investment events all fed on each other. Canadians awoke to discover that finance and investment were not only a large part of North American middle-class culture — in many ways they *defined* much of the culture.

Other factors intervened. After decades of constantly expanding social programs from all levels of government, the cradle-to-grave concept began to pall for Canadians. When it came to dancing through fiscal matters, federal and provincial governments were seen to have two left feet, and both were flat. During the Reagan administra-tion Canadians watched in envy as, across the border in the US, vast personal wealth began to accumulate, and

millionaires become as common as cocker spaniels. Under
the guidance of a president who favoured jellybeans over
social programs, Americans grew more wealthy and financially adventurous while Canadians stared at a deepening
sinkhole of personal and public debt.

Canadians began to change from prudent savers to
risk-taking investors. Massive government deficits helped
propel them in that direction, when accountants, political
columnists, and outraged editorialists began declaring the
Canada Pension Plan a hoax and a sham. They pointed
out that money collected by the federal government to generate pension income was either being spent to buy votes,
or lent to the provinces at laughably low rates of interest
— and who knew if the provinces would ever pay it back?

Registered Retirement Savings Plans promised potential salvation, but for years the contributions and investment options were severely limited. Something else had to
be done, especially with the arrival of mid-1980s' prosper-
ity when incomes rose, property values skyrocketed, Greed
Was Good and Poverty Sucked. It was a fine time to be
employed, and a fine time to set higher financial goals.

Depressed interest rates in the early 1990s produced
single-digit annual earnings from bank accounts and
insurance policies, which lost whatever appeal they still
held for many people who realized they could make money
faster by investing, not saving. With time and luck, you
could even achieve financial independence and not give a
fig for government deficits, or worry about an anemic
Canada Pension Plan.

The chartered banks were determined to change the
face and nature of the country's investment activities.
Their program was two-pronged. First, the banks
launched their own mutual fund families, expanding their
retail investment opportunities beyond the safe and familiar world of savings accounts and GICs. Next, the banks

began acquiring the country's most highly respected brokerage firms one by one, effectively assuming control of
the RRSPs of millions of Canadians, and eventually leaving Midland as the only nationally located and independent brokerage in the business.

The combination of Canadian tradition and financial
clout created when Royal Bank absorbed Dominion
Securities, for example, proved immense. Small-town
Canada might consider Bay Street brokers as shysters and
stock promoters, shell-game exponents in three-piece
suits, but the banks were different. They held your hand,
and best of all they promised that they — and your money
— would always be there when you needed them. Soon
Canadians, even those with only a few thousand dollars in
their RRSP portfolios, were being wooed by investment
advisors from bank-owned brokerage firms, the introduction often made by the customer's branch manager. Every
Royal Bank customer with sufficient funds sheltered for
his or her retirement was connected with an RBC
Dominion Securities salesperson; every CIBC account
holder was introduced to a Wood Gundy representative,
and so on down the line.

Midland Doherty management wanted no part of
Canada's chartered banks. They wanted independence,
not paternalism, and to achieve it they had to grow as
large as the rest of the sharks in the pond. They fostered
a more aggressive resolve to work harder, be smarter, and
make money faster than the bank-backed competition.
They had no choice. Each of the five major banks had millions of prospects on their customer lists available to be
swept up by the banks' brokerage operations, leaving independents like Midland Doherty to snag clients as best they
could. The difference was like farming and fishing.
Farmers harvested their crops and herded their livestock
right in their own backyard; fishermen had to hook their

catch, one by one. Midland and First Marathon had to fish for prospects, which fostered a proactive approach among the independents.[4]

Michael Holoday, toiling in the company's back office, liked that attitude at Midland. As soon as he qualified, Holoday registered for the securities course leading to a broker's licence, permitting him to deal with clients and leave the dull routine of the back office behind.

An $18,000 salary doesn't carry a young man far in Toronto, and it was especially limiting for a bright, ambitious guy who couldn't wait to show Bay Street how fast and how far the quiet kid from Revelstoke could go.

Michael Holoday's first apartment was conveniently located at Gloucester and Church Streets, permitting him to walk the few blocks back and forth to work each day. But elbowing his way through the ranks of hookers and street people who congregated in the area became too much to bear for a soon-to-be-recognized investment genius, and he moved to a cheap basement apartment in suburban Scarborough.

In some ways, this location irked him even more. Now he had to commute to his office by TTC subway, jostled by students and housewives on his way from the flatlands of the eastern Toronto suburb to Bay Street each morning, and back again at night. He couldn't fail to notice that many Midland Doherty hotshots appeared not even to know where a subway stop could be found, let alone ride the trains each day. They wore tailored clothes from Holt Renfrew and Harry Rosen, paid for lunches with platinum American Express cards, and travelled back and forth from their condos on Queens Quay or their Tudor homes in Forest Hill in Porsches, Mercedes-Benzes and BMWs.

For a year and a half, Holoday watched them with envy. Normally impatient, he forced himself to relax and wait. He studied hard, he kept notes, he observed those around him who wore the aura of success like an alpaca topcoat, and he took small steps toward his goal of joining them.

First, the daily subway ride had to go. When his salary rose high enough to afford it, Holoday purchased a Chevrolet Camaro, a gauche car to other brokers, a joke to drivers of Porsche Carreras and BMWs, but he wasn't ready to join them yet so it didn't matter. The car gave him freedom, it provided a means of transportation when dating the few women he associated with during those months in the wilderness, and it enabled him to cruise through better neighbourhoods on weekends, choosing the home he would live in someday. Best of all, it took him off the subway and away from the crowds.

Following his training period, Holoday was appointed cash clerk, a standard back-office position for rookies in the brokerage business. The work was dull and repetitive, devoid of the glamour and big bucks enjoyed by traders and licensed brokers. But the work revealed two important elements of the brokerage business to Holoday. One was the enormous volume of money that flowed almost unencumbered through the firm between brokers and wealthy, active investors. The other was the mechanism of making transfers between clients, advisors, traders, and the brokerage itself. Anyone who wanted to track the routes of money as it moved between various destinations needed just a few days as a cash clerk to grasp the picture. And anyone searching for a weakness in the system, for a method of circumventing the traditional methods of safeguarding clients' money, would learn almost all they needed to know.

Holoday made few friends at Midland, and he rarely participated in organized social events during these early months. Instead, he bided his time and studied hard, alone in his suburban apartment like a recluse or a banished child. When he won his securities licence and joined Midland's sales force in April 1989, it was as though he stepped directly from the subway platform onto an express train that barely slowed before hauling him aboard.

For Christmas that year, Michael returned to Revelstoke to visit his family. Borrowing his father's car, he drove west to Kelowna to shop for gifts, and as he emerged from a downtown shop he heard a familiar voice call his name. It was Ervin Schleith, the high school buddy whom he had last seen in the UBC library. Schleith, in the middle of obtaining his multi-engine commercial pilot's rating at a flight training facility in Florida, had also returned home for Christmas. Unlike at their previous chance meeting, Holoday now had time to spare for his friend, so they went for a beer and Ervin invited him to a New Year's Eve party. Michael agreed. But on arrival, instead of celebrating the advent of the 1990s, Holoday seemed more intent on discussing his friend's investments.

"I told him I had about fifteen thousand dollars invested with a local broker," Schleith recalled several years later. "They were looking after me all right, I thought, but Michael started convincing me to give him my money to invest. His argument was, 'Your money needs to be in Toronto where the action is, not in Kelowna.' I trusted him one hundred percent, so I transferred everything to him."[5]

Michael, for his part, promised his old friend that he would invest the money wisely.

Each working day, Holoday sat crowded among other small-volume brokers in the "bullpen" in the centre of Midland's 32nd floor of Scotia Plaza, their small desks shoved against low dividers. The also-ran brokers envied the heavy hitters, large-volume brokers who occupied private offices on the perimeter of the floor, with larger desks, potted plants, picture windows, and, most valued of all, privacy.

Residents of the bullpen depended on sales assistants to handle much of their routine paperwork, with three or four lower-level brokers sharing one often-harried assistant. Holoday was one of four brokers relying on the administrative support of Tanya Sargent, an engaging and attractive young woman from Saint John, New Brunswick. Tanya's formal education was in travel and tourism, but when that industry failed to prove rewarding, she was pleased to find herself working in Toronto's investment industry. She was also, to some degree, smitten by the apparent polished confidence of Mike Holoday. Holoday reciprocated. He bought her flowers on her birthday and from time to time escorted her to lunch at trendy downtown restaurants.

"Mike knew what he wanted from the very beginning," Tanya Sargent recalled. "He wanted to be rich, he exuded confidence and ambition, and he dressed just a little sharper than the other brokers."

In 1990, Midland Doherty merged with Walwyn Stodgell in a move that stunned many Bay Street observers. It seemed like a marriage of opposites. Midland had been an old-school kind of investment house, where wearing a patterned shirt suggested an unhealthy, rebellious nature. Midland clients tended to introduce their children to their financial advisors, cautioning their offspring to pay attention to the wisdom of the Midland investment expert. Walwyn Stodgell, in contrast, was loose and aggressive, more attuned to the wilder dreams of younger boomers than the careful conservatism of old money. The merger was like Glen Miller sitting in with Elvis Presley, like Johnny Carson eloping with Madonna.[6] Michael Holoday might have been a Midland man, but he preferred the Walwyn technique, the get-it-while-you-can philosophy, the if-you-got-it-flaunt-it lifestyle.

Clark Gilmore had opened Holoday's eyes to the possibility of making large sums of money in short periods of time, but during his early years at Midland a man named Tim Miller served as Holoday's role model, a breathing, back-slapping paragon of the life that Holoday wanted to lead.

Barely 40 years old in 1989, Timothy I. Miller was already a Bay Street legend. President of Midland Walwyn Capital Inc., Miller was audacious, flamboyant, and rich. His sales commissions alone were rumoured to have exceeded a million dollars annually for several years, and he supplemented this income with a large executive salary and earnings from personal investments. He was the classic Walwyn Stodgell man, dropped into the Old Boy's Club atmosphere of Midland Doherty and determined to shake up the conservative way of doing things.

Miller lived in a mansion bordering the Rosedale Golf Club and drove a fire-engine red Porsche with customized licence plates that read WALWYN. At six-feet six-inches and two hundred and sixty pounds, Miller's physical presence added to his larger-than-life image.

"He was the perfect symbol of the nineteen-eighties," one colleague described Miller. "He was a deal-maker who lived on the edge and packed a lot into his years."[7]

The more Michael Holoday watched and learned about Tim Miller, the more alike they seemed to be in Michael's mind. And, as time proved, the more alike they became in every way but one.

Orphaned at an early age, Tim Miller had proved a lacklustre student with no hint of the powerhouse he might become, until he earned his Bachelor of Commerce degree from St. Mary's University and, at age 23, joined Wood Gundy as a retail sales trainee. Within four years, Miller rose to become the firm's top salesman, a position he continued to hold through his appointment as vice-president and executive director of the firm.

By 1983, Miller had grown bored with the straitlaced brokerage business, and he managed to persuade Wood Gundy management to launch an outrageous experiment, at odds with the firm's personality. Miller's pitch was this: members of his generation were entering their high-income years and growing aware of the need for financial planning. These investors couldn't relate to the sombre, three-piece-suit mentality of traditional stockbrokers — especially Wood Gundy's. They were, after all, kids of the rock-and-roll generation whose record collections were built around the Beatles and Stones, not Sinatra or Mozart. They wanted action and rhythm, a sharp edge to their style, and an attitude.

As convincing with Wood Gundy management as with his clients, Miller was awarded the entire 42nd floor of the Toronto-Dominion Centre, where he launched an experimental boutique operation dealing in stocks and bonds, designed to snare high net-worth clients in the under-40 generation. Given the go-ahead, Miller quickly selected the most talented of Wood Gundy's brokers from among the firm's ranks, inviting them to join him in the new venture. Few could refuse.

Everything about Miller's creation, from its name — *42nd Street* — to its furnishings, catered to yuppies. Instead of Canadian landscape prints and dark oak furniture, visitors to 42nd Street offices were greeted with bubble-gum machines, childhood photographs of staff members, and live cockatoos. Wood Gundy top management were aghast, until they saw the performance figures. Miller's 42nd Street creation was not only the brashest marketing strategy in the history of Canada's investment industry, but also among the most successful. The firm's client roster grew and its profits rose, all a direct result of Miller's foresight and style.

Four years later, Miller grew bored once again and, taking the core of the boutique firm's sales staff with him, he fled to Walwyn Stodgell Cochrane Murray Ltd. Recently acquired by Financial Trustco Capital Ltd., Walwyn promised to be the ideal vehicle for Miller's next fireworks display of sales and marketing genius.

The same Black Monday that welcomed Holoday to Bay Street had a sobering effect on Miller's disposition. He began to express serious concern for people, both those working beneath him in the hotbed of stocks and bonds, and those who lacked the skills and opportunity he and his family enjoyed. "I'm trying to pay a lot of attention to people," he told the *Globe and Mail*'s *Report On Business,* referring directly to the effects of the 1987 crash. "I've seen emotional stress before."[8]

Miller had nothing to prove when it came to his social conscience. While at Wood Gundy, he helped raise hundreds of thousands of dollars for the Canadian Special Olympics, and then went on to pioneer *The Children's Miracle* which, once each year, diverted one full day's commissions earned by Wood Gundy sales staff to charity. Within seven years of its launch, *The Children's Miracle* had generated over $4 million in contributions. Miller had such charisma, and was so committed to assisting others, that he even managed to raise $13,000 for the Special Olympics with a single haircut, when he auctioned off his long golden locks at a charity event.

No one on the Street during the late 1980s could miss this fast-living, hard-driving, and generous personality who headed Walwyn Stodgell and then, following its merger with Midland Doherty, was named president of the new firm, Midland Walwyn. Michael Holoday became as enraptured by Tim Miller's personality and achievements as anyone, recognizing and, perhaps at times, rationalizing the parallels between himself and the president.

Both men had grown to adulthood bereft of biological parents. When Miller claimed his rapport with underprivileged children grew from his own unhappy childhood, Holoday determined that his experience had been almost as miserable.

But where Miller framed his success against the challenge he had faced in being orphaned at an early age, Michael Holoday treated his adoption as a stigma, seemingly convinced that his life was not as fulfilled as it might have been, had he been raised by biological parents, whatever their status. He expressed resentment at being adopted, claiming he had always wanted to be part of a large, loving family. He made a point of informing everyone who knew him, even on a casual basis, of his adopted status. Early in his career, it was a method of obtaining sympathy. Later, it was a rationalization for his excessive generosity to clients, friends and in-laws. In the end, it became something else — a justification, an appeal for mercy.

Miller's ambition and sales abilities towered over those of everyone around him, and Holoday determined to set his sights just as high. Tim Miller loved to host parties, especially at Christmas and Halloween. He also loved to ski and race powerful speedboats.

Holoday emulated Tim Miller's characteristics, determined to enjoy the same rich and flamboyant lifestyle and the same high regard by everyone in the industry. He was especially intrigued by Miller's success at creating a separate brokerage arm. Surely the height of success and achievement would be to set up your own independent firm and apply your own standards of service and success.

Holoday managed to copy almost every attitude of his mentor, but among those he failed to imitate was this one: throughout his entire career, Tim Miller never generated a whisper of speculation about his integrity and honesty when dealing with clients.

Tim Miller blazed across the sky over Bay Street like a flaming rocket until, on March 30, 1991, while attending an NCAA basketball tournament in Indianapolis with his son, he succumbed to a massive heart attack.

"There'll never be another like him," voices said on the Street when the news broke. Michael Holoday thought otherwise.

With his securities trading licence, new car, and rising income, Holoday abandoned the suburbs to take a lease on a small condominium on St. Clair Avenue at the southern perimeter of Toronto's fabled Forest Hill. He had always dressed as well as he could on his limited salary, and now he paid even more attention to his grooming. Rather than furnish his condo he furnished his closet, choosing conservative blue suits, striped school ties, and pristine shirts, usually with French cuffs sporting gaudy cufflinks. He had to make that ideal first impression, the one that spoke to new clients with two messages. "I am very successful," it said in one ear, and "I can make you as rich as I am," it whispered in the other.

A good haircut is always a sign of good grooming, and Michael kept his hair trimmed as neatly as his polished fingernails. His choice of barbers was haphazard, based more often on his need than their talent or style. One day, soon after obtaining his securities trading licence, Michael took a break from his office to stroll through the underground shopping complexes linked with the Midland offices, searching for someone to trim his straight, dark-brown hair. He headed for a barbershop on the lower level of First Canadian Place, a popular spot for other Bay Street brethren. The shop was located just beyond the Birks store, and he arrived to find all four barber chairs occupied.

Men in three of the chairs were having their hair

styled by other men. But one young fellow — "Lucky guy," Holoday thought briefly — was being tended to not by a male barber, but by a young woman. And not just any young woman either. Tall, slim, and blonde, she laughed and joked with her customer in an engaging manner. At one point her eyes caught Michael's, and her smile seemed to grow wider.

"Next," one of the male barbers said as his customer slipped into a coat and headed for the door.

Michael glanced up at him, smiled, and shook his head. "I'll wait for her," he said, pointing at the blonde woman.

Hearing him, she offered a smile. Then, when she was finished with her customer, she gestured for him to sit down and relax.

Michael learned her name was Maureen Boczan, and he returned for another haircut the following week. And the week after that. Soon they were dating steadily. Now, in addition to having the job he wanted in the town he wanted to be in, Michael Holoday also had an attractive girlfriend who craved wealth and luxury every bit as much as he did.

Maureen Boczan was 22 years of age when Michael entered the barbershop in First Canadian Place. The fourth in a family of six children of John and Carole Boczan, Maureen had been raised for the most part on the family farm near Cobourg, Ontario. Successful farming demands substantial quantities of hard work and good luck, and while the Boczans invested as much as they could spare of the former, they were unfortunately lacking in the latter.

John and Carole Boczan had married in the fall of 1960. He was the bright, ebullient son of sturdy Hungarian immigrants (the family name is pronounced "Boe-zan") who settled in Aldershot, a community long ago

absorbed within the city of Burlington, Ontario. Through
the 1940s and 1950s, Aldershot was one of the most pro-
ductive farming areas in southern Ontario. The sandy soil
and close proximity to Lake Ontario created near-ideal
growing conditions, free of early frosts and the risk of
drought. As a result, John Boczan's memories of local
farming were invariably positive, and although he had
acceded to his parents' wishes and earned a university
degree in chemical engineering, he always believed himself to be a farmer in his soul.

In 1957, while John Boczan was still attending university, a new family moved into the Aldershot neighbour-
hood, overflowing a small bungalow on nearby LaSalle
Park Road. Their last name was Soucie, and they were
descendants of a French-Canadian father and a mother
whose ancestors included prominent settlers in Southern
Ontario (the towns of Jarvis and Hagersville bear their
names). Newly arrived from the New Liskeard area,
members of the large family seemed to be everywhere at
once. At one time, all nine Soucie children resided in the
tiny house along with their parents, Wilf and Bessie.

None of the Soucie children, ranging in age from 2 to
23, was a shrinking violet. Without exception, all were
bright, energetic, talented, and exceptionally attractive,
the offspring of a piously Catholic father and a warm,
although often overwhelmed, mother. Three of the four
eldest sons were dispatched to seminaries in the US, and
all were encouraged to pursue higher education.

When John Boczan appeared on the Soucie doorstep to
date his eldest daughter Carole, Wilf Soucie lent both his
approval and encouragement. The young Boczan was def-
erential, ambitious, and from a solid Catholic family. The
Cyanamid chemical company had offered the new engineer a position at their Montreal plant, and the elder
Soucie gave his blessing to John and Carole's marriage,

even if it meant watching his little girl move more than three hundred miles away.

By the end of the decade, John Boczan had a family of his own, a suburban house, and a secure job. But amid the fervent atmosphere of Montreal in the late 1960s, John and Carole Boczan grew disenchanted with city life, and began planning a move to the country. Children raised on a farm grew up more balanced and moral than city or sub-urban kids. They learned the dignity and rewards of hard work first-hand, watching their father go off to work across fields of crops, and not vanish into a city of concrete and steel. For himself and for his children, John Boczan was determined to fulfill his dream and bring a better life to his family.

The farm they chose near Cobourg, Ontario, was pur-chased with every asset John and Carole Boczan owned in 1970 — his pension fund, their savings, the proceeds from the sale of their home in Montreal, and a substantial bank loan. Covering 450 acres, the property included a dilapi-dated farmhouse, said to be haunted by the ghost of a woman who had died, alone and despondent, within its walls several years earlier. Ghost or no ghost, John Boczan set to work restoring the property, helped by friends, family, and neighbours. He would later replace it with a brand new home built with his own hands.

Choosing commercial corn as their main crop, John and Carole launched into years of hard labour leading to one disappointment after another. Crops failed, corn prices plummeted, costs rose, droughts descended, and on and on. Later, the Boczans added cattle, which led to new disas-ters. Long nights spent nursing sick calves or assisting in difficult births often produced nothing more than another dead animal. If hard work alone could guarantee success, the Boczans would have become wealthy landowners. It is never enough, of course, as the Boczans discovered.

Impressed by John's abilities and hard work, a neighbouring farmer made them an offer: if John and Carole would rebuild an old farmhouse on the farmer's land — the farmer would provide money for building materials — the Boczans could work the land for a salary and rent the refurbished house for a few hundred dollars a month.

Her parents' struggles fostered in Maureen's heart a streak of rebellion as wide as any swath cut by her father's combine, and when the first few months of high school failed to satisfy her hunger for something more than the farm could offer, she was gone. At age 16 she dropped out of school and abandoned the family farm for Toronto, where her eldest sister Suzie was already living. Overnight, she was in a world that pulsed to something more interesting than the engine of a John Deere tractor.

Toronto was bustling with growth, and there was always room for another teenage farm girl, even a high school drop-out, especially if she were tall, slim, and blonde. Rooming with her sister, Maureen found work at Yorkville's exclusive Via Condotti boutique, where an inherited sense of colour and fashion, along with an engaging personality, made her a favourite of many customers.

Still a teenager, Maureen sold multi-thousand-dollar wardrobes to the wives and mistresses of Toronto's business elite, women who drove off in Mercedes and BMW sedans on their way to lunch at the Four Seasons. She assured herself that some day, somehow, she would be the one to slap a Platinum card on the counter and jangle her keys impatiently while some overworked sales clerk packaged her selection of blouses, scarves, sweaters, and gowns.

Conspicuous among the twentysomething sales clerks at Via Condotti was Connie Gould, an older woman whose demeanour suggested that she did not belong on the sales side of the retail counter. Indeed, she had once played the customer's role at the city's most elegant boutiques, thanks to her late husband, Albert Gould.

Gould, part-owner of the Hotel Barclay, a mid-level downtown hotel on Toronto's Front Street, was convicted in 1959 of attempting to scam half a million dollars from a Toronto development company. He promised high levels of interest for short-term loans, claimed possession of off-shore assets, stalled payments for purchased investments, submitted documents of non-existent corporations, and generally scrambled to construct an ever-widening shell of deceit.

Gould's plan worked, for a while. When it began falling apart, Gould's fast talk and fancy footwork were no longer enough to keep him dancing away from the police and, in November 1959, he was sentenced to six years in prison. On his release he made a second attempt at stock fraud, was arrested and convicted, served another penitentiary term, and died soon after his release, leaving his wife little more than a box of baubles.[9]

Connie Gould grew fond of Maureen, who had arrived from the farm determined to enjoy all the pleasures and excitement of the big city. And Maureen, far from her parents, responded more warmly to the older woman than to the other sales clerks her own age. Soon, Maureen began introducing Connie as "my second Mom," and together they shared gossip and dreams.

Albert Gould, Connie told Maureen, had promised to take her to Paris someday and never did. Connie dreamed of waking in a five-star hotel, browsing shops on the Champs Élysées and sipping wine at a sidewalk café. Wearing Givenchy or Dior, of course. Someday, she said, if she ever became wealthy again, she would take Maureen with her to Paris and they would have such fun.

Retail sales would never make Maureen wealthy.

Neither would barbering and hairstyling, but she felt she had a knack for it so she enrolled in barbering school, acquiring a skill with scissors and comb.

The upscale environment of Yorkville attracted wealthy men, and many swung their eyes in admiration at the sight of Maureen Boczan. Soon she was stepping directly from the Via Condotti into an expensive foreign car, on her way to Pronto or Scaramouche for drinks and dinner, and maybe dancing at whatever new club was attracting Toronto's young elite.

John and Carole Boczan were delighted at their daughter's apparent happiness, concealing their disappointment at her failure to obtain a high school diploma. In its place, Maureen had acquired something as good and maybe even better — a veneer of sophistication, a taste for the good life, entry into an influential social circle, and an apparently wealthy boyfriend.

The new boyfriend proved physically abusive and demanding, and Maureen finally fled his domineering ways, abandoning her career and her relationship to return to Cobourg and the safety of her family's arms.

She discovered her parents working as hard as ever. While John continued to farm his neighbour's land in return for a small salary and rental on the home he rebuilt himself, Carole Boczan had obtained a Merle Norman cosmetics franchise and opened a popular and successful shop in Cobourg. While John enjoyed working the land in return for a small income and reasonable rent, they depended for much of their income on earnings from Carole's beauty salon.

Maureen eventually returned to Toronto and began work at a barbershop in First Canadian Place. It was a perfect location to meet the market traders and financial analysts who spilled through the concourse area from the Bay Street brokerage houses and the TSE itself. They

were aggressive, ambitious men who had never over-
hauled a hay mower or crawled under a tractor in their
life, and never would. They were the men Connie had spoken of, and one of them, the one who saw Maureen as
another expression of his success and achievement, was
Michael Holoday.

FOUR

*Finance is the art of passing money from one
hand to another until it finally disappears.*
– ROBERT SARNOFF

"Turning a thousand dollars into two thousand dollars," an investment wag once remarked, "is hard work. Turning a million dollars into two million dollars is inevitable."

Novice investors understood the truth of this statement, even if they failed to grasp the mechanics involved. The basic premise was: the rich get richer. The challenge was to first get rich.

"The street is driven by raw greed," explained Doug Cunningham, a former senior vice-president and director of telecommunications and media at Midland Walwyn (now Merrill Lynch Canada). "End of story. You encounter kids in their twenties who are making more money, three or four years after getting hired, than their parents ever made in their best years. These kids see the acquisition of material things as a game, a way of keeping score. If the guy next to them buys a Benz, they get a Porsche, then the next guy gets a Ferrari, and so on. It never ends. Once you're in the game, you don't dare slow down. You either run faster or you drop out."[1]

One of Holoday's first lessons as a licensed broker was recognizing the importance of establishing trust with his

clients. Michael cultivated it with all the energy and dedication that Maureen's parents were devoting to the struggle on their farm back in Cobourg. But with substantially
more success.

"You have to establish trust," Holoday emphasized.
"When you establish trust, and the client respects your ability to understand markets, they'll give you their account."
Then he made a comment that would be revealing in light
of his later actions: "From that point on, clients will agree
with most of your recommendations. They may not go along
with you all the time, but if you were to talk to a thousand
successful stockbrokers, they'll tell you that ninety-five
percent of the time, clients follow their recommendations."[2]

Along with his awareness of the significance of trust,
Holoday discovered something else about himself and the
financial trading business. It stemmed back to Clark
Gilmore's luncheon lesson on the ability to make several
thousand dollars in minutes in an industry that constantly lectures its clients on the virtue of patience. "Invest in
good, solid companies or well-managed mutual funds,"
financial advisors often suggest, "and don't try to rush
things. Think long-term. Look at the big picture. Be
patient."

On Bay Street, patience may be a virtue but it's not an
especially valued one, among the younger crowd at least.
The adrenaline kick of doing deals and making money
doesn't come bottled with patience. It comes wrapped in a
futures warrant or option with a market value of $100 this
week and either $1,000 or nothing at all next week.
Dealmakers enjoy the rush that's ignited by purchasing
bonds in the morning, flipping them after lunch, and
watching the value of their account being kicked upwards
by several thousand dollars before dinner.

Many traders and clients seek this kind of action, making the business more reminiscent of the Las Vegas strip

than a stuffy investment firm. Michael Holoday thrived in the environment. "I was more interested in being right or wrong on short-term movements in the markets. You earn good commissions and at the same time offer clients the opportunity to make profits or expose themselves to losses." Short-term movements meant using derivatives, the same arcane instruments that sank Barings Bank. A derivative is a form of side-bet, a wager made on the outcome of larger, more direct actions. It is a financial arrangement between two parties whose profits and losses are based on (or "derived from") an underlying asset or benchmark. Buying and selling shares in companies listed on the Toronto Stock Exchange moves the TSE's index up or down — that's investing. Two people betting against each other on which direction, and by how much, the index moves are engaged in derivatives.

"Derivatives give you quick results," Holoday observed. "You have the opportunity to maximize both your returns or losses in a very short time. The secret is to stay one step ahead of the pack on interest rate volatility."[3]

Among hundreds of other young and aggressive traders on Bay Street, Holoday knew he needed a forte, a niche to separate him from the crowd of generalists. Holoday's niche was derivatives based on US T-bills, and eurodollars backed by T-bills and issued by the US government. It was a heady, glamorous choice, heavy with both risk and opportunity.

T-bills and eurodollars represent the most liquid asset in the marketplace, delivering the biggest trading volume. Holoday, who had studied the complexity of 30-year interest rate curves while studying at UBC, revelled in this environment. But he needed to know more, needed a depth of understanding that would permit him to make snap decisions on every opportunity that arose. Each evening he carted reports on volatility patterns and trading models back to his apartment for study, growing familiar with constraints and strategies, and implementing them on behalf of clients the following day.

Market knowledge was only half the equation. He needed salesmanship as well, so he became, in his own words, an expert at selling his concepts, many dealing with currency futures, the most volatile and high-risk instruments available. He wasn't perfect. But he was close enough often enough. "Even if I was wrong," he recalled later, "it seemed that I was never wrong by more than a month, which is pretty accurate." Then, he added telling-ly: "But in the futures game, that can be life or death."[4]

Futures are both simpler in their structure and more complex in their application than any other investment option. At its simplest, a futures contract is a wager, shar-ing many qualities with a stack of chips riding on a chosen roulette wheel number. You are, in essence, staking something of value on a future outcome. In gambling, the outcome is just minutes away; in a futures contract, the time frame may be measured in days, weeks, months, or even years.

The appeal is the same: a relatively low initial capital risk may earn substantial multiples of the original invest-ment. Two bucks to win on a five-to-one horse brings you ten bucks at the end of the race, if you were correct. The concept also applies to land speculators and, with the broadest of interpretations, to any investment carrying no guarantee of return and an acknowledged risk of loss. Futures have been accurately described as "one of the last frontiers of capitalism,"[5] promising virtually unlimited opportunities for wealth, and requiring no assets beyond a desk, a telephone, and a personal computer.

Purchasing a futures investment means making a con-tractual commitment to acquire something of value — a commodity — at a fixed point in time. In reality, futures dealers rarely take possession of the commodity in the contract. It's the contract that is bought and sold.

Suppose you own 100 shares of XYZ Inc., a solidly managed manufacturing company in a volatile industry. You paid $30 per share for the stock last year and you plan to sell the shares, hopefully at a profit, six months from now to cover an anticipated expense. If I'm bullish on XYZ and expect their price to rise between now and then, I might offer you $300 for the option to purchase all your shares at $40 in six months. That's not a bad deal for you; you'll make $13 a share — the $10 increase in price, plus the $3 per share I pay for the option. (For the sake of clarity, I am avoiding broker commissions.) If you agree, you write a *call* on the shares, which I buy because I am gambling that the value of the shares will rise above $43 each ($40 for the share plus $3 for the option). Owning the call provides me with the option to purchase the shares under the agreed-upon conditions. (A *put* provides the option to sell under certain conditions, and is used when the investor is shorting the market — that is, believes the future price of the stock or commodity will be lower than today.)

One of three things occurs. First, I'm wrong, and six months from now the shares don't reach $40 (known as the strike price); in fact, they sell for $28. I don't want to purchase them at the strike price of $40 if their value is only $28, so I don't exercise the option, and lose my $300. Meanwhile, the market price for your shares has dropped $2 per share but you have earned $3 as a result of the option you sold me. You win.

Or perhaps I'm correct and, when the option date arrives, the price is $45. I exercise the option and pick up the shares for $40, plus the price of the option. You sell your shares for a 33 percent profit over the original purchase price, plus the $3 per share you earned from the option. Meanwhile, I paid $43 for shares worth $45 each.

This can be construed as a rare "win-win" situation.

In the third situation, I strike it rich when XYZ Inc. is selling at $50 per share in six months. Under the option agreement, you sell me your shares at $10 beneath the current market price, and I laugh all the way to the bank. But hey — you've still made a profit two ways: from the increase to the strike price, and from the option fee I paid you.

Once written, options can be traded as freely as shares in XYZ Inc. The price of the options will vary according to the option's intrinsic value (the difference between the market price, when the option is purchased, and the strike price) and the time value (the weeks or months before the expiry date arrives).

By purchasing the call for your stock, I exercised more leverage than I could by buying the stock alone. If I had simply purchased the stock at $30 and held it until the price rose to $50, I would have realized a 66 percent profit on my investment. The intrinsic value of my option, however, is $10 per share, the difference between the strike price and the market price, and that's an increase of more than 300 percent over the $3 per share option price I paid. It's this leverage factor that drives the options market, and makes traders starry-eyed.

The same process works if you are bearish about the stock, expecting its market value to decline by the expiry date. In that case, you sell an option to trade your stock at below market price — say, $25 per share for XYZ Inc. — six months from now. Many investors may scoop up that option at a premium, but if your bearish inclinations prove correct and the stock drops to $20 per share — $5 per share beneath the strike price — you'll pocket those option fees and still retain your shares.

Quick profit opportunities make the futures market irresistible to people whose confidence and egos overpower their ability to recognize the darker aspects of the game.

These include the highly complex nature of the trades, and all the influences to which they are subject.

Traders who ignore two fundamental aspects of futures trading do so at their peril. These two realities are the following (and wise futures traders keep them either at the forefront of their consciousness or on a printed sheet above their computer monitor):

• Unlike a simple wager on horses or a roulette wheel, you can actually lose more than your initial investment in futures.

• There are nine losers for every winner in the futures market.[6]

This evidence should be sobering enough. But while dangers loom in the background of every deal in commodities futures, they grow far more menacing when applied to trading in currency futures, Michael Holoday's chosen area of expertise.

The futures market grew out of commodities trading, stimulated by farmers seeking a guaranteed price for their crops while the seeds were still germinating in the ground. During the 1970s, the explosion of international trade and the relative instability of currencies launched a new definition for the term *commodity*. Instead of being restricted to corn, wheat, and pork bellies, the word now included money itself. Traders around the world began looking for assurances that the value of the currencies they were using to sell and purchase goods in other countries would remain predictable in future months. Without this assurance, a contract signed today, promising a profit six months from now, could produce a loss if the relative value of one currency rose or fell substantially against another. It could also, of course, provide a windfall bonus, but manufacturers and traders generally prefer to deal with fixed values, exchanging a possible upside bonus for assurances against a potential downside loss.

Thus, a market developed for currency futures that is similar to markets for pork bellies, wheat, corn, and corporate shares, but with one critical difference: unlike agricultural products and stock market shares, no underlying commodity exists in currency futures. No vehicle will arrive on the appointed day to deliver a material or product, with a value subject to some appraised value. There is only the money itself.

Every foreign traveller encounters the reality of currency fluctuation. In the relatively small quantities of money used by tourists, short-term currency fluctuations represent little more than an annoyance. But to savvy traders dealing in currency futures — remember the exceptional leverage they enjoy — these fluctuations represent a tremendous opportunity for profit.

Currency fluctuations are driven by several factors, but especially by interest rates at the international level, and these were Michael Holoday's bread and butter. He grew convinced that he could predict, with reasonable accuracy, the direction that interest rates would take for major world trading currencies, and he would trade puts and calls on bonds based on this information.

Holoday began promoting currency options to every potential client he encountered. Suddenly the brash kid from Revelstoke, who used to blush beet-red after public speaking events, was doing million-dollar deals with other peoples' money. "I became an expert at quickly selling my concepts to clients," he recalled, "who always seemed to appreciate my view on interest rates. We had profits and losses, but the clients became addicted to profit periods. When they were in the profit periods, they never experienced such quick profits in their lives. So naturally referrals came in."[7]

Whether or not the clients became "addicted," Holoday and Midland Walwyn both profited from the surge in business through the commissions earned. Commissions, based on a percentage of the trade, were taken by the brokerage at both ends: when the client bought the options, and when the client sold the options. Whether the trade was profitable or not to the client, the brokerage made money by pocketing a portion of the trade; the balance was paid to the individual broker. Holoday's success led to referrals, referrals led to new clients, new clients led to new respect and bigger commissions, and bigger commissions led to more income and prestige for Holoday.

"When we started the derivatives strategy, I was on a roll, I got eight hits in a row," he boasted. "I went from having ten clients to over a hundred. Other brokers assigned some of their clients to me, and it got to the point where I had twelve associate brokers selling my abilities, splitting commissions with me. When we had a meeting, there would be fourteen or fifteen people sitting with me at a boardroom table, and I was supposed to be just one junior broker."[8]

Holoday applied two investment tools from his arsenal, depending on the situation. One was his comprehension of cyclic interest rate patterns; the other was a technique called "strangles," sometimes referred to as "straddles." Both proved effective over the short-term, but neither was foolproof.

Cycles in commodity prices and interest rates have been known for decades, based on the work of Edward R. Dewey, who created The Foundation for the Study of Cycles in 1941. The availability of computer programs to analyze and predict these cycles has made Dewey's theories accessible to novices and experts alike. But, as one astute observer points out, the application of cycles to the marketplace is not nearly as simple a matter as the demonstration of their existence.[9] Price cycles vary widely in length, depth, and height. The price of some commodities, such as silver, can trace cycles as short as four to five days, overlaid on longer cycles stretching across more than 50 years, with multiple cycles of varying lengths oscillating along the way.

Applying cyclic analysis to futures trading demands three skills: projecting the cycles; forecasting the next peak or valley; and timing market entries and exits according to the cyclic pattern. To investors with a gambling instinct, it all sounds like a foolproof system. But engaging in futures trading based on an analysis of cycles is like betting on a horse race based on the observation that the number seven horse tends to win the third race every ten days or so. This may be enough to persuade a racetrack bettor to plunk down a few dollars on the number seven horse according to the cycle. But his dreams of growing rich by applying this knowledge will likely remain just that. And Michael Holoday was persuading clients to invest tens of thousands on the same "system."

Holoday's use of "strangles" in futures trading worked like this:

A futures option contract is based on the investor's belief that a given commodity's price will either rise or fall by the time the contract matures. The key word here is *option*. The investor can choose not to exercise the option, which is the logical decision if the investor's prediction proves false. The buyer simply permits the option to expire, writing off the option cost as a loss.

The strangle technique seems to defy logic, because the investor chooses to option both a buy and a sell on the same commodity. It's like betting both teams on the Super Bowl. How can the investor win? Only by choosing to exercise the option that generates a profit, leaving the other option to expire. If the price rises, the investor exercises the right to sell and allows the option to buy to expire. If the price falls, the option to sell is discarded and the right to purchase is exercised — again, producing a profit.

In a highly volatile market, the profit realized by exercising one transaction will more than cover the cost of discarding the other option. The investor doesn't care which way the market moves, as long as the movement is substantial enough to cover the cost of the discarded option and generate profit.

In a stagnant ("sideways") market, disaster strikes. Little or no price movement means the investor loses both ways. The loss may be relatively small, but a series of small losses can add up to a substantial amount.

Obviously there can be no "system," only short-term and long-term success. And for a period in the early 1990s Michael Holoday enjoyed spectacular short-term success.

"I was good at pricing strangles," he claimed, recalling his heyday at Midland Walwyn. "I graduated from trading against other people to trading against Morgan Stanley or Salomon Brothers. It got to the point where Morgan Stanley used to buy my positions from me. I was dealing against Salomon or Goldman Sachs. We had a good little club down there (at Midland Walwyn). People knew when we were in the market."[10]

According to Holoday, his success raised him to the status of corporate celebrity. "I became, in effect, a division of the firm. I had my own traders clearing trades for me, because the volume I was dealing with was so huge. On a national basis, the rest of the group and I became thirty to forty percent of the firm's total volume. When I started in nineteen-eighty-nine I was at the bottom of the totem pole. But by the end of December nineteen-ninety-one, I was the top national producer in the firm."[11]

Holoday was long gone from the bullpen. He was awarded an office with a window overlooking downtown Toronto. His newly acquired Chairman's Club status,

earned by generating a million dollars in commissions for
the firm, carried enough clout for him to have Tanya
Sargent's desk relocated outside his office door.

In his professional life, Michael Holoday was supposedly
an investment genius; in his personal life, he was
Maureen Boczan's Prince Charming. Within a few weeks
of dating Holoday, Maureen graduated from standing on
her feet eight hours a day in a barbershop to dining in
some of the city's finest restaurants and shopping at its
most exclusive boutiques. Michael replaced her wardrobe
with new fashions from top designers, surprised her with
jewellery from Cartier and Tiffany's, and paid for expensive dental work. He scooped her away for weekend shopping trips to Montreal and New York City and promised
they would travel first-class to Monte Carlo for their honeymoon. It was all an intoxicating experience for a somewhat starry-eyed farm girl.

Maureen was slow to introduce Michael to her parents.
Perhaps she was unsure of the relationship, frightened
that it might lead to a repeat of her earlier experience. In
fact, almost a year passed between the day Michael
entered the First Canadian Place barbershop and the day
Maureen arrived back in Cobourg to introduce her exciting
new boyfriend to her family. It was the day her brother
Paul was to ship out for service in the Gulf War; Michael
offered to drive the young soldier to Trenton where he
boarded a flight to Kuwait. Maureen announced that she
and Michael were planning to marry. Michael had a brilliant future on Bay Street. He was already making more
money than her hard-working parents could imagine, handling millions of dollars on behalf of grateful clients who
grew richer each month, thanks to Michael's talents. He
and Maureen were jetting off on weekend shopping sprees
to Montreal and New York, and Michael was about to

replace his Camaro with something more suitable to his style — a Mercedes maybe, or a Porsche or Jaguar.

The family was stunned by the news. Maureen had always seemed the most brash of the Boczan children, a girl filled with wild dreams. Maybe ambition, good looks, and luck were all you needed to succeed. If so, Maureen was on her way. She'd had the good luck to meet this Holoday fellow, who carried himself with confidence and had a way of talking that suggested he knew more than you could ever learn, but if you and he hit it off, if you'd care to pay attention, he might share it with you.

When Michael and Maureen weren't escaping for weekends elsewhere, they motored down the highway to visit Maureen's family. Holoday seemed to revel in the atmosphere created by the five sisters, all teasing each other. Driving back to Toronto one Sunday evening, Holoday announced that he wanted to do something for Maureen's family — all of them, her parents and her siblings. In many ways, he told Maureen, she was lucky. Her family may not be wealthy but they were warm and caring, united by love and blood, sharing a common struggle to succeed, sharing everything in fact — glory, failure, joy, tragedy. It was this blood-related intimacy that he envied so much, he told her. He had craved a true family relationship like this all of his life, had felt starved for it as a young child. He had been adopted, after all, and adopted children, even in the best of situations, always carry a hollow spot within them that can never be filled.

Maureen replied that she could hardly wait to introduce him to all her vibrant and artistic aunts and uncles. When her mother's family, the Soucies, were present, parties would erupt spontaneously, brimming with games, music, and laughter, and children clambered on and off the laps of familiar aunts and uncles, sometimes more than two dozen kids in all. It sounded like The Brady

Bunch and The Mickey Mouse Club all in one venue, with
a dash of Jake and the Kid.

By the time they reached Toronto that evening,
Michael was vowing to see that John and Carole Boczan
would never have to scrape and save or worry about farm
prices and crops again. Michael would take care of them
for the rest of their lives. He made that promise to
Maureen and swore to repeat it to Maureen's parents.

The Boczan family were fascinated by Holoday's success
and impressed by his constant generosity, which was overwhelming at times. Michael looked forward to spending
weekends at the Cobourg farm, feeling more and more like
part of the family.

Michael began showering Maureen and her family
with extravagant gifts. Each time Maureen arrived back
in Cobourg, it seemed, she had another bauble to display
to her parents and sisters. Her engagement ring was a
massive solitaire from Tiffany's. Holoday took pride in
revealing its cost — $33,000, paid in cash by the way. He
added more diamond rings to Maureen's jewellery box,
along with opal and diamond-drop earrings, diamond solitaire earrings with stones almost as large as the one in
Maureen's engagement ring, and several necklaces and
bracelets of sapphires and diamonds.

Not everyone felt the allure of Michael Holoday's
charm and success. Even his most ardent admirers admitted that Michael was not the warmest or most commu-
nicative person. His gaze seemed to avoid your own, and
he was uncomfortable discussing details of his work. But
no one questioned Michael's success.

"You'll need to live off your savings soon," he told his
future in-laws over coffee at the farmhouse one weekend.
"You could be making a lot of money right now, if I handled it for you." He raved about opportunities to be earned

from "the inefficiencies of the market" by applying "maximum leverage," and promised to "watch over your money for you."

"How much would it take?" the Boczans asked. They had never dabbled in investments more complex than savings accounts and GICs.

"Fifteen thousand, minimum," Holoday told them.

The Boczans replied they had managed to accumulate about $5,000 in their savings account.

Carole Boczan had an idea. "I'll borrow the difference from Mom's estate," she said. A few years earlier, Carole's father had died from a massive heart attack while bending to kiss his wife on their golden wedding anniversary, with the entire family in attendance. It was a chilling, melodramatic event that left the family shattered. Careful financial man that he was, Wilf Soucie bequeathed a substantial estate to his widow, the balance to be divided among the children at their mother's death. Two Soucie sons were named co-executors for the estate, and at Carole's request they released $10,000 of the family's inheritance to her for Michael to invest.

First, there was some paperwork to complete, the most complex being the Know Your Client (or KYC) form, a standard document used by all investment firms. On the surface, the KYC form appears to safeguard the interests of the small, inexperienced investor.

In addition to personal information, including name, address, SIN, birth date, telephone, and some means of identification such as a driver's licence number, the KYC form records the potential client's financial means and investment acumen. It asks clients to list their approximate net worth, gross annual income, investment objectives (Liquidity, Income, Stability, Long-Term Growth), risk tolerance (High, Medium, Low), investment knowledge (Excellent, Good, Fair, Nil), and Estimated Risk

Capital, or ERC. The completed form is signed by the investor and returned to the brokerage, where it is reviewed by the firm's compliance officer, who fills a watchdog role.

After Holoday completed the KYC form and the Boczans transferred the $15,000 to him, Michael assured them he could generate enough earnings from this seed investment to produce a healthy nest egg for their retirement years. This was fine with the Boczans. With no experience in stock market trading and no knowledge of trading rules, they were content to leave every decision up to their future son-in-law.

Soon they began receiving account statements from Midland Walwyn. "We couldn't figure them out," Carole Boczan recalled. "Every time we received a statement I'd set it aside, and the next time Michael and Maureen visited I'd show it to him and say, 'Michael, what the heck does this mean anyway? It's all gibberish to me.' And Michael would say, 'We're having trouble in the accounting department. Don't worry about it. I'll always know how much you have.' Michael said we were making two or three thousand dollars a month and that everything was fine. So we eventually just ignored the Midland Walwyn statements."

They had little reason to mistrust their daughter's fiancé, and they encountered a new, more pressing reason to draw him even closer within their family when the farm owner announced he would be resuming operation of the property later that year. No longer needing John Boczan to manage the operation for him, the farmer had promised the house to his own son. Once again, the Boczans were about to find themselves homeless — until Michael made a generous suggestion.

Carole and John Boczan had borrowed $10,000, enough for two-and-a-half acres of woodlot land in a rural area north of Cobourg where they planned to erect a prefab house on the property. It would be a cozy bungalow in the country, the fulfillment of a postponed dream. Seventy thousand dollars would buy the basic shell, and John's handyman skills would erect and finish it. When one of Holoday's handwritten statements indicated the Boczan's original $15,000 investment was nudging $70,000, they asked him to withdraw that amount for the purchase.

Michael considered it for a moment, and then announced that he had a better idea. Instead of withdrawing the funds in their account, the Boczans should permit him to finance the building materials for a splendid new home, something more elaborate than a run-of-the-mill prefab box. "Make it a big farm-style home, with lots of bedrooms," he suggested. "We'll fill it with antiques. It'll be a place for the whole family to gather on weekends. Won't that be terrific?" His face softened, his eyes glowed, and his smile grew wistful. "I've always wanted to be part of a big happy family like that."

Holoday's proposal grew more detailed and alluring. John Boczan's "sweat equity," he suggested, would entitle him to half ownership of the property and residence, which, of course, he and Carole would occupy. Michael and Maureen would consider the home their weekend retreat.

It seemed as though every good luck charm in the Western world was shining on the Boczans. Michael's plans for the house in Cobourg were opulent. It would be a showplace, built with John's own hands. The Boczans would reside in comfort beneath its roof. Their income would be generated by the fruits of their investments, selected and husbanded by Holoday himself, who reminded Maureen's parents that the more they invested in their account, the more profit they could expect to reap in the future. So every penny John and Carole could spare was signed over to Michael, who accepted it with assurance that their account was growing in value at a spectacular rate.

The Boczans couldn't resist sharing news of their good fortune with almost everyone they knew. "You have to approach Michael and ask him to look after your money for you," Carole Boczan would say to customers in her salon. "He won't come to you. You have to go to him." She provided Michael's name and telephone number. "Tell him I said to call him," she would add. Her motive was understandable: She wanted everyone to become as wealthy as Michael promised she would be.

Most of the Boczans' friends and family members had only relatively small amounts of money, to be sure — not enough for a Bay Street Whiz Kid, an advisor to major big-city investors, to be concerned about, unless he were providing the service as an act of kindness, which seemed to be the case. In essence, Michael appeared to be doing everyone a favour simply because they were friends, customers, or relatives of John and Carole Boczan. "Michael wants to share the wealth," Carole Boczan might say. "He's doing this just for us and our friends. He makes his real money from big clients on Bay Street. This is his way of helping out the little people, by handling their accounts for them. He's that kind of person, sweet and generous."

Some people began to ask questions about Michael's magic. How does he do it? they wanted to know. How can he double or triple the value of an investment in just a few weeks? "It's too complicated for ordinary people to understand," Carole Boczan would reply. "Michael knows how. I've got the statements from him to prove it."

Indeed she had. Some were scribbled on notepaper in Michael's strange angular handwriting. Others arrived wrapped in the foggy jargon of a Midland Walwyn client statement. The actions and instruments were arcane in the extreme, their movements impossible for novices to decipher, but it didn't matter, really. Invariably, the investor's eyes dropped to the bottom line, where the balance always showed astounding growth.

One day, Holoday paid the Boczans a visit, explaining that Midland Walwyn had requested a financial statement from the couple to update the brokerage's records. "Just a formality," he said. "I'll help you fill it out."

The Boczans owned few assets beyond the value of the Cobourg beauty salon operated by Carole and the undeveloped woodlot in the country. Nevertheless, Holoday assessed the couple's net worth at $135,000, entering $20,000 as their risk capital. He asked Carole how much the beauty salon grossed. "About eighty thousand a year," she replied. And how much did John earn from working the farm for its owner? "Thirty thousand a year." Michael added them up and reported that the Boczans, farmers and part owners of a small-town beauty salon, earned a combined annual net income of $110,000. He also affirmed that their investment knowledge was Good. In reality, the income and net worth of the Boczans were a fraction of the figures Holoday claimed, but he dutifully filed them with the authorities at Midland Walwyn.

When John Boczan's widowed mother disposed of the family home, son John signed over his portion of the sale's proceeds to a reassuring Michael Holoday. "You're doing great," Michael assured the Boczans a few months later. When John Boczan asked how great, Holoday said they had over $50,000 in US funds, more than three times their original investment.

Holoday was apparently making as much profit for himself as he was for his family-connected clients. He and Maureen were planning to marry in the fall of 1991, and their wedding would be an event to remember. Everyone in Maureen's large family would be invited: aunts, uncles, cousins, dozens of them.

Holoday appeared concerned, almost fatherly, toward

Maureen's youngest sister, Rebecca, now a high school student. "You shouldn't be going to school here in Cobourg," he
suggested during one visit. "You would do better at a private school, like Bishop Strachan in Toronto."

Maureen told her youngest sister and parents that
Michael was making no idle promise. They had already discussed the idea, and agreed it would be a wonderful opportunity for Rebecca. Bishop Strachan was the favoured private school for Toronto's bluest-blooded families to entrust
with their daughters' education. Rebecca could live with
Michael and Maureen in Toronto while attending the prestigious school to complete her Grade 13 studies; after graduating from there, she would have little trouble being
accepted at almost any university she desired.

Carole and John Boczan gave their blessings to the
idea. Why not? Michael appeared to love his future in-laws
without reservation. As proof of his generosity, he signed
over the ownership of his Camaro to Rebecca, after taking
delivery of a new Jaguar V-12 convertible in British
Racing Green.

"She's too young," John and Carole Boczan said when
Michael announced his gift to their daughter. "She's only
fifteen years old."

Holoday shrugged. "When she's sixteen and gets her
licence, she'll have a car to drive."

Now, really. Who could help but love a man like that?

Some of Carole's family — her brothers and sisters and
their spouses and offspring — reserved judgement about
Michael. Some responded with enthusiasm and money.
Others weren't so sure.

Paul Legere, an outdoorsy fellow with Marlboro Man-
rugged good looks, had married the Boczans' daughter
Rosemary in 1990. In 1991, Legere found himself with
$10,000 in cash, thanks to the sale of a house. He and

Rosemary tossed around the idea of locking it safely in the bank, but future brother-in-law Michael persuaded them that he had a better idea: invest it with him and they would soon be living in a new home, mortgage-free. During one weekend visit, Holoday slid a Midland Walwyn New Account Application/Know Your Client form across the kitchen table to Legere. "Sign it now and I'll fill the information in later," Holoday said while pocketing a cheque transferring all of the Legeres' savings to him. Paul Legere did, and Midland Walwyn soon confirmed that they had indeed opened an account in the name of Paul and Rosemary Legere.

The Legeres, according to Midland Walwyn records, were ideal new investors. Their New Account Application stated they had "Fair" investment knowledge, some experience in trading stocks and bonds, an annual income between $50,000 and $100,000, net worth between $100,000 and $200,000, $25,000 available for investment, and dividend income of $15,000 annually. Not a word of it was true.

From the beginning, neither Rosemary nor husband Paul was able to decipher the Midland Walwyn monthly statements they received. Holoday suggested they ignore the statements, they didn't mean anything anyway. The back office had screwed up, the accountants were incompetent, the computer system was breaking down all the time, and all they needed to do was ask him, Michael Holoday, the status of their investment. When they did, his most frequent reply was: "Relax, you're making money."

Within weeks of opening their Midland Walwyn account, the actual value of their investment had declined to $23.70.

When Howard Desmond[12] lost his job with the closing of Maher Shoes, he and wife Suzie, Maureen's eldest sister, at least enjoyed the comfort of a healthy RRSP balance and a reasonable severance settlement from his employer. Howard was nudging 40, with two small children and another on the way. With about $45,000 to invest in their future, he and Suzie needed the rare combination of high growth and high security from their investments. Michael Holoday claimed he had the answer.

"Write me a series of cheques," Holoday told his future in-laws, "no date and no amount. I'll fill them out and cash them as I need them."

Howard Desmond, who has a degree in Business Administration, blinked at that suggestion.

"The money you have really isn't a very big amount," Holoday explained, "so I'll put it under an umbrella of pooled funds and invest it that way."

Desmond said he wasn't clear how such a pooled fund worked.

"It's a high earning, low-risk strategy of making puts and calls," Holoday said. "It's very volatile, but I have a system to minimize risk, based on timing. It tells me when to get in and get out of the market." When Desmond asked for proof of the system, Holoday snapped: "That's privileged information." And when Holoday began to fill out the details of a New Account Application form for his future in-laws, and wrote "$400,000" as their net worth, a figure not even close to reality, Howard Desmond declined to sign it, saying he could not be a party to such a blatant lie.

"It's just a formality," Holoday claimed. "It's done all the time," and Howard Desmond said, "Not by me."

Bessie Soucie, matriarch of Carole's family, had been diagnosed with Alzheimer's disease and placed in a nursing home near Dundas, Ontario. The balance of her husband's estate was yielding unimpressive earnings in an account at Richardson Greenshields, a fact that galled Carole. She collared her brother Jacques, co-executor of the estate, during a family party: "Give mom's money to Michael," she pleaded with him. "It'll make so much more for her and for us."

Jacques told his sister he felt uncomfortable risking the entire estate in that fashion, and Carole assured him there was no risk, not with Michael giving it his full attention, as he promised. She was so insistent that Jacques finally agreed to approach Michael with the idea, and they set up a meeting at Michael's Midland Walwyn office for the following week. Uncomfortable about making an investment decision for the family on his own, Jacques invited older brother Lowell to accompany him to the meeting.

On their arrival at Holoday's office, Michael hosted them to an elaborate lunch at a nearby restaurant, and then brought them back to the Midland Walwyn building where he had reserved the boardroom. To Jacques and Lowell's surprise, Holoday launched into an aggressive sales presentation involving a series of complex charts and graphs, all created to assure the two brothers that their investment would grow dramatically and risk-free if placed in his hands.

"I used to be a salesman," Jacques Soucie recalled later, "and I know a hard-sell when I see one. We were expecting a quiet chat, maybe a discussion of ways we could take care of Mom's money, and here was Michael giving us a big-time sales pitch, the whole nine yards. We just weren't comfortable with the idea. This was our parents' money, and he was treating it like it was just another business deal." After leaving the Midland Walwyn offices, Lowell and Jacques agreed they would leave the estate in the same hands it had resided in since the death of their father.

The next day, Carole Boczan phoned her brother to ask how the meeting had gone and how much of their parents' estate he had transferred to Michael.

"None," Jacques replied.

Carole couldn't believe it. She was flabbergasted. She demanded to know why.

Jacques replied that he and Lowell felt uneasy about the sales pitch. Michael's high-pressure sales approach had turned them off the idea.

Carole told him he was crazy. "You've just wasted the best chance everybody had of getting rich, like John and I are going to be," she snapped, and things were cool between brother and sister for a while after that.

A few of the family members who met Michael at the Boczan's house in Cobourg thought him aloof, even a little weird, especially when playing his favourite board game, Monopoly. Day-long Monopoly games became a tradition during the weekend sessions. Michael would come alive with a pair of dice and a wad of Monopoly money in his hands, and he usually won, ruthlessly bankrupting the other players one by one. On those rare occasions when he lost, when he had to rise from the table and admit defeat, he would grow sullen and not speak for the rest of the evening, or sometimes he'd throw the board game to the floor.

Hey, some of the family might say. It's only Monopoly. It's only a game.

And others might permit themselves to wonder, just how did this kid get so rich, so fast?

FIVE

Money doesn't always buy happiness. People with
ten million dollars are no happier than people
with nine million dollars.
– HOBART BROWN

Michael Holoday's rise from raw credit department recruit to fully licensed financial advisor and trader within two years was not unique on Bay Street. In the late 1980s, candidates for a securities licence needed only to complete a Canadian Securities course and demonstrate a basic knowledge of the *Conduct and Practices Hand Book,* published by the Investment Dealers Association. In the early 1990s, the industry mandated a 90-day training program, tightening the requirements somewhat. The programs, however, remained administered by the brokerage houses according to the individual standards of each investment firm, and the new rules were not made retroactive. Advisors like Holoday who rose through the ranks according to the old standard simply continued what they had been doing all along.

Large investment firms such as Midland Walwyn maintained in-house training courses. While these might have been designed to correct failings in some applicants, they were also valuable in earmarking candidates who could be fast-tracked to become registered representatives, or RRs.

Holoday's elevation to RR status, futures trader, and

financial advisor at age 25 marked him as a comer at
Midland Walwyn. "Typically, the average age for a new
financial advisor these days is about thirty-seven,"
explained Brad Doney, senior vice-president, general
counsel, and director of risk management at Midland
Walwyn. Among the awkward titles employed by the brokerage business, Doney was the firm's Ultimate
Designated Person, or UDP, identifying him as the individual responsible for ensuring that Midland Walwyn's
hundreds of ambitious commission-paid sales staff
remained in compliance with the rules.

New financial advisors, Doney suggested, often acquire
experience working for insurance companies, banks, or
accountancy firms. "Here they are, maybe an assistant
branch manager at a bank, earning perhaps forty-five
thousand dollars a year," he explained, "and one day they
realize they could do virtually the same job in the securities industry, but making two, three, or four times that
amount. They're people with financial experience, they
know the industry, they know how to put together a financial plan, and so they come to a company like Midland
Walwyn where they can develop their entrepreneurial side
and make a lot of money."[1]

Academic training, financial experience, and a degree
of maturity (the kind a bank or trust company middle-
manager would acquire by his or her mid-30s) are not sufficient in themselves to ensure success, according to
Doney. "A good financial advisor also needs an ability to
develop strong relationships with clients," he continued.
"An RR must create financial plans, assume allocation of
assets, and manage client relationships."

There was little in Michael Holoday's background, and
nothing in his training, to suggest that he possessed
exceptional skills in building relationships and generating
sales. Being associated with a firm such as Midland

Walwyn, whose advertising theme promised clients the value of "Blue-Chip Thinking," provided Holoday with a lustre of trustworthiness that inspired confidence.

"It's a huge benefit for a client to come to a firm like Midland Walwyn or RBC Dominion Securities or Nesbitt Burns, and deal with financial advisors who function as your contact," Doney said. "Ninety-nine point nine-nine-nine percent of the time, that person is a thorough professional, the same as a lawyer or a doctor or any other professional."

Deborah Thompson's experience in the financial sector includes stints as a correspondent for *Knight-Ridder Financial News,* and vice-president in charge of institutional marketing for Royal Bank Investment Management. She has viewed misconduct in the financial marketplace from both inside and outside the industry, and this special perspective inspired her to write *Greed: Investment Fraud in Canada and Around the Globe* (Viking, 1997), a review of investment frauds and scandals. She agreed with Doney's claim that a large firm like Midland Walwyn brings benefits to clients when they deal directly with a qualified financial advisor who draws on the investment firm's research, analysis, and trading resources.

"I think there is an implicit trust when clients go to a large brokerage house and initiate a relationship with a broker representing a large company that has been around for a while," Thompson said. "There's a sort of unspoken, unwritten message (from the brokerage houses) that says, 'We know what we're doing with your money, regardless of the fact that the investment advisor might be under the age of thirty, and has not been at it for a long time.' That's why people are willing to give these individuals and companies the benefit of the doubt."

Clients and patients tend to give lawyers and doctors "the benefit of the doubt" as well, of course. But that's where the similarity ends.

The legal and medical professions operate in the public eye more than financial advisors do and, although their records are hardly unblemished, both doctors and lawyers are subject to strict rules of conduct by their professional associations. Legal clients and medical patients are also, by nature, more familiar than clients of investment houses with the reasons behind the professional assistance they are seeking. You don't have to understand every statute of the law to suspect someone has committed fraud against you, anymore than you need someone to tell you when your arm is broken. Many financial clients remain much less aware of their financial position than of their legal or medical needs — which, of course, is why brokerage firms shout, "Trust us!" at every promotion opportunity.

Doctors and lawyers are paid by direct fees, as are most independent financial advisors. In large brokerage houses, however, income is earned primarily by commissions generated from trading activity. The more activity created, the more commissions earned for both the advisor and the brokerage firm. When the activity exceeds a reasonable level, and its principal objective is clearly to produce commissions for the brokerage and sales representative, the practice is referred to as *churning*. Everyone in the brokerage business has a favourite story about the rapid and unnecessary buying and selling of securities, in a process that depletes the client's account while building income for the financial advisor and brokerage house.

Traders need clients, and most traders build the foundation for their client list by exploiting existing relationships. With trading licence in hand, neophyte brokers contact friends, family members, frat brothers or sorority sisters from university, anyone with money to invest and a latent trust in the new trader's skills.

Michael Holoday, the kid from Revelstoke, had few

opportunities to exploit a network of potential clients in Toronto beyond his future in-laws, so he was forced to depend on making cold calls to strangers and receiving over-the-transom clients via referrals. This latter source could generate significant numbers of new clients, since Midland Walwyn was among the most actively promoted investment firms in the early 1990s. Its high profile, and its ubiquitous promise of "Blue-Chip Thinking," pulled in more than its share of first-time investors responding to the firm's advertisements.

One of these calls was made by Roger Gordon, a millwright in nearby Bolton, Ontario. Gordon and his wife Debbie, a nurse specializing in organ transplants, were precisely the kind of clients the investment community needed to expand its client universe. The Gordons were investment novices; they had cash on hand; and, most important, they mistrusted banks.

Roger Gordon had operated an industrial services business with reasonable success until crippled by the onset of record high-interest rates. He found himself paying more than $50,000 annually to the banks to cover an operating loan, yet the banks, Gordon noted, were not paying depositors nearly as much as they were earning in interest from borrowers. The experience convinced him that chartered banks grew rich on the substantial spread between paying low interest to depositors and squeezing high interest rates made from struggling small businesspeople like himself. If he ever accumulated a significant amount of cash, Gordon vowed, he would never let the banks get their hands on it.

As it turned out, just a few weeks after Michael Holoday obtained his licence as a broker, the Gordon family found itself with $75,000 in cash through an inheritance and profit from the sale of some family real estate. True to his vow, Roger Gordon sought to keep his money out of the grasp of the hated banks, choosing to place it instead in the hands of someone who would provide a reasonable return for the family. With three active children, the Gordon family had dreams to fulfill — a modest home in the country, perhaps on a hill with a view you never get tired of looking at, and lots of room for growing kids to play safely. The Gordons also wanted to provide their children with quality education, including sending all three to a good university.

The $75,000 wouldn't buy their dream, but it represented a solid step toward it. Perhaps, with a few years of solid investment growth, it could top $100,000, bringing the dream closer to reality. Roger and Debbie were damned if they would trust the banks to do it for them. They began reading about a company on Bay Street that promised "Blue-Chip Thinking," and that's who Roger Gordon called in late 1989. "We have some money to invest," Roger told the person who answered the telephone at Midland Walwyn, "and we'd like to talk to somebody about it." The receptionist thanked them for calling and put them on hold. Inquiries from non-clients were assigned to the sales staff on a rotating basis. She checked the next name on the list, dialled an extension, and connected it with the caller.

There was a pause before a dispassionate voice on the other end of the line said, "Michael Holoday here. How can I help you?"

Roger Gordon introduced himself and explained his position. He and his wife had $75,000 and they wanted to put it into a low-risk investment, one that would return a few points better than the banks were paying. "We can afford to lose ten percent of the money and not feel uncomfortable," Roger told Holoday. "But if, at any point, we lose any more than ten percent, stop right there. Just put it back into cash for us. I'm not expecting to double our money in one year, nothing like that. If the bank is paying ten percent, I'll be happy to make twelve or thirteen percent, okay? Just keep it liquid. If it's not liquid, you're not doing it right."[2]

Holoday proposed strip bonds, the interest coupons removed from long-term bonds and traded like IOUs. The coupons, whose maturity date may be 20 or more years in the future, are sold at a discount from their face value. The difference between the discounted rate and the face value, divided by the number of years until maturity, represents the annual interest earned. Strip coupons removed from high-quality bonds issued by governments or major corporations are about as risk-free as investments can be.

Holoday agreed to open an account for the Gordons, and arranged to send a Know Your Client form to be completed. Only when the form had been signed and returned to Midland Walwyn would their money be invested.

A few days after the Gordons completed and returned their KYC form, Midland Walwyn arranged for the transfer of $75,000 from the Gordons' bank to an account under the management of its most youthful investment advisor, Michael Holoday. In exchange, the Gordons received a receipt and a thank-you note from Holoday, who at this stage was still a toneless voice on the telephone and a scrawl across the bottom of a Midland Walwyn letterhead.

Other investors landed on Holoday's client list through reassignment from various Midland Walwyn brokers. Thomas Rice, a real estate agent, hadn't spoken with his Midland broker in several years, so Rice was only mildly surprised to discover the broker was no longer with the firm. He had only a little money to invest, just over $5,000, so he didn't investigate very thoroughly when directed to Michael Holoday. "Forget about putting your money in the stock market," Holoday advised his newest client.

"Futures are the way to go," and Holoday slid a blank Commodities Account Application form across the desk to Rice, a document needed for trading in high-risk commodities. "Sign the bottom, and I'll fill in the rest," Holoday said. "It's just a formality." Rice gave Holoday a cheque covering his initial investment. He never saw either the money or the account application form again.

Reading Rice's application form today is revealing. It was early in Holoday's career, but he was already employing the tactics he would use over the next four years. Filling in the form himself, Holoday lowered Rice's age by 12 years, wiped out Rice's $100,000 mortgage on his home, inflated Rice's real estate equity to $400,000, and set his newest client's investment objectives as "25 percent income, 75 percent short-term trading."

In theory, all trades made by a broker on behalf of clients must reflect information provided on the KYC form. Trading in commodities, for example, would be totally inappropriate for investors seeking liquidity and stability, no matter what level of investment knowledge they may claim to have. A special waiver form would be required for this kind of trading, protecting the client from making bad decisions, and protecting the brokerage from claims of poor investment advice.

Each brokerage follows a prescribed method of reviewing KYC forms, comparing the information they provide with actual trades to confirm that the investments reflect the investor's goals and knowledge. They also apply rules-of-thumb such as the 10/40 guideline, which dictates that the total exposure to risk should not exceed either 10 percent of the client's total net worth or 40 percent of liquid assets, whichever is smaller. Thus, an investor with a million dollars in net worth should not be permitted to risk more than $100,000, which, in turn, should not exceed 40 percent of the investor's liquid assets. Inappropriate trades and excessive exposure to risk set off red lights in a compliance officer's head, triggering a visit with the broker in search of an explanation — or so goes the strategy. In reality, the system is a sieve.

Neither Brad Doney's nor anyone else's attention was drawn when Rice's account balance was wiped out within a year. Rice, according to the document bearing his name, was young enough to survive a paltry $5,000 loss, especially with almost half a million dollars in real estate equity. And anyone weighting their investment opportunities 75 percent in favour of short-term commodity trading had to accept the risk of major losses.

Greg Weber was another client directed Holoday's way. Weber, in his mid-20s, was a chartered accountant intent on securing an MBA.[3] When the financial advisor who previously handled Weber's account moved on to another brokerage, Weber's file was given to Holoday. In September 1991, Holoday persuaded Weber to redeem his $15,000 in strip bonds and invest it all in put/call options on 30-year US bonds, using a straddle strategy to reduce risk. Weber's CA background provided him with the understanding and insight to appreciate Holoday's actions, and he agreed to the plan.

When Bruce Clark, one of the most popular salesmen at Midland Walwyn in the late 1980s, encountered serious health problems, he began reducing his client list, and several found themselves dealing with Michael Holoday. "He's young but really bright, really good," they were told by Clark, and Holoday's cool demeanour and smooth patter put Clark's former clients at ease.

Among Clark's clients transferred to Michael Holoday was Martin Karp. In his late 40s, Karp had been a Toronto cab driver until he inherited a substantial estate from his parents. At that point, he stepped out from behind the wheel and invested a portion of his inheritance in a number of taxicabs, hiring others to drive the routes he had toiled for several years. Swarthy and stocky, Karp's appearance may have matched the stereotype of a big-city hack driver, but it belied his shrewd approach to business. He felt comfortable both with Midland Walwyn and with this young upstart Holoday, whose silk ties and bespoke suits contrasted with the ex-cabby's favoured leather jackets and sport shirts.

Any concerns Karp may have had about moving out from under Bruce Clark's wing to Michael Holoday's guidance were dissipated during his first meeting with Clark's successor. Holoday described various investing vehicles and tactics with more confidence and authority than the older and vastly more experienced Clark. Besides, Holoday suggested they make no immediate change in Clark's investment strategy, which favoured steady growth through shares of blue-chip stocks. Karp knew this line of thinking wouldn't make him fabulously wealthy in the short term, but he could sleep nights without worrying about excessive risk and the loss of his inheritance, and there was a value to that. I don't want to risk any of my capital, Karp instructed Holoday, and Holoday replied there was no way that could happen, no way at all.

Former teacher Tony Noxon and Manufacturing Engineer Gary Davidson were two more clients of Bruce Clark who succumbed to the rave reviews of Michael Holoday's investment skills. Both men hoped that Holoday's vaunted acumen would produce passable returns for their money when they opened Midland Walwyn accounts in early 1991. Holoday's manner appeared to reflect the high praise; he was confident, somewhat reserved, and helpful. "Don't worry about filling all this stuff in," he said, presenting the men with blank KYC and New Account Application forms. "Just sign them and I'll look after the rest." And he did. Tony Noxon was identified as President of his own real estate operation, and agreed to risk $250,000 of his capital in commodities trading; Gary Davidson's application misspelled the name of his employer, claimed he had a net worth of $770,000 (almost four times Davidson's actual net worth), and as a credit reference listed Holoday's own branch of the Royal Bank.

In fact, about the only true information listed in both application forms were the signatures at the bottom, placed there at Holoday's urging while the documents were blank.

Davidson was sufficiently impressed with Holoday to refer Tony Honeywood, to the broker. Honeywood, an industrial photographer, eventually transferred his entire savings to Holoday.

Robert McIntosh, employed by CBC Radio as director of finance and administration, was added to Holoday's roster around the same time. McIntosh handed over $25,000 in US funds. Within a few months, McIntosh noted that he had managed to make a profit, according to the almost indecipherable Midland Walwyn statements, of $4,000. During the same period, McIntosh realized, Holoday and Midland Walwyn pocketed $11,000 in commissions from his account. Who the heck was really making money here?

Brokers were expected to use their initiative to pull in new clients, usually through dreaded "cold calls." Talking to a stranger on the telephone, and persuading him or her to seriously consider entrusting their nest egg with you, is not the activity most Economics graduates had in mind when they chose their field. It certainly didn't appeal to Michael Holoday, but he swallowed his pride and began prospecting.

He started by accessing a list of investors in National Investment Management, a popular Canadian tax shelter during the 1980s, where he obtained the name and address of Helen Rentis, who became one of Holoday's earliest clients and, as things became unravelled, one of his angriest, most vociferous critics.

Helen Rentis had reason to be proud of herself. In her early 50s with just a high school education — her first job was as a secretary with a small brokerage firm later absorbed within Burns Fry — Helen Rentis had built a strong career with Butterworth's, the leading distributor of law books in Canada. After the breakup of her marriage, she succeeded in raising two children as a single mother, remained a fashionable dresser, and retained her youthful appearance and slim figure. She was especially proud of her financial discipline, having salted away the maximum RRSP contribution each year during most of her working life, and of her close relationship with her aging parents.

Michael Holoday's initial cold call to her, and his boast about using an advanced computer program to track investments, did little to impress Rentis, who was pleased with the service she was receiving from Richardson Greenshields. Holoday persisted in calling and the following year, when her Richardson broker was transferred from the downtown office to a suburban location, Helen decided to move her investments — virtually all of them in T-bills and government bonds — to Midland Walwyn and Michael Holoday.

Almost from the beginning, Holoday ridiculed her highly conservative investments. Commodities trading and futures were the way to make money and reduce risk, he almost scolded her. Helen Rentis had no experience with commodities trading and derivatives, but she knew that they were inherently risky. Not so, Holoday lectured.

Using an investment strategy he had developed himself, one he called strangles, he could guarantee her initial investment would never be lost.

His persistence paid off, and in September 1990 Helen Rentis agreed to purchase options on US government bonds. Within a few weeks, Holoday announced she had made a substantial profit, and encouraged her to leave the funds in play, employing the strangle strategy to build her assets. She was becoming a rich woman, Holoday assured her. If so, she asked, why wasn't it showing up on the Midland Walwyn statements she received each month? Because, Holoday explained, commodities trading was too difficult to track for the Midland Walwyn computer system. Whenever she needed to know the value of her investments, all she had to do was call Michael, who tracked his clients' accounts on his own system, and then confirmed them with handwritten monthly statements.

He was convincing. Or maybe Helen Rentis, like Holoday's other clients, wanted to believe everything he told her. In any case, in April 1991 Helen Rentis, caring mother and dutiful daughter, asked Holoday to open new accounts for each of her children and her parents. Each account would be started with $10,000 deducted from her personal account. The funds were withdrawn as instructed, and Helen Rentis began receiving personalized statements from Michael Holoday for accounts in the name of her son, daughter, and parents. The balances in these accounts, it appeared, were growing as steeply and as steadily as Helen's own.

Helen Rentis didn't know that Michael Holoday had followed only one-half of her instructions. He had indeed drawn funds from her account. But the funds were not transferred into the three new accounts, because he never opened them. The statements he sent were totally fictitious.[4]

One day around this time, Roger Gordon received a curious telephone call from his Midland Walwyn broker.
Michael Holoday wanted to visit Gordon at his home that
very evening. It was important, he explained. He could
make some big money for the Gordons, but they had to act
quickly. Could Holoday drop by that evening for a visit,
say around seven?

Gordon agreed. In part, he was curious. He still had
never met his broker.

Holoday appeared at the Gordon's door as promised.
The younger man was clean-cut and well dressed, as
Roger Gordon expected, but he seemed to be restraining
some deep emotion within himself. It was more than
excitement and less than panic. "When he was talking, it
seemed as though he couldn't take a deep breath or something," Roger Gordon recalled years later.

When Deborah Gordon arrived home from her work at
Mt. Sinai Hospital, she was surprised to find Holoday in
her living room, awaiting her arrival with her husband
Roger. After introductions, Holoday asked Deborah
Gordon what she did for a living.

"I'm a nurse," she replied.

"Really?" Holoday said. "My wife Maureen is a nurse.
She works at St. Michael's in the Intensive Care Unit." In
reality, of course, not only was Maureen not his wife, she
was far from filling the demanding role of an ICU nurse; a
few months earlier she had been cutting hair in the basement of First Canadian Place.

The lie about Maureen's nursing position made
Holoday more convincing, and the Gordons more vulnera-
ble, as he launched into his pitch. The Gordons, Holoday
assured them, were doing well. The new house, the children's university education, it was all going to be within
their means, if they could just raise the size of their investment to a new, higher level. It was one of these critical

mass things, where you couldn't cash in on bigger earnings until you had a little more money on the table. Banks
do it all the time when they tell you they'll pay an extra
percentage point more in interest when you get your
deposit up to $10,000, $100,000, whatever. Except, if the
Gordons moved up to the next level they wouldn't be earning just a lousy percentage more, they could be earning
twice as much.

How much more do we need to invest? the Gordons
asked, and Holoday said about another $20,000.

The Gordons made it clear that they had no cash to
invest. Millwrights and nurses don't have a spare $20,000
or so tucked away in the cookie jar. They wanted to maximize their investment, of course, but this was one opportunity they would have to pass up.

Perhaps they could borrow it from their families,
Roger's or Deborah's parents, Holoday suggested. He
made it all seem so plausible, so logical, that Roger Gordon
agreed to borrow $25,000 from his father to take advan-
tage of Holoday's opportunity. Then they thanked him for
looking after their interests and, a few days later, sent a
cashier's cheque for Holoday to add to their burgeoning
account.

Holoday's pitch to the Gordons was a complete fabrication. In reality, Holoday had been making bond trades on
behalf of the Gordons without their consent, and that
month the trades had gone spectacularly sour. Midland
Walwyn had instructed Holoday to obtain $16,696.57 from
the Gordons to cover the losses on their account. Holoday's
trades were not only at odds with their instructions but
illegal, since he did not possess the right to make discretionary trading rights on their behalf.

Discretionary trading means the broker is essentially
operating the client's account as though it were his
own, deciding what and when to sell or buy. Having

discretionary authority over an account is highly unusual and tightly restricted. Brokers require forms to be completed and filed, and the authority is usually limited by time or portion of funds available. As an indication of how rarely brokerage firms grant discretionary trading status, of 800,000 accounts under management by Midland Walwyn/Merrill Lynch Canada in 1999, only about 100 had discretionary status. Discretionary trading without proper authority is against the law.

Instead of either admitting his wrongdoing or covering the losses out of his own pocket, Holoday created the charade of new investment opportunities, using funds borrowed by the Gordons from their family to conceal losses they neither had approved nor even knew existed. Without the Gordons' extra $20,000, a Midland Walwyn credit manager would have called them, demanding payment and revealing that the Gordons' investment had vanished.

When the cashier's cheque for $25,000 from the Gordons arrived a few days later, Holoday used it to wipe out the delinquent charges and drafted a new handwritten statement for them. Their investments, he assured them, were doing better than ever, just as he had predicted.

Over his first couple of years as a registered representative, Holoday expanded his roster of clients from various sources. Advertising executive Ray Kundinger was pulled in through an advertisement promoting Holoday's "controlled risk strategy," which appeared in a financial publication above the Midland Walwyn logo. Others were snared through satisfied clients convinced they were, or were becoming, wealthy, thanks to Holoday's remarkable investment skills. Holoday's future in-laws also proved fertile ground for cash investments; Mary Gehring, John Boczan's sister, invested several thousand dollars with

Holoday, trusting him to watch over it for her and her family.

Cold calls, broker referrals, and family connections were proving fruitful, but they were no way to build a heavy-weight client list. If Michael Holoday were to achieve everything he planned in the business, and become a legend like Tim Miller, he could never rely on clients to whom $15,000 seemed a large amount of money. Yet he had no network of wealthy frat buddies from Upper Canada College to tap, like some of the other young brokers at Midland. He was still a new boy in Toronto, a notoriously difficult city for a newcomer to establish himself in at the best of times.

Patience may be a virtue, but to a young Bay Street broker whose head was turned by every passing Porsche, patience was for losers. So in 1991, Michael Holoday employed a basic tactic used by savvy investment sales-people and bank robbers alike: Go where the money is.

Much of Toronto's money, or at least much of its independently owned wealth, resides among members of the city's most prestigious clubs. The list includes The Ontario Club, whose facilities sprawl throughout an entire floor of Commerce Court at the intersection of King and Bay Streets.

The business of The Ontario Club is business. Founded in 1909, its original quarters were officially opened in 1913 by Sir Wilfrid Laurier himself, and the club's mandate remains "to create a permanent meeting place where members could gather at will and enjoy all the amenities of Club life, including the now diminishing art of conversation." The model for The Ontario Club was the quintessential club of London, where "gentlemen" gathered to ponder the state of the world over roast beef, brandy, and cigars. The Ontario Club offers its members a spacious lounge, three dining rooms, seven meeting rooms, and a large ballroom. The food is good, if not spectacular, and members can lunch at their tables in the lounge area if they prefer, seated in leather armchairs gathered around walnut coffee tables. It makes for easy table-hopping and casual acknowledgement of acquaintances across the room.

Membership in The Ontario Club includes privileges at over 200 similar clubs around the world, plus access to facilities at local sites such as the Cherry Downs Golf & Country Club, The Island Yacht Club, and the Bayview Country Club. All of this comes at a reasonable price, considering the location and amenities. In 1999, members under 35 years of age paid an entrance fee of $275 and annual dues of $285, plus a monthly obligation of $45 for food and beverages. (The club obviously seeks to lower the median age for its members; upon reaching age 36, members are charged entrance fees and dues of $775 and $890 respectively.)

Along with being a source of valuable business contacts, the club is also a soothing refuge from the hurly-burly of the financial world just beyond its soaring sound-proofed windows. Walls are painted in gentle beige, carpets are woven in rich wool Axminster, doors are solid oak and nine feet high, and service is gracious and subtle. The Ontario Club may not reside at the summit of Toronto's social pyramid — the Toronto and Granite clubs vie for that position — but it exudes class, success, and establishment values.

Holoday became a member of The Ontario Club in early 1991. His motive for joining was strictly pragmatic: He wanted to meet wealthy people with money to invest. Nothing in Holoday's past qualified him as a social animal, a joiner of organizations dedicated to providing a common venue for people with shared interests. Neither Holoday's comparative youth nor his somewhat aloof personality suggested he would easily slide into the camaraderie of a moderately exclusive club, but neither did they prove a barrier to acceptance among the owners of old or recently acquired money, who sat absorbing *The Wall Street Journal* in the club's reading room before taking a light lunch in the dining area. Holoday's position at Midland Walwyn, his somewhat reserved manner, and his fastidious appearance all fitted neatly into the club's atmosphere. Only his youth seemed out of place among the most prominent members. Michael, after all, was still some distance from his 30th birthday, and most of the Ontario Club's members were at or well beyond retirement age. These were precisely the people Michael began to cultivate.

The club, together with Holoday's office a block away, served as the axis of his life from Monday to Friday. Instead of gravitating toward the few members who were close to his own age, Holoday began chatting up the most elderly of those he encountered in the bar and club rooms. Soon he was lunching among men whose names represented the very foundation of Canada's industrial and financial establishment, and he was especially pleased about exploiting his friendship with fellow Midland Walwyn broker Jack Labatt, who had arrived a few years earlier through the acquisition of Davidson Partners Ltd.

The name Labatt carries a special cachet in Canadian business and social circles, and Holoday began boasting to Maureen and her family about his new friend's charm and wealth. But Jack Labatt, while he may have admired Holoday's apparent intelligence and ambition, was not a promising candidate to become a Holoday client. This didn't prevent Labatt from sharing meals, drinks and conversation with the young newly licensed trader. Holoday, for his part, showered Labatt with near-fawning respect, and a hunger to acquire whatever wisdom the older man might choose to pass along.

Labatt, in his 80s, appeared to enjoy his encounters with the much younger Holoday, and the relationship grew closer and warmer each day until Labatt introduced young Michael to a friend of his, another club member named Ken Roberts. Holoday shifted his attention from a man whose name was linked with a prominent brewery fortune to a former MD more than half a century older than himself, a man who had moved from medicine to finance with spectacular, near-legendary success, and now controlled a chain of brokerage houses and bond dealers.

Kenneth Alexander "Doc" Roberts possessed both a keen intellect and remarkable business acumen. Born in the eastern Ontario hamlet of Actinolite, Roberts sailed through his education, graduating as the Gold Medallist winner from Queen's University School of Medicine at age 22 before moving to Toronto, where he became one of the city's most prominent allergists.

As brilliant a physician as Roberts was, he also harboured the soul of an aggressive entrepreneur, and when one of his patients, a stock promoter by trade, began providing the allergist with tips on the stock market, Roberts listened, learned, and invested. At the end of the Second World War, Roberts partnered with a mining engineer to launch Elder Gold Mines near Noranda, PQ. Less than five years later, the good doctor wrested control of the mine from his partner after a bitter proxy fight, and his world of skin rashes and respiratory problems gave way to balance sheets and stock options.

Doc Roberts made his most brilliant move in February 1959, when the Canadian government killed the Avro Arrow project without warning. Besides crippling Canada's advanced aviation industry, the move depressed both morale and land prices in and around the town of Brampton, where many of the released Avro employees lived. Roberts watched with interest as Brampton's entire economy sagged. Then, accompanied by a band of US investors, Roberts swept in and purchased over 1,000 acres of land at fire sale prices. Applying the profits from his gold mine to develop the property not for Avro workers, many of whom had fled to the US and Britain with their skills, but for Toronto residents seeking the joys of suburbia, Roberts created Peel Village, one of Canada's first and most profitable planned communities. He reaped millions from the deal.

Roberts was not a man to sit on his laurels and dividend cheques. By the mid-1970s, he had parlayed his Peel Village profits into Canadian Goldale Corporation, a land development company; Aetna Investment, a real estate firm; Tokar Ltd., which held interests in a chain of lumber supply stores, financial operations and, of all things, the Ontario Conservatory of Music; Ontario Trust Ltd., created by merging smaller trust companies; and a substantial stake in the Ponderosa chain of restaurants.[5]

In his early 60s, with a second wife and growing family, Roberts began, as he put it, to "loosen up financially." He used his substantial personal wealth to launch a merchant bank in conjunction with the British Hambro Bank, accepting the position of vice-chairman while a 40ish member of the original Hambro family, who founded the bank in the 1600s, actually ran the show. By this time, Roberts' assets were estimated at between $400 and $500 million.

Playing figurehead in a banking operation, even one as notable as Hambro, wasn't enough for the doctor, who turned his attention to Sheep Creek Gold Mines, a British Columbia operation whose gold production was about as rewarding as its corporate name was glamorous. Doc Roberts, as usual, saw well beyond the moribund mine. True wealth, he knew, wasn't hacked out of some rocky ravine in Northern BC or scooped from a mountain stream in the hinterlands; it was made on the trading floor of the New York Stock Exchange. The productivity of a mine was limited by the size of its vein of rich ore; the economic rewards from finance, Roberts recognized, were ever flowing and infinite.

Roberts wrapped Sheep Creek into Goldale Investments Limited, now registered as an Ontario corporation, which purchased the outstanding shares of Fahnestock & Co. Inc., a broker-dealer whose roots extended one hundred years back to its founding at Two Wall Street in New York City, and combined them with Edward A. Viner & Co., another New York brokerage. The merger created Fahnestock Viner Holdings Inc., which began acquiring bond dealers, investment advisory services, and retail brokerages throughout the US Midwest. He managed to oversee the entire operation with a staff of three: himself, his eldest daughter from his second marriage, Elaine, and a secretary named Rhonda.

Doc Roberts raised his second family in a sprawling Tudor stone mansion at 2 Old Forest Hill Road, one of the most prestigious addresses in Toronto. He installed Elaine, his eldest daughter from this marriage, as president and chief financial officer of Fahnestock Viner. The father-daughter team ran the holding company, with Doc Roberts making the critical business decisions and Elaine, a chartered accountant, handling regulatory filings, issuing press releases, and dealing with investor inquiries.

Two daughters from Doc Roberts' first marriage resided in faraway California and Arizona, but Elaine remained close both emotionally and physically. She occupied a large Georgian-style home on Forest Hill Road, just a few blocks from the family residence, and spent each working day at a desk adjacent to her father's. She also acted as her father's chauffeur, picking him up at the family's mansion, driving him to the office, and then taking him home at the end of the day.

Of his seven children, Roberts' two sons caused him special heartaches. One had grown to become estranged from the family, refusing any contact with his father; a second son suffered from severe schizophrenia. Entering his ninth decade of life in 1991, Doc Roberts may have had little to lament, but the effective loss of two sons must surely have cast a shadow over his achievements.

Michael Holoday could relate to the grief Roberts felt over the shattered bond between father and sons. Holoday himself, as he pointed out soon after meeting Doc Roberts, had been wrenched from a biological family he had never known and inserted into an artificial family unit with a younger brother, regrettably dead now, and two sisters with whom he shared neither blood link nor deep emotional connection. Like the impoverished child who longs most for luxuries he can never own, Michael valued the idea of a close, loving family above everything else. He was being married in a month and while he loved his future wife dearly, he told Roberts, he especially looked forward to the prospect of becoming a member of her extended family, connecting with numerous aunts, uncles, and cousins, all united by a shared heritage. He anticipated raising a family in an atmosphere of love and devotion, and he would see to it that he had the means to provide everything his family needed for a rich and rewarding life — private schools, extensive travel, exposure to the arts, and most of all, security.

As for the tragedy of Roberts' ill son, well, Michael had experienced loss in his own way — a terrifying, mind-numbing loss when, as a boy of 11, he watched as his 5-year-old brother David, for whom he held a special affection, was crushed beneath the wheels of a truck.

Whether or not David's death scarred Holoday as

deeply as he suggested, he was never reluctant to describe it, leaving it to his listener to determine its impact. In fact, his description of his brother's death varied in the telling. Some heard that David had been struck by a speeding express train on the CPR main line. Others were told the accident happened on the Trans-Canada highway, when an 18-wheeler slid out of control, narrowly missing Michael himself. In each version, Michael was able to do nothing more than watch, and know in the instant that he would always recall that time, that place, that incident. Each telling seemed designed to garner sympathy for Michael, the successful businessman who had once been a traumatized young boy.

Doc Roberts was entertained, amused, and at least somewhat impressed by his new protégé's dreams and ambitions. He was also flattered by the attention being paid to him by Holoday. Almost daily, it seemed, Michael would phone and suggest they meet for lunch, or would approach Roberts' table at The Ontario Club to pay his respects should the older man be dining with someone else. If neither encounter could be arranged, Holoday might call Roberts at the Fahnestock Viner office to seek his wisdom on an investment opportunity, or trade a little gossip from Bay Street.

Holoday could never fill the void left by Doc Roberts' sons, but he was similar in age. He might have been the son Doc Roberts wished he had, a young man familiar with the same financial dealings that intrigued and enriched Roberts himself, someone who could be sitting in the chair now occupied by Roberts' eldest daughter. Holoday saw himself that way, at least. He would become the male heir Doc Roberts deserved, with the same ambition and financial acumen as Roberts himself, someone who deserved to live among the privileged residents of Forest Hill.

The attention Holoday paid to Roberts, and the older

man's warm response, was not lost on other members of the Roberts family. "My impression was that my father held Holoday in very, very high regard," Elaine Roberts recalled, "almost like a surrogate son. He spoke to him in the way that a father would speak to a son."[6]

With Roberts' assets and his trading skills, Holoday suggested, they could set Bay Street on its ear, and soon Doc Roberts became the target of various investment proposals made by the young Midland Walwyn broker.

Roberts might have been impressed with the younger man's grasp of futures trading opportunities, but he was also cautious. He had not, of course, acquired his wealth without exercising shrewdness and power where money was concerned. In some quarters, much of his investment success was attributed to his ability to bend rules and swing situations in his favour, right up to the legal limit. But he listened to Holoday's proposals with interest and trust. "I think you should seriously consider this one," Holoday might say over lunch in the dining room, sliding a proposal across the damask tablecloth. "Strangles can't lose in this position. Notice the volatility." Roberts might study the figures on the sheet, smile, and shake his head. "Interesting, Michael," he would say. "But I think I'll pass."

Perhaps a week later, Michael might call him on the telephone or approach him at lunch, clutching a printout of the same deal he had proposed, and shaking his head. "Look at this, Ken," he would say, jabbing at the paper with his finger. "We netted sixteen percent on a put. You could have been part of it." Roberts would read the figures, arch his eyebrows, nod in admiration, and agree that Michael had been right after all. "I usually am," Michael would say. "I understand this stuff. There's another one coming into play. I can make you part of it, if you want."

Roberts would shrug and say, "We'll see."

Within weeks of first meeting Doc Roberts, Holoday invited the older man to attend his upcoming wedding. It was vital that Ken Roberts attend, Holoday said. The presence of no one else would be more important to him.

Doc Roberts may have wondered about the sincerity of Michael Holoday's intentions, but he seemed to enjoy playing a fatherly role to this young man with the Sammy Glick ambition. Roberts agreed to attend although he wondered why Michael Holoday had to work so hard to surround himself with people he knew, people he trusted. Could he not attract friends and acquaintances like other people, just by being himself?

SIX

If Michael Holoday had charted his career in the same manner that he charted long-term bond yields, the graph line would have reached its apex in the month of August 1991. Twenty-seven years old, engaged to a woman who drew admiring glances from other men, he was barely four years out of university and generating annual commissions exceeding one million dollars. This qualified him to become the youngest member in history of Midland Walwyn's Chairman's Club, an inner circle of Big Swinging Dicks who commanded respect and attention from everyone in the organization. He was lunching almost daily at The Ontario Club with the legendary Doc Roberts, who was introducing him to Bay Street moguls, predicting great things for this bright young man from somewhere on the other side of the Rockies.

Holoday could sit back and review an impressive list of clients he had managed to assemble, two years after being awarded his trading licence. They included his future in-laws the Boczans and their relatives, friends, and clients; over-the-transom people like Roger and Debbie Gordon; transfers from other financial advisors; and new clients attracted by stories praising Holoday as an honest-to-goodness financial phenomenon, a Whiz Kid with money, the guy to see for the surest way to turn a modest nest egg into a pot of gold. His clients represented a cross-section of Canadians, all of whom were ready, willing, and wealthy enough to pursue the dream of financial riches, both inside and outside their RRSPs, being peddled by Bay Street.

One of them, Ray Kundinger, was pleased but confused. His investments with Michael Holoday appeared to be doing well. Holoday assured him of that fact constantly, and showed Kundinger the results on customized statements. A recent statement from Holoday to Kundinger and his wife had indicated the Kundingers' account boasted a profit for that month, using two put options dated September 1998, of $60,500 from a net equity of just $119,826.05, all of it in US funds. At least, that's what Kundinger thought it meant. None of the statements prepared by Holoday matched the official Midland Walwyn statements, which indicated the Kundingers' account was something less than US$15,000.

Ray Kundinger needed advice, and he had the ideal source. Kundinger's friend Jim O'Donnell was president of Mackenzie Financial, a giant in the Canadian mutual fund industry. During the merger between Midland Doherty and Walwyn Stodgell, O'Donnell had spearheaded an investment of more than $20 million by Mackenzie into the newly merged brokerage. The move earned O'Donnell a seat on the Midland Walwyn board of directors, a position he held until the firm was acquired by Merrill Lynch.

O'Donnell, Kundinger believed, would be able to assess Michael Holoday's ability to generate massive returns for his clients. When Kundinger brought up the matter of Holoday's confusing statements with him, O'Donnell recalled that another Holoday client and O'Donnell acquaintance, lawyer Jeff Lyon, had similar comments about Midland Walwyn's hot young broker, the youngest-ever member of the firm's Chairman's Club.

O'Donnell offered to chat with Holoday, fathom his techniques, and pass his discoveries along to his friends Kundinger and Lyon. But after visiting Holoday in the broker's office a few days later, O'Donnell came away no more enlightened than Kundinger or Lyon. Holoday explained that he was dealing in derivatives, which were not products that O'Donnell, for all his 40 years of experience in the securities industry, knew much about. O'Donnell admitted that the young man's demeanour was impressive. He appeared confident, and dropped arcane terminology and complex strategies from time to time, but in other areas he seemed vague to the point of obfuscation. Was Holoday afraid his investment strategies might be copied by someone? Perhaps.

O'Donnell told Lyon and Kundinger that he was unable to fathom Holoday's technique. The best advice he could offer, if they had questions regarding their accounts, was to call the broker's compliance department. "Any compliance officer can give you answers within twenty-four hours," he assured them.

O'Donnell wasn't prepared for the telephone call he received from an annoyed Michael Holoday a few days later. One of Holoday's clients, either Kundinger or Lyon, had repeated O'Donnell's advice to their broker, promising to check with Midland Walwyn's compliance department the next time they had a problem. "He gave me hell for telling them that," O'Donnell recalled. "He said giving that kind of advice to his clients was 'not nice,' and then he added that he was tired of having clients like Kundinger and Lyon anyway, they weren't the kind of clientele he should be dealing with." Holoday calmed down during the brief conversation, but after he hung up, O'Donnell remained struck by the anger the young broker had vented, and to a member of the Midland Walwyn board of directors at that. Well, you had to give the young man credit, O'Donnell shrugged. He wasn't easily intimidated.[1]

Roy O'Hearn knew the importance of personal financial planning. As a salesman of law books, he carried no corporate-funded safety net to protect him against bad times or provide financial security. Having passed his 60th birthday, O'Hearn was also alert to the wisdom of prudent investing and the preservation of capital.

In the spring of 1990 when Helen Rentis, another book salesperson, began boasting of the gains she was making with her investments at Midland Walwyn, O'Hearn listened with interest. A new, young financial advisor at Midland Walwyn was exceeding her wildest expectations in growth and earnings, Rentis told him. The young man was smooth, bright, and confident. His name was Michael Holoday, and Roy should give him a call.

Roy O'Hearn did just that, suggesting that Holoday visit him at O'Hearn's home. He invited an old friend, Dr. Oswald John, to meet this investment Whiz Kid. Born in Nepal and raised in Guyana, John was a respected medical doctor and astute investor. As impressed by Holoday's confidence as Helen Rentis had been, O'Hearn and John both transferred their accounts to Holoday, after laying down a basic rule: Holoday would submit recommendations, but he must always consult with the two men before making a trade. Holoday agreed, thanked his new clients for the business, and went to work.[2]

Ted Gittings had parlayed his elegant stature, native intelligence, and sense of style into an outstanding career in advertising and publishing, and at age 63 he was determined to enjoy the fruits of it. A child of the Depression to whom a university education was beyond his financial reach, Gittings used his high school diploma to secure a job as assistant advertising manager at Eaton's in 1947. Over the next ten years he earned degrees and certificates from the University of Toronto, Ryerson Institute, and the University of Montreal, all through extension studies while holding down a full-time job and progressing upward through various advertising and marketing positions. His ambition and dedication paid off when, in his 40s, he was named President of Comac Communications Ltd., publishers of *Homemaker's* and *Quest,* two of the most successful magazines in the Canadian publishing field.

Gittings held the title until 1985 when, with their five children grown, Ted and wife Joyce decided Ted would leave the corporate world to work on small undemanding projects generating a modest income, leaving him and Joyce enough time for travel and regular rounds of golf with friends at the Mississauga Golf & Country Club. Gittings formed a company called Ad Planner Corporation, watched with satisfaction as the value of his RRSPs and other investments nudged the million-dollar mark, and assumed the duties of director of marketing for the Treasury Management Association of Canada, or TMAC.

One day in 1990, while scanning a proof of TMAC's publication *Canadian Treasurer,* Gittings noted an unusual advertisement. The ad's heading was direct, if not creatively inspired: *(See Fig. 1, page 94).*

Advertisements for investment houses in *Canadian Treasurer* magazine were not unusual. Its readers were financial professionals responsible for the stewardship of

THE OPPORTUNITY TO EARN SUBSTANTIAL INVESTMENT RETURNS

The Index trading arena has remained the sole domain of sophisticated institutions for two reasons:

1. Relatively high risk

2. Significant amounts of risk capital required

Michael Holoday of MIDLAND WALWYN CAPITAL INC. enables qualified individual investors with as little as $30,000 to participate at the same level as these institutions. This is facilitated through a controlled-risk trading strategy. The opportunity to participate in this specialized investment service is made available at Midland Walwyn through Mr. Holoday.

For more information call:
MICHAEL HOLODAY
(416) 369-8975
MIDLAND WALWYN

CANADA'S LARGEST RETAIL BROKER WITH OFFICES COAST TO COAST

Fig. 1

billions of dollars held in pension funds and corporate portfolios, people who boasted both knowledge of, and familiarity with, various investment strategies and opportunities. But identifying one individual within the brokerage house, promoting a single investment strategy, was surprising.

Ted and Joyce Gittings had begun dealing with Midland Walwyn a year earlier, and following the suggestion of their financial advisor, Bruce Clark, they placed a substantial part of their assets in strip bonds. "Solid, secure, and highly liquidable," Clark pointed out. They

were also as boring and predictable as cold mashed pota-
toes, he might have added. Now this Holoday fellow at
Midland Walwyn was promoting substantial returns with
a low-risk strategy and an entry level of just $30,000.

Bruce Clark had been making noises about withdrawing from the investment business due to health concerns.
Soon after noting the advertisement, Gittings received a
telephone call from Michael Holoday himself. "Bruce
Clark is getting out of the business," Holoday said in his
flat, unexpressive voice. "I'm assuming his client list,
including yours. Perhaps you should drop in for a chat and
we can review your portfolio." Gittings agreed, and they
set a date and time.

With extensive experience in top-level corporate and
financial matters, Ted Gittings was not a man easily
impressed. Nevertheless, his first meeting with Michael
Holoday made a memorable impact on Gittings. Once the
older man got over Holoday's surprising youth — he had
expected to encounter a more mature individual based on
the Midland Walwyn advertisement — he found the financial advisor's intensity and enthusiasm highly convincing.
"And he appeared to be very successfully financially,"
Gittings recalled, "a well-paid senior level employee of
Midland Walwyn which, of course, was a major brokerage
firm."[3]

Ted and Joyce Gittings were sufficiently impressed
that they agreed to transfer their assets to Holoday's
account listing, most of it in bonds to be reinvested on
their maturity date and mutual funds, using Holoday's
heavily promoted controlled-risk strategy.

Did it work? The Gittings couldn't tell. None of the new
Midland Walwyn monthly statements they received made
any sense to them. Each time Gittings received a statement, he would call Holoday to complain about it.

Holoday invariably blamed Midland Walwyn. "It's a

real problem here," he replied, sounding annoyed. "I'm trying to change it." After several calls, and sensing Gittings'
growing exasperation, Holoday said, "Look, why don't I
take your account balance directly off my computer read-
out each month and send you a statement you can understand?"

Gittings agreed, and soon Holoday was forwarding his
own statements, listing the value of the Gittings' accounts.
Some arrived typed, others were scrawled on plain bond
paper, but they all had one thing in common: None agreed
with the valuations shown on the official Midland Walwyn
statements, which continued to arrive. All of Holoday's
statements indicated that the Gittings had a much higher
balance in their account than claimed by statements from
the brokerage.

"We're having a real screw-up in the accounting department," Holoday explained when the Gittings continued to
express frustration. "They're running way behind. But
trust me — you're making money. Lots of it."[4]

Margaret Raines had enjoyed teaching. She loved seeing
the light of discovery in the eyes of students, and being
part of a noble and honoured profession. Corny stuff these
days, but that was her motivation nevertheless.

After obtaining a Bachelor of Science degree in
Chemistry, she taught several years in her native Britain
before emigrating to Canada in 1972, where she resumed
her teaching career. By 1990 she had sold her home,
invested the $260,000 realized from the sale, and retired
to live off her investments. She supplemented her income
with a small salary earned as an accountant/bookkeeper
with Canadian Executive Services Organization, a non-
profit organization of volunteer business advisors.

She, too, had been a Bruce Clark client at Midland
Walwyn, and during a discussion with her financial advi-

sor, Clark mentioned Michael Holoday's name. "He said
Holoday was a young broker doing brilliant work,"
Margaret recalled.[5] A few months later, when Clark
became ill, he passed her account along to Holoday.

Clark, as with most of his older clients, had recommended strip bonds for Margaret's portfolio. Holoday correctly pointed out that strip bonds were inappropriate for
her needs because they triggered annual tax obligations. A
strip bond maturing in ten years generates taxable
"imputed interest." Even though the bond's owner has not
realized any income from the bond, and won't until it is
either sold on the secondary market or held until maturity, the imputed interest must be declared as taxable
income.[6] Inappropriate they might have been, but this was
the investment option that Holoday had proposed for the
Gordons, who were also investing outside an RRSP. The
difference? Bruce Clark had actually purchased strip
bonds for Margaret Raines; the Gordons' investment had
vanished into thin air.

After pointing out the unsuitability of the bonds for
Miss Raines' needs, Holoday asked her to sign a blank
Account Application form, explaining that he would complete the rest of the information and get to work "earning
back the money Bruce Clark lost for you." Margaret
Raines agreed, knowing the brokerage had the information they needed in their files. Indeed they did. But the
data entered in her New Account Application bore little
resemblance to reality. The application claimed she held
the position of vice-president, that she had extensive experience in trading options, and that her annual income was
between $50,000 and $100,000 (it was actually $35,000).
Finally, in what could be construed as either an act of
chivalry or a justification for placing his client in high-risk
investments, Holoday chopped seven years from Margaret
Raines' age.[7]

The first few Midland Walwyn statements Margaret Raines received indicated that Holoday's strategy was indeed outpacing his predecessor's. Clearly, she had made a wise decision to follow the young investment dealer's advice. But while Margaret Raines was pleased with the results, Holoday's expectations were higher still, and in May 1991 he wrote to say that substantial returns at low risk could be earned by applying his controlled-risk strategy to bond spreads. The strategy was based on current spreads in US bond prices, and it all sounded very complex and esoteric. When Holoday followed up his letter with a telephone call, he grew so insistent and persuasive that Margaret Raines gave in, but only if Holoday could promise a maximum loss protection of 4 percent of capital. She confirmed this direction with a letter to Holoday, who agreed to her restrictions.[8]

Almost immediately, the Midland Walwyn statements for her account, which Margaret Raines had followed to this point with ease, grew complex and confusing. Was she making money? Losing money? She couldn't tell. And what happened to the maximum four percent capital loss protection? How was that accounted for? When Margaret Raines complained about the statements to Holoday, he promised to forward a simpler version, which he did. She also insisted on receiving copies of all trading slips issued for her account. An astute and prudent investor, she recorded the trades and compared her records with the personal statements from Michael Holoday, pointing out any discrepancies as soon as she spotted them, and insisting that they be corrected on the next statement he issued to her.

By September 1991, Margaret Raines marvelled at her good fortune in being assigned Michael Holoday as her broker. She was delighted to accept his invitation, along with several other clients, to his elaborate wedding to

Maureen Boczan. Marriage, Margaret Raines believed, would be a stabilizing influence on the free-spending Holoday.

According to the personalized statements issued to her from Holoday, her original investment had almost doubled to over $150,000 in less than a year. Margaret Raines, needless to say, was rather pleased with herself.

Mona O'Hearn had been one of Canada's leading dramatic actresses in the 1940s and 1950s and had worked alongside legends such as John Drainie, Lorne Greene, and Andrew Allan during the CBC's golden era when it was the pre-eminent leader in radio drama and stage productions. Her finely articulated voice, professional attitude, and dramatic skills qualified her for first call through hundreds of CBC productions, and her beauty would have earned her leading-lady status had she ventured into television or feature films. For some time in the 1950s she was romantically linked with future Hollywood comedy star Leslie Nielsen. When CBC's radio drama productions began to die away, Mona switched to commercials before withdrawing from performances to console herself with her memories and her theatrical reviews.

During Toronto's real estate frenzy of the mid-1980s, Mona O'Hearn bought and sold a series of houses, leaving her with a net gain of $200,000. This was more money than she needed, although it represented a level of financial security she had never known as an actor. Having nurtured an admiration for the Jesuits over several years, Mona decided she would generate as large a nest egg as she could to leave as a bequest to the movement.

When her brother Roy O'Hearn began boasting of the investment returns he was generating, thanks to the special skills of some hotshot kid at Midland Walwyn named Holoday, Mona grew intrigued and asked to meet the broker. Perhaps, she believed, the magic that Holoday was working for Roy could be put to use for the greater good of the hard-working Jesuits.

Roy brought Michael Holoday around to Mona's Thornhill condominium in November 1990. Mona served the young man tea and told him of her $200,000 nest egg, which intrigued Holoday, and of her plans to leave it as a bequest to the Jesuits, which appeared to bore him. By the end of the evening, Mona agreed to transfer $100,000 of her savings to be invested by him at Midland Walwyn. "Put it in good quality bonds," she instructed. At her age, Mona O'Hearn knew a thing or two, after all, about the importance of preserving capital.

Holoday said she should be in commodity futures. Futures were his specialty and he had a way of controlling risk.

"Bonds," Mona O'Hearn repeated. "Commodities scare me. I knew someone in New York whose boss invested in commodities and lost every cent he owned. I don't like commodities, and I don't understand futures. But I know about bonds, and that's where I want my money."

Holoday nodded, asked her to sign the bottom of the application form, and told her he would fill in the details later.

Familiar with investing Mona O'Hearn might have been, but she still had difficulty deciphering the statements she began receiving, one from Midland Walwyn and another from Holoday himself. When her statement indicated that $17,000 of her initial $100,000 investment was in commodity futures and not in gilt-edged bonds, where she wanted it to be, she phoned Holoday, determined to get to the bottom of it.

Holoday explained that Midland Walwyn's back office had screwed up a little. "But it's all right because you're making lots of money," he assured her. Mona O'Hearn's

initial investment was doing so well, Holoday suggested,
that she should consider transferring the rest of her
$200,000 nest egg to him, just to help those hard-working
Jesuits. So she did.[9]

Chester Hooper would never use the term, but he was in
some ways a Renaissance man. After obtaining an engineering degree, Hooper earned an MBA from Harvard
University. Forty years later, following a successful professional career, Chester accepted a position as a dispute
administrator with the Ontario government where he
used his attention to detail, his articulate language, and
his concern for fair play to pursue a second career in
labour relations.

Both Chester and wife Jean had been clients of
Midland Walwyn, where their accounts were handled by a
young woman who decided to abandon the business within a year. When her accounts were distributed among
other registered representatives at Midland Walwyn, the
Hoopers found themselves in the hands of Michael
Holoday. They didn't have a great deal of cash to invest;
Chester had $26,000, Jean just $20,000, all of it in bonds
and T-bills. Holoday virtually sneered at their conservative investment approach and suggested, if they really
wanted to build Chester's pension and their RRSP, they
should add an aggressive element to their portfolio by
investing in commodities.

The idea was disturbing to the Hoopers, who were concerned about preserving their capital. But Holoday first
described his controlled risk strategy in great detail, then
flashed cheques for several thousand dollars each at them.
These cheques, Holoday boasted, were being distributed to
clients who had invested little more than the Hoopers had
now.

It was a powerful story. So after signing a blank New

Account Application form, which Michael Holoday promised to complete later, the Hoopers handed over $26,000 for investment in commodity trades. Chester Hooper, had he seen the completed form, might have been flattered: Holoday had taken eight years from the man's age, and added $50,000 to Chester's annual income, according to the form filed with Midland Walwyn's compliance department. More ominously, Holoday listed the Hoopers' credit reference as a branch of the Royal Bank at 20 King Street West where Chester Hooper, as far as he knew, had never set foot.

Things looked good, however, when the Hoopers began receiving Michael Holoday's personalized statements, mailed on Midland Walwyn letterhead, at their high-rise apartment. Their investments appeared to be growing rapidly. The official Midland Walwyn statements said otherwise, but the Hoopers never saw them because their New Account Application form failed to include their 14th-floor apartment number, although Holoday's personalized statements did. So the fictitious, positive statements found their way to the Hoopers; the real, negative statements sat in the lobby, where they were eventually discarded as junk mail.

Lee Cowie may have had a blue-collar beginning to his work career, but he had no intention of ending it that way. From his first full-time job at de Havilland Aircraft as a labourer, Cowie worked his way up first to assembler and then to a supervisory position, gaining skills as an electrician along the way. He also managed to set aside a portion of his income on a regular basis and by early 1991, when he was on a disability leave from de Havilland, his investments exceeded $44,000, most of it in safe low-yielding government-backed T-bills. Not bad for a 36-year-old guy with a family and no formal financial training.

Early that year, Cowie had been discussing financial matters with an old friend, Gary Davidson. "I've got this broker," Davidson said, "who can't seem to miss. The guy's incredible. He can't be much older than twenty-five and already he's a member of the Chairman's Club at Midland Walwyn. That's reserved for the top five percent of their brokers. You should talk to him. Here, I'll give you his number. Name's Holoday."

Cowie called Michael Holoday, who invited him into town for a visit at the Midland Walwyn offices. "You're wasting your money in T-bills," Holoday said in a clipped, almost abrupt, delivery. "You should be trading in bond futures. That's where the smart money is."

Cowie replied that he wasn't much of a risk-taker, and was concerned about preserving his capital.

"We're not talking risk, we're talking about doubling your money every six months," Holoday countered. "The only risk you face is losing commissions on the deal. These are US government T-bills and quality bonds, as solid as anything you can invest in."

How, Cowie wanted to know, could Holoday promise to double his investment every six months with virtually no risk?

"Futures," Holoday said. "Leverage. Derivatives." He sketched words and figures on a sheet of paper as he spoke. "You want to just play around, stick with T-bills," Holoday almost sneered. "You want to make real money, I'll put you into futures."

Cowie was convinced. He handed over $44,000 in T-bills to Holoday. Less than two months later, his Midland Walwyn statement showed a balance of $52,421.

Son of a gun. This kid really had the stuff.[10]

Holoday began using the idea of hedging his clients' losses as a means of persuading them to accept an admittedly high-risk venture. Later, he used this strategy to explain wide variations between the value of their accounts as indicated by the brokerage house statements, and the amount Holoday assured him they "really" owned.

Hedging is an investor's form of insurance. A manufacturer depending on foreign sales, for example, may count on a deflated Canadian dollar to provide a price advantage needed to show a profit down the road. If the Canadian dollar increases in value, margins will be squeezed. To hedge against that possibility, the manufacturer might purchase options based on a higher Canadian dollar six months from now. If the dollar's value remains the same or falls, the manufacturer lets the option expire; if the dollar rises in value, the option will be exercised, and the resulting profit will help balance against lost sales.

This is a proven and generally shrewd business decision. It is also, at heart, based upon the manufacturer betting against himself. In essence, that is what all hedges are: a wager that the future will bring the opposite of what you are seeking.

Whenever Michael Holoday boasted that he could minimize potential losses on the part of his clients by using his own funds and account to hedge their investments, he was betting against his own clients. None of Holoday's clients seemed to grasp this concept. They were simply pleased to learn that their financial advisor, Michael Holoday, had found a way to ensure some degree of safety in a high-risk trading area.

Dianne Sone believed in the benefits of hedging. A client of Carole Boczan's, she considered Carole more than a good aesthetician. To Dianne, who shared duties in a sales and marketing consulting firm with her husband Gershon, Carole was a trusted friend, eager to share views on topics such as choosing cosmetics, raising children, pursuing a holistic lifestyle, and, in 1991, investing money.

This was new. Carole Boczan may have been knowl-
edgeable and enthusiastic about many things, but she had
never discussed investing opportunities until her daughter Maureen became engaged to Michael Holoday.

A few years earlier, Dianne had sold her home and
placed the cash in GICs and Canada Savings Bonds, a
classic conservative Canadian decision. Perhaps she could
earn a little more if the funds were managed by the brilliant young Holoday. "You can afford to risk a little," a
banker friend of hers agreed. "Consider fifteen thousand
dollars in an aggressive investment, keeping the balance
in safer vehicles to preserve capital."

"Maybe even have a little fun with some of the money,"
Dianne thought. GICs and CSBs sure weren't fun. But
investing in the stock market might be. So in the summer
of 1991, she asked Carole Boczan for Michael Holoday's
telephone number.

On September 2, 1991, Dianne Sone met Holoday at
Midland Walwyn and opened a trading account with him.
She handed over two cheques — one for $100,000 and the
other for $15,000. The $100,000, she instructed in her soft
English accent, was to be invested in conservative instruments. Blue-chip stocks and bonds would be suitable. As
for the $15,000, it was something to play with, to measure
just how far and how fast Holoday could turn a relatively
small amount of money into . . . well, into a large chunk of
money. Holoday suggested commodity futures.

Dianne Sone said that was fine with her, but she wanted one thing made clear: The two investments were to be
kept separate from each other. One was for security, and
the other was "to have some fun with."

Holoday said he understood perfectly. The commodities account, he assured her, would be handled in a unique
manner. By constantly hedging his clients' investments,

Holoday explained, he created a floor to protect them from major losses. The hedging method ensured that none of his clients could ever lose more than 8 percent of their original investment. On the upside, however, the sky was the limit. He noted that the Sones had substantial equity tied up in their house, and asked if they ever considered mortgaging their home and investing the cash. Absolutely not, the couple responded. They were not the kind of people who borrowed money to invest, and they suggested that Holoday forget about that idea entirely. Holoday quickly withdrew his suggestion and opened a futures account with the $15,000, and a stock account investing in "very conservative securities for long-term growth and some income" with the $100,000.

At the end of the meeting, Dianne told him how much she appreciated Michael taking the time to deal with her, considering his marriage to Maureen was just a couple of weeks away.

Michael smiled and said it was no trouble. No trouble at all.[11]

Whatever Michael Holoday needed to ensure an unforgettable wedding in September 1991, he bought. The things he couldn't buy, like a perfect mid-September day beneath a porcelain-blue sky, he enjoyed through sheer luck.

Over three hundred guests crowded into Our Mother of Perpetual Help on St. Clair Avenue. Doc Roberts was there, of course, along with several selected clients. Holoday's parents and two sisters, whom Michael had virtually ignored after his brokerage career began skyrocketing, flew in from BC for the event. A dozen or more guests were accommodated overnight in first-class hotels, at Michael's expense.

Virtually every aunt, uncle, and cousin of Maureen's family attended the no-expenses-spared wedding, which struck many as more of an opportunity for Michael and Maureen to flaunt their assets than to tie a knot. A Forest Hill wedding for little Maureen Boczan, who hadn't even completed Grade 10? Wearing a diamond solitaire as thick as the bottom of a Coke bottle? ("He gave her a solid gold Cartier Panther watch for her wedding present, did you see it?") And how about that white Rolls-Royce for the bride and groom, and the parade of stretch limos to carry the wedding party and the parents to the reception?

Michael's best man was his old school chum Ervin Schleith, a handsome young man with a gentle manner and keen intelligence. Ervin had achieved his dream of becoming a commercial airline pilot, and still lived on his family's Kelowna farm when not chauffeuring Boeing 727 aircraft on scheduled trips around the continent. Many of his flights took him into Montreal for overnight layovers, and one evening earlier in 1991 he had decided to call his old school buddy Mike Holoday, five hundred kilometres away in Toronto. The $15,000 Schleith had invested with Holoday at Midland Walwyn seemed to be earning a reasonable return, but Ervin wasn't interested in talking business. He just wanted to touch base, trade stories, and relieve the monotony of watching late-might television alone in his hotel room.

Michael had seemed pleased to hear from Schleith, and eagerly asked about his childhood friend's success as a pilot. Then, just a few minutes into the conversation, Holoday had told Schleith that he was getting married in the fall. Almost before Ervin could congratulate him, Michael had announced that he wanted Ervin to be his best man.

Taken by surprise, Ervin agreed. How could he have said No? "It'll be a big wedding, first class all the way," Holoday gushed. "We'll have the reception at The Ontario Club, which is really exclusive, you have to be somebody important to become a member, and I'm the youngest member in their history."

The conversation had left Ervin puzzled. Why choose him as his best man? Had Michael made no new friends in Toronto? And what if Ervin hadn't called out of the blue like that? Who would Michael have turned to then?[12]

Mona O'Hearn was among several of Holoday's clients who responded to the wedding invitation. She chose to pass up the reception, but as a practising Catholic decided to witness the wedding ceremony. Like much of Holoday's life, the wedding struck Mona as extravagant and not especially tasteful. Maureen's gown was stunning, but the bride and groom sat at the altar during much of the ceremony, Maureen "sprawled on a chair, the better to show off her train." The behaviour of Maureen's parents, John and Carole Boczan, seemed to Mona to be outlandish. "At most weddings," she recalled later, "it's a bittersweet occasion for the parents of the bride, who get teary-eyed and all of that. But the Boczans couldn't have been happier. They were grinning and laughing with delight, and my only thought was, 'They must be so happy to be rid of her!' Although perhaps they were just delighted to be acquiring Michael and his money in the family."[13]

At the reception in The Ontario Club, guests were greeted in the oversized foyer by massive ice sculptures, strolling musicians playing romantic songs, and waiters circulating among the guests dispensing hors d'oeuvres of caviar, shrimp, lobster, and oysters. A camera crew large enough, some suspected, to shoot a Hollywood feature, scurried here and there to capture the event on film. On cue, the musicians led guests toward the reception line, where the wedding party waited to greet them, all smiles and tuxedos and lace, at the entrance to the grand ballroom.

The banquet was everything Michael and Maureen

boasted it would be — elaborate and ostentatious. Musicians roamed among the guests, the multi-course dinner service seemed to go on for hours, and at one point Michael rose to announce that guests should feel free to order anything they wanted from the club — cigars, cigarettes, extra bottles of wine — and charge it to him. Then he delivered an extended speech to praise a man whom he admired without reservation. He wanted to recognize someone who had provided Michael with wisdom and guidance, and who served as Michael's role model and inspiration, a man to whom Michael owed so much of his success. Everyone assumed Michael was about to introduce his father. They were mistaken. The object of Michael's excessive praise and gratitude was Kenneth "Doc" Roberts, whom Michael had known for less than two months. Some guests noted the elder Holoday's response to the snub, an understandable blend of anger and resentment.

Who could blame him? Holoday's parents and sisters were treated like after-thoughts. All of Maureen's bridesmaids were her sisters. All of the ushers were Boczans, or husbands and boyfriends of the Boczan daughters. Michael and Maureen's wedding was less a fusion of two families than a repudiation of Michael's adoptive parents.

It was after midnight before the wedding guests began drifting away, each impressed with the wealth and generosity of Michael and Maureen, who flew first-class to Monte Carlo for their honeymoon. One of the biggest topics of conversation was a guesstimate of the cost of all this luxury. Fifty thousand dollars? Probably. A hundred thousand dollars? Possibly.

Upon his return, Holoday resumed wooing Ken Roberts and the multi-millionaire's assets, and in the autumn of 1991, Holoday's persistence and apparent good record at profiting from option strangles began to win Ken Roberts over. The young trader seemed to be scoring an impressive number of victories with his option strangles — too many for the older investor to ignore — and Holoday finally persuaded Roberts to open a commodities trading account at Midland Walwyn. "We'll trade together," Holoday promised. "When I profit, you profit."

"And when I lose?" Roberts asked with a grin.

"I lose too," Holoday replied. "But don't worry. We're going to score so many wins, we won't even be aware of the losses." In fact, Holoday boasted, he would know their profit before the trade was actually made, because he would see the future price coming down. In other words, Holoday would know how much he could get for his options even before he purchased them.

Roberts asked how the devil he could do that, and Holoday said it was all a matter of timing, and working on short turnaround schedules, often no more than a day or two. He had been doing it for some time, Holoday assured the older man. And he never lost. If the Roberts would match his investment dollar for dollar, they could double their clout in the market, virtually setting the options price on their own.

Roberts said he would have to discuss it with Elaine. Holoday replied that would be great, he was looking forward to meeting her. He had heard so much about her talent and abilities that he thought he knew her already. Almost like a sister, he might have added.

Elaine Roberts admitted that most of the prejudices she had built up toward Holoday, based on her father's description, were dispelled when she met the younger man in person. He shook her hand and actually bowed, and during the lunch conversation that followed he was unfailingly polite, answering her toughest questions without hesitation.

"Commodities trading is risky," she said at one point. "It's a risk we don't need. We don't need the money and we don't need the risk."

In reply, Holoday detailed his straddling strategy, demonstrating how volatility presented a no-lose situation and sketching his risk-analysis formula while Kenneth Roberts smiled and nodded his head, encouraging the younger man to win his daughter over to their side.

Two more things impressed Elaine Roberts, dissolving her latent suspicion toward the younger man and softening her opinion of him as an opportunistic gold-digger. First, he treated her father with deference and admiration, and her father revelled in it. Doc Roberts' face shone, his eyes sparkled, and his entire demeanour grew more youthful in the wake of Holoday's praise. Whatever else Michael Holoday may have been, whatever tales true or false he may have spun, it affected Elaine's father like an elixir, and what daughter could resent that for very long?

The other impression Elaine Roberts garnered from her first meeting with Michael Holoday was one of image and appearance. "He looked well-off," she recalled years later. "He looked successful."

Holoday's aura of success and achievement, his steady persuasion, and the trust he generated in her father finally won the sceptical daughter over. "It's your decision," she said to Doc Roberts at the end of the meal. "I'll leave it to you."

Her father seemed more pleased than he could express. "It will be in your name," he said. "We'll open the account with Michael for Elaine Roberts In Trust."

"It's your decision," Elaine repeated.[14]

Michael bit his bottom lip, almost as though he were afraid to express all the joy he was feeling.

Later, Holoday revealed his long-range career plan to Doc

Roberts. Midland was a good firm, but you can never become really wealthy by working for others, Michael said. Of all people, Doc Roberts knew that true wealth is achieved by those who create something of their own, who strike out to make their own mark in the world. Michael Holoday announced he would do this by launching his own brokerage firm. He could never make up for the pain of being an adopted child — a tale he rewove and returned to on a regular basis — but he could compensate for it by reaching pinnacles of success unattainable by others.

Roberts found Holoday's dream of launching his own brokerage amusing. The younger man had arrived on Bay Street from university four years earlier, and now he was talking about opening his own brokerage? Michael Holoday may have thought he knew a good deal about the investment business, but he had much to learn. Most of his experience, after all, had been based on shuffling papers in the back office of Midland Doherty. As time passed, however, Michael's persistence grew less amusing and somewhat grating. He was asking for more than Doc Roberts' business acumen in launching a brokerage, after all. He was seeking an investment in hard cash from the older man, several million dollars perhaps, to get things off the ground.

Trading stories and absorbing a young man's outlandish dreams of success over a luncheon salad and a glass of decent wine was one thing. Signing your name to a cheque for several million dollars to finance these dreams was something else again, something far too risky for a man like Roberts, who had built his substantial fortune by accurately assessing risk and avoiding pie-in-the-sky dreams.

One day, several weeks after meeting Holoday, Doc Roberts discussed the younger man and his dreams with daughter Elaine, mentioning the increasing pressure he was under to bankroll Holoday's plans of launching his own brokerage.

Elaine Roberts inherited her father's keen business sense, and she blended it with a direct, plain-speaking manner. She informed her father that she was totally opposed to the idea. Not only that, but so were other family members. They would object to Michael Holoday receiving even one penny of the family's assets for his plan. Moreover, Holoday's initial positive first impression had begun to wane. Elaine was growing suspicious not just of Holoday's abilities, but also of his motives. "He's a young man, still in his twenties, hanging around men in their eighties as though he's their best buddy," she said. "What's that all about?"[15]

By the end of 1991, Doc Roberts made his decision clear to Michael. He enjoyed the relationship with the younger man, he admired Holoday's intelligence and ambition, and he wished him well in his endeavours. But if Michael Holoday were to launch his own brokerage firm, he would not be doing it with any of Doc Roberts' money.

Michael said he understood. He was disappointed, of course. But he would not give up his dream of operating his own firm, and he didn't. He simply changed tactics.

SEVEN

It is physically impossible for a well-educated, intellectual or
brave man to make money the chief object of his thoughts.
– JOHN RUSKIN

During the newlyweds' first Christmas, fissures in
Michael Holoday's career began to develop.

Most of Holoday's clients continued to be confounded
by the statements received from Midland Walwyn; only
the handwritten supplementary statements issued by
Holoday calmed their concerns. Differences between the
two could not be reconciled, no matter how much the
clients and, in some cases, their accountants pored over
them. Each received personal assurances from Holoday
that their investments were generating major returns,
and most chose to uphold their trust in him. He was
Midland Walwyn to them, the only contact they had, the
man the brokerage promoted as something of a genius
in its advertisements, a member of the prestigious
Chairman's Club.

The trust was fostered by the somewhat cavalier
approach many investors took to the monthly statements
they received from the brokerage house. This attitude by
investors astonishes Gregory Clark, former senior vice-
president, member regulation, for the Investment Dealers
Association of Canada, the industry's self-regulatory
watchdog. "I'm amazed that anyone can manage to steal

thousands of dollars from another person who receives monthly statements and reviews their transactions, whether it's their VISA card or their investment account," Clark said, in response to allegations against Michael Holoday. "If somebody took seventy dollars out of my account, I would demand to know why they did it, yet investors sometimes shrug off unexplained losses of much more than that. Sometimes I wonder if people take these statements seriously enough."[1]

Many of Holoday's clients were taking their account statements seriously — they just couldn't understand them.[2] Tanya Sargent, Holoday's sales assistant, was constantly fielding calls from clients who were unable to make heads nor tails of their statements, or who simply could not believe their accounts had been so depleted. Not yet licensed for securities trading, Sargent could do little more than assure the clients their concerns would be looked after, and pass the messages on to Holoday. In several cases, clients asked to withdraw money from their accounts when the account balance was clearly much less than the requested withdrawal. "What do I tell these people?" she would ask Holoday.

"Tell them their money's in the market," he would say. When he fielded their questions directly, he always ensured that his door was tightly closed.[3]

Just before his wedding in September 1991, Holoday had approached Tanya with an unusual request. Handing her a sheet of scribbled figures with a client's name at the top, he asked her to type the document on plain white paper. Tanya asked what this was all about.

"It's just an annual account summary," Holoday said. "The clients can't understand the trading that's going on, so this explains it for them."

Soon he was asking her to prepare summaries for all of his clients on a regular basis, even obtaining a special computer for her. It seemed every client of Holoday's received a summary, and each summary indicated substantial earnings. When the documents were completed and printed, she handed them to Holoday, who never revealed what he did with them.

As part of their internal audit operations, financial institutions and investment firms send letters to clients asking the respondents to compare their records with those of the company's. This is an ideal time for clients to assure themselves that their financial picture is, in fact, accurate.

In mid-January 1992, the accounting firm of Deloitte & Touche distributed two types of confirmation letters, along with copies of their most recent account statement, to every member on the investor list of their client Midland Walwyn. Most clients received the "negative" form letter, requesting no direct response unless the balance on the attached statement differed from the investor's own records. Others, selected at random, were sent "positive" versions, instructing the Midland Walwyn client to sign and return the statement acknowledging either agreement or disagreement with the statement balance. The positive version read:

> *Dear Sir/Madam:*
> *Re: Midland Walwyn Capital Inc.*
> *In connection with our annual audit of the accounts of the above company, we require confirmation of your account with the Company as at December 31, 1991.*
> *A copy of your statement is enclosed. Please examine the details of your account balance and/or security position(s) as at December 31, 1991. If you agree, would you please sign this letter in the space below. Should you disagree with*

*any of the details, please note your disagreements
at the bottom of this letter or on the reverse side.*

*Would you then kindly return this letter directly
to us in the envelope enclosed for your convenience.*

*As Stock Exchange Regulators require that our
examination of the accounts be completed within a
very short period of time, your early attention to
this request would be greatly appreciated.*

Yours faithfully (etc.)

Margaret Raines received one of these "positive" letters. On reading the letter and attached statement, the meticulous former schoolteacher began comparing the Deloitte & Touche figures with her own records. The difference between the amount Deloitte & Touche claimed she owned and the balance provided by Michael Holoday was substantial. Margaret Raines sat down, pen in hand, to express her concerns on the auditors' letter in her customary precise manner:

*Account balance = $206,938.40 as of Dec.
31/91, not $68,844.40.*

Securities positions were correct. These discrepancies have been worrying me all year — the monthly commodity statement has never agreed with the Commodity Account Summary as provided by my broker yet both are reporting the same account.

There is no comparability of trade price so that the client can compare any statement to the other.

To this she attached examples of trades she believed were being made on her behalf, reported in both the statement provided by Deloitte & Touche and the one supplied by her broker, Michael Holoday. In one, Holoday reported that an August 27th purchase of T-bill options cost $140,625.00; the Deloitte & Touche statement showed two smaller purchases of the same options on the same day, costing a total of just $25,734.80. She added:

> *Yet the two wildly different versions are reporting the same trade! I have to take on trust*
> *a) the number purchased*
> *b) the cost*
> *c) that the same trade is being reported.*
> *Please assure me that next year's reports will agree!*[4]

This wasn't the first time Margaret Raines had expressed concern over differences between the amount of money she believed was in her account at Midland Walwyn and the amount that Midland Walwyn reported in its statements to her. Each month, when she saw that her account balance was much higher on statements provided by Michael Holoday than those distributed by Midland Walwyn, she would call Holoday at his office. Each time she did, Holoday would blame "the mess in the back office," or assure her that "our computer people are working to reconcile the situation."

He was convincing. In October 1991, she had written Holoday expressing thanks for the remarkable returns he seemed to be generating. The results, she acknowledged, were better than she expected, with 130 percent gross earnings on her original investment and 70.7 percent net return, all within little more than one year. "Wow!" she added. Yet the balances on the two statements she was receiving differed by more than $63,000 in US funds. "I have made detailed notes of all the discrepancies between (your) summary and my records," she wrote to her investment dealer, "and hope that the records can be set straight by year end. Meanwhile, I shall base my calculations on the amount given in the attached notes . . . It is a cheerful picture! Thank you so much for all the work you are doing on my account."[5]

Holoday never replied to this letter.

But within a few days of returning the Deloitte & Touche positive response letter, Margaret Raines heard, by telephone, from a distressed and panic-stricken Michael Holoday, who begged her to meet with him as soon as possible. Margaret Raines at first declined. She had an especially heavy workload plus some social engagements, that sort of thing. Holoday was frantic. He pleaded, he cajoled, he almost broke down while demanding that she *must* see him until, responding to the desperation in his voice, she agreed to meet him at The Ontario Club the following day.

The Michael Holoday she encountered at his club was not the confident young man she had come to know over the past year. This one reminded her of cowering young boys she would see during her teaching days, standing outside the principal's office. Visibly shaking, his voice trembling, his eyes threatening to overflow with tears, Michael told her that he had been locked out of the trading floor at Midland Walwyn as a direct result of the letter she had returned. His career was ruined, or about to be.

"You did something very serious by sending that letter," he said. "If you had a problem with your account, why didn't you tell me about it?"

For a moment, Margaret Raines felt like the guilty party in this matter. She reminded first herself, then Holoday, that he had never answered her October letter, nor had he provided a reasonable explanation for her concerns. Besides, she told him pointedly, this was her money they were talking about. More than that, it was her future security. Didn't she have a right to know the status of her investment, whether from Deloitte & Touche or from Holoday? And what was going on here anyway? How could Midland Walwyn take such drastic action on the basis of a simple bookkeeping error . . . if that was all it was?

The lecture seemed to help Holoday gather his thoughts and emotions together and he began, calmly this time, to explain the situation.

Holoday had been operating, he told her, a pooled account in which he combined all the assets of participating investors. Instead of each member of the pool owning separate balances, distinct from those of others, they owned a portion of the total amount, similar to investors in mutual funds. This enabled Holoday to provide various benefits for his clients. But Midland Walwyn had not given him permission to operate a pooled account. That's why they were locking him out of all trading until Margaret Raines verified, in writing, that no discrepancy existed between the balance she believed was in her trading account, and the amount that Midland Walwyn's records stated.

And here was the real bombshell: Only Michael knew what proportion of the pooled account belonged to Margaret Raines, and thus the true value of her assets. If he were fired, it would never be sorted out. She could lose everything. She owned every penny that Holoday said was hers in his personal statements to her, but she would never get it back unless Midland Walwyn restored Holoday's access to the trading floor.

Margaret Raines absorbed all of this with shock and unease.

To this point, no one else from Midland Walwyn had contacted her directly. Given that fact, Holoday's story about the pooled account was at least plausible. Her first concern, of course, was to reclaim the money she believed was rightfully hers, and she told Holoday that, in no uncertain terms.

Holoday had a solution. All she had to do, the young broker explained, was sign the bottom of the Deloitte & Touche letter where it said *The account balance and/or security position(s) were correct as at December 31, 1991,* and return the document. This would be satisfactory for Midland Walwyn, who would grant Holoday access to the trading floor once more. Without that access, all was lost.

In response, Margaret Raines played her trump card. There was a difference of $138,000 between the amount Midland Walwyn assured her she had in her account and the amount Holoday *said* she had. "You give me the one hundred and thirty-eight thousand dollars, Michael," she said, "and I'll sign off on the letter."

Holoday explained that he couldn't get the money from her account because he couldn't get onto the floor to request the cheque. And he couldn't get on the floor until she signed the letter.

"Then," she said, "you will have to raise the money yourself."

Holoday turned away, wiped his brow, and said, "I'll see what I can do."

Leaving him sitting there, Margaret Raines returned home with mixed feelings. On the one hand, she felt guilty about jeopardizing the career of a bright and somewhat pleasant young man. On the other hand, she had to protect herself, and $138,000 was a lot of money to be accounted for.

Two days passed, and no one from Midland Walwyn contacted her about the $138,000 discrepancy. Then Holoday called to say he had been able to scrape together $120,000 and would she accept this and his promissory note for the remaining $18,000, please, so he could be admitted back onto the trading floor and straighten things out?

Margaret Raines didn't want a promissory note; she wanted the entire amount of her missing money. But if Holoday wasn't on the trading floor, who would be looking after her investments? So she agreed, and later that day Michael handed her a bank draft for $120,000 and his promissory note for the difference before asking her to meet him that evening at the Midland Walwyn offices.[6]

It was after business hours when Margaret Raines arrived. Most of the Midland Walwyn offices were darkened and unoccupied. Greeting her at the entrance to the brokerage, Holoday appeared as tense as ever, and he escorted her down a corridor and into an office, where two stern-faced Midland Walwyn executives were waiting. "We understand this matter has been settled to your satisfaction," the man Holoday introduced as Scott Sinclair said to her. (The other man was Ken Broaderip, head of futures sales, in whose office the meeting took place.) Sinclair, Midland Walwyn's vice-president, internal audit, handed her the Deloitte & Touche letter she had returned, the one noting the discrepancy and her concern. After confirming the losses indicated in the letter, and asking if she indeed understood their significance, he said: "Would you now be willing to sign off on this?"

When she replied that she would, a pen was placed in her hand. She scratched out her original concerns, and signed her name. With this action she was agreeing that the balance and/or security positions recorded by Deloitte & Touche in their audit were, in fact, correct. Ken Broaderip watched from behind his desk and Michael Holoday blinked from a chair in the corner. When she finished, the two senior Midland Walwyn men snatched the letter from her hand and disappeared down the corridor, leaving Holoday to escort her to the elevator. Less than five minutes after her arrival, the retired schoolteacher was back out on King Street, alone in the cold January night.

Strange, she thought. No one mentioned the pooled account.[7]

(Scott Sinclair, in his testimony at Holoday's trial, recalled the event with significant differences. Sinclair claimed the meeting took place during the day, not at night; that he spent "perhaps ten or fifteen minutes" reviewing every aspect of the letter and its significance with the client, and not the few minutes Margaret Raines remembered; that the mood of the meeting was friendly and affable, not cold and businesslike; and that he, not Holoday, escorted Margaret Raines to the elevator.[8] All this places Sinclair and Midland Walwyn in a more favourable light, but Margaret Raines was far more precise and convincing in her recollection of these same events, and her version deserves credence.)

By this time Brad Doney had joined Midland Walwyn, arriving from Dean Whitter Canada. As the Ultimate Designated Person (UDP) at Midland Walwyn, he was assigned to ensure compliance with rules and regulations. The buck stopped on Doney's desk. When he wasn't dealing with compliance problems brought to him by others, he was expected to go looking for them on his own, sniffing the air for any indication that greed might be winning out over prudence.

Doney's background was exemplary for his position. Armed with a newly acquired law degree, he had joined the Canadian Bankers' Association before moving on to the Toronto Stock Exchange, where he worked on market policy. Later, he served as counsel for Merrill Lynch Canada, jumped to Dean Whitter as general counsel, and assumed the top-level legal position at Midland Walwyn in 1991.

Among the items that interested Doney were the levels of commissions earned by the firm's ranks of financial advisors. Depending on your point of view, Doney's role was to act as either a counterweight or a wet blanket. High levels of commissions were good, because the firm's profitability was based upon the trading activities of its representatives.

There were two ways to generate high commissions: by building a large roster of wealthy clients over several years, and by churning client accounts through excessive trading. Doney's eye swept down the list of Midland Walwyn advisors earning a million dollars or more in commissions in 1991. The majority were long-term staff, men and women in their 40s, 50s, and 60s whose service skills had built a large and loyal clientele. Doney noted that Michael Holoday was more than a million-dollar man; he was the highest-grossing financial advisor among the hundreds employed by Midland Walwyn all across Canada. Yet he had been licensed barely two years earlier. How could someone so young and inexperienced generate so much income so quickly?

When Margaret Raines' reply to the Deloitte & Touche form letter landed with Richter-Scale impact on Doney's desk in January 1992, his reaction was one of "consternation." Discrepancies of a few hundred dollars between the client's perception of an account balance and the actual value were not unheard of, and were usually attributed to poor memory or sloppy bookkeeping on the part of the client. A difference of almost $140,000 was extraordinary. How could such a massive misunderstanding occur? And what was this "Commodity Account Summary as provided by my broker"? It made no sense. Midland Walwyn did not provide Commodity Account Summaries. Scott Sinclair was assigned to get to the bottom of it.

Sinclair belied the familiar image of internal auditors as suspicious gum-shoes determined to unearth every hint of indiscretion. In this instance at least, he was almost forgiving to the broker. "Anytime we have response like this one (with Holoday), it's disturbing," Sinclair explained later. "But clients get confused by statements, and futures statements are even more complex." Why didn't Midland Walwyn probe more deeply into the rampant "confusion" among Holoday's clients? "It was our objective, as part of the overall strategy," Sinclair said, "to try not to 'spook' any of the clients, that we were trying to do this as much as normal course (*sic*) or have it appear as normal course to them."[9] His response to the Raines event was to direct Deloitte & Touche to send positive response letters to all of Holoday's clients.

The reply to this new series of letters indicated that, if Margaret Raines was losing her marbles, almost everyone else on Holoday's client list was just as mindless. Ted Gittings, employed with the Treasury Management Association of Canada — now there's a guy who should know the status of his investment — was claiming the same thing as Margaret Raines. So was Lee Cowie, the aircraft assembler, who signed and returned his positive response form, noting that Midland Walwyn had been making major errors on his account for some time. The attached statement, Cowie claimed, reflected only a portion of his account. Holoday had explained this to Cowie just a few months earlier, when Cowie was stunned to discover massive losses reported on his Midland Walwyn statements. The Midland Walwyn statements, Holoday assured him, covered only a portion of his investment, which had grown from Cowie's original seed money of $44,000 to $52,421 in US funds. Holoday had been so convincing that Cowie handed more money over to him, adding $8,000 in August and another $25,000 in September. Why? Because he was making so much money, or so Michael Holoday had told him.

Thomas Rice was as confused as anyone when he received his positive response letter. How could he have just a couple of hundred dollars in his account, as Deloitte & Touche were claiming? Michael Holoday's last personal statement to him claimed a balance of well over $10,000. "Administrative errors," Holoday explained to the real estate agent when Rice called to enquire about the situation. "Certain transactions weren't attributed to your account. Just write that on the bottom of the Deloitte & Touche letter and send it back." Later that day, Holoday visited Rice, pulled a cheque from his briefcase and handed it to his client. It was for a few thousand dollars. "That's part of your profit for the year so far," Holoday said with a smile and a handshake. Naturally, Thomas Rice signed.

As replies to the second Deloitte & Touche letter began arriving, Sinclair categorized them according to a numbered code:[10]

1. Balance confirmed correct by letter
2. Balance confirmed correct by telephone
3. Balance confirmed correct, with reconciled exceptions
4. Balance confirmed correct, with unreconciled exceptions under $50,000
5. Balance confirmed correct, with unreconciled exceptions over $50,000
6. Outstanding, unable to contact
7. Other

Most clients who responded to the second Deloitte & Touche letter stated they had been receiving two monthly statements on their account: one from Midland Walwyn that was indecipherable, and one from Holoday that was not much clearer, but which indicated substantially higher returns on their investment. Naturally, they chose to believe Holoday's statements. And by the way, some asked, when would Midland Walwyn start catching up to the facts, and stop sending erroneous information? When would they make their statements easier to read, and reflect the true value of their accounts, like Holoday's did?[11]

When confronted with discrepancies in client accounts, Midland Walwyn followed the industry practice of directing the registered representative to resolve the situation directly. The rationale for this stance was to avoid upsetting clients with an official "Head Office" investigation.[12] Most complaints, so the theory went, were the result of poor record-keeping by the client, and the RR was best-positioned to deal with them. A corporate-level investigation might trigger concerns by the client, blowing the situation out of proportion.

But when the client's complaint was the direct result of fraudulent activity or major incompetence on the part of the RR, this industry practice provided the opportunity to conceal any fraudulent activity from both sides, which is precisely what Holoday was managing to do.

Following this "Don't upset the client" policy, Doney assigned Scott Sinclair to ask Holoday for his side of the story, and Sinclair reported back with a remarkable tale.

Holoday, Sinclair explained, claimed he had been sending "simulations" to about 20 of his clients on a monthly basis. The simulations, according to Holoday, were designed as "model portfolios" to demonstrate the earnings Holoday's clients would have achieved had they followed his investment advice, instead of acting on their own initiative. "Here is what you earned," the Midland Walwyn statements would say. "Here is what you might have earned, had you listened to me," was the message of the Holoday statements. Sometimes he told them by telephone, sometimes he sent a letter, sometimes he trusted his own statements to make the point. Hey, Holoday told his internal audit chief, it's not an attempt to fool anybody. It's just a marketing device.[13]

Doney and Sinclair had never heard of such a thing. Nor had Midland Walwyn CEO Bob Shultz, Chief Operating Officer Bill Packham, Head of Retail Operations Bill Hatanaka, or Head of Futures Sales Ken Broaderip. Doney conferred with them all, and the general consensus was to ban Holoday from any trading activity until the matter was cleared up — meaning the clients had been calmed down and agreed with the Deloitte & Touche statements. "Traditionally, deference was given to the registered representative in the broker-client relationship," Doney recalled. "We tried to avoid any action that might undermine the RR's relationship with the client."[14]

Helen Rentis called Holoday as soon as she received the disturbing second Deloitte & Touche letter, asking him for an explanation. Holoday, of course, had one. In early 1991, Holoday explained, he had opened an "institutional" account to protect his clients in the shaky market conditions prevailing that year. By harbouring a substantial portion of their investments in the institutional account, his clients could continue to trade in commodities without being exposed to the risk of down-market conditions that were shredding the assets of other, less fortunate clients. Midland Walwyn's statements, which formed the basis of the Deloitte & Touche evaluations, did not include assets in the institutional account; these would be provided in supplementary monthly statements direct from Holoday's office.

Helen Rentis and other clients accepted this explanation. Moreover, many expressed gratitude for Holoday's prescience, and the special attention he was paying to their investments. Would they sign the second Deloitte & Touche letter confirming that the balance shown in the auditors' letter was correct? Of course they would. The rest of their investment, thanks to the shrewdness of their young Whiz Kid financial advisor, was sitting safely out of the storm.

Holoday had done what he promised to do. He had put out the fires and calmed his clients. Things were back to normal.

Still, there was the matter of those "simulations." How could a bright guy like Holoday do such a thing?

Holoday attempted to justify his actions with a memo to Doney and others dated January 24, 1992, titled "THREE SOURCES OF DIFFERENCE" and addressed "TO WHOM IT MAY CONCERN."[15] The Commodity Account Summaries sent out by Holoday, he claimed, "were meant to be a simulation of the use of all available cash . . . confirmed to me as usable funds for commodity trading." The amount of cash used in the actual trade "may have been less than the cash used in the simulated trade." The reason for the whole exercise, Holoday said "was to stress the positive performance of my combination strategy in the markets, as client confidence in understanding the firm's commodity statements was declining."

The "three sources of difference" between his simulations and the actual account balances were never clearly articulated by Holoday in his defence. He stated that the simulations "assumed full investment of available client cash," which was clear and understandable, and "assumed that I feel that given the time to expiry on a combination position, and volatility levels in the market, a 40 percent of available cash to investment constraint be used to set the upper limit on how much cash I will trade into the combination position for the client," which was gibberish.

Sensing this explanation was cutting no ice with top executives at Midland Walwyn, Holoday next composed a rambling, almost pleading, three-page document addressed to the entire group. Neither in tone nor literary style did it sound like one of the investment industry's most dynamic and successful financial advisors. Instead, it bore the aroma of a desperate schoolboy, with middling communication skills, attempting to avoid punishment.

"I wish to prove my innocence regarding the whole matter of statements or misunderstanding," it began.[16]

> *Please allow me my input to you or other's (sic) to prove that nothing underhanding (sic) has been done. I am proud of my dealings with my clients and they are very happy with me.*
>
> *I acknowledge and admit that I am sloppy with my paperwork and because of this I have put the firm at risk when I did not mean to. I've made a mistake. I should have shown the client simulation of available cash invested statements to the commodity department . . . I get the feeling that people beleive (sic) I am lying and I want to prove to everyone that I am not. I'd like to get this all out of the way to continue to do business with my client's (sic) on the firm's terms, and continue to keep my clients happy.*

For two pages, Holoday virtually lectured the top executives at Midland Walwyn on his investment strategy, as though the CEO and COO of Midland Walwyn were freshman students in an Economics course. Holoday said "the constant monitoring of the volatility of a given financial futures index is key to profitable trading. This involves ones (*sic*) knowledge of economics, interest rates and international politics."

He rambled on for several more paragraphs before introducing the core of his defence, which suggested that he was too valuable to the firm to be banished from it:

> *In general (my) average client is wealthy. I've tried to select high net worth clients, who have*

capital to risk, even though the strategy uses cal-culated risk constraints. In general, this is their risk money.

This was an astonishing statement to make on behalf of Margaret Raines, John and Carole Boczan, Lee Cowie, Diane Sone, and other clients of Holoday's who were investing for their retirement years. The message seemed to be: They can afford to lose it all anyway, so why be concerned about it?

He went on:

The strategy works to (sic) well. The number of accounts basically doubles every six months. Trading capital doubles every eight months. I've doubled my account base with the help of Three (sic) broker's (sic) that have been allowed to participate with their selective clients. My business is getting so big I'm starting to feel like a hedged index trading money manager.

The account summary's (sic) I sent out were ment (sic) to show the opportunity cost of not investing total available risk cash per client involved in my strategy. I should have put this proper disclaimer in the summary statements. I hope when everyone understands my strategy and how I do it, that there will be a better trust and comfort in my operations. I hope that after everything has been checked out and my innocence proven that I will be allowed to come back to Midland Walwyn Inc. This experience has been a learning curve to me.

Yours Truly,
(signed) Michael Holoday

Nowhere in his letter did Holoday invite Midland management to speak directly to his clients and ensure that they were both cognizant of and agreeable to his activities.

While the Midland Walwyn executive team was absorbing the letter, Holoday was attempting to extinguish fires. In early February, Lee Cowie received a telephone call from Holoday, who insisted that Cowie meet him at his Midland Walwyn office "to straighten things out."

Cowie agreed, and on February 13, 1992, Holoday paced his office, lecturing his client on the foolishness of returning the Deloitte & Touche positive response letter. Holoday claimed the Midland Walwyn statement attached to the Deloitte & Touche letter showed only a portion of Cowie's total investment. Leading the discussion at every stage, Holoday explained again that Cowie was invested in two different accounts. "Those people," and he waved his arm in the direction of the executive suite, "don't realize that this is a pooled account. They don't understand my strategy, and how I'm making you money. They're just dealing with one account here, and it has nothing to do with our pooled investments."

He berated his client for returning the positive response instead of calling Holoday first. "You should be happy with what I'm doing for you," Holoday said. "These guys, these auditors, they're like cops. Trust me, your money is safe. They're watching over it for you."

Cowie asked how much money was in his account as of that day. Holoday sat down at his desk and, keeping the screen of his computer monitor hidden from Cowie's view, snatched a piece of paper from a drawer and scribbled some figures while referring to the monitor from time to time. Finally, he shoved the paper across his desk to Cowie.

Three columns, headed Trades, Weighting, and % Return/Loss were filled with hastily written numerals. In some cases, the Weighting and Return/Loss figures were scratched out and replaced with new data. None of it made any sense to Cowie. But at the top of the sheet, Holoday had written the date and "Account Value: $76,600 Cr."

"That's what you have in the pooled account," Holoday assured him. "All you had to do was come to me." He asked if Cowie understood that Holoday was making money for him, and that it had been a mistake for Cowie to return the Deloitte & Touche letter with his claim that it showed only a portion of Cowie's assets. Cowie said he understood.

With that, Holoday picked up the telephone, had a short conversation with someone on the other end, hung up, and told Cowie there was just one more thing to do "to straighten this mess up."

Within minutes, Scott Sinclair arrived in Holoday's office. After a perfunctory introduction, Sinclair asked Cowie if he were satisfied with Michael Holoday's performance on his account. When Cowie replied that he was, Sinclair handed him the copy of the Deloitte & Touche response letter, instructed him to cross out Cowie's claim that the Midland Walwyn statement showed only a portion of the value of his account, initial the correction, then sign and date the declaration that he agreed with the Midland Walwyn statement of December 31.

Cowie did as he was instructed; Sinclair added his own initials and the date, and left without any further comment.[17]

Holoday's clients might have been pacified by this time, but Brad Doney and the rest of the team could not stop there. Million-dollar commissions level or not, Holoday had been damn foolish in distributing his own account statements and his career, not only at Midland Walwyn but in the securities industry itself, was in severe danger. While Holoday was composing his two defence documents, Doney and Sinclair were reviewing the status of several of

Holoday's accounts, comparing the earnings he reported
on his "simulations" with the actual balance according to
the Deloitte & Touche audit.

Client Balance	Holoday Simulation (from his "statements")	Actual (from MW records)
Boczan	$56,765.63 (64.31%)*	$12,059.41
Davidson	$215,323.75 (109.43%)*	$33,590.03
Gittings	$148,377.53 (75.38%)*	$21,190.00
Hastings	$79,290.15 (62.12%)*	$35,603.64
Hooper	$44,253.50	$146.25
John	$97,497.29 (84.93%)*	$8,608.74
O'Hearn, M.	$136,268.83 (46.98%)*	$66,525.95
O'Hearn, R.	$242,710.51 (87.61%)*	$145,266.00
Raines	$219,048.55 (103.78%)*	$ 68,844.40
TOTAL	**$1,239,535.60**	**$391,834.42**

* Holoday's calculated one-year return on investment

This was not a complete list; several other clients held
only a fraction of the assets they believed they owned,
according to Holoday's simulations.[19] He had exposed the
firm to significant credit and compliance risk, and his distribution of simulations directly contravened brokerage
and industry rules. Stumbling explanation or not, Holoday
needed to be punished, and the hammer fell on Valentine's
Day, 1992. In a memo from Brad Doney, Holoday received
the news:[19]

> *Your Performance Enhancement Bonus
> ("PEB") will be withheld until April 30, 1992.
> You agree that your PEB and any other commis-
> sions or payments in respect of your employment
> may be credited toward any client settlement or
> unsecured debt in respect of your clients.*

You will be liable for the costs of additional audit expenses incurred as a result of the actions described above. Such amount shall not exceed $5000 and will be deducted from your PEB.

All marketing materials prepared by you shall be approved by Ken Broaderip or other designate of the firm, as well as by your Branch Manager or his designate.

The firm will review your client accounts and impose whatever trading restrictions it deems appropriate. Such restrictions may include determining that individual clients are unsuitable.

You will not be permitted to accept client referrals from other brokers or enter new commission sharing arrangements for three months.

Your employment will be probationary for three months and you will be subject to "strict supervision" in accordance with the provisions above. The successful completion of this probationary period will be contingent upon no further negative findings in respect of the transaction summaries described above.

You will be relocated to the Liberty Branch in Scotia Plaza. This move will be effective as soon as possible.

Finally, Holoday would be suspended without pay for two weeks.

Then, a little salve to soothe the blows:

We believe these steps are both appropriate and fair, Michael. We also believe that you have the abilities to be an extremely successful financial advisor. In the 1990's, however, a "successful" broker must be extremely aware of and comply with

all applicable rules and procedures and industry
standards. We look forward to your cooperation
with your new Branch Manager . . . and ultimate-
ly putting this unfortunate episode behind us.

Holoday's antics were serious enough to be discussed at
the very top of Midland Walwyn's management pyramid.
At a board of directors' meeting around this time, his
name and a description of his unacceptable activities were
raised and discussed. On the one hand, the directors
heard, Holoday might be intercepting his clients' statements, an activity which, at the very least, could be considered suspicious. On the other hand, Holoday was the
firm's top commissions producer, and all the clients who
responded to the second Deloitte & Touche positive
response letter appeared satisfied. His activities could not
be ignored; something had to be done to express the firm's
displeasure with Holoday's escapades. The Solomonic
decision: Holoday would be permitted to retain his
Chairman's Club member designation, thus continuing to
impress present and future clients of his high status within the organization, but he would not be permitted to take
part in activities enjoyed by other Chairman's Club
members. No luxury vacation junkets to exotic resorts. No
banquets. No close camaraderie with other Midland
Walwyn overachievers.[20]

Holoday still had his licence and a career at Midland
Walwyn. The biggest punishment he was about to suffer,
in fact, was banishment to the Liberty branch office, two
floors above Head Office in premises formerly occupied by
Dean Whitter Canada.

At no time were Holoday's clients asked if they understood that the account statements he sent to them each
month were mere simulations and not actual records of
their earnings. None of the clients was ever afforded the

opportunity to discuss the benefits of the "pooled accounts" that Holoday claimed to be managing for them.

Later, Scott Sinclair was asked why he failed to raise the questions of Holoday's simulations with Margaret Raines, who would have declared that they were not simulations, not in her mind at least, but a partial accounting of pooled funds, thus blasting Holoday's cover story and career into confetti. Sinclair's response: "I didn't want to legitimize them. . . . At the end of the day, we're just interested in resolving the situation."[21]

To be fair, many of Holoday's clients employed something less than due diligence on behalf of their investments. Only 39 percent of the clients who were sent a positive response letter following Margaret Raines' revelations responded to it; the rest ignored the request to confirm the recorded value of their investments. One client pointed out that his investment was actually worth $906 more than the figure indicated by Deloitte & Touche; this amount was deemed "insignificant" and not worthy of follow-up. Another client indicated he would talk to Holoday first, then discuss the matter with Deloitte & Touche, but failed to follow up. A third noted a difference of $100,000 between the statements; he discussed the matter with Holoday before confirming that the original statement had, in fact, been correct. Others appeared similarly lackadaisical in their response.

Or perhaps they were simply confused. After all, both Deloitte & Touche had been instructed to, in Scott Sinclair's words, resolve the situation. In defence of Holoday's clients, it may have been easier and more reassuring to accept Holoday's explanation and high account balance than respond to the entreaties of Deloitte & Touche. The auditors simply sent letters, filled with potential bad news. Michael Holoday visited them, looked into their eyes, assured them that he was marshalling their investment for them, earning profits, making money. It was not only easier to believe Holoday; it was more comforting.

Holoday had one more chore. Contacting Margaret Raines, he reminded her that the $120,000 (of the missing $138,000) he returned was no longer earning money. Now that she understood the situation, he proposed, why not put it back in the account and restore the balance?

It made sense. So on February 17, Margaret Raines wrote a cheque for $120,000 payable to Midland Walwyn, and handed it to Holoday.[22]

Before starting his two-week suspension period, Holoday called several of his clients to inform them that he had enjoyed a spectacular year at Midland Walwyn, and that he was about to take some well-deserved R and R. "I'm off to Barbados," he told Gary Davidson. "Just gonna lie around in the sun for a couple of weeks." He would be checking his messages every day, though, so if Davidson or anyone else had a question, they just needed to call in and he would get back to them, *tout de suite,* which didn't sound like much of an escape from the pressures of work, but that's the way Holoday wanted it.

Holoday wasn't in Barbados at all. He was an hour's drive away, staying with the Boczans in Cobourg, where he boasted about his new appointment to the Scotia Plaza Liberty office. It was a major promotion, he claimed, a reward for all his achievements with the firm.

EIGHT

It is possible to own too much.
A man with one good watch always knows what time it is;
a man with two watches is never sure.
— LEE SEGALL

oloday's encounter with Brad Doney over the Deloitte & Touche audit and his "simulations" was not the kind of tale to be spread loosely around Midland Walwyn, or any brokerage firm for that matter. Most staff members knew little of Margaret Raines' visit to the office, or the repudiation of her allegations. Nor were they aware of other consultations with Holoday's clients, all mollified on one side by the financial advisor's claim to his employer that the statements were mere simulations, and on the other side that his clients' money was earning eye-popping profits in a pooled fund, separate from the investments shown on their official monthly statements. Still, rumours spread among the staff, traded at washroom sinks, copying machines, and coffee makers. Holoday was transferred to Liberty branch? That was nothing for a top producer to brag about. And what was behind all those closed-door meetings he was having with Doney and others?

Specific details of Holoday's difficulties did not reach Albert Robinson, credit manager of the Midland Walwyn Futures Department. He knew only that Holoday had breeched some rule or another. Otherwise, why would he have been sent two floors up to the Liberty branch? That was no way to treat a member of the Chairman's Club in good standing.

Albert Robinson arrived in Canada from Belfast in 1951, at a period when Irish workers were considered by many employers to be unreliable drunks, suitable only for the most basic labour. Robinson snared his first job when he managed to persuade a foreman to hire him for the assembly line at Massey-Ferguson, whose farm equipment assembly plant sprawled among several city blocks in Toronto's west end. He married an Irish girl, and the two settled among others in the Irish community to raise a family.

Industrial labour in the 1950s was cyclical and uncertain, and in search of more secure and less strenuous employment, Robinson moved into the financial area, joining Bache & Co. as a clerk in 1961. With a talent for assessing debits and credits, Robinson began moving among firms in the brokerage business, finding his niche in the credit departments, where his Irish lilt softened the hard edge of his demands that clients live up to their obligations and pay their debts.

Robinson became credit manager of the futures division at Doherty Rodehouse & McQuaig. Through a series of mergers the company morphed into Midland Doherty and, when conjoined with Walwyn Stodgell, became Midland Walwyn.

Midland Walwyn, in Albert Robinson's terms, became a "brother and sister kind of place," meaning it was rife with intrigue and politics. "Two people would be in line for the same job, and whoever didn't get it, they'd be mocked by others," Robinson said. "They'd come by just to say 'I see you didn't get that position, eh?' whether you were after it or not. It was very different from the old way of doing things, where people acted like gentlemen and ladies all the time."

Midland reflected an earlier era when much investment counsel was traded over brandy and cigars, and when the major institutional purchasers were insurance companies represented by grey-haired men in three-piece suits. Some Walwyn brokers, in comparison, were like young cowboys riding through Bay Street in sports cars, their car stereos tuned to punk rock or rap music.

Fast and loose had never been Albert Robinson's style, and entering his 60s in the early 1990s, he was not prepared to change it, no matter who was involved. As credit manager, Albert spent much of his time monitoring client margin accounts and taking action where necessary to protect the firm's assets.

A margin account is basically a loan arrangement between client and broker. An investment of $10,000 in a margin account can be used to purchase up to $20,000 worth of securities, doubling the client's leverage and thus the client's profits, should the value of the security increase. While the brokerage charges interest on the unpaid $10,000, the interest rates are low because the brokerage retains the securities under the margin agreement, securing the outstanding balance. (The brokerage, of course, also doubles the commissions it earns under this arrangement, which is why brokerage houses promote margin accounts to qualified clients.)

When the value of the securities held in a margin account rises, everyone is happy; the client realizes a capital gain on paper at least, and the loan made by the brokerage grows more secure, because the securities they hold are now worth much more than the loan they advanced.

A drop in the value of the securities triggers bad news in a margin account. If the proportion of the loan to the client — $10,000 in the above example — is more than half the market value of the securities, the client will receive a

margin call, requiring cash payment to restore the account
to its proper 2:1 value-to-loan ratio.

It was Albert Robinson's duty to make margin calls
under these conditions, and it may well be the least
desirous chore in the brokerage business. Clients resent
margin calls, financial salespeople fear them, and senior
management demand them.

Albert Robinson never enjoyed it, but he pursued margin calls diligently. "I'd call the client on the phone and
explain the situation," he said. "If it was an equity
account, they'd have seven days to make the payment and
restore their margin account position. If it was futures,
they only had three days." Albert did more than make a
telephone request. If the amount owing was substantial,
and the client claimed to have the money on hand, Albert
announced he would be arriving in a taxicab within the
hour to pick up the cheque and deposit it in Midland's
account. "You don't wait around for a hundred thousand
dollar cheque to show up in the mail," he explained. If a
client failed to return the margin account to its correct balance, Albert Robinson had the authority to "sell the client
out," by liquidating the securities without notice — an
action he took on several occasions, leading to complaints
from outraged clients that "the cheque was in the mail,"
and demands from sales staff that Robinson "show a little
bit of flexibility, for Christ's sake!"

Most of the complaints about Albert Robinson's diligence at fulfilling the mandate of his job originated on the
Walwyn side of the newly merged company. As Albert
Robinson put it, "The Walwyn people started running the
flag in all directions — the sales staff, the sales managers,
all of them. I'd look at an account that was overextended
on its margin, notify the client, ask for payment, and if the
money didn't arrive when it was supposed to, I'd sell them
out to recover the loss. Sometimes I'd check the account

the next day and the position would be back again, reinstated by some sales manager."

As time passed, Albert Robinson became more of an anomaly than ever, seemingly out of step with the looser approach of the Walwyn culture. Eventually the Walwyn style dominated, as older Midland employees began moving to other brokerages or retired, their duties filled by Walwyn adherents. The Irishman's determination to follow the rules earned him some respect, much resentment, and a nickname used by some brokers whenever he "sold out" one of their clients' margin accounts to restore it to its proper balance: That Irish Bastard.[1]

When Brad Doney arrived at Midland Walwyn, Albert Robinson assessed him as a Walwyn man, even though Doney's background was in the legal area and his brokerage experience limited to Merrill Lynch Canada and Dean Whitter Canada. Doney had the Walwyn look: superb tailoring, perfect grooming, shining confidence, unlimited optimism. Robinson foresaw difficulties ahead; he was running out of people who would support his actions against the highest-flying brokers out of the Walwyn Stodgell stable.

Robinson was concerned about his ability to work with Doney. He asked his Credit Supervisor if he could be transferred somewhere else within the company. His supervisor broached the idea with Doney, and returned with Doney's response. "He wants you to stay," Robinson was told. "He needs you."

Robinson stayed, but over the following year both the workload and pressure grew more intense. His insistence on selling clients out to recover margin imbalances encountered growing resistance until, convinced that management would not support him, Robinson began making three copies of his daily worksheets. One set was filed with the operations supervisor, and a second set forwarded to the manager of the futures division. This should have been sufficient. But concerned that he could be sold out by his superiors as easily as he sold out the positions of defaulting clients, Robinson took a third set of documents home and stored them in his basement.

Even Albert Robinson's wife questioned his actions. Was he perhaps edging toward paranoia? "I told her," Robinson said, "that one of these days something's going to happen and they'll say it was all Robinson's fault, and I'll be out the door. I was keeping those files for my own protection."

To Robinson, Michael Holoday was straight out of the Walwyn mould, although perhaps a little cooler and more distant than most. He was young and confident, with a demeanour that said he knew something you didn't know, or could do something you couldn't do, or owned something you would never possess. None of this really mattered to Albert Robinson, but it coloured the older man's opinion of Holoday's character on at least two occasions.

The first occurred when Albert Robinson telephoned to inform Holoday that he was under margin in his own equity trading account, and it would take either a fresh infusion of cash or the liquidation of some of Holoday's positions to bring it back to balance. "I'll look after it right now," Holoday promised. A few days later, when Robinson noted the problem continued to exist in Holoday's account, Holoday claimed he had sent the cheque to the accounting department, located on an upper floor. It took several telephone calls to confirm that no such cheque had been received for deposit into Holoday's account. When Robinson called Holoday yet again, the younger man promised that he was "on my way up there with the cheque right now." It took more telephone calls and threats for Holoday to finally show up, promised cheque in hand, weeks after claiming his account had been settled.

Whenever Albert Robinson encountered an imbalance in Holoday's margin accounts — a far more frequent occurrence than with other registered representatives at Midland Walwyn — Holoday used the same stalling tactics, the same pattern of lies and deception. "Over and over again, I kept catching him in these lies," Robinson said, "and I wondered how long he could get away with them."

It wasn't only the lies that disturbed Robinson, who discovered that other Midland officials were monitoring Holoday's futures trading accounts, a job Robinson normally performed. One day, chatting with Holoday in the hall, the credit manager asked how a particular stock Holoday held was doing. "Great," Holoday replied. "It's up to three bucks. Why don't you get a couple of thousand shares?"

Albert Robinson, growing prudent with his money, pointed out that he didn't have $6,000 available to invest.

"Don't worry about it," Holoday scoffed. "Just put some shares in your account."

There were ways to slide a security into an account, Robinson knew, without laying out cash. While Holoday never provided details, Robinson recognized the implication and was shocked. From that day on, he started watching Holoday carefully.

What he saw made him almost ill. Holoday was identified as one of the two or three top producers at Midland Walwyn, a genuine million-dollar-a-year guy in commissions. In many ways, this made Holoday almost untouchable when it came to relatively minor indiscretions, such as being late with a margin payment cheque. But when Albert Robinson heard that Holoday had been caught distributing "customized" statements, he assumed that was the end of the Whiz Kid's career. "In other times," he pointed out, "salesmen have been fired for using the brokerage letterhead for more innocent purposes than

Holoday. Sending out statements? That has to get him sacked. He'll be out of the business in no time."

He wasn't. Two weeks later, Holoday surfaced at the Liberty branch of Midland Walwyn, and soon recovered his position among the top echelon of the firm's producers.

Albert Robinson grew outraged. Not only had Holoday broken a cardinal rule in the brokerage industry with his false statements, he continued to flaunt various edicts, permitting his margin account to topple out of balance and lying to Robinson over and over about making deposits to correct the situation, until Robinson was on the verge of liquidating his positions.

One day in November 1992 Albert Robinson, having encountered yet another of Holoday's deceits, blurted out to the compliance officer, "Why don't we just fire this fucking guy?"

"He (the compliance officer) looked at me kind of funny," Robinson recalls. "Didn't speak, just looked at me."

Two weeks later, on November 25, 1992, Albert Robinson was handed a letter ending his brokerage career. *This letter,* it began, *will serve to confirm the discussion which you have had with your immediate supervisor concerning the termination of your employment with Midland Walwyn Capital Inc., effective November 25, 1992.*[2]

"I had no such discussion," Robinson explained, still bitter eight years later. "As soon as I finished reading the letter, I was escorted to my desk where I was given just enough time to get my jacket and some personal things, and marched out the door, just like that."

In shock, Albert Robinson made his way home and broke the news to his wife. Neither could believe that a single imprudent comment would end a 25-year career so abruptly. When the shock began to wear off, Albert consulted a lawyer, who agreed that he had a strong case for wrongful dismissal, and stood a good chance of recovering a much larger settlement than the one described in his termination notice. "But as soon as you launch the suit," the lawyer warned, "Midland Walwyn will halt any payments they owe you. It could take a year to settle this. Do you have enough funds to survive on till then?"

The answer was no, not without dipping heavily into the Robinsons' retirement savings.

They decided to forego the legal route. Albert Robinson brooded about his dismissal for weeks, wavering between anger and despair, blended with a sense of failure. He didn't want to remain in a city where he had been treated so badly, where every exposure to Midland Walwyn reminded him of the abrupt and painful end to his career. So, with their children fully grown, Albert and his wife decided to return to Ireland, for a while at least. And they did.

Between the day Albert received the brusque dismissal from Midland Walwyn and his departure with wife Margaret for Ireland, a courier arrived at the Robinsons' front door with a gift-wrapped package. Inside was a selection of expensive men's toiletries, elegantly presented. Curious, Robinson read the message on the gift card accompanying the package.

"Best wishes," it said, "from Michael Holoday."

nine

The ability to divorce one's mind from one's actions
is a symptom of psychological aberration.
– WALTER GOODMAN

I f Brad Doney and the rest of the Midland Walwyn executive group expected Michael Holoday to fall into line
like a chastened miscreant for the balance of his career,
tugging at his forelock and adhering to every rule of both
the brokerage and the industry watchdogs, they were very
much mistaken.

At the end of Holoday's three-month probationary period, Doney released Holoday's Performance Enhancement
Bonus of several thousand dollars to him, less $4,500 for
audit expenses attributed to the "simulations" incident.
Then he loosened the restraints somewhat, but kept the
leash fastened, adding new rules as conditions for
Holoday's continued employment at Midland Walwyn.
Among the restrictions Doney demanded from Holoday, in
a May 1992 memo, were that Holoday update his client
information; assign no more than 25 percent of any client's
investment into a single market; refrain from distributing
simulations of client accounts; and obtain approval before
placing any advertising or promotional material on his
behalf in the media. What's more, he could not accept any
client referrals from other brokers until further notice.

Holoday's Chairman's Club perks may have been

taken from him, but the young broker's large commissions still carried sufficient weight for Holoday to have Tanya Sargent accompany him in his banishment to the Liberty branch. During Doney's investigation of Holoday's antics with simulations, Tanya Sargent had been instructed that such documents were not to be prepared for clients. Within a few weeks, however, Holoday asked her to prepare new summaries, following the same format as before.

"I refused to do it anymore," Tanya Sargent says. "I said, 'No, you've got to get it okayed with the managers, you just can't send out that kind of thing.' Then I called a meeting with Ben Kizemchuk to say that (Michael) was starting to do this again, but I wouldn't have any part of that. I said I think he might be doing it again, he's asked me to do it again."[1] If any action was taken against Holoday as a result of her information, no record remains.

In addition to apparently repeating his simulations, Holoday broke another of Doney's orders by placing an advertisement promoting his "Limited Risk Option Combination Strategy" in the *Financial Post* the same month that Doney wrote his memo. He also welcomed a referral from a Midland Walwyn broker named John Speck, who spoke in awe of Midland Walwyn's hotshot broker to one of Speck's clients. "You won't understand what he's doing," Speck warned, "because we don't understand it ourselves."[2] Speck's client, a Mississauga dentist named Randy Lang, had accumulated over a million dollars from his various investments, and he didn't let the fact that Holoday's own superiors appeared unable to determine the secrets of his investment success sidetrack him from wanting to climb aboard Holoday's money train. Following Speck's introduction to his colleague, Holoday signed Lang on as a client.

Lang brought with him a commodity account he managed on behalf of his sister Jan Miller, who resided in the

US, and together they transferred almost $300,000 in funds to Holoday. Lang was as baffled by Holoday's trades as anyone else, and confused by Midland Walwyn's monthly statements, but he and Holoday connected socially and enjoyed each other's company.

Holoday continued to issue his "personalized" account statements to clients in direct contravention of Doney's orders. Lee Cowie, for example, was informed at the bottom of a totally incomprehensible document dated March 21, 1993, that his account balance totalled $110,756.77, a remarkable increase in the $76,700 balance reported just two months earlier. Holoday did note, however, in a hand-scrawled memo attached to the "statement" that the figure "does not include transfer out of funds for Fahnestock Viner purchase."

Fahnestock Viner, of course, was Doc Roberts' company. Holoday was promoting shares in his mentor's company to his clients as an outstanding investment, while at the same time making all the decisions on buying and selling investments in his clients' accounts without their knowledge or approval.

Holoday had not written off the large, long-term opportunity he saw in using Roberts' immense wealth to launch his own brokerage firm. But at some point in 1992, he saw a new way to fulfill his ambition while side-stepping the stiff resistance that Elaine Roberts and the rest of Doc's family had raised against bankrolling Holoday's dream. It was called Eastbridge, and it was a superb operation.

Eastbridge Capital Inc. had been established in 1989 by Nippon Credit Bank as a foothold for the Japanese firm in the rich US investment market. The company's original goal was to function as a corporate money manager specializing in bond arbitrage — trading in futures and options on government securities.

In setting up the operation, headquartered near the Plaza Hotel on East 57th Street in Manhattan, the Japanese Bank assembled an exceptional management team from several US financial and investment firms, including Goldman Sachs, Shearson Lehman, and others. From Citibank, they recruited Paul DeRosa as vice-president and managing director, eventually elevating him to president. DeRosa, who boasted a PhD in Economics from Columbia University, had served in the US Federal Reserve and as a senior vice-president with E. F. Hutton; at Citibank, he was hailed as a "fixed-income trading wizard," a man whose wisdom, intelligence, experience, and instincts qualified him to commit tens of millions of other people's money for relatively short periods of time with the prospect of earning substantial profits.[3] In his late 40s when appointed *de facto* chief at Eastbridge, he was at the top of his form and the pinnacle of his career.

Unlike the high-rolling cowboys depicted in books such as Tom Wolfe's *Bonfire of the Vanities* and Michael Lewis's *Liar's Poker,* DeRosa was a thoughtful and methodical professional. Despite his Mediterranean-sounding name, he projected an anglophile appearance, favouring tweed suits and sporting a distinguished handlebar moustache.

DeRosa and his Eastbridge partners functioned as proprietary traders, dispatching money under their management to purchase bonds based on their projections. It was the style of their investment strategy that set Eastbridge apart. Instead of following the arbitrage technique of purchasing bonds only to sell them almost immediately for a few pennies profit, repeating the exercise over and over, DeRosa and his Eastbridge traders might hold a position for days, weeks, even months. They could choose to reject an immediate razor-thin profit in search of larger, longer-term profits, basing their decision on a technical aberration in the market, such as a sudden flood of quality securities, or on a view regarding interest rates that was contrary to the rest of the market.

Success in this métier rewards a measured, intellectual approach over the get-rich-quick knee-jerk tactics of day-traders. At Eastbridge, the measured approach was even more important because the firm typically operated on a leverage factor — the ratio of cash on hand versus the potential downside loss — that was more than twice the maximum permitted in Canada. As a result, it would be difficult to obtain regulatory approval to market and manage the product here.

Even the most methodical bond trader accepts the inevitability of risk. Firms such as Eastbridge are evaluated not by return on capital, but by return on *risk*. Anticipated profits are weighed against maximum potential loss, and some degree of loss is anticipated and factored into the strategy. Typically, an arbitrage firm such as Eastbridge will look for a 4 to 5 percent positive return with a potential downside of 1 to 2 percent. Or, as one observer put it, "The idea is to make money seventy percent of the time, not fifty-fifty."[4]

DeRosa and his team had the insight and experience to achieve and often exceed the magic 70 percent success level, and with $50 million in seed money provided by Nippon Credit Bank for the firm's trading account, they had the opportunity to prove their talents. Corporate investors were soon attracted to the firm by its record of scoring monthly returns of 10 percent or more over several months in succession.

In mid-1992, Eastbridge leaped a major step in prestige and influence when it joined the exclusive ranks of "primary dealers" in US government securities, one of a handful of companies authorized to do business directly with the Federal Reserve Bank. Later that year, capitalizing on its achievements, Eastbridge launched a product called The Southbridge Fund. Located in the Cayman Islands,

Southbridge pooled money from individual investors, and followed the same strategies as the Eastbridge traders, meaning that anyone with minimum initial capital of $5 million could share in the gilt-edged talents — and much of the profits — of Eastbridge investment managers. Eastbridge charged an annual management fee of 2 percent of assets from the Southbridge Fund, plus a performance fee of 20 percent of all profits earned beyond the first 5 percent. In other words, investors kept 100 percent of the first 5 percent of profits, and 80 percent of all profits above that level. The charges were hefty — typical bond mutual funds operating in a similar manner charge 2 percent as a management fee and apply no performance fees — but the returns were worth it, because the performance of Eastbridge easily outpaced similar funds.

Michael Holoday was familiar with bond arbitrage, and he boasted that he made a specialty of it through his study of long-term interest rate cycles. Under different circumstances, he might have applied for a position at Eastbridge, a prestigious house that not only made money on a fairly steady basis for its clients, but also did it with an element of class.

Holoday wanted to transfer the Eastbridge investment magic across the border and market it to Canadian investors, with himself at the helm. The timing couldn't have been better. Canadians were chasing a wide range of investment options beyond GICs and savings accounts, especially for their Registered Retirement Savings Plans. Almost overnight, mutual funds had become the choice of savvy investors, and the relative merits of Trimark and Mackenzie became as much a part of cocktail party gossip in many homes as the emergence of Ontario wines and the introduction of the GST.

The basic appeal of mutual funds is easy to understand. Individuals cannot turn a thousand dollars into two thousand dollars without a lot of hard work. But a thousand individuals investing a thousand Loonies each can drop a million dollars into the lap of a fund manager who, with her expertise, databank, and skills, can convert it into two million dollars over time — or so the claim goes.

Most mutual funds are promoted as long-term performers. In this case, long-term usually means five years or more, especially for an equity-based fund. Five years, as the joke goes, isn't a long time — for a tree. Many people keep looking for a better formula than one that advises mixing equal measures of patience and prudence.

By mid-1992, the total investment in Canadian mutual funds had reached $70 billion, and was growing in spectacular fashion. Many observers predicted that assets under management by the country's mutual funds would easily exceed $300 billion by 2000. A solidly managed fund reflecting the performance record of Eastbridge, dealing in quality bonds and demonstrating consistent above-average profits, would be a natural for Canadian investors. All it would need to succeed would be a corporate structure provided by a well-established brokerage, a lower entry level for investors, a management team familiar with bond arbitrage strategy, and a suitable name.

Midland Walwyn could provide the structure, and Michael Holoday was the ideal person to head it. The fund would mirror the Eastbridge/Southbridge strategy under the Canadian firm's corporate umbrella, which provided the perfect name: The Northbridge Fund.

Through the balance of 1992, Holoday continued to woo Doc Roberts with promises of wealth and success via a brokerage firm to be called Holoday/Roberts Securities. Most of his time and efforts, however, were devoted to pacifying clients who, though they may have been calmed by his previous explanations, continued to pester him with niggling concerns about the value of their accounts and ongoing discrepancies between the two statements they were receiving. In the midst of it all, he was still fighting rear-guard actions with pesky Midland Walwyn compliance officials.

One of these sessions arose in June 1992, when someone in Midland Walwyn's compliance area noted that Holoday appeared to be making discretionary trades on Margaret Raines' account without any authority on file. Holoday was asked to explain his actions, and in response he submitted a letter dated June 15, 1992 reading:

> *Attn: MICHAEL E. HOLODAY*
> *This letter is written to request you to trade $65,000 US plus any profits realized in account SCO 11636 from this date on until I further instruct you to change the amount of capital to be traded in this account.*
> *This represents approximately 20% of my liquid net worth as of June 15, 1992.*
> *Yours truly,*
> *(SIGNED) Margaret Raines*[5]

Instead of calming Midland Walwyn's watchdogs, this set off another flurry of flashing red lights, and a memo from Compliance landed on the desk of J. McCabe, manager of the Scotia Plaza branch office where Holoday had been reassigned. Issued by D. Davis and dated June 25, the memo read:

> *I attach a copy of the latest letter received from this client (Margaret Raines). According to my records the client has net deposits life to date of $104,000. As of 6/22 the options have a value of $47,000, which indicates that client is presently*

down approx. $57,000 life to date.

The manner in which the client has composed her letter indicates that only $65,000 of her capital is to be used. No mention is made of any previous losses. Assuming that the client means what she says, there remains only $8,000 to be placed at risk, but we have placed $39,000 at risk.

My point is that the letter from the client is unacceptable as it is written. It makes no reference to prior losses, only to (non-existent) realized profits. If we accept what the client says then the account should be liquidated now before we exceed the $65,000 limit imposed. Please discuss the matter with Mike Holoday and advise me ASAP. Thanks.[6]

Copies were sent to Brad Doney and, conveniently, to Michael Holoday.

Before either McCabe or Doney could confront Holoday with this problem — Holoday had contravened one of Doney's key directives to him — Holoday produced a document absolving him of any blame and eliminating the concerns of the compliance officer. Unaddressed and undated, except for a handwritten notation claiming it had been received on August 30, 1991, the letter read:

This is to acknowledge that my current losses to date have exceeded $53,000 for which I take full responsibility.

Furthermore, I wish to continue trading futures. I am prepared to risk an additional $100,000.

Please find enclosed an updated financial statement detailing my position.

Yours sincerely,
(SIGNED) Margaret Raines[7]

Nothing else was said on record about the matter. Remarkably, no one appears to have found it curious that the June 15th letter from Margaret Raines had been written on a Midland Walwyn letterhead. Nor did anyone compare the signatures on that letter, and the August 30th note acknowledging responsibility for Ms. Raines' losses, with a verified signature on file. Because, while both documents were signed "Margaret Raines," she had no knowledge of their existence. And, of course, neither signature was hers.[8]

Michael Holoday sailed through the summer of 1992 on a new wave of success and achievement, as recorded in his personal account statements to clients. He nurtured his warm relationship with Doc Roberts, and kept attempting to thaw his rather more frosty dealings with Doc's daughter Elaine. In spite of periodic missives from Brad Doney, his work at Midland Walwyn re-established him as a bright, if somewhat tarnished star.

More important, his high volume of trades continued to generate sufficient commissions to qualify him once again for membership in the Chairman's Club, a distinction he trumpeted from the letterhead of his Midland Walwyn stationery. To remain a member, he had to generate over one million dollars annually in commissions. "He was creating incredible sales," Tanya Sargent remembers. "I think once we broke the record (in commissions for the brokerage). It was two-hundred and sixty thousand dollars for the month, or something like that, a record for the firm."[9]

He needed those commissions because his personal expenditures were escalating with all the abandon of the proverbial drunken sailor.

Some of his expenses were nickel-and-dime stuff, compared with Holoday's purported income and wealth. When one of Maureen's cousins was married in the summer of

1992, Michael provided Rolls-Royce limousines for the entire wedding party. And when Maureen's uncle Jacques phoned Michael about purchasing $100-a-plate tickets to support a local political fund-raising dinner, Michael insisted on purchasing an entire table, mailing Jacques a cheque for $1,000. A few weeks later, when Jacques informed his nephew that the dinner had been called off due to lack of interest, Holoday told him not to worry, just forget about returning the $1,000 cheque and "spend it any way you want." Jacques contributed the money to a local charity.[10]

Other examples of Michael's generosity became legendary among the family, including his birthday present to Connie Gould, Maureen's older friend from her days at Via Condotti. Maureen recalled her friend's dream of shopping in Paris, and suggested that she and Michael take Connie there for a long weekend. Michael had a better idea. Why not make it an entire week? If they were going to France, forget about flying economy. They would take the Concorde out of New York. And what's the best hotel in Paris? Book a suite there for the week. Michael, of course, was much too busy to join them. He simply paid the bills, well over $25,000 for flights, luxury right-bank hotel accommodation, meals, and shopping. For several weeks afterward, he and Maureen delighted in describing the journey and its expense, its lavishness, to friends and relatives, watching the expression on their faces, the shock and the envy.

If Michael couldn't afford the time to visit Paris, he could afford the expense of dining as well as anyone in Toronto. He was not among the social set who delighted in discovering unknown *boîtes* and favouring them before the crowds followed. Holoday stuck to the tried and the true, trusting the taste of the established elite who, in the mid-1990s, were lending all their support to the Centro grill

and wine bar on Yonge Street above Eglinton. He and
Maureen were regulars at Centro, usually in the company
of a selected client or two. He delighted in ordering an
expensive bottle of wine, savouring it, and ordering another for his friends, for his clients, for someone at the next
table whom he knew in the investment business. He
favoured the main dining room, decorated like a resplen-
dent Venetian palace with ceilings 18-feet high, where he
sampled Centro's exotic and expensive menu: Imported
Buffalo Milk Mozzarella and Vine-Ripened Tomatoes with
a Julienne of Basil, Extra Virgin Olive Oil and 120-year-
old Balsamic Vinegar, a splendid appetizer for $17.50. To
his guests, he recommended the Roasted Squab and
Seared Quebec *Foie Gras* with a *Fricassee* of Seasonal
Mushrooms, Quince Compote and Lavender Honey
Essence for $39.50, or the Nunavik Caribou Chop Seared
with Juniper Berry Oil, Alsatian *Spatzle* and Arctic
Cloudberry Sauce for $42.95, and isn't that Harrison Ford
sitting over there in the corner?

Michael, it seemed, was not only Midas. He was also a
latter-day Odysseus, achieving wealth and riches in spite
of obstacles placed in his path by other, less competent,
error-prone associates. At a Boczan family gathering during the summer of 1992, Paul Legere pulled his wife's
brother-in-law aside and pointed out that his most recent
Midland Walwyn statement claimed that Legere's account
was virtually empty. What, the muscular Legere demanded, was going on?

"It's the accountants," Holoday explained. "They're
idiots, making mistakes all over the place. I'm in the
process of getting them all fired. But don't worry, Paul,"
Holoday added. "You're making money. Lots of it."

Holoday rediscovered his love for hockey, and he would
rent the Chesswood Arena first for pickup games and later
for teams made up of players from Midland Walwyn and

other brokerages. Sometimes only four or five players would show up, skating around and around the empty arena, not even playing hockey. Holoday would pick up the bill, often several hundred dollars, without batting an eye. He created and bankrolled his own hockey team, the Bruins, and at one point, according to Holoday, arranged a trip to Europe for the team, chartering a jet and covering the entire expense out of his own pocket. Holoday was to be captain and player/coach on the junket, but the evening before they were to depart Maureen told him of a dream she had, a dream of a horrific plane crash. Fearing it was a premonition, she begged him not to go, so he reluctantly stayed home. But he paid for the entire trip nevertheless.[11]

In the autumn of 1992, the Holodays needed a new home. Maureen was expecting their first child at the end of the year, and the tiny St. Clair Avenue apartment was already cramped. A suburban tract house was out of the question. Michael wanted a house that reflected his elevated status and income, and he and Maureen settled on 265 Forest Hill Road, a square stone-faced residence with severe lines. They submitted an offer at the full asking price of $1,295,000, which was almost twice the amount the previous owner had paid to acquire the property less than two years earlier. The best feature of the three-bedroom home was its location, backing onto a shallow ravine and nature trail, and just a few minutes from the homes of both Kenneth and Elaine Roberts.

On the afternoon of Thursday, October 8, 1992, Doc and Elaine Roberts were in their Fahnestock Viner offices on University Avenue when they received an urgent telephone call from Michael Holoday. He and Maureen, Holoday explained, were spending Thanksgiving weekend with his parents in Revelstoke, and an urgent matter had come up. The Holodays had placed an offer on 265 Forest Hill Road, and the deal was scheduled to close the following day. The mortgage had been arranged, but the bank screwed up and a scheduled transfer of funds had not taken place. He and Maureen were unable to get a flight back to Toronto because of heavy Thanksgiving traffic, and they risked losing out on the deal and forfeiting their down payment. Could Doc Roberts help them out?

Roberts asked what kind of help they needed.

If Roberts' company, Elka Estates Ltd., would lend the Holodays $170,000 for two weeks, from October 8 to 22, Holoday would repay the amount plus 2.5 percent interest per week, which worked out to $8,500. Michael would fax an agreement directly back to him, and provide details regarding delivery of the cheque and so on.

Ken Roberts was wealthy beyond the wildest dreams of the average Canadian, but making $8,500 profit with the stroke of a pen still appealed to him. Besides, he had grown to like and trust Holoday and his succeed-or-be-damned style. If he could help the young man and pocket a few bucks (at a pro-rated annual interest of 130 percent), why not?

As usual, Elaine Roberts was not as enthusiastic and trusting as her father but, again as usual, she left the decision to him. When he agreed, Holoday faxed a handwritten note from BC, acknowledging that he was to pay Elka Estates Ltd. the sum of Cdn$170,000 on or before October 22, 1992, plus interest at the rate of 2.5 percent per week from October 8 to October 22, 1992.[12] This was good enough for Ken Roberts, who issued a cheque for $170,000 and forwarded it to the real estate agent the following day.

Holoday achieved a number of things with this single telephone call. First, he avoided losing the house he and Maureen planned to make their family home, with the birth of their first child just weeks away. More significantly, he managed to borrow $170,000 from his benefactor with ease, and by long distance. Finally, he had leveraged the purchase of a $1.3 million home with only $150,000 of his own cash. He failed to inform Roberts that the Royal Bank had issued a first mortgage on the property of $650,000 and a second mortgage of $325,000, leaving Holoday with a $320,000 down payment. If Roberts' $170,000 loan at 130 percent annual interest was needed to close the deal, this meant the Holodays had put up just $150,000 for the purchase.

On their return from BC, the Holodays moved into 265 Forest Hill Road and became neighbours of Doc Roberts and Elaine Roberts, among other Toronto notables. And when Holoday repaid the loan on time with interest as agreed in the note, he cemented his trust with Doc Roberts more solidly than ever. He had also broken a cardinal rule in the brokerage industry against borrowing money from clients. But who would know?

Holoday drew closer to Doc Roberts and his untapped millions. On November 4, he visited the Fahnestock Viner offices at 181 University Avenue and brought an intriguing proposition for his mentor.

Holoday claimed he had a US$160,000 "yield curve arbitrage" deal ready for closing that afternoon, one that would profit from Holoday's familiarity with interest rate cycles. He was setting up the trade in his "pro" account, a special trading account for the exclusive use of selected brokers at Midland Walwyn. The deal would wind up the following Monday, November 9, and net Holoday $6,000. Holoday had already made the trade but, due to a short-term liquidity problem, he couldn't cover all of it right away. So here was the deal: If Doc Roberts kicked in $80,000 in US funds, Holoday and he would split the $6,000 net in five days.

Doc Roberts thought it sounded fine, but again Elaine was hesitant. For one thing, she still had reservations about Holoday, whom she believed was "stalking" her father and other wealthy elders at The Ontario Club. For another thing, she had no idea what "yield curve arbitrage" meant. If her father insisted on loaning Holoday $80,000 he should at least get something down on paper.

Holoday agreed, and Elaine typed a form for him to complete and sign:[13]

> *I, Michael Holoday, promise to pay the sum of eighty thousand United States dollars (US$80,000.00) plus interest of three thousand United States dollars (US$3000,00) to Kenneth A. Roberts on November 9, 1992.*
> *Dated this 4th day of November, 1992.*
> *(SIGNED) Michael Holoday*

A few minutes later, Holoday walked out onto University Avenue with a cheque for $80,000 in his pocket, made out to him by his friend and new investment partner Doc Roberts. The following Monday, he returned with a cheque for $83,000 in Roberts' name and a suggestion: Why not do this on a regular basis? They would call it their daily trades, parlaying the original investment on new deals each day. Michael would locate the deal, discuss it over lunch with Doc Roberts, fix the anticipated net profit, and exchange cheques. Roberts' cheque to Holoday, bearing that day's date, would represent his share of the trade; Holoday's cheque, made out to Roberts and postdated by one day, would repay Roberts' investment and add his share of the profit.

It didn't take long for each side to drop the discussion about trade details, because Holoday couldn't seem to lose. He made a profit on every deal, and when Doc and Elaine

Roberts asked how he managed to do it, Holoday attributed it to "a mathematical formula. When you do the math
right, it's a sure thing."

Could a man who had accumulated hundreds of millions of dollars through shrewd financial manoeuvring
accept the concept of "a sure thing" in any investment
based on commodities and futures? Doc Roberts did, and
the size of the cheques he exchanged virtually every day
with Holoday grew as he and daughter Elaine continued to
plough their earnings — designated as "loan interest" —
back into Holoday's scheme.

At some point, Ken and Elaine Roberts wanted more —
more comprehension of Holoday's secret, more assurance
that they were dealing with real assets and not fiscal
smoke and mirrors. Neither knew much about yield curve
trading and interest arbitrage, but they knew that nobody
could turn a profit on trades day after day, week after
week, without losing even a penny.

"I'm mirroring a trading strategy designed by
Eastbridge in New York," he explained. Had they heard of
Eastbridge? They hadn't, but it would be easy to confirm
its existence and status on Wall Street. When they did,
they discovered it was blue-chip all the way.

Why would Eastbridge open the books on its trading
strategy for Michael Holoday, a young broker from
Toronto? Because, Holoday explained, he was establishing
a fund to be named Northbridge, which would provide
Eastbridge with a minimum $50 million in fresh capital. In
exchange, Eastbridge management agreed to provide
Holoday with information about their proprietary trading
system, on the understanding that he would use this
knowledge for his own trades only. Technically, by including the Roberts in his own trading account, he wasn't breaking the agreement. He just wanted them to share in the
largesse. That's what you do for your closest friends, right?

That's how you reward those you care about and admire.

The Roberts were so pleased with Holoday's investment performance that they ignored any problem that arose from time to time, even if the problem concerned cheques whose value represented small fortunes to most Canadians. Two days before Christmas 1992, for example, a cheque from Holoday for $302,490 in US funds was returned NSF, followed by another for $578,275 the following March. In both cases, Holoday issued new cheques to cover the arrears, and neither event appeared to disturb the Roberts greatly, as long as Holoday made good on his promise to replace the cheques. This set the stage for a later deluge, in the spring of 1994, when four cheques from Holoday totalling almost $2.5 million in US funds were returned NSF, and still no alarm bells sounded.

In spite of the positive face he was wearing for the benefit of Ken and Elaine Roberts, Holoday was finding himself in trouble again with Brad Doney. A memo issued by the Midland Walwyn senior vice-president in early 1993 was almost weighted down with exasperation.[14] *Your repeated violations of requirements,* Doney lectured in his memo, *either through carelessness or deliberate attempts to circumvent restraints, have seriously undermined the level of trust that must exist between you and the firm. Further violations of these continued conditions of employment will result in further disciplinary action and may result in the termination of your employment.*

Doney listed ten conditions, expanding the memo he had sent when he lifted Holoday's probationary terms. Holoday had to maintain a record of all conversations with clients where orders were concerned, and must not invest more than 25 percent of available funds in any account to a single market. Doney closed Holoday's personal trading account when the risk factor — the amount of money

Holoday might lose from his trades — exceeded $250,000. He also expressed concern that, of 22 of Holoday's clients, only 6 were showing a profit based on their original investment. One was at a break-even point, and the remaining 15 had lost money. He could have gone further, by noting that the profits generated by Holoday's "controlled risk" strategy totalled only $124,223 while the accumulated losses measured $878,831. What's more, three of Holoday's clients not only suffered losses, but their assets had been depleted. Whether they knew it or not, they were broke.

Still, Doney could not ignore Holoday's large influx of commissions, which reached well over a million dollars annually.

When Maureen Holoday gave birth to their first child, a boy, at the end of 1992, Michael appeared as content as he had ever been. The troubles with the Deloitte & Touche audit and Holoday's "simulations" were almost a year in the past, and he simply ignored Doney's complaints. Holoday had a Forest Hill home, an attractive wife, and a fine healthy son. Needing a family car, he acquired a Jeep Grand Cherokee for Maureen and the baby, and he celebrated his new status as a father with the purchase of a Ferrari 328 GTS for himself. For his beaming in-laws John and Carole Boczan, he bought Cartier 18-carat gold watches to commemorate the birth of their grandson.

Carole Boczan displayed her Cartier watch and photos of weekend skiing vacations in the Laurentians to her clients with understandable pride. She described Michael's Forest Hill home and his plans to take everyone to Europe the following year, and antique-hunting Sundays with daughter Maureen. If a customer grew sufficiently impressed, Carole would urge her to contact Michael to handle her investments.

Paul and Joanne Simpkin entered their 60s in good financial shape. Paul had just retired from operating a manufacturing company in partnership with his brother, and
both he and his wife were enjoying their home near
Campbellford, Ontario.

Joanne Simpkin frequently treated herself to visits to
Carole Boczan's Cobourg beauty salon. Carole was an
expert beautician and, lately, an exceptionally proud
mother-in-law, gushing about the ability of her daughter's
husband to generate high returns for his clients' investments. If the Simpkins were smart, Carole suggested on
several occasions, they would transfer their investments
to him.

Joanne Simpkin began relaying these messages to her
husband after visiting Carole Boczan's salon. Paul
Simpkin was sceptical. Anybody could boast about making
money in the market, but delivering on the promise was
something else. Besides, when you invested your money,
you chose the firm as much as the individual. "Next time
she starts bragging about her son-in-law," Simpkin
advised his wife, "ask if he works on his own or with some
big investment house."

When Joanne Simpkin reported that Holoday was
employed with Midland Walwyn, where he was the
youngest member of the company's Chairman's Club, Paul
Simpkin grew interested. Holoday was no lone wolf hus-
tler, but an apparently highly regarded trader with a big,
solid brokerage house. Perhaps they should meet with
Holoday after all.

On Easter Monday 1993, Holoday greeted the
Simpkins at his Midland Walwyn office. He was only mildly surprised when Paul Simpkin announced that he
planned to tape their conversation. Totally without guile,
Simpkin explained that he often taped these kinds of
meetings for review later, to ensure that he fully under-

stood the facts as they were presented. Holoday shrugged, said "Sure, why not?" and got started.

The Simpkins made their objectives clear from the outset. They had $350,000 in assets held outside their RRSP to entrust to Holoday, and they emphasized they wanted to use it to generate income and preserve capital. This meant no undue risk, no high-flyers.

Holoday responded by suggesting they put $250,000 in bonds and the balance in commodity future options. Commodities? The idea seemed far-fetched to the Simpkins. They had never traded commodities in their lives. Weren't commodities a high-risk investment?

Not with Michael Holoday watching things, they were assured. He went on:

> *I'll merely report to you when we are buying, when we take an open order at that point and tell you what we are going to sell it at. It's merely a compliance thing. I'm basically going to just inform you on what's going on, once I trade. But the overall money management of the main account, I can't expect your clients to understand the intrinsic and the small properties that you have to know to officially make money in that market. We take care of that for you. But we still call and let you know how it's going and what we've bought at what price, what the results were, and if we get into a risk situation where I've recorded a loss, we'd call you and let you know what you're down, and how we're going to get you out of it. It is something . . . you'll never have gotten more mail in your life then. You get three to four pieces of mail a week on that program, because there is so much activity in it.*[15]

All of this was both impossible and illegal: It was impossible to determine what the selling price would be; and it was illegal because Holoday was proposing discretionary trading, the buying and selling of client assets without their prior knowledge and approval.

Holoday assured the Simpkins that he used a technique designed to reduce risk to a minimum. The trick, he said, was to use strangles. Out of nine trades using his system, Holoday explained, five will be profitable and four will lose money. But the difference can be substantial. In fact, the most the Simpkins could lose would be 25 percent. The upside, of course, would be considerably more than that.

The Simpkins may have been impressed, but they still weren't convinced. Futures options in commodities or, as Holoday had been proposing, international bonds, still carried a whiff of unacceptable risk. So Holoday dragged out another option, a service new to Canada and coming in the current quarter:

> *We're finishing the legals on it, though I know it will be a green light it's not, it's about a month away. It services large minimum accounts . . . and it's a very professionally run operation out of New York, in trading again, but in cash bonds and Government mortgage-backed securities, and what we have there is, we have an operation, joint association with a company in New York with an eighteen-year track record. They used to run the bond division for twelve years at Citibank and they ran the bond division of E. F. Hutton. Then they formed their company just now with a major Tokyo bank document, and I have the Canadian division of that operation. We have forty traders on the Bond Street, New York*

and Wall Street, and they try and spin the capi-
tal probably as much as a hundred and fifty
times a year, but they're . . . what we'll do is, we'll
take a minimum account of five hundred thou-
sand dollars, it used to be one million, and we'll
put it into that structure and give you a unit.
Their four-year track record is sixty-two and a
half percent return per year . . .[16]

This was outrageous fabrication from beginning to end. He
was speaking of Eastbridge, which lacked both an 18-year
track record and a four-year average return of 62.5 percent. Bond traders who "spin the capital 150 times a year"
are wild speculators, not brilliant and prudent investors
like the Eastbridge management. And, of course, Holoday
was neither the Canadian representative nor a month
away from finalizing legal requirements.

It all sounded both true and tempting. And the
Simpkins were, after all, sitting within the walls of
Midland Walwyn, one of the country's largest brokerage
houses. Holoday roared on:

You need three months' notice to withdraw
funds out of our operation. It uses the repo
finance rate, so if you were to give me five hun-
dred thousand dollars, I am going to lend you fif-
teen million dollars inter-day. With that, you'll
do a bond trade of fifteen million dollars for six
hours or so. We'll charge you two to two-and-a-
half percent overnight interest on a daily basis
for an annualized. (sic) So it's a real big boys'
market down there. It is all discretionary, we
report to you monthly and quarterly, and it is the
most professional division and the only one of its
type in Canada. That is where you would expect

to see very consistent, well above market rates of return over the years to come. That risk program goes back to 1974 and we'll be running over the next three years as much as one to one hundred fifty million dollars Canadian capital into that operation. So the trades, you know, on a one hundred million dollar deposit of Canadian investors, we're doing three-point-six billion dollars a day tradings. So we're pooling you in with the big boys in that operation, but that's the best division, that's, I mean if you want to get into, I'm tired of, even I don't want the eighteen percent, I would even though it's risk-managed, it's diversified over forty people including the two of us.[17] . . . If you're still looking at the million-dollar figure, you put five hundred (thousand) in there, three hundred (thousand) into the bond portfolio and then two hundred (thousand) into the options program. Your net return could be anywhere from thirty-five percent to God only knows, depending on the year.[18]

No one in the brokerage business can define the term "repo rate," nor explain how to provide $15 million of leverage with a $500,000 investment.

Having portrayed himself as an investment genius for cornering the Canadian operation of Eastbridge, Holoday sprinkled a little modesty on the mix:

The New York operation is very successful, very. It's run by people of an average age of fifty years who have been in the business twenty-three years and, I mean, a young whippersnapper like myself is like a fluke dealing with them. I think at a very young age I got my hands on a mass of

experience that has not, only taken somebody fif-
teen, twenty years in this business. It is odd for
them to be playing with a guy my age but it hap-
pened, and that's the way it is, and I'm happy for
it.[19]

Later he cannot resist elevating his boasting to outrageous levels:

> *When it comes to trading, those guys have*
> *been at it for twenty-three, fifteen, twenty-three*
> *(sic) years. Ninety-seven percent of the time I'll*
> *agree with them on anything they want to do*
> *down there. They are the real pros, and I cut a*
> *deal with them, because one of our men is on the*
> *advisory to the US Treasury, on the (board) of the*
> *Treasury. We are involved in the quarterly*
> *options, which may become semi-annual. One of*
> *the forty firms in North America which, which*
> *the US government comes to finance from the*
> *public, they phone Eastbridge, and you know*
> *Eastbridge will take down X-billion dollars of*
> *the issue.*[20]

Holoday continued in this manner for over an hour, spinning dreams of small risk, big returns, brilliant manoeuvres, and friends in high places, finally convincing the
Simpkins to shift their entire investment portfolio to him.

Carole Boczan was ecstatic when Joanne Simpkin
revealed, during her next visit to Carole's salon, that she
and her husband had placed all their investments with
Carole's son-in-law. She congratulated Joanne and Paul
on their wisdom, and assured the couple this was one of
the best moves they could ever make.

When the first Midland Walwyn statement arrived at

the Simpkin residence, it indicated substantially less money in the account than they had transferred. They immediately phoned Holoday who promised to send his personal statement showing the actual balance in the Simpkin account. "You're making money," he assured them.

Holoday's statement, when it arrived, indeed showed their investment was generating a profit. But it never agreed with the monthly statements from Midland Walwyn, which always indicated a significantly lower balance.

Roger and Penny Campbell[21] also became intrigued by tales of Holoday's wizardry. A customer of Suzie Desmond's salon, Penny Campbell had been listening to her boast about Michael Holoday's magic with money for several weeks. She and her husband saw the Desmonds socially, and Suzie often talked about her brother-in-law Michael, who was a complete gentleman, very personable, and wonderfully generous with his in-laws. "He was also somewhat of a whiz in the investment field according to Suzie," Roger Campbell recalled. "Very, very successful as an investment broker, living in a Forest Hill mansion . . ."[22]

Owners of a video production company, the Campbells were in their mid-40s and aware of the need to maximize their investments, both to stave off inevitable downturns in their business and provide for a retirement income. While they owned several shares of blue-chip stocks managed by a small investment firm, the returns were never as substantial as they hoped. Everyone around them seemed to be earning more than the Campbells. Why not at least meet this Michael Holoday, who Suzie said was successful, wealthy, and a good family man?

A week before Christmas 1992, Michael and Maureen Holoday accompanied Suzie and Howard Desmond to the Campbells' home, where Roger Campbell took charge of the cooking and roasted a turkey inside a brown paper bag. Holoday was "very easy going and personable, very low key," and he appeared to express keen interest in Campbell's cooking techniques and recipes.

Eventually, the discussion drifted to financial matters. "We talked about investments during the nineties," Campbell said. "Of course, when you are dealing with someone who is reputed to be a very successful investment analyst, you are talking to him about, you know, what's the secret of his success?"

Holoday responded that he was customer-focused. He never took commissions unless he made money for his clients and he believed that, if his clients were successful, he would be successful.

The Campbells continued to be impressed. Not impressed enough to move their investments to Midland Walwyn a few months later, when Holoday called to propose the idea, but that's because 1993 was an exceptionally busy year for their video production company. They wanted time to think about things before shifting their fairly substantial investment portfolio from their current broker. Maybe later, they suggested, and Holoday said sure, he would stay in touch in case something came up.

On December 30, Holoday made a pitch to Ted and Joyce Gittings, claiming that he planned to bring an outstanding investment fund into Canada under his management. The fund was operated by a New York company called Eastbridge, which had an exceptional record of profitability in arbitrage trading. Holoday's plan, he told the couple, was to combine his strategy for controlled risk with the extensive facilities and track record of Eastbridge, a firm beyond reproach. In 30 years of operation, the fund had never lost money, and over that period it averaged monthly gains of 2 percent on its investments.

Eastbridge management were enthusiastic about the

prospect of entering Canada, Holoday told them, but he wanted to run a test before committing himself and his clients. He was planning to check the results with a small short-term investment in Eastbridge — maybe a week or ten days, that's all — to measure growth under real market conditions, and do a market projection based on the results. There could be no possibility of loss; if a loss occurred, Holoday would cancel the plan, cover the loss himself, and write it off as a business expense. Any profits made during the test would be passed on to the Gittings and other selected clients of Holoday's who chose to participate, and profits earned would be treated as interest returned from a loan to Holoday.

If Eastbridge proved as successful as Holoday anticipated, the Canadian version would be launched as Northbridge and the Gittings, of course, would be among the first invited to participate. It was a no-lose offer, made only to a handful of Michael Holoday's most prized clients.

Holoday, as usual, was convincing, and Ted and Joyce Gittings handed him a cheque for $44,000 in US funds.

The next day, New Year's Eve, Michael and Maureen Holoday treated Maureen's parents, Connie Gould, and several other invited guests to a splendid ski vacation in the Laurentians. It was first-class all the way.

TEN

We are born brave, trusting and greedy,
and most of us remain greedy.
– AUTHOR UNKNOWN

B y early spring 1993, Holoday's star status at Midland Walwyn was clearly fading. Soon after Albert Robinson was dismissed, Brad Doney began noting that more of Holoday's clients than ever were recording losses in their accounts, and Holoday's paperwork still wasn't adequate. Doney also ordered Holoday's personal trading account closed when, once again, his $250,000 risk factor was exceeded.

Of Midland Walwyn's hundreds of registered representatives, Michael Holoday had become Brad Doney's most serious disciplinary problem, eating up more of the senior VP's time and resources than anyone else. He remained, Doney had to admit, among the firm's top five producers in earned commissions. Still, Doney began making the first veiled suggestions that Holoday's future in the securities industry might lie elsewhere.

A chance meeting between a Midland Walwyn branch manager who knew of Doney's exasperation with Holoday, and W. David Wood, executive vice-president of First Marathon Securities, presented an opportunity for everyone involved, with the exception of Holoday's trusting clients.

Wood, a chisel-featured man with fashion-model looks and impeccable wardrobe, had been assigned a special project at First Marathon, one that would provide an ideal opportunity for Michael Holoday to expand his income and activities far beyond the limitations of a traditional brokerage house like Midland Walwyn.

First Marathon Securities boasted a distinctive personality in the securities industry, representing the Canadian epitome of the "eat what you kill" ethos that had originated in the hardest-headed Wall Street brokerages.[1] In the late 1970s Lawrence Bloomberg had used an MBA, ten years' experience in securities research and sales, and a million dollars in seed money to launch First Marathon, naming it after his obsession for long-distance running. Marathon running suited Bloomberg's attitude perfectly. All you needed to participate was a good pair of shoes, a reservoir of energy, and a determination to go the distance.

Bloomberg began building his firm into the leanest, meanest investment outfit on the street by recruiting partners and staff who shared his vision, and he set up a compensation system to reward them appropriately. Success meant an income of a million dollars or more a year, if you deserved it. And the concept worked. First Marathon grew into a powerhouse brokerage, going public on the TSE and launching subsidiaries in the US, UK, and Germany. Quickly reaching the critical mass stage, it didn't need to recruit star performers who would operate without hand-holding supervision; the most aggressive arrived on First Marathon's doorstep, prepared to run with the fastest thoroughbreds in the business.

Free spirits come in all shapes, sizes, ages, and genders, but the same skills that qualify them as lone wolves become a hindrance when they are asked to become conforming team players. Nor are they attuned to qualities such as vision, loyalty, and submission to the rules of other people. All of this led to a constantly recurring series of investigations launched, and charges filed, against First Marathon by the Toronto Stock Exchange, the Alberta Securities Commission, and even the FBI.[2]

When David Wood encountered the Midland Walwyn branch manager at a social function in December 1992, Wood was involved in setting up a correspondent network at First Marathon, designed to make it easy for ambitious financial advisors to become independent brokers. The correspondent network would provide trade execution and back-office services — accounting, administration, research, compliance assurance, and so on — for small brokerages and independent financial advisors. In return, First Marathon would charge a commission on the total amount of business processed through its facilities, plus fees on individual transactions.[3]

The premise was this: Major investment dealers were being swallowed up, first through amalgamation and then by the chartered banks. Many strong-willed and ambitious brokers resented this corporate fusion, especially where the despised chartered banks were involved. If they had a loyal client base, an ability to function without close super-vision, and subscribed to the "eat what you kill" philoso-phy, they could avoid the suffocating atmosphere inflicted by bank ownership, and boost both their ego and their income substantially. All they needed were the services being offered by First Marathon's correspondent network.

Wood was shrewd enough to recognize the risk in quickly associating the firm with a tribe of gung-ho entre-preneurs, eager to leap off a brokerage merger using his or her client list as a parachute. He suggested that, while these independent entrepreneurs represented a major source of potential profit for First Marathon, the firm ran the risk of becoming associated with a group of investment

cowboys who could cause First Marathon more headaches
and expense than they might be worth. So Wood, appointed president of the new correspondent network, proposed
that all members of the new division undergo an incuba-
tion period before they earned full independence. During
this time, the registered representatives would function
under Wood's supervision; when they were deemed to be
sufficiently trustworthy and competent, they would be
permitted to operate with greater independence, continuing to employ First Marathon's service facilities.[4]

As it happened, the Midland Walwyn branch manager
to whom Wood outlined the new correspondent network
knew someone who might be interested in participating.
This guy was the premier producer at Midland Walwyn,
the youngest member of the Chairman's Club in the firm's
history and determined to head his own independent brokerage some day. Wood should talk to him. His name was
Michael Holoday.

A few weeks later, Wood met with Holoday and made
a presentation to the young broker. Holoday seemed
impressed with the opportunity presented by the correspondent network. Wood, in turn, was impressed with
Holoday, who carried himself well, had high production
capabilities, and appeared smooth in his observation and
responses.

For Holoday's part, running comparatively free of
restrictions and earning big-time rewards appealed to him
more than snapping to attention every time Brad Doney
sent him another "Shape up!" memo. Holoday proposed
setting up his firm within the First Marathon correspondent's network, handling futures and following the pattern established by Eastbridge Capital. Wood, who was
aware of Eastbridge and its high status in the financial
community, was intrigued. Did Holoday have a working
relationship with Eastbridge?

Holoday assured him he did. And there was more, he said. Kenneth "Doc" Roberts and Holoday were planning to launch their own futures trading firm, to be called Holoday/Roberts Securities. Roberts had already committed $2 million to the venture, Holoday boasted, and its operation could benefit First Marathon by filling the role played by Refco. Refco, a US firm, acted as middleman for First Marathon in dealings with the Chicago Board of Trade. In its place, Holoday/Roberts could function as a partial "in-house" futures operation, improving both trading efficiency and First Marathon profits. To sweeten the deal further, Holoday predicted that eight Midland Walwyn brokers would join him in moving to First Marathon, bringing $6 million in annual commissions and $120 million in assets under management along with them. Wood declined to offer Holoday a position at First Marathon immediately, but he was clearly impressed.[5]

Holoday, while disappointed at Wood's response, shrugged it off. And why not? He appeared to have tapped an unending supply of cash to spend in a lavish, over-the-top fashion.

Maureen and her acquired glamour were a trophy to Holoday, as much a measure of his whiz-kid success as his armada of expensive cars, Forest Hill address, expensive suits, and first-class vacations.

To clients and co-workers, he announced that his wife was managing to spend enormous amounts of money on her wardrobe. "I give her ten thousand dollars to go shopping with," he would claim with amused concern, "and she spends eleven thousand."

When Maureen began redecorating their new Forest Hill home, she hired Pat Soucie, married to Maureen's uncle Robert, as design consultant. "Let's start with the master bedroom," Maureen said. She wanted something elegant and unique, something suitable for Canada's wealthiest young stockbroker. Pat Soucie, a highly regarded talent whose contracts include acting as design consultant for VIP suites in major luxury hotel chains, suggested covering the walls with padded raw silk, "if money were no object." It wasn't. Maureen loved the idea. Silk wallpaper — what a contrast with life on the farm. After Pat Soucie finished her work on Forest Hill Road, the Holodays suggested they would hire her to do a Barbados villa they were planning to construct.

Michael included Maureen in client meetings, both at their home, and when visiting the homes of others. She was young, slim, blonde, attractive, and full of life, but Holoday wanted something more for a wife. An actress, perhaps.

In the winter of 1993, Holoday asked Mona O'Hearn if he might drop around with his wife for a visit. They arrived for tea, Mona seeing Maureen up close for the first time and assessing the younger woman as "a pretty little girl, but with more money than taste when it came to dressing herself."

She was still assessing Maureen's appearance when Michael explained the reason for their visit. Maureen, it seemed, wanted to be more than a housewife, even if the role identified her as the partner of Canada's most successful young stockbroker. Maureen wanted to be an actress.

Mona O'Hearn was blunt. Maureen's voice was tiny, not authoritative. She had no experience and, while she was pretty, her looks weren't stunning. Plus, she was the mother of a small boy. "Forget about becoming a professional," Mona said. "You're too late for that. But you might get some experience and have some fun in amateur productions." Mona wrote the names of several amateur theatre companies she knew on a sheet of paper, and handed it to Maureen. "Call them and let me know how you make out," she said.

Maureen appeared thankful, but disappointed. Having fun in amateur productions? Is that how Michelle Pfeiffer got started? Not likely. She crumpled the list in her purse and forgot about it.

Michael's only comment was to complain about Mona's small dog bouncing on the floor beneath the table where they sat. Michael, his wife explained, couldn't stand having small furry animals near his feet; it gave him the creeps.

As they were leaving, Michael shrugged into a new Midnight Blue alpaca coat and mentioned that it had been custom-made to emphasize the width of his shoulders, narrowing at his hips to echo the Italian cut of his suits. "How do you like my coat?" he asked, and he spun on the spot, displaying its lines, detailing, and expensive tailoring. "Don't I dress for the part?"

You're showing off, Mona wanted to say, but she told him it was very nice and bade both of them goodbye. *What a strange couple,* she thought when they left.

In early February 1993, the value of each cheque that Doc Roberts exchanged with Holoday to cover their "daily trades" exceeded US$500,000 and was climbing day by day. Since Doc and Elaine Roberts believed they were buying into just half the total daily trading, they assumed Holoday was generating similar profits for himself. They had even more reason to believe it when, to Doc Roberts' surprise and his daughter Elaine's consternation, Michael announced he and Maureen had booked their vacation at the exclusive Sandy Lane resort, just down the beach from the Roberts' villa in the elite St. James area of Barbados. During each of Doc Roberts' visits to Barbados that winter and spring, Michael Holoday seemed to be always nearby, wanting to discuss the market over drinks, or appearing at Roberts' elbow during the older man's solitary strolls on the beach. More than ever, Michael Holoday was Robert's protégé, his fawning fan club, and his unbidden shadow, filling the role of quasi-son and potential heir.

Back in Canada, Holoday decided it was time to establish himself with Eastbridge — a prudent move, since he had been accepting funds from clients to be invested in the company for several months, and had boasted of his connections at Eastbridge with David Wood. Returning from his Barbados vacation, Holoday and Jim Fitzgerald, a Midland Walwyn senior vice-president, flew to New York for a meeting with Paul DeRosa, ostensibly to discuss the prospects of initiating bond trades between Eastbridge and Midland Walwyn. Discussions among the three men concluded this would not be a profitable strategy for either firm. Then Holoday proposed the idea of creating a fund to mirror Eastbridge, made available exclusively to Canadians through Midland Walwyn. Investment strategies and decisions would remain with Eastbridge, who would collect both a management and performance fee from the Canadian fund — which would be named, of course, Northbridge.

DeRosa expressed interest in that idea. His firm had no inclination to enter the Canadian market on its own, but if Midland Walwyn wanted to set up the organization, stick-handle its way through various regulatory requirements, market the product to its clients, and kick back a share of any profits generated, it was worth pursuing. And that's how it was left: Holoday and Fitzgerald would prepare a proposal to be made to Eastbridge on behalf of Midland Walwyn, and DeRosa and his partners would evaluate it.

Midland Walwyn and Eastbridge were close to putting a deal together in the spring of 1993. In a letter addressed to Holoday, Eastbridge suggested creating a fund to trade in US Treasury bills and bonds; one-quarter of the fund would mirror the actively traded Southbridge fund, and the balance would be personally managed by Paul DeRosa. Midland Walwyn would pay the usual management and performance fees; the minimum investment required to participate would be $5 million in US funds.

Holoday returned from New York City elated at DeRosa's encouraging response and the prospect of launching Northbridge. But life at Midland Walwyn was becoming more vexing than ever, thanks to Ted and Joyce Gittings, who continued to complain about not getting records of trades on their accounts at Midland Walwyn. They wanted details of every transaction, a summary of all month-end holdings, a rundown of interest earned and paid, dividends earned to date, and a listing of current cash balances. Holoday had already issued a statement showing that Joyce Gittings had a balance of $141,810 in her commodity account, an increase of almost 50 percent over her original investment. Now he scurried about, providing the Gittings with figures to calm them down, before calling to propose a neat idea. Why didn't Joyce Gittings transfer $100,000 of her commodity account into the ongoing Eastbridge "test" investment? It would leave her with a substantial balance in her commodity account at Midland Walwyn, and provide better growth opportunities via Eastbridge. When Northbridge was launched, she could simply roll her Eastbridge funds into that, if she wished.

Joyce and Ted Gittings agreed this was a good idea, and signed a letter approving the transfer of $100,000 to Michael Holoday, to be placed in his special Eastbridge pool. Now Holoday could control things, by discounting any apparent losses in Gittings account against spectacular gains in their Eastbridge investment. Which, of course, didn't exist.

With that blaze under control another popped up, this
one fanned by Brad Doney and his exasperating complaints about — well, about damned near everything. And
with good reason. Doney's review of Holoday's accounts
noted that 24 out of 26 of his clients were in a loss position.
What's more, the losses weren't mere blips in a volatile
market. Most had lost at least half their original investment, and three accounts were virtually wiped out, including Holoday's personal trading account, which was down
more than $380,000 or 98 percent of its original capital.
Doney once again closed Holoday's personal trading
account when its losses exceeded his $250,000 limit.

Another concern of Doney's was Holoday's insistence
on "batching" his trades, grouping hundreds of Sell and
Buy options, or "tickets," at the same price and at the
same time for multiple clients. When all the securities
were either bought or sold, according to the transaction,
the earnings or losses were distributed among the clients
in the proper proportion. Batched orders can be filled more
efficiently, and they ensure that all clients buy or sell at
the same price, if possible. But batching was expected to
represent the exception, not the rule, in trading options.

Doney instructed Holoday to cease the practice.
Holoday and his trader Chuck Oliver defended batching in
a memo obviously composed by Oliver — there was no evidence of Holoday's poor spelling and fractured syntax —
claiming it was more efficient and promised better returns
for clients than submitting individual tickets.[6]

Doney responded with barely controlled rage. The
issue, he said in his memo, was not batching tickets but
"the fundamental way in which you are doing business
with your clients. We agreed that you would discuss individual strategies with individual clients and enter orders
forthwith upon receiving them. This means that your business would conform to industry requirements and be con-

sistent with that of other futures financial advisors. You explicitly agreed to this procedure, especially in light of your current strategy. I thought, perhaps incorrectly, that you understood the reasons behind our decision."[7]

Doney had reached his limit with Midland Walwyn's Boy Wonder. On June 29, 1993, he drafted a confidential memo to the firm's legal counsel, Brigitte Geisler, and CEO Bill Packham, proposing that they begin working toward Holoday's termination with Midland Walwyn. To support his proposal, Doney attached a number of memos dating from February 14, 1992, to December 3, 1992, covering disciplinary action taken against Holoday, as well as reference to misleading statements made by Holoday to clients and a letter from Joseph Mariash, dated June 21, 1993, alleging "inappropriate trading practices."[8]

The steps had to be taken prudently, and the timing had to be perfect. Should the termination be premature and without appropriate cause, Holoday could launch a lawsuit demanding up to $1 million in severance pay.[9] While they waited for the right time and conditions to make their move, Holoday remained free to continue wringing money from his clients.

Whether Holoday was directly informed of Doney's decision, or picked up his intentions via instinct and osmosis, is unclear, but he had already taken steps to protect his career and conceal the true status of his clients' accounts.

His first move was to strengthen the relationship with David Wood at First Marathon. Ignoring the fact that Jim Fitzgerald, who accompanied Holoday on his visit to Paul DeRosa at the Eastbridge office in New York, had exchanged correspondence expressing Midland Walwyn's intention to manage and distribute an Eastbridge product, Holoday presented himself to David Wood of First Marathon as the *de facto* Eastbridge representative in

Canada. Wood was as impressed with Holoday's abilities and confidence as before, and the two men began serious discussions about Holoday leaving Midland Walwyn and joining First Marathon, bringing his supposed trading expertise, his Eastbridge connection and, of course, all of his wealthy and satisfied clients with him.

Holoday had made another important move earlier, when he proposed a small but significant change to the daily trades he was conducting with Ken and Elaine Roberts. By April, the value of each daily trade exchange had reached $725,000 in US funds, yielding an overnight profit, or "interest," for that day's trade of $3,850. The daily trades continued to be appealing, and profitable, to the Roberts (the $3,850 overnight gain represented a pro-rated annual interest of more than 190 percent), so they weren't unduly upset by Holoday's request.

"My bank's telling me they want bank drafts for our trades," he explained to Ken and Elaine Roberts in their office.

Elaine Roberts asked why the banks cared. What was the difference?

Holoday shrugged. You know what banks are like, he explained. "Gotta keep 'em happy." If the Roberts didn't mind, he said, could they begin issuing bank drafts in his name instead of cheques?

Elaine Roberts said it wouldn't be a problem, it was all the same to her and her father. It seemed like such a minor request that she never thought of asking Holoday to recip-rocate, by providing her and her father with bank drafts as well. The next day, Elaine Roberts handed Holoday a bank draft for $725,000 in US funds, issued by Bank of Montreal out of the Roberts' personal chequing account, in exchange for a post-dated cheque for US$728,050 written on the Holodays' personal chequing account.[10]

Elaine Roberts' response, especially in light of her

training as a chartered accountant, reveals how extreme
levels of trust can hide dangers that might easily be
detected in normal business relationships. The difference
between the Roberts' bank drafts and Holoday's reciprocal
post-dated cheques was measured in time and worth. The
bank drafts were liquid; within reason, they could be
exchanged immediately for the same value in cash.
Holoday's cheque, on the other hand, was delayed by one
day due to post-dating, and another day or two while it
cleared the Canadian banking system. Moreover, should
Holoday's cheque be dishonoured due to insufficient funds,
it would become simply a small piece of paper bearing a
few printed words, scribbled figures, and a signature.

So each day for more than a year, Michael Holoday
handed Elaine Roberts a potentially worthless scrap of
paper in exchange for as much as $5.5 million in US funds.

For summer fun, Michael and Maureen took a multi-year
lease at $2,500 per month on a five-bedroom waterfront
cottage on Lake Simcoe, near Orillia, Ontario. An Ontario
cottage needs a boat or two, so Michael went shopping for
three vessels. He purchased an Aqua-Ski for riding the
choppy waves, an inboard-powered bow-rider for sedate
relaxation on the water and, for his personal amusement,
ordered a custom-made "cigarette" boat, 38 feet long and
powered by twin super-charged V8 engines each generating 600 horsepower, enough to push the craft through the
water at more than 80 miles an hour. Holoday christened
the vessel *Bad Company*. Tim Miller had once owned a cigarette boat but, as Holoday pointed out to everyone, *Bad
Company* was bigger, faster, and more expensive than
Miller's.[11]

Summer weekends were an opportunity for Holoday to
display and share his wealth with family and clients.
Most Friday evenings saw the Boczan family members

streaking north from Toronto to Michael and Maureen's cottage, along with a raft of clients.

Jacques Soucie, Carole Boczan's brother, spent many summer weekends at Holoday's cottage. "Michael would be off to the side, watching people having fun," Soucie recalled. "He would just sit there in a lawn chair, look around, and smile, and say, 'I love this. I really love this!' while everybody else was eating and drinking and dancing and swimming, having a great time. He was looking after his in-laws, and that was important to him. I think that was more important to him than the money he was making."[12]

Howard Desmond, married to Maureen's sister Suzie, enjoyed the family weekends but felt he should contribute in some way. One Sunday morning, Desmond rose before the others and drove into Orillia for food to prepare breakfast for the dozen or so guests. When he returned, laden with groceries purchased with his own money, Holoday mocked him. "What're you doing?" he said, laughing at Desmond's efforts to compensate his host in some small way. "Are you crazy? Nobody pays for anything here except me." Desmond, a warm and gracious man with strong ethics, had been trying to reciprocate his host's generosity, but Holoday ridiculed Desmond's gesture for the rest of the weekend.

Roy O'Hearn was unimpressed by his broker's efforts to impress and entertain his in-laws. "He married this girl Maureen, who he called 'Sugar' all the time," O'Hearn remembered, "and introduced me to her whole family at his wedding, and I used to see them hanging around his cottage all summer. Holoday was paying for all of them, I think. The mother worked; she had a beauty parlour somewhere east. The father said he wanted to build a house down near Cobourg, but he didn't have any credit, so Holoday was loaning him the money."[13]

O'Hearn's impressions were telling. Holoday indeed

appeared to be the sole supporter of a vast clan of in-laws, distant relatives, vaguely connected friends, and bemused clients, all of them on the periphery of the Holodays' luxurious lifestyle . . . and all convinced that it was financed by the Whiz Kid's brilliant investment acumen.

In reality, of course, the bills were being paid directly out of the investment accounts of many of Holoday's weekend guests.

ELEVEN

Who is rich? He that is content.
Who is that? Nobody.
– BENJAMIN FRANKLIN

When not heading north for summer weekends at Holoday's cottage, John Boczan was busy putting the finishing touches on the house near Cobourg — the one that had been planned as a small retirement home for himself and Carole, but which was now being expanded into a large country retreat for the entire family. Supervising the construction, John signed receipts for shipments of materials, and negotiated contracts for tradesmen. He grew concerned from time to time when contractors began to complain that the bills weren't being paid on time, or even that a cheque sometimes bounced. Naturally the suppliers and contractors blamed John, who had to reassure them that his son-in-law was good for the money, that he was one of the hottest traders on Bay Street. Michael was just distracted, that was all, John Boczan would say. He's good for it, Boczan kept repeating. Michael has the money.

"The money" was growing at astonishing speed, as far as Doc and Elaine Roberts were concerned. They and Holoday continued to exchange personal cheques to finance the "daily trades" Holoday claimed to be making on his "pro account."

Each bank draft Elaine Roberts handed Holoday in the Fahnestock Viner office was accompanied by a blank form, identifying the money as a loan, and the fixed profits as interest:

> *I, Michael Holoday, promise to pay, in United States dollars, the sum of $ _____*
> *plus interest of $_____ to E. K. Roberts, on*
> *_____, 1993.*
>   *Dated this _____ day of _____ 1993.*
>
> _____
> *Michael Holoday*
> *Payment received this _____ day of _____, 1993*
>
> _____
> *E. K. Roberts*

Payment was always set for the day after the date of the loan. On the 4th of February, for example, Elaine Roberts handed Holoday a personal cheque for $515,000 in US funds; the following day, Holoday presented her with his personal cheque for US$518,862, the $3,862 difference representing the Roberts' overnight profit on his daily trades. If amortized over 260 days — 52 five-day weeks — the $3,862 daily earning represented an annual yield of 100 percent.[1]

Holoday's daily trades never lost a penny. They were executed without delay, and without apparent risk. When investors were happy to earn 10 to 12 percent annually and accept some degree of risk, Holoday was generating twice that return, day after day, week after week, for his good friends the Roberts, who never questioned either their good fortune or Holoday's remarkable talents.

The reality was this:

Holoday was no investment genius. He was not even

an original or creative con man. From the beginning, he had been employing a fraud technique as old as banking itself, one often used by friends who require short-term funds and use the banks to finance them. In the banking profession, it is known as "kiting" cheques.

Kiting is defined as "any act that takes advantage of the time required for a cheque to clear through the banking system." Via his so-called daily trades, Holoday received bank drafts from the Roberts and handed them his personal cheques. The bank drafts were immediately credited to Holoday's account balance. The time it took for Holoday's cheques to be deposited in the Roberts' account at Bank of Montreal, move through the clearing system, and arrive at Holoday's Royal Bank branch at 2 Bloor Street was sufficient for Holoday to pocket the difference between the previous bank draft and the new one, leaving funds from the earlier draft in his account to cover his personal cheque when it arrived.

Here is an example: On August 18, 1993, Holoday handed Doc and Elaine Roberts a cheque for $1,908,550, representing their return on a bank draft for $1,900,000 given to him two days earlier. By the time the August 18 cheque cleared the Roberts' account at Bank of Montreal and arrived at Holoday's bank, the next bank draft had been deposited and credited to Holoday's account, providing sufficient funds to cover the debit. Each Roberts bank draft was used to cover the previous trade's cheque, including principal and "profit" provided by Holoday. Sidetracking a portion of the funds from each transaction, Holoday accumulated millions of dollars from the Roberts over a two-year period.

Over less than two years between October 12, 1992, and August 12, 1994, Holoday and the Roberts exchanged 418 bank drafts and personal cheques totalling an astonishing $818,645,094 in US funds (over $1 billion Canadian).

The cheques exchanged with the Roberts family were written on Michael and Maureen Holoday's personal chequing account, the same type of bank account millions of Canadians employ to pay their household bills. For the month of May 1993, the Holoday's joint account recorded total debits of $44,606,535.26 and deposits of $38,300,142.19. In spite of this massive cash flow, the Holodays' personal chequing account remained overdrawn by $1,037,538.72.[2]

Where did the money come from, and where did it go? A portion of Holoday's income was being earned by commissions he continued to generate at Midland Walwyn, but the majority came from the pockets of Doc and Elaine Roberts and the accounts of various Holoday clients.

During 1992, Kenneth and Elaine Roberts handed Holoday bank drafts totalling $6,343,974.92 in US funds. Kiting enabled Holoday to return only $5,062,439.00, keeping the difference for his own use. In 1993, the value of bank drafts written by the Roberts in Holoday's favour was $389,097,357.38, but they received only $385,619,279.60 in return. And for the first six months of 1994, they issued bank drafts of $404,939,694.27 while Holoday paid them back only $400,664,568.50.

If any genius can be attributed to Michael Holoday for his dealings, not only with the Roberts but over his entire career as a Bay Street Whiz Kid, it is this: He managed to persuade one of Canada's wealthiest men and the man's chartered accountant daughter that he was adding to their already substantial asset base when he was actually stealing millions from them.[3]

The money went for toys — Holoday added a Jaguar sedan and a white Porsche Turbo to his fleet of cars — plus gifts and entertainment. Everyone was welcomed to the Lake Simcoe cottage on weekends that summer, especially members of the Boczan family. Guests, including several of Holoday's favoured clients, wanted for nothing. Anyone craving excitement might find themselves skimming across the lake at 60 miles an hour or more in *Bad Company,* the roar of the boat's twin turbocharged engines echoing back from the shore, with Michael at the wheel and Maureen clinging to him, the two of them laughing like schoolchildren.

In early May 1993, Tanya Sargent required a three-month leave of absence for major surgery. Prior to leaving, she earned her securities trading licence, placing her on a similar footing, when it came to advising clients and handling documents at least, as Holoday himself. During her absence, she was replaced by Tracy Ellis, brought in by a temporary employment firm.

Soon Midland Walwyn made it clear that Holoday had no future with their firm. Holoday simply smiled at the news. He was already negotiating a move to First Marathon and, on August 9, 1993, Michael Holoday resigned from Midland Walwyn to join First Marathon Securities, taking Chuck Oliver with him as trader and Tracy Ellis as sales assistant. Tanya Sargent, who had stuck to her guns and refused to produce any more account "simulations," was left behind.

Holoday and his two Midland Walwyn cronies represented First Marathon's entire futures division, occupying a suite of corner offices on the 30th floor of The Exchange Tower. The space had been recently vacated by the immensely wealthy Reichmann brothers, whose multi-billion-dollar real estate empire was in temporary disarray thanks to their development of Canary Wharf in London, England.

Oliver and Ellis trod in Holoday's footsteps over the next 14 months, actively participating in his trades and client services. Oliver, whose dress and carriage suggested an upper-class English heritage, performed the mechanics of Holoday's trades, placing them through Refco Canada who, in turn, completed them on the floor of the Chicago Board of Trade.[4]

Whatever else Holoday might have done on August 10, 1993, only his second day with First Marathon, much of it was spent purchasing bank drafts in the names of 14 former clients whose accounts remained at Midland Walwyn. A series of mysterious deposits were made in these accounts. Margaret Raines received $26,000; Helen Rentis' account grew by $138,000; Elaine Roberts' account gained $41,198. A total of almost $350,000 in US funds found their way into the accounts of Holoday's clients at Midland Walwyn, all payable by a Citibank branch in Syracuse, New York, and all bearing the initials T.E., for Tracy Ellis. And all, by coincidence, just managed to wipe out the bad debts in these accounts. The accounts immediately followed Holoday to First Marathon, where presumably the confirming transfer documents matched, or nearly so, the expectations of the former Midland Walwyn clients.

While withdrawals from investment accounts may only be made by authorized individuals following fixed procedures, anyone can make a deposit to client accounts on the theory, perhaps, that no client will complain about receiving money, whatever the source. Had a system been in place to detect it, someone at Midland Walwyn would have noticed that all the funds arrived simultaneously from the same bank and individual — a curious occurrence. Nor did anyone question the almost immediate transfer of these client accounts out of Midland Walwyn and up the street, following Michael Holoday's footsteps.

Where did the money come from? From Holoday's good and generous friends, the Roberts.

During the first week of August 1992, while exchanging bank draft and post-dated cheque to carry out the "daily trade" Holoday and the Roberts were sharing, Holoday asked for a small favour. He was about to assume direction of the new futures division at First Marathon, he explained. He was sure to succeed. (In fact, he had already told some clients and family members that he was being groomed to become successor to First Marathon founder and president, Lawrence Bloomberg, something that would have been too far-fetched for Doc and Elaine Roberts to believe.) Meanwhile, the new division needed capitalization to get things started.

Kenneth and Elaine Roberts understood, of course. How much did Holoday need?

Not much. About $420,000 in US funds should do it. Could they lend him that much at, say, 5 percent annual interest?

The "day trades" Holoday was sharing with the Roberts had reached $1,850,000, which was the amount of the bank draft that they had handed him in exchange for Holoday's personal cheque for $1,857,875. The overnight profit of $7,875 represented better than 150 percent annual interest earned. Every business requires start-up capital, and US$420,000 to launch a futures division at Lawrence Bloomberg's operation seemed reasonable. So Ken Roberts cut a cheque on the spot, without collateral or any security at all. Michael Holoday's word was good enough.[5]

Holoday spent the rest of the day dividing the money among all of his Midland Walwyn clients whose accounts were in a debit position, restoring them to a positive balance, and enabling him to move them out of Midland Walwyn to First Marathon without alerting anyone.[6]

Holoday joined First Marathon as a member of the firm's correspondent network, but with the intention, as stated in David Wood's offer of employment to Holoday, that his employment was ultimately leading to the creation of his own securities firm.

A prime motive behind First Marathon's offer was Holoday's promised capture of Canadian rights to the Eastbridge pooled fund. In essence, Eastbridge was the bait and Holoday was the hook. Wood made this clear when, in his confirming letter to Holoday, he wrote:

> *We expect you will abide by a strict philosophy of "non-compete" in all products and services with our accounts without our prior written approval. We will respect a similar philosophy in those situations where you have developed an exclusive relationship. Such understanding would include any relationship we develop on your behalf with Eastbridge Capital Management. You will have the option to acquire, at anytime, our interest in Eastbridge Capital Management at our unamortized cost plus $1.*

For his operations, Holoday would rely on First Marathon's administration services, which included responsibility for compliance, regulatory, and accounting procedures. In exchange for these services, he would pay First Marathon commissions on futures business conducted by him, according to a sliding scale. The maximum commission of 14 percent applied if the annual business volume remained under $1.5 million, but dropped in intervals to a base of 10 percent at $4.5 million annual volume. Expenses such as office rental, employee benefits, communication costs, stationery, and the like would be charged to Holoday at cost. In effect, Holoday was operating a brokerage within a brokerage.

Wood's enthusiasm at securing Holoday was evident.

"Michael," Wood closed his letter, "we are very excited by the prospect of working with you as a partner in building your business."[7]

One thing Holoday insisted on receiving was an appropriate title. It was needed, he explained, to entice clients to follow him from Midland Walwyn. At Midland, Holoday had been a member of the Chairman's Club. Arriving at First Marathon as a mere account executive or financial advisor would be a demotion. Holoday needed a title worthy of a "Big Swinging Dick," someone whose name would soon be emblazoned on Bay Street's newest brokerage.

Wood made a suggestion: How would Holoday feel about becoming "managing partner, futures division"? Holoday thought it sounded fine. *Managing Partner*. It carried more clout than vice-president. Wood considered it an essentially empty gesture, a no-cost incentive for a guy capable of delivering a million dollars annually in earned commissions.

The securities industry is cavalier about providing staff with impressive-sounding titles, based on the assumption that clients prefer dealing with someone who has attained elevated status within the organization. It is flattering to have one's account managed by a senior vice-president rather than a lowly registered representative, but the title is more illusory than real. In 1996, for example, Midland Walwyn's employee roster listed 98 company directors, 141 senior vice-presidents, and a staggering 206 vice-presidents. Did clients of these vice-presidents assume their financial advisor was actively involved in management of the company? Almost certainly. Did the 347 vice-presidents and senior vice-presidents ever gather together in a single decision-making activity? Not very likely.

So if Michael Holoday could burst his buttons by calling himself managing partner, futures division, at First

Marathon, what was the big deal? It was only a title.

To the clients Holoday brought with him on his trek from Midland Walwyn to First Marathon, it was a big deal indeed, if only because Holoday told them so. Only a title? Holoday's clients assumed he had clambered several more rungs up the ladder, joining a senior management group at First Marathon as a partner — that's what the title said. The assumption accounted for some extraordinary decisions by Holoday's clients, and some outlandish deceptions by Holoday.

Before David Wood could make his offer to Holoday and thrust First Marathon into the risky but lucrative — for the brokerage at least — futures commodity market, First Marathon required a compliance officer qualified for, and experienced in, commodities trading. Wood assigned David Burnes, vice-president of the correspondent network, to locate someone to fill the watchdog compliance role.

Burnes didn't have to look far for his candidate. He found the correspondent network's new compliance officer literally next door at the Toronto Stock Exchange, and a sharper contrast to Michael Holoday would have been difficult to locate anywhere in the financial industry.

Joseph Thurman, ten years older than Holoday, started his career in the brokerage trade at the Ottawa office of Richardson Greenshields at age 24. A commodity trader encouraged Thurman to obtain specialized registration for commodities, and Thurman was employed seven years at Merrill Lynch Canada and two years at Dean Whitter before landing at the TSE as a compliance officer. Most of his TSE duties consisted of visiting member brokerages to ensure that compliance rules were being followed, no doubt making his visits to the brokers as popular as those of an uninvited in-law who arrives to drag a finger across the furniture, looking for dust. The TSE claims it has "very strict standards of conduct for its member brokerage

firms. For example, the Exchange monitors members'
sales and business practices; investigates investor complaints; disciplines members when TSE rules are broken;
and audits their finances to make sure they have enough
capital to operate safely."[8]

Thurman had spent five years at the TSE when David
Burnes dangled the position of compliance officer, correspondent network, in front of him. Though qualified for
the job, Thurman had been a commodities trader in a brokerage house, and a compliance officer with the stock
exchange, but there is no evidence that Thurman had been
a compliance officer with a brokerage house to this point.

Upon arriving at First Marathon in August 1993,
Thurman realized he had encountered Holoday's name,
and a hint of his reputation, while at the TSE. One of
Holoday's clients, a man named Joe Mariash, had filed a
complaint with the TSE two months earlier, charging
that Holoday had engaged in unauthorized trading in
Mariash's account. The TSE was in the process of investigating the charges, and noted this in a letter to First
Marathon on August 11, 1993, confirming Holoday's status as a registered representative, futures contract
options. This was serious enough for Wood to call Jim
Fitzgerald, and ask the Midland Walwyn executive if
there were any other blemishes on Holoday's record that
Wood should be aware of. Well, Fitzgerald admitted,
there seemed to be a few. While Holoday had replaced
unacknowledged (to his clients) debits in their accounts in
order to move them to First Marathon, he had left a few
uncovered tracks.

Dr. Oswald John was complaining that his account
was short by $150,000. A woman named Marcia Dixon
claimed that her account was missing a $60,000
T-bill. Then there was Gary Davidson, rumoured to be
boasting that Michael Holoday had paid Davidson

$44,000 to cover losses in his account.[9]

These were serious charges, extending well beyond disagreements covering a few hundred dollars in apparent
losses or bookkeeping errors. Wood called Holoday into his
office and asked if he had heard about them and, if so, how
he could explain them.

Sure, Holoday said, he had heard the rumours, but he
laughed them off. "It happens in this business, you know
that," Holoday said. "A top producer leaves one house to go
to another, taking his clients with him, and the next thing
you know, his old firm is saying, 'That guy wasn't so hot,'
stuff like that." Every broker has at least a couple of
grumpy clients, Holoday went on. Some people at Midland
Walwyn were upset that Holoday had jumped to First
Marathon, and now any complaint that anyone ever had
about him was being blown out of proportion.

Holoday had a point. "The first thing that happens
when a registered representative leaves a brokerage,"
Wood reflected later, "is that his accounts are redistributed
among other RR's. They call the clients and tend to express
concern about the security and performance of the client's
investments, and the quality of advice the client might
have received in the past. It's a cut-throat business."[10]

Still, these were not the kind of rumours Wood could
ignore. Wood called Midland Walwyn again, this time
speaking to Midland's corporate counsel Brigitte Geisler.
Geisler promised to investigate these rumours, determine
if there was any substance to them, and report back to
Wood.[11]

Geisler's response was generally reassuring. Oswald
John could not have lost US$150,000 as he claimed,
because the balance in his account had never approached
that amount. Marcia Dixon had spent most of her
US$60,000 T-bill via a series of cheque-withdrawal privi-
leges. Geisler couldn't comment on Gary Davidson's situa-

tion, but she had found no evidence of wrongdoing in his account either. Geisler was basing her information on Midland Walwyn documents alone; no one contacted the clients directly. As for the charges of Joe Mariash, it came down to the client's word against the broker's, and Midland Walwyn chose to accept the broker's word that Mariash had been aware all along of the trades in his account. Case closed. Holoday's clients, the verdict seemed to say, were either muddle-headed fools or out of touch with reality.

Wood thanked Geisler for her assistance, but Gary Davidson's claim of a $44,000 pay-off still bothered him. It was, after all, an unusual situation. Most clients were concerned about money missing from their accounts. Here was one who claimed money was being put back into his account by his broker.

Wood decided he would break the unwritten rule of leaving direct client contact up to the RR, and call Davidson himself. He had never made such a call to a client before, but this was too serious to ignore. First he needed a telephone number, so he asked Holoday to provide one. After much procrastination by Holoday and prodding by Wood, Holoday scribbled a number on a sheet of paper and handed it to Wood, warning that Wood might have difficulty reaching Davidson.

Holoday was correct. It was several days before someone answered calls to the number Holoday provided. Wood asked if the individual on the line was Gary Davidson, and the man confirmed he was. Wood introduced himself and explained that he was investigating a serious rumour regarding Davidson's broker, Michael Holoday. Did Holoday, Wood asked, ever provide Davidson with a substantial amount of money — $44,000, to be exact?

The man replied that he had never received such a sum from Holoday. "The only thing I ever got from Mike," he said, "were four Blue Jays baseball tickets, good ones too, that Mike said he couldn't use and wanted to know if I'd like them. I said 'Sure,' so he gave them to me. They were worth about two hundred and fifty dollars, as I recall."

Nothing else? Wood asked.

"Nothing else."

Wood thanked him for his time, apologized for any inconvenience, and hung up.

Something still bothered him. He called Holoday and confirmed that Davidson had denied, over the telephone, receiving $44,000 from Holoday. "I need something in writing, Mike," he said. "Something for the file. Ask him to supply a letter confirming that he received no money from you, and that he's happy with your services as his broker."

Holoday agreed to do it.

Wood called Brigitte Geisler again. Would she check her records at Midland Walwyn to confirm that no cheque from Holoday was ever deposited to Davidson's account? Geisler called back to confirm that no record existed of Holoday making a payment to Davidson from Holoday's personal bank account.

Wood was both relieved and concerned — relieved that his new managing partner, futures division, appeared to be cleared of serious charges against him; concerned that such rumours could be freely spread by former colleagues. "This sounds like defamation of character to me," he told Geisler before hanging up.[12]

Had David Wood encountered Gary Davidson around this time, his concern would have been much deeper, tinged with outrage perhaps. Because whomever Wood had spoken to on the telephone, it was not Gary Davidson. Davidson had neither heard of nor spoken to anyone named David Wood at First Marathon. In fact, on the day Wood claimed to have spoken to him at a local number, Davidson and his wife were visiting relatives hundreds of kilometres away in Kirkland Lake, Ontario. Davidson had, however, received an unexpected personal cheque from Holoday for $250 on August 17, which was just about the time Holoday learned that David Wood was attempting to reach his client.

Davidson asked Holoday what the cheque was for. "It's a gift," Holoday explained, "from me to you, for being a loyal client. Go out and spend it on your kids, maybe take them to a Blue Jays game. Have some fun with it. Your investments are doing well, and I'm glad you're coming with me to First Marathon."

It seemed a strange gesture from a stockbroker, but of all the people Davidson knew, Michael Holoday was wealthy enough to toss a few hundred dollars in the direction of his clients.

The following Saturday, August 21, Davidson and his wife were attending a wedding reception, sharing a round table in a large banquet hall with five other couples whom they had never met before. Everyone was enjoying themselves, trading stories and gossip about work, family, and friends, but Davidson's attention was drawn to an adjacent table, where scandalous things were being said about someone in the investment business. The conversation seemed to centre on a young hotshot broker being investigated, the words spiced with ill-concealed delight. When one of the guests mentioned Midland Walwyn, Davidson began to listen closely. A broker who used to be at Midland Walwyn, Davidson heard, was in trouble. The SOB will finally get his, they said, and then Davidson heard someone mention the broker's name: Michael Holoday.

Davidson called over to them. He knew Holoday. What was this about?

"He's in deep shit over at Midland Walwyn," one of the guests grinned.

"Michael Holoday?" Davidson said. "I'm one of his clients."

One guest claimed he was part of a task force assigned to investigate Holoday's dealings at Midland Walwyn. "Will you be investing with him at First Marathon?" he asked Davidson.

Davidson said sure he would, and mentioned that Holoday had covered some of Davidson's losses in the past.

The table fell silent. Looks were exchanged. One couple got up to dance, another headed for the bar. Gary Davidson felt ill.

As soon as the Davidsons arrived home after the wedding reception, Gary called his buddy Lee Cowie. It was Davidson who had suggested Cowie should invest his life savings with Holoday, and if Holoday was really in trouble, Cowie should know about it, even if it was one in the morning. Davidson told his friend about the disturbing talk at the wedding reception. They both agreed to raise it with Holoday, first thing Monday morning.

"I've heard that stuff before," Holoday told Davidson when he called. "Happens every time a big producer leaves a broker and takes his best clients with him. It's sour grapes. Ignore it."

Davidson wanted to, but couldn't. Later, he discussed the situation with Lee Cowie, who was just as concerned as his friend. Cowie's suggestion was to be simple and direct: "Let's ask for our money," he said. "Let's tell Holoday we need cash out of our accounts for one reason or another. If he stalls, maybe there's something to it."

The next day, Davidson and Cowie each called Holoday, planning to employ different reasons for withdrawing their investments from First Marathon. Lee Cowie claimed he had a real estate deal closing and he needed the $130,000 Holoday said was in Cowie's account. "No problem," Holoday responded. "Where do I send the cheque?" Cowie gave him an address and within three days a cheque for the full amount arrived in the mail. Ten days later, on September 8, Cowie reinvested the money in his First Marathon account again, satisfied that Holoday was on the level.

When Davidson asked for his money, Holoday replied that a bank draft in Davidson's name was waiting for him. The value: $57,952.40 Canadian or, at the current exchange rate, a neat $44,000 in US funds. "That's your profit from the pooled account," Holoday told Davidson. "By the way," the broker added, "I'm managing partner, futures division, here at First Marathon. Things are better here. They have a better computer system, for one thing, so we won't have as many problems tracking your investment and getting cheques to you."

Davidson had yet to follow Holoday from Midland Walwyn to First Marathon. When Holoday informed him that his account was showing a profit of almost $60,000, Davidson asked Holoday to transfer his account to First Marathon in spite of his misgivings — misgivings that were heightened later that day when Davidson received a telephone call from Jim Fitzgerald at Midland Walwyn. Fitzgerald began asking disturbing questions. Was Davidson a client of Michael Holoday's? Were Davidson's accounts in order? Was he happy with his broker's service? Had Michael Holoday provided Davidson with any money, any unusual payments? "Only for some Blue Jays tickets," Davidson replied.

Fitzgerald asked Davidson to come down to the Midland Walwyn office for a chat. But Davidson and his wife had just begun their vacation, and the drive to downtown Toronto from Aurora and back would take the better part of the day. Besides, they were heading north later that week to visit family in Kirkland Lake, and he had chores to complete around the house before leaving.

He couldn't make it. Maybe some other time.

Fitzgerald called Davidson again the following day, August 24, saying he really would like to have a chat about Holoday. Could Davidson possibly get downtown and talk about Holoday? Davidson explained that he was too busy. He was also getting a little annoyed at these telephone calls. Holoday had already left Midland Walwyn for a competitor, and it seemed to Davidson as though he were caught in the middle of one firm's efforts to hold on to business that was going to another firm. He didn't need this. He called Holoday at First Marathon to complain about it. He and his wife were planning a much-needed holiday, he had things to do, he didn't want to keep fielding calls from this Fitzgerald guy, and he certainly didn't want to waste a day of his vacation driving into downtown Toronto and back.

Holoday seemed amused at the situation. "Relax," he said. "It's all business. I'll speak to somebody and get them to stop harassing you." Holoday asked where the Davidsons were heading. "Give me a number where I can reach you up there," Holoday said, "just in case something comes up."

Sure enough, Holoday called the Davidsons at the family home where they were vacationing in Kirkland Lake. "Don't worry about Fitzgerald," the broker assured Gary. "He won't be calling you again. I've taken care of him."

Davidson thanked him.

"But I need a favour from you," Holoday said. "I need a letter saying you're happy with the service you've been getting from me. Just for the file, kind of a reference from one of my best clients."

Davidson wondered why Holoday would need a reference letter after he had already made the move to First Marathon. Davidson said he was sorry but he was on vacation. He didn't feel like taking time to draft some letter and get it typed up, all of that. No problem, Holoday assured him. Holoday would compose it himself, for Davidson's signature and approval.

That weekend, Davidson and his wife returned home to Aurora, Ontario. Labour Day was sunny and warm, and Davidson was busying himself in the front yard, raking lawn clippings and trimming the hedge, when Holoday roared up in his Jaguar V-12. He squealed to a stop and leapt from the car clutching two sheets of paper, leaving the engine running. He practically ran to where Davidson was standing, a rake in his hand.

"Here's the letter," Holoday said. He pulled a pen from a jacket pocket. "Just sign it here. I really appreciate this." He seemed out of breath, as though he had run all the way instead of driving the Jag.

"I should read it first," Davidson protested, but Holoday said it covered the things they had talked about, nothing special, no big deal, sign it on the second page, okay?

Davidson ran his eyes over the single-spaced typewritten first page: *Michael Holoday phoned me at work . . . informed me he would be leaving Midland Walwyn . . . signed new account agreements at First Marathon . . . $250 Blue Jays tickets . . . phone calls from Jim Fitzgerald . . . wedding conversation . . . Holoday leaving Midland Walwyn . . . firm criticizing his poor business practices . . . intended to invest $44,000 to $45,000 with Michael in whatever he recommended.*

Davidson scrawled his signature on the second page.

Holoday snatched the letter from his hand, took back his pen, and looked around. "Nice day, eh?" He climbed into the Jag, revved the engine, and tore off again, barely a minute after arriving.

Gary Davidson, who kept a detailed diary of events and prided himself on his ability to recall dates, had scanned the letter so quickly that he missed two errors. The letter, for example, claimed the wedding at which

Davidson heard about Holoday's troubles took place on
August 7, two weeks earlier than the actual date.

The day after Labour Day, Holoday handed Gary
Davidson's letter over to Wood. Nothing in it referred to
Holoday covering his client's loans, or to the existence of a
pooled account. The mention of the $250 Blue Jays tickets
confirmed the comment Wood believed Davidson had
made to him during the telephone call.[13]

Wood filed the letter. Holoday appeared to be clean.

One of Joe Thurman's key functions at First Marathon
was to review all the documents necessary before a new
account could be opened in the name of Holoday's clients.
He would look for evidence that the clients were not over
their heads due to insufficient capital or inexperience in
trading commodity futures. While First Marathon had
been licensed for some time to trade in commodities,
Michael Holoday's arrival marked its entry into this market, and almost as soon as the firm's new managing partner, futures division, was settled in his office, its expensive redecoration supervised by wife Maureen, a series of
requests to open new accounts began arriving on
Thurman's desk. Thurman scanned the Know Your Client
forms, identifying the new clients' investment knowledge
and goals, then flipped to, as Thurman described, "the
main supervisory signal": the amount of capital the client
was prepared to risk in commodities trading.

Before accepting a new client, Thurman was to examine the Risk Capital Figure (RCF) and determine if it was
suitable for the new client's financial situation. Obviously,
an individual with $50,000 net worth who set his or her
Risk Capital limit at $75,000 would be rejected. Even
where an individual's net worth was greater than the Risk
Capital Figure — for example, agreeing to risk $50,000 of
a total net worth of $75,000 — Thurman's response would

be to reject the application for commodities trading if the Risk Capital Figure represented a disproportionate share of the net worth. It was a response he exercised only once during Holoday's tenure at First Marathon, and the applicant turned out to be a university student conducting an experiment.[14]

Once a client's account was opened, Thurman was required to note the Risk Capital Figure inserted in each client's account opening document, keep track of losses suffered in each account, and halt trading once the loss limit was reached or exceeded.

Thurman assumed that all data on the account opening documents provided by Holoday was correct because each bore the new client's signature. In doing so, he overlooked the fact that most of the applications had been completed by two different people. The contrast between the handwriting styles was not subtle; it was, without exception, startling. Moreover, the handwriting where the Risk Capital Figure was entered — the "main supervisory signal" in Thurman's own words — was consistent from client to client. The Risk Capital Figure represented the limit that the client was prepared to lose through trading. As compliance officer, Thurman had both the authority and the responsibility to halt trading in the account once the RCF had been exceeded. Was someone filling in blank documents either before or after the clients' signatures were entered? If so, how confident could the brokerage be in the accuracy of the RCF, or any other data used to monitor accounts? "It's very rare for a client to sign a blank document," Thurman observed later. "But sometimes if a client lives at a distance (from the broker), the registered representative may mail a document, ask the client to sign it, and complete the figures later."[15]

Confirmation of these figures with the client might be in order, but it was rarely pursued. "The standard in the industry," Thurman explained, "was to have the registered representative maintain an exclusive relationship with the client. It would be distressing to clients to have anyone else talk to them about this information."[16]

Brokerage houses routinely, as with the Midland Walwyn/Margaret Raines/Deloitte & Touche incident, ask clients to verify the balance in their account as part of an annual audit. If a brokerage truly wished to avoid upsetting clients, why approach them in this fashion? The client, in such an audit, is asked to verify the existence of funds trusted to the registered representative in an "exclusive relationship." How did this differ from confirming a client's stated risk capital, even through random checks? Credit card companies routinely call cardholders to confirm a purchase that does not match the cardholder's established buying patterns. The goal is to protect the interests of the cardholder, and virtually every credit card customer who receives such a call understands and appreciates this.

As for Thurman's fear that clients would find it distressing to discover that others had access to their net worth or RCF, Thurman addressed this point whenever the risk capital limits were reached, some within a few months of Holoday's arrival at First Marathon. When this happened, Thurman forwarded letters noting the fact and pointing out that, unless the client provided signed authorization for a higher limit, trading in the client's account would be halted. This effectively protected the brokerage against risk, should a client's losses exceed those shown on the RCF — assuming, of course, that the RCF was accurate in the first place.

All firms, in every industry, avoid distressing clients, or damaging the close relationship between client and sales representative. But the industry's standard, as described by Thurman, represented a fatal flaw where Holoday's clients were concerned.

TWELVE

The covetous man is ever in want.
– HORACE

Whether it was the "eat what you kill" climate, the irresistible temptation of the Roberts family's immense wealth, or a growing confidence that, regardless of his audaciousness, he would never be caught, Holoday's arrival at First Marathon launched a bold spiral of swindles and spending.

First, Maureen oversaw the furnishing and decorating of her husband's office, using the movie *Wall Street* as inspiration. Holoday worked from behind a 16-foot doughnut-shaped desk constructed of black-topped cherry wood with copper footings, the entire edifice set upon a riser so that clients looked up at Holoday, as he put it, "as though I were on a spaceship. The coffee table was a solid block of steel, and I had a wet bar that matched the desk, so people could come in, and while they were making or losing money, they could have a good drink."[1] He took pride in announcing that the suite's previous tenants had been the legendary Reichmann brothers, pointing out the holes still visible in the heavy walnut doors where the brothers had mounted their *mezuzahs,* and claiming the elusive real estate moguls called on him for investment advice from time to time.

Seated beyond Holoday's glass-walled office and out of direct view of his computer monitor were the two personal assistants who had followed him from Midland Walwyn. Tracy Ellis served as Holoday's personal secretary, and Chuck Oliver handled futures trading.

Holoday's first action was to circulate letters to Midland Walwyn clients whom he had not automatically transferred to his new brokerage, formally inviting them to transfer their business to First Marathon. "I am delighted to announce I have been appointed to a new position as *Managing Partner, Futures Division* [his italics], at First Marathon Securities Limited," Holoday wrote. "My association with First Marathon will enable me to access new derivative products and to strengthen the brokerage and futures services you currently enjoy." Holoday's letter went on to praise First Marathon ("an enviable record of consistent profitability"), and invite the client to complete and return the attached account application form.

Most of Holoday's clients agreed to transfer their accounts. And why not? Midland Walwyn's statements may have been confusing and inaccurate, but Holoday always provided data confirming that their investments were growing at a phenomenal rate. What's more, their investment dealer was now a managing partner of First Marathon. The Whiz Kid was riding higher than ever, and his clients naturally wanted to cling to his coattails.

Holoday's clients may have been pleased about his move to First Marathon, but at Eastbridge, Paul DeRosa was confused, and more than a little upset. After dealing with Midland Walwyn for several weeks, he received a letter from David Wood of First Marathon proposing an identical relationship with Wood's firm, indicating that Michael Holoday would lead the project. Apparently, Holoday had assumed ownership of the Eastbridge proposal for himself, applying it as a lever in his negotiations with First Marathon. Acting with integrity, DeRosa wrote to Holoday in mid-August 1993, backing his firm out of any deal under the current circumstances. *Subsequent to your move from Midland Walwyn to First Marathon I have learned,* DeRosa wrote, *that your former employer has asserted its claim to distribute the fund we had planned while you were employed there.* Eastbridge, he emphasized, would deal with neither firm under the circumstances. Eventually, Jim Fitzgerald of Midland Walwyn wrote Eastbridge to formally withdraw his firm's proposal, leaving First Marathon on its own to develop the concept. Of course, unknown to DeRosa, Wood, Fitzgerald, or anyone else in the picture, Holoday had chosen not to wait for formalities such as business agreements and legal authorization. He had been operating his own version of Eastbridge for several months, promoting the firm's success, establishing himself as the Canadian representative, and accepting deposits targeted for a non-existent arm of Eastbridge.

Between throwing parties, taking vacations, escorting his wife and in-laws on shopping sprees, hosting dinners at Centro, and maintaining a near-constant round of inveigling and account juggling, it's surprising that Holoday had time to pursue any trading activity following his arrival at First Marathon in mid-August 1993.

He did manage, however, to call Roger and Penny Campbell, owners of a video production company and the couple he had hosted at a dinner party the previous Christmas. Holoday said he was now with First Marathon Securities, where he had been "hand-chosen by the Chairman, Lawrence Bloomberg" as Bloomberg's heir-apparent, and he was sitting on the executive committee. "He was on his way to the top," Campbell recalled, "and he was a Managing Partner, which is a very high ranking position, he indicated, in that field."[2]

Campbell had been impressed by Holoday at Christmas, but this latest revelation astonished him. The next chairman of First Marathon? He wasn't 30 years old yet. Hand-chosen by Lawrence Bloomberg? It sounded like adolescent boasting, except that Holoday appeared to back it up with all the trappings you expect in someone geared for success — the house in Forest Hill, the Jaguars, Ferrari, and Porsche, the boat and cottage, the property in Barbados, even the svelte blonde wife dripping in diamonds. "I thought, boy, he must be really something special," Campbell remembered, "and I was very flattered that he was pitching me to handle our account."

Still, the Campbells held back. They weren't flighty when it came to investing. They couldn't afford to be; the nature of their business often meant swinging like a pendulum between extremes of feast or famine, and today's nest egg might be tomorrow's source of income.

Holoday persisted. At a barbecue at his Forest Hill home, Holoday promised Campbell weekends in Muskoka, and perhaps a trip to Barbados, all compliments of First Marathon's new managing partner, futures division. Holoday always found ways to tilt the conversation toward investment matters, his future at First Marathon, the importance of maximizing growth, and his ability to minimize risk.

Martin Karp's account didn't follow Holoday to First Marathon, because it held a positive balance. Instead, Midland Walwyn cashed out the account and sent the balance to Karp, who immediately noticed a $6,400 shortfall. "How could this happen?" Karp asked his broker, who was now at First Marathon. "You told me it was impossible to lose money in this account."

"Something happened with the British pound," Holoday said. "I couldn't see it coming, it was out of my control." Holoday had a suggestion. "Listen," he told the former cab driver, "the way they let me operate here (at First Marathon), I'll get you back your sixty-four-hundred bucks in three weeks or less, if you'll invest another twenty thousand dollars."[3]

The following month, Holoday hosted and paid for a second wedding reception in the ballroom at The Ontario Club, this time for brother-in-law Paul Boczan and his bride Toni. Once again, over a hundred guests crowded the facility, enjoying an elaborate dinner at Michael Holoday's expense while the host beamed from the head table.[4] Almost as elaborate as his and Maureen's wedding two years earlier, the celebration was only the first half of his gift to the newly married couple. The other half consisted of an all-expenses-paid honeymoon in Hawaii, including accommodation in an exclusive multi-bedroom villa costing $3,000 a night and vacated just a few days earlier by comedienne/actress Roseanne Barr.

Michael and Maureen chose to accompany the newlyweds on their honeymoon, sharing the villa, and touring the island with them from behind the wheel of a rented luxury sports sedan. This may not have been as intrusive as it sounds, since Holoday rose each morning at 2 a.m. to call Toronto on his cell phone, muttering instructions and "doing deals" in the darkness while the others slept.

He and Maureen had barely returned to Toronto before they began planning an elaborate Halloween party for Holoday's clients and Maureen's extended family of aunts, uncles, and cousins. Later, Holoday boasted that the party cost $20,000, which meant he spent more money on one evening's food, drink, and decorations than he had earned in his entire first year of employment six years earlier.[5]

Preparations for the Holodays' party created some apprehension among their neighbours. To many, it appeared that the residents of 265 Forest Hill Road were permitting their home to be used as a film location. Toronto had long ago become Hollywood North, and not a day passed without oversized white vans, mobile homes, and portable electric generators being trundled into place in Riverdale, Cabbagetown, or The Annex, disrupting traffic and attracting star-struck gawkers. This was unheard of in Forest Hill, however. So it seemed curious when crews in large trucks arrived at 265 Forest Hill Road bearing outrageous props, some carried into the house and others set here and there in the front garden. Hour by hour during October 30 and 31, 1993, the square stone mansion was transformed into an outlandish monster's lair. Workers crawled up and across the entire facade, draping the house in heavy black netting as though it were the domain of some immense spider. Powerful spotlights were set among the shrubs, their beams aimed at the structure, while oversized evil-looking masks were suspended above the windows and, most disturbing of all, tombstones were erected in the front garden.

Relief washed up and down Forest Hill Road when residents discovered the props were not intended for a film production. Some neighbours passing the home later in the day even smiled at the sight of workers installing a mock guillotine, complete with bloodstains on its shiny metal blade, near the front entrance. A Halloween party. Well, why not?

On Halloween night, over 200 invited guests in costume were greeted at the door by a stern security guard and a smiling Maureen Holoday dressed as Edith Prickly of SCTV fame in the same *faux* tiger-skin costume worn by TV star Andrea Martin.

Inside, the house buzzed with laughter, gossip, music,

and envy at the Holodays' wealth. Early guests button-
holed later arrivals. "Have you seen Michael yet?" they
would ask. "It's a hoot! Guess what he's dressed as? A
tramp! A bum!" It was true. Michael Holoday, the not-yet-
30 Bay Street Whiz Kid, was indeed costumed in the
clichéd garb of a hobo clown. Wearing a tattered tailcoat
over gaudy checked trousers, and a frayed striped vest held
closed with an oversized safety pin, he spent the evening in
a corner of the living room, accepting the thanks and con-
gratulations of his guests, rarely speaking except to say,
"Enjoy yourself. Have some food. Get a drink," as he welcomed Ted Gittings, Roy O'Hearn, and other clients, saving
a special welcome for Roger and Penny Campbell.

George Gunn was not a client of Michael Holoday's.
He wasn't even an investor, of any kind. Gunn was
engaged to Maureen's aunt Christine, a younger sister of
Carole Boczan, and he dealt with down-to-earth reality in
a manner alien to Michael Holoday. Gunn averaged $20
an hour installing floor and ceiling trim for a builder of
tract houses in the Kitchener-Waterloo area, while
Christine pursued her career as a watercolour artist.
During the same eight-hour day that Michael Holoday
might boast of generating million-dollar profits trading
Yankee greenbacks and eurobonds with unseen brokers
at the other end of a transatlantic computer link, George
Gunn earned less than $200 for measuring, cutting, nail-
ing, and finishing wooden baseboards and window trim,
hustling up and down ladders, breathing sawdust and sol-
vent fumes in dark, unfinished, and unheated houses.
After work and on weekends, Gunn carved blocks of bass-
wood into replicas of songbirds so lifelike that they
seemed prepared to fly from his hands. Many of his carv-
ings won Best In Show awards at woodcarving contests in
Canada and the US.

George Gunn had an eye for detail, and a knack for

transforming what his eye could perceive into something his hands could realize. He also possessed a wry scepticism about excessive wealth and ostentatious display. Relatively new to the Holodays' extended family — he and Christine had met only the previous year — Gunn was still acquainting himself with the various members of Maureen's family, their names, their relationships, and their occupations, when he attended the 1993 Halloween celebration.

During the party, Gunn wandered among the guests dressed as a circus clown. He watched couples dance to a hired DJ in the music room, nibbled on gourmet snacks in the high-tech kitchen, enjoyed a drink at the bar, and eventually settled himself on a sofa in a relatively quiet corner of the house, sitting between Maureen's mother Carole Boczan and Maureen's long-time friend Connie Gould, who was invited to every social function the Holodays hosted.

"What did you say Michael does for a living?" George asked Carole Boczan, who was costumed as an angel, complete with diaphanous wings.

"He's a stockbroker," Carole Boczan said. "A managing partner at First Marathon. They practically begged Michael to leave Midland Walwyn. He was the hottest trader there. Two years after he got his trading licence, he was a member of the Midland Walwyn Chairman's Club. You have to be in the top five percent of traders in the whole company to make the club. And he did it in just two years." She waited for an admiring reaction from George Gunn. When there was none, she continued: "Michael makes a lot of money, and he loves spending it on his family and friends. Michael is so sweet, so generous." She went on to explain that her son-in-law promised to provide for her and her husband "for the rest of our lives. That's how he put it." On the strength of her son-in-law's promises, Carole had sold her Cobourg salon.

"How can he make so much money and be so young?" George Gunn asked.

"He's just smart," Carole Boczan answered. "It's too complicated to understand. If you and Christine have any money, give it to Michael."

"Why?" George asked. "What'll he do with it?"

"He'll invest it for you."

"In what?"

"In futures, derivatives, things like that."

"What the hell are they?"

Carole Boczan waved the question away as though it were irrelevant. "It has to do with bonds and currency values, I don't really understand it myself. He buys bonds in Europe, and sells them in other places at a profit. You have to know interest rates, the way money moves, how the dollar does against German marks, British pounds. Michael knows all of that stuff. And he's into futures. That's when you know what the price on something will be next month, so you buy it cheaper this month. He's a genius at it."

"So if I give him my money, how do I know what he's going to do with it?" George asked. "How do I know he's making the right decisions?"

"It doesn't matter," Carole Boczan explained. "You just give him the money, and let him decide what to do with it. Leave everything up to him."

"That's right," added Connie Gould.

George Gunn twisted to look at the older woman. Connie was dressed as a flapper with elbow-length gloves and strings of pearls hanging to her waist. "Michael's a genius and the most generous man you can imagine," she said. "He loves to make money so he can spend it on other people. He flew Maureen and me to Paris last year, on the Concorde. We stayed for a week in the best hotel in Paris, in the same room that Johnny Carson had just vacated. Some famous rock band was staying down the hall from us . . ."

"Guns 'n' Roses," Carole Boczan said, and George Gunn turned back to her. "Maureen told us all about it." She leaned forward so Gunn could catch every word. "Did you know Michael is taking a bunch of us to Lake Louise at Christmas? He'll fly us all out, John and me and some of the family and a bunch of Michael's friends. We're taking an entire floor at Chateau Lake Louise."

"How does he make so much money?" George Gunn frowned.

"Through commissions and his own trades." It was Connie Gould. "Don't waste time trying to understand it. It's too confusing. Just give him your money and tell him to make trades for you."

"He can take five thousand dollars and turn it into eighty thousand dollars in six months," Carole Boczan added. "Guaranteed."

George Gunn looked at her and blinked. "No, he can't," he said. George might work on suburban construction sites and not on Bay Street, but he knew a thing or two about money in the real world. One thing he knew for certain was that you cannot turn a $5,000 investment into $80,000 in six months, guaranteed. Not without a pair of loaded dice in your hands, and an angel on your shoulder.

Carole Boczan began to lose her patience. "He already has," she said. "He did it for Maureen, and he's doing for John and me. He's taken our money and he's doubling it every month."

"No, he's not," George said, shaking his head. "Nobody can make money that fast unless they're gambling with it."

This was too much for Connie Gould, who seized George's shoulder and twisted him to face her. "Don't you ever doubt Michael!" she hissed. "Who are you to say he can't make money for his family and friends? Michael has made a lot of people here wealthy, and they're grateful to him." Her hostility rose another notch. "I will not hear anything bad about Michael Holoday! How dare you say a thing like that right here in his own home, while you're enjoying all his generosity? *Don't you dare say anything against Michael Holoday!*"

George Gunn rose from the sofa and walked away. Maybe he wasn't the type to move in these circles after all. Maybe it was time for him and Christine to head home to Kitchener in their van. For another half-hour George stood alone, watching the guests as they laughed and danced and drank and partied. Some were talking of plans to invest money with Michael, trusting his wisdom to multiply it over and over again in the coming months.

George Gunn was not disappointed that he and Christine had no money invested with Michael Holoday. He preferred the solid reality of a weekly paycheque. But he wondered over the next few months just why Connie and the others were so defensive about Holoday, and whether it was because they had their own doubts.

Among the guests at the Halloween party was a woman named Glennis MacLean.[6] Until a few weeks earlier, she had been Michael Holoday's private banking account manager at the Royal Bank branch where the Holodays maintained their personal chequing account.

Glennis MacLean had completed the Canadian Securities Course and successfully passed the examination to become a registered representative, qualifying her to advise clients on potential investments. MacLean had plans to move from banking to RBC Dominion Securities, Royal Bank's brokerage firm, plans made all the more attractive each time she reviewed the monthly cash flow in Maureen and Michael Holoday's accounts. In September 1993, almost $83 million in US funds — $41,317,648.91 in deposits and $41,372,591.40 in withdrawals — moved through one of the couple's several accounts at Royal Bank's 2 Bloor Street West branch. True, this represented a shortfall of almost $60,000, but you have to be doing something right to generate that kind of cash flow. Just a few months earlier, the Holodays' balance in that same account exceeded a million dollars Canadian. MacLean desperately wanted to move into securities, even if 1993 was not a hiring year for brokerages.

When Holoday heard about MacLean's qualifications and ambition, he made a proposal to her: Why not work for him at First Marathon? "I head the futures division," he boasted. "Hire, fire, and pay my own staff. Come and work for me."

MacLean knew little about futures, and wasn't qualified to sell them.

"You'll learn," Holoday boasted. "I'll teach you. In the meantime, you can become my marketing assistant and bring in new clients. Every broker needs new clients." He promised she could earn as much as $400,000 a year and, just to sweeten the deal, he would lease a Mercedes-Benz for her, at his expense.

MacLean jumped at the offer, and in early October 1993 she transferred her investments, including her RRSP and non-registered accounts, to First Marathon before joining Holoday's team. She began by mailing solicitation letters and making telephone calls to wealthy potential investors who might want to take advantage of Michael Holoday's "risk-free" investment strategy.

David Wood and First Marathon management had no objection to Holoday hiring MacLean. Holoday was paying MacLean's salary directly out of his own earnings, just as he was covering those of his trader, Chuck Oliver, and his personal assistant, Tracy Ellis.

But First Marathon's attitude changed when manage-

ment received a complaint that, before leaving Royal
Bank, MacLean had copied client names, addresses, and
telephone numbers from her employer's records and was
using them to build her prospect list for First Marathon.
This was an unacceptable breach of business ethics, and
when First Marathon confirmed the facts, they insisted
that Holoday fire his marketing assistant immediately.

Holoday agreed. Ethics are important. Glennis
MacLean had to go. And she did (leaving her leased
Mercedes-Benz behind for Holoday to cover the pay-
ments). But this was not the last that either First
Marathon or Michael Holoday would hear from her.

Paul Simpkin received a telephone call from Holoday the
Monday morning after the Halloween party. Holoday had
an excellent opportunity for the Simpkins, he announced.
A new fund called Northbridge Unit Trust was being
launched under Holoday's direction and, because of various needs to achieve a targeted capital balance, it was
offering to guarantee a pre-dated payment schedule to
selected first-time investors. Those who signed on would
be able to build profits even before the fund was officially
launched in Canada. In fact, the deposit would be back-
dated two months, generating an extra earnings bonus.

Before Simpkin could ask a number of pointed questions, Holoday completed his sales pitch and promised to
forward a letter of intent for the Simpkins to sign, adding:
"You'll need a minimum of five hundred thousand dollars
to participate."

When the Simpkins explained they didn't have
$500,000 tucked away in a kitchen drawer, ready to hand
over on short notice, Holoday suggested they borrow the
funds. "Your guaranteed returns," he assured them, "will
more than cover the interest payments." The Simpkins
remained apprehensive. Half a million dollars was a large

amount of money, especially to this retired couple. Holoday said his letter would alleviate their concerns. The letter, dated November 2, 1993, and printed on Holoday's "managing partner, futures division" letterhead, arrived a few days later:

> *Dear Mr. & Mrs. Simpkin,*
>   *This letter is written to confirm your intended $500,000 cdn (sic) investment in the "Northbridge Unit Trust" under Ontario Security Commission laws and regulations. It is understood that return on principle will commence from September 1, 1993 at a preferred interest rate of 10% per annum on the $500,000 cdn (sic) at First Marathon Securities Limited. As well a rate of 10% per annum will be paid on $250,000 cdn (sic) for June, July and August 1993.*[7]

The letter gave them 40 days to withdraw from the agreement. But why would they? Holoday, as "managing partner, futures division," was offering to pay more than two months' back interest on $500,000, plus an additional three months' interest on half that amount, which worked out to $18,750 profit starting on the date of the letter, plus an additional $50,000 earned interest per year. On that basis, the Simpkins signed the letter with confidence and high expectations, not knowing that "Northbridge Unit Trust" existed only in Michael Holoday's imagination.

The charade continued. Holoday's clients grew so elated over the growth of their investments under his management that they sent friends and colleagues to him, money in hand. Among those approaching Holoday, seeking to take advantage of the Northbridge offer was Brian Rocks, a 32-year-old building contractor married to Ray Kundinger's daughter. On the advice of golfing buddy John Keen, who worked at an auto body shop in downtown Toronto, Rocks contacted Holoday in mid-November. During an early meeting, Holoday repeated his boast about occupying office space that formerly housed the Reichmann brothers, who had moved one floor down to make way for Holoday's futures division. "He told me the Reichmanns would come up and ask him about interest rates, and where the economy was going," Rocks recalls. "He said they would bring their partners, and sometimes twenty or thirty of them would stand around his office, just to pick his brains."[8] Sufficiently impressed, Rocks deposited a total of $150,000 in two First Marathon accounts managed by Holoday.

Roger and Penny Campbell had overheard several guests at the Halloween party praising the investment wizard's ability to generate massive returns. When Holoday called the Campbells yet again the following week, they gave in. Yes, they would talk about investments with Michael. But only at their office, and with their accountant present. Would Holoday agree to that?

Of course he would, Holoday assured them, and he congratulated the couple on their astuteness.

At the meeting on November 26, 1993, Roger Campbell made his goals clear: Whatever funds he committed to investment on behalf of his and his numbered company — wife Penny controlled her own finances, and she too was eager to entrust money to Holoday's management — 90 percent was to be placed in safe, conservative investments, and the balance in something more aggressive, more risky.

As luck would have it, Holoday replied, the Campbells' timing couldn't be better. In his position as managing partner, futures division, at First Marathon, Holoday had the exclusive rights to one of the best investment vehicles in North America. It boasted a 15-year record of never losing money, averaged 20 percent earnings annually, and was managed by the top bond dealers in the world, working out of Wall Street. First Marathon was the exclusive sanctioned dealer for all of Canada. Entry was available only once or twice a year and, by the way, it took a minimum of one million dollars to buy a position. If the Campbells could assemble that much in cash, Holoday would see that they profited. Of course, they would want to examine past performance of the fund, so he promised to fax data to them. Its name? Northbridge, operated by Eastbridge Financial Management.

The following day, the Campbells' fax machine stuttered out a series of charts for the Northbridge Fund, confirming the earnings figures in Holoday's presentation. For 1989, Northbridge had generated a return on investment of 21.68 percent. Impressive? Not really. For the next four years it returned 85.92, 85.35, 27.91, and 46.0 percent for 1993 to date.

It would take, Holoday repeated, a minimum of one million dollars to get in on the action at Northbridge, and the investment window closed at the end of January. "You've got until then or you miss the boat," Holoday lectured the couple, and Roger and Penny Campbell began assembling their assets, setting a cool million as their goal.

Later, the Holodays went Christmas shopping for their clients. Mona O'Hearn and Helen Rentis received hamper-sized baskets filled with luxurious body lotions, creams, toiletries and soaps, set among fine porcelain bowls and hand-painted containers. Others received expensive crystal, fine wines, sterling silver, and rare brandies. Michael Holoday, everyone agreed, certainly knew how to look after his clients.[0]

In December, Michael and Maureen Holoday celebrated

Christmas with the Boczan family. Carole Boczan was thrilled to open her gift from Michael and Maureen to discover a superb full-length mink coat. After Christmas, Carole and John Boczan flew with Michael and Maureen and other members of the family to Calgary and drove to Chateau Lake Louise, where they spent the week between Christmas and New Year's. The Holodays booked nine rooms on one floor, including an expansive suite for themselves, their son, and his full-time nanny.

Ervin Schleith was invited to drive up from Kelowna and join them. "It was one of the last times I saw Michael," Schleith recalled. "He asked me and my fiancée to join him at Lake Louise. My fiancée was somewhat uncomfortable. We were staying in a small room, but it was costing two hundred and fifty dollars a night. The Boczans were there, Carole and John, and their son Paul and his wife, and some others as well. Mike and Maureen were staying in a suite as big as a house. It was immense!"

Holoday's generosity may have pleased others, but it left Ervin Schleith and his fiancée feeling uneasy. Holoday wouldn't let the couple pay for anything; he seemed intent on demonstrating how much money he had, and how frivolously he could spend it without regard.

After two days, Schleith tried to tell his old school chum that he and his fiancée had decided to return to Kelowna. Michael's hospitality and generosity weren't unappreciated, Schleith wanted to explain; it was just too excessive.

"Michael was on the telephone all the time, talking to Toronto," Ervin said, "and I didn't want to bother him. Besides, I had a sense he was under a lot of pressure, so the only time I got him alone to say we were leaving was when I was riding beside him on the chairlift, on our last day there. I told him this kind of living was out of our league. We were uncomfortable because Mike was paying for everything, picking up the tab for dinners for twenty people or more." The price for this outing, Ervin knew, would run to tens of thousands of dollars, all out of Holoday's pocket.

Holoday's response, when told his oldest friend was departing that day, proved curious. He told Ervin to send his father up to Lake Louise in Ervin's place.[10]

Ervin's father, Kurt Schleith, had invested with Michael more than two years earlier. Having bought his dream home — a picturesque cottage on a hill overlooking Okanagan Lake — with the proceeds from the sale of his Revelstoke sawmill, Kurt invested his remaining assets in government T-bills. They generated enough cash flow that it didn't matter if his orchard produced little more than blossoms each year.

Almost sneering at Kurt Schleith's cautious approach, Michael Holoday assured his friend's father that he could double his money in a short period of time with virtually no risk. He had already convinced another of Kurt's sons, Danny, to invest with him, and Danny seemed to be making as much profit as brother Erv. So in August 1991 Kurt had agreed to give Holoday $20,000, and later $60,000, to invest, just to see how well this hotshot kid would do.

Ervin replied that he didn't think his father would want to make the long drive from Kelowna to Lake Louise.

"No problem," Holoday said with a wave of his hand. "I'll charter a helicopter for him. It'll drop him off right here on the ski run."

Ervin thought this was an outrageous idea. He declined to pass along the invitation, and he and his fiancée left that day.[11]

As beautiful as Lake Louise might have been, snowmobiles and ski hills were not enough for Michael and Maureen Holoday. The sun and sand of Barbados were

more alluring, especially with Kenneth Roberts nearby.
Roberts had purchased a large beachfront property on the
island, adjacent to Sandy Lane, from the Rothschild
family several years earlier, and constructed a family villa
facing the ocean. The property was large enough to be
divided, at some future date, among Roberts' various offspring.

In late 1993, Michael Holoday (to his chagrin) did not
qualify as a Roberts family member, but he craved owning
a piece of the expansive landsite, and he began to pressure
Roberts to sell a parcel of land to him. The rest of the family was outraged at the idea. Had Michael Holoday enjoyed
their favour, their genuine affection, they might not have
objected. But many regarded Holoday as an interloper, a
hustling sycophant exploiting the quiet good nature of Doc
Roberts, and they opposed not only the sell-off of a portion
of their birthright, but also the proximity of Holoday and
his family in Barbados. They couldn't get away from the
guy, his constant talk about launching a brokerage, and
his glitzy blonde wife.

Doc Roberts eventually agreed to sell a portion of the
family's Barbados land to Holoday for something over a
million dollars in US funds. To mollify the family, Roberts
severed the land beyond a public road that paralleled the
shore; Holoday may be a neighbour, but he would not be a
shoulder-to-shoulder oceanfront neighbour.

Holoday didn't care. He had access to the beach
through the Roberts villa property. Better still, he had
access to Ken Roberts. Next year, Holoday announced, he
and Maureen would build their own villa on the newly
acquired land, luxurious enough to fit in among all the
other moneyed residents of Sandy Lane.[12]

Expensive gifts, extravagant parties, and first-class vacations weren't the only drain on Holoday's assets during

this period. He also made investments of his own, all foolish and costly. He purchased 275,000 shares at $6.25 per share of SDI Virtual Reality, a Toronto-based company listed on the NASDAQ exchange, whose sole product was a Formula One racing car ride designed for video arcades and shopping mall locations. The company faded out of sight in the mid 1990s.

He sank $600,000 in shares of Consolidated Madison, a Canadian mining company dedicated to locating mineral reserves in Brazil, and $175,000 in Wye Resources, a shell game that earned notoriety as one of the most outlandish in a long line of stock frauds aimed at gullible US investors. Wye and its president, a Newfoundlander named Rehan Malik, were convicted by US authorities in 1995 of selling four million shares of unregistered stock through a New Orleans-based Internet site on the basis of ten gem-quality diamonds from Wye-owned property in Zaire (now the Republic of the Congo). In reality, no one from Wye, or any of its contractors, had set foot on the property. The "gem-quality diamonds" were purchased from vendors on the black market, and Holoday and all other Wye Resources investors lost every penny they entrusted to the venture.

Holoday scored some coups as a bond trader during this time, most in commissions earned from trading in his client accounts. In January 1994, he grossed $106,426 in commissions, boosting this to $778,000 and $721,000 for the months of February and March respectively, slipping back to $607,000 for April. When it came to investing for himself, however, he was extraordinarily incompetent.

In mid-January Joe Thurman, correspondent network compliance officer at First Marathon, received a telephone call from Glennis MacLean, the former Royal Bank Account Manager who had been recruited by Holoday as a

*The Holoday family home in Revelstoke.
Holoday said his childhood was
"like growing up in Pleasantville."*
CREDIT: J. L. REYNOLDS

M. HOLIDAY

*Holoday's graduation pic. He was
so low-key in school that no one
noticed his name was misspelled.*
CREDIT: J. L. REYNOLDS

*Dr. Kenneth Roberts in 1974.
As a result of Holoday's fraud
he died "a broken man."*
CREDIT: BRIAN WILLER

*Sophisticated investors were lured
by Holoday's personalized
advertisements, supported by
"Blue Chip Thinking."*

020183

THE OPPORTUNITY
to EARN SUBSTANTIAL
INVESTMENT RETURNS

The Index trading arena has remained the sole domain of
sophisticated institutions for two reasons:
1. Relatively high risk.
2. Significant amounts of risk capital required.
Qualified individual investors with as little as $30,000 can
now participate through a controlled-risk trading strategy.
To participate in this specialized investment opportunity and
for more information call:

Michael Holoday
(416) 369-8975

MIDLAND WALWYN
BLUE CHIP THINKING™

*Tanya Sargent in 1992 – a
Maritime girl caught up in
the whirl of Bay Street.*

*Mona O'Hearn, circa 1955, when
she was one of Canada's leading
radio and stage actresses.*

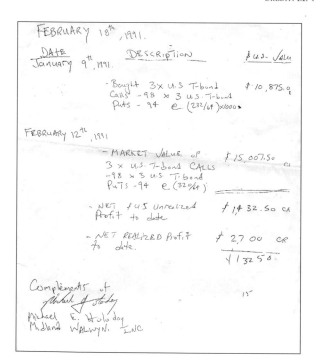

*Holoday's scribbled personalized
statements had one advantage over the
brokerage's: they always showed a profit.*

*Albert Robinson claims he was on
to Holoday earlier than others.
His reward was unemployment
and a surprise gift.*

*The Holodays'
Forest Hill home.*
CREDIT: J. L. REYNOLDS

*Exterior of the Forest Hill house
decorated for a 1993 Halloween party.*
CREDIT: PRIVATE COLLECTION

*Michael Holoday (centre)
hosting his Halloween party
costumed as a hobo clown.*
CREDIT: PRIVATE COLLECTION

*Maureen Holoday at the same
Halloween party dressed as
Edith Prickley of SCTV fame.*
CREDIT: PRIVATE COLLECTION

020184

Consider Index Trading to Increase Your Investment Returns

Today, qualified individual investors with as little as $30,000 can participate in the Index Trading arena through a specialized controlled-risk trading strategy.

Interested?

To find out more, please call:

Michael Holoday

(416) 369-3022

Toronto   Halifax   Montreal   Regina   Calgary
Vancouver   London   Paris   Zurich

First Marathon

At First Marathon, Holoday used the same "specialized controlled-risk trading strategy" in his advertisements.

Michael (front left), Maureen (front right), and their $300,000 cigarette boat BAD COMPANY on Lake Simcoe.
CREDIT: DOUG BUNKER

The mansion at 61 Park Lane Circle.
Holoday's $500,000 deposit cheque bounced.
CREDIT: J. L. REYNOLDS

Michael and Maureen's wedding –
a perfect day, a Rolls-Royce, and
a honeymoon in Monaco.
CREDIT: THE TORONTO STAR

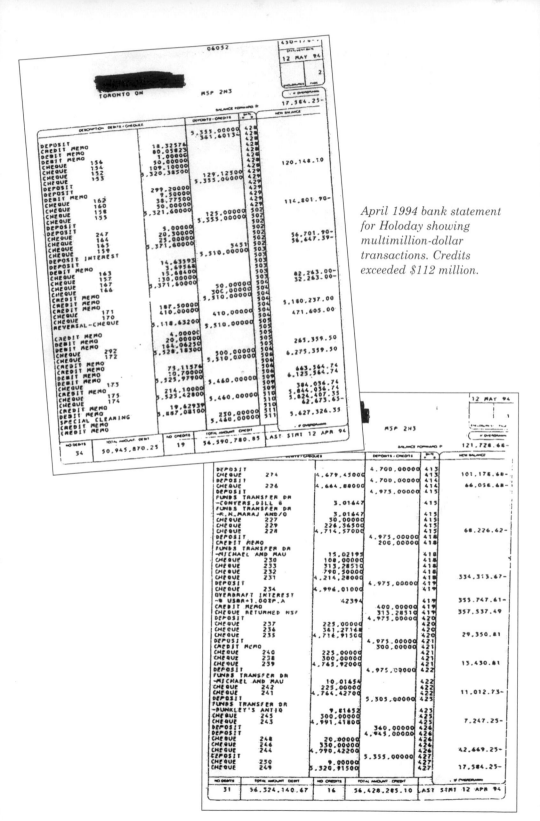

April 1994 bank statement for Holoday showing multimillion-dollar transactions. Credits exceeded $112 million.

The Holodays leaving bankruptcy court in July 2000.
CREDIT: THE TORONTO STAR

Fraud detectives Gary Logan and Jeff Thomson. Logan let Holoday underestimate him. Thomson was blunt and direct.
CREDIT: J. L. REYNOLDS

Holoday on his way to trial, October 2000.
CREDIT: J. L. REYNOLDS

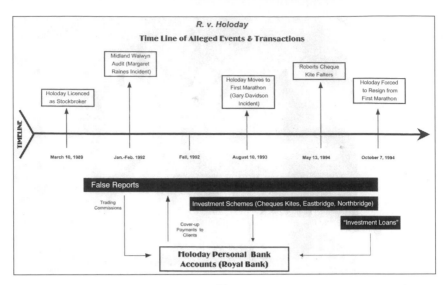

R. v. Holoday

Time Line of Alleged Events & Transactions

TIMELINE

- Holoday Licenced as Stockbroker — March 10, 1989
- Midland Walwyn Audit (Margaret Raines Incident) — Jan.-Feb. 1992
- Fall, 1992
- Holoday Moves to First Marathon (Gary Davidson Incident) — August 10, 1993
- Roberts Cheque Kite Falters — May 13, 1994
- Holoday Forced to Resign from First Marathon — October 7, 1994

False Reports

Trading Commissions

Investment Schemes (Cheques Kites, Eastbridge, Northbridge)

Cover-up Payments to Clients

"Investment Loans"

Holoday Personal Bank Accounts (Royal Bank)

Time-line chart used by Crown to track Holoday's tactics during his criminal trial.

TSE
Toronto Stock Exchange

December 16, 1997

Mr. L.S. Bloomberg
Member Seatholder
First Marathon Securities Limited
2 First Canadian Place
The Exchange Tower, Suite 3200
Toronto, Ontario
M5X 1J9

Dear Mr. Bloomberg:

Re: **First Marathon Securities Limited - Supervision of Michael Holoday**

This is to inform you that the Investigations and Enforcement Division of the Toronto Stock Exchange (the "TSE"), has completed its investigation into the supervision of Michael Holoday, formerly a Registered Representative in the Toronto, Ontario office of First Marathon Securities Limited between August 11, 1993 and October 7, 1994.

Having reviewed the findings of the investigation, TSE staff has determined that First Marathon Securities Limited properly supervised Michael Holoday while he was employed with them. As such, disciplinary proceedings will not be initiated.

If you should have any questions regarding this matter, please do not hesitate to contact me.

Yours very truly,

Tom Atkinson

Tom Atkinson

TA:dw

cc: Mr. Joel Wiesenfeld
Fogler, Rubinoff

Ms. Melanie Sampson
Manager, Registrations
Investment Dealers Association

Mr. Michael Haddad
Chief Investigator
Investment Dealers Association

** TOTAL PAGE.01 **

The TSE letter sent to First Marathon more than three years after Holoday was asked to resign.

After the verdict. Later, it was Logan's turn to say, "He's not too smart, is he?"
CREDIT: J. L. REYNOLDS

marketing assistant, and whom Holoday was instructed to fire when it was discovered that MacLean had taken Royal Bank client files with her.

MacLean was angry. Michael Holoday, she charged, was engaged in illegal discretionary trading, among other things. Holoday was getting away with murder, and First Marathon should do something about it.

Thurman didn't want empty accusations. If MacLean had a complaint, he instructed her, she should put it in writing to him, and he would conduct a thorough investigation into her accusations.

A few days later, Thurman received a letter from MacLean in which she stated that several trades were made in her RRSP account, without her knowledge, around the time she left First Marathon. She wrote:

> *Upon receiving notices regarding the trades I was puzzled, however, I decided to wait until my monthly statements in order to clarify the trades. In December, I made several attempts to get further information regarding the status of my accounts, to no avail. Finally, after several telephone calls, I asked Michael's assistant Tracy (Ellis) to provide me with a breakdown of my account, as I did not understand the trades that were placed in my account. During all of this time I was advised that Mike could not speak to me. . . .I am concerned about the dealings in my account. Tracy advised me that the balances shown on my statement do not include accrued interest. However, my understanding is that the balances shown on my statement includes interest to the date of settlement. Please clarify.*

It took two weeks for Thurman to respond to MacLean's

letter, and his reply rejected her concerns out of hand.

> *I have undertaken to investigate your written complaint of January 17,* Thurman began, *and have been unable to determine any regulatory violations by our representative, Michael Holoday.*

Thurman's investigation did not extend much beyond discussing MacLean's letter with Holoday and asking if there was any substance to it. Not surprisingly, Holoday denied the charges; to accept them would have meant the end of his career. MacLean was still mad, Holoday suggested, because he had to fire her. She was just trying to get revenge. Thurman asked Holoday to submit a letter explaining his position.

> *You state in your letter,* Thurman went on in his reply to MacLean, *that several unauthorized trades were made in your account by Mr. Holoday "around the same time" that you left the employ of First Marathon Securities Limited. Mr. Holoday has indicated that he specifically discussed each and every trade in your account and was of the opinion that you fully understood what was happening in your RRSP accounts.*
>
> *You also indicate in your letter that Mr. Holoday represented that certain investment strategies bore "no risk." Mr. Holoday denies that he has ever stated that any investment was riskless. A check of your registration records indicates that you have successfully completed both the Canadian Securities Course and the examination based on the Manual for registered representatives. I would expect that anyone who has*

passed these examinations ought to be reason-
ably expected to be aware of the fact that no stock
or bond investment can be totally riskless.

Thurman dispensed with MacLean's claim of lost interest
by directing her to discuss the matter with Holoday's
assistant, Tracy Ellis, and dismissed concerns about
excessive commissions charged to MacLean's account by
saying the commissions were within industry standards.

Three days after Thurman mailed MacLean his
response to her charges, Thurman received the written
explanation he had requested from Holoday, who wrote:

Mrs. Glennis MacLean did authorize the
trades in her RRSP around November 9th. The
trades were discussed with Mrs. MacLean by me
before the bond positions were purchased.
Mrs. MacLean indicated that she did not
want to purchase speculative or high risk invest-
ments in her RRSP, but that she understood that
she must tolerate some risk on her RRSP invest-
ments if she was to make returns greater than the
T-bill rate of interest. The investment put in her
RRSP in my opinion had conservative risk relat-
ed to it.
Mrs. MacLean was aware that other clients of
mine were investing in the bond portfolio recom-
mended for her RRSP and at no time was there a
statement by me to any client that there was no
risk attached to this portfolio.[13]

Nothing else was heard from Glennis MacLean.

During the short time Glennis MacLean was at First
Marathon, she managed to generate one important new

client for Holoday — a real estate developer named
Sheldon Fenton.

In January 1994, Sheldon Fenton was rich in both liquid assets and shrewdness. Impressed with Holoday,
Fenton agreed to open a futures trading account. Fenton
had traded in futures and understood the investment principles Holoday outlined for him. In fact, he understood
them too well for Holoday's comfort. When Fenton grew
curious about Holoday's apparent success record in futures
dealing, Holoday suggested an alternative: Eastbridge, out
of New York. Fenton asked his lawyers to look into it, but
when they informed Fenton that a minimum US$5 million
was needed to participate in Eastbridge, Fenton declined.
He'd stick with futures for a while.

By January 28, 1994, the Campbells had done it. Roger
Campbell liquidated his investments, Penny Campbell did
the same with hers, and they cobbled together various
other assets until the total came to just over one million
dollars. When Roger Campbell called Holoday at First
Marathon to announce they had the million dollars in
hand, Holoday suggested they come downtown to his office
and open an account. When they arrived, Holoday was
cool; Roger Campbell was not. In fact, he was so nervous
that he insisted his office manager accompany him on the
ride. Once in Holoday's opulent office, he was unable to
hand the cheque across to Holoday and asked the office
manager to do it for him.

Holoday seemed amused by Campbell's nervousness.
There was nothing to worry about, he assured his newest
client. Campbell, he suggested, had just taken the first
step toward immense future wealth.

Later that month, Holoday was again tripped up by a routine audit, this time at First Marathon. Greg Weber, the

young CA whose $906 discrepancy in his Midland Walwyn account had been dismissed as immaterial by Deloitte & Touche, was randomly selected to receive a confirmation letter from First Marathon's auditors in January 1994. Weber had grown unhappy with losses in his account due to Holoday's trading. Even after Weber instructed Holoday to make no further trades in the account, the next month's statement always indicated more trades had taken place, leading to more losses and more complaints from Weber. Holoday's excuses were consistent. "Errors," he would mumble. "Damn back-office guys. I'll fix it on the next statement."

So Weber was not hesitant in faxing the auditor's letter back to them in early February 1994, noting the account balance as he believed it to be.

The response was immediate . . . and surprising. Within five minutes of faxing the document, Weber's telephone rang. It wasn't a member of First Marathon's auditors on the line, or Joe Thurman, the company's compliance officer. It was Michael Holoday himself, and he was outraged at his client's actions.

"Why did you do that??!!" Holoday screamed across the line at his own client. "Why did you send that damn letter to the auditors?"

Weber tried to explain. The auditors asked if he agreed with his account balance, and he hadn't. So he told them. What was wrong with that?

Holoday, regaining control of himself, advised Weber that, in future, any questions about Weber's account must be directed to Holoday, okay? *Okay??!!* Holoday, after all, was the managing partner, futures division. He was the one responsible for maintaining and supervising all the Division's accounts. Every inquiry about account balances must be directed to Holoday alone, was that clear? By the way, Holoday added before Weber could respond, a First

Marathon cheque for $2,101 was being sent out to him as part of his profits.

Later, Weber wondered why Holoday had been upset with him for contacting the auditors directly. Obviously, the auditors had passed Weber's faxed message on to the managing partner, futures division. If Holoday were responsible for its operations, as he claimed, why should he become angry about a client responding directly to an auditor's inquiry? Why would it make a difference? And what was behind the $2,101 cheque? Weber hadn't asked for any money from his account.

In early 1994, Holoday realized a potential personal profit of almost $1 million in a single day, earned from trading options on interest rate futures. He walked, gloating, into David Wood's office to boast of it, then asked the First Marathon executive for advice. Should he take his profits now, or let the deal ride, maybe make more money if the bidding went higher?

"I think you should crystallize it," Wood replied, meaning Holoday should sell the options and take his profits.

Holoday wasn't so sure. He wanted time to think about it, and he rode the elevator downstairs and walked around the block a few times, criss-crossing Toronto's financial district in the mild spring air, pondering the alternatives and weighing his options. By the time he returned to his computer, others had flooded the market with their own options and the price of Holoday's deal had collapsed, wiping out his brief million-dollar bubble. Such was the life of a currency options trader.

From that day forward, Holoday's personal substantive losses began to soar, and Holoday's activities at First Marathon became a frantic shuffling of assets from one hand to another, supported by forgeries, delays, and outright lies.

Holoday earned over $700,000 in commissions from his futures trades during March 1994, but this wasn't nearly enough to offset his losses and expenditures in other areas. After encouraging his father-in-law John Boczan to entrust the last $25,000 of Boczan's inheritance to him, Holoday dispatched his in-laws to Barbados where, for a monthly salary of $5,000, they were to oversee the construction of Holoday's custom villa on the property sold to him by Ken Roberts. Meanwhile, Holoday's day-trades on behalf of Doc and Elaine Roberts were exceeding $4 million.

He needed more money, and his only remaining source was the quickly dwindling balance in his clients' accounts.

By now, Holoday's clients had grown accustomed to his explanations regarding discrepancies between the statements they received from the brokerage and those provided by Holoday. The suspicions of some weren't as easily diverted as others. Several of Holoday's clients began recording their conversations, both over the telephone and face-to-face.

Among them was Paul Simpkin, who continued to be concerned about losses in his account. Late in the afternoon of Thursday, March 24, 1994, Simpkin called Holoday and recorded their conversation. Holoday's convoluted explanation, delivered in his flat, authoritative voice, demonstrates his style and technique:

> SIMPKIN: *With the last (First Marathon) statement that came in today, from March the twenty-first with another profit and loss debit, I'm up to thirty thousand, nine hundred and seven dollars now in loss.*
>
> HOLODAY: *Your Friday position, that was bought Thursday, carries forward Tuesday, Monday . . . the market dropped a point and a half plus four yesterday . . . and*

> *that whole thing reverses, it's part of the same strategy with an April, May rollover from Thursday last week.*
>
> SIMPKIN: *Yeah . . .*
>
> HOLODAY: *The thirty comes back and you go up another twenty grand as of today. So we actually made you a chunk of money today and you'll see that, in one or two days I guess.*

When this gibberish failed to impress clients, Holoday's fall-back position was to blame the brokerage for a book-keeping error. He would dangle the promise of anticipated profits, neutralize their concerns, and whet their appetites, as he did with Simpkin later in the same conversation:

> HOLODAY: *I know where the account sits today. And I know about the error, and that's all I can say, and I can make the adjustment for 'ninety-four, and if I take the cash balance in the morning and add that adjustment, uh, as far as I'm concerned it's in line . . .*
>
> SIMPKIN: *Well . . . if I started out with seventy-three thousand, and I had a twenty-two percent profit, in cash, it's gotta be up to, what? Another seventeen and seventy-three, that would have got me up to ninety thousand in cash then.*
>
> HOLODAY: *That's right.*
>
> SIMPKIN: *Huh?*
>
> HOLODAY: *That's where you should be . . . it's been a pretty . . . like, the last six months have been a very active trading period, and all I can say is that all the accounts, before, at the middle of last week . . . were up*

> *twenty-two percent. They did a profit*
> *today.*
> SIMPKIN: *Yeah . . .*
> HOLODAY: *They're up higher. . . . So the account could*
> *be as high as forty percent as of today.*
> SIMPKIN: *Well gee, I'd love to see it.*
> HOLODAY: *All I'm going to do, I'm not going to make*
> *another trade on your account, Paul,*
> *until we fax you your credit balance,*
> *and then we'll move forward from there.*
> *But I know that it's going to be a hell of*
> *a good-looking picture.*

There was nothing "good-looking" about the picture at all. Simpkin's accounts with First Marathon had already lost almost $100,000 of their net investment of $515,000, and within 60 days the losses had mushroomed to $325,000. All the while, Holoday kept assuring Simpkins that his account was earning a substantial profit.

In April 1994, Holoday paid a visit to his mother-in-law's friend Dianne Sone to announce a great investment opportunity for her: shares in SDI Virtual Reality, a company on the cutting edge of the technological revolution. They had a computer chip that was years ahead of anybody's, one that was going to revolutionize the entertainment industry by putting players right in the middle of the action.

Dianne and her husband were cautious — she intended, she reminded Holoday, to focus on conservative investments only, and this one sounded risky.

Holoday explained there is risk, and then there is risk. SDI promised big dividends, and that's the only kind of risk to take. "Personally, I'm the biggest single shareholder in the company," he said. He claimed to own over a million dollars in SDI stock. "That should speak for itself, right?"

Maybe it spoke for Holoday, but it didn't convince Dianne Sone.

Holoday smiled and said he understood. But this might also be a good time to review Sone's other investments, and along the way Dianne Sone mentioned a Canada Savings Bond she had purchased in 1987. Its value at maturity, in 1997, would be $50,000.

When Holoday asked its location, she replied that it was tucked away in a file drawer. Holoday was aghast. Don't leave it there, he warned her. Didn't she know that a burglar could carry it off and cash it? Or what if she had a fire? The bond was nearing maturity, it would be worth $40,000 by now. The only place to keep the CSB was in a safety deposit box.

Dianne Sone explained that she didn't have one, wasn't sure if one was available from her bank.

"Keep it on deposit at First Marathon," Holoday said. The value would show up on her monthly statement, and she would never have to worry about losing her bond in a fire or due to a burglary.

It made a lot of sense, the way Holoday put it. A few days later Dianne Sone delivered the bond to Holoday at his First Marathon office. Remember, she told him. Under no circumstances was he ever to cash the bond. She was expecting to have $50,000 from it in 1997.

Holoday agreed. Of course, he understood. The bond was safe with him.[14]

Jim O'Donnell, the Midland Walwyn director who endured Holoday's wrath for advising two of the broker's clients to discuss their account problems with a compliance officer, had left Mackenzie Financial to launch his own line of mutual funds. O'Donnell Fund Management Limited was one of several operations sprouting up in the spring of 1994, responding to the awareness of Canada's baby boomers of the need to invest for their retirement years.

O'Donnell claimed more credibility than most, given his long-time association with the largest mutual fund operation in Canada. In spring 1994, he leased offices in The Exchange Tower, a few floors below First Marathon Securities, and was looking for $6 million in US funds to expand the business. The response was generally favourable, but a telephone call O'Donnell received in mid-April was surprising, to say the least.

It was from Michael Holoday. "I hear you're looking for capital," Holoday said to the somewhat startled O'Donnell. Holoday claimed to have money available. "By the way," he added, "I'm now a managing partner with First Marathon. Why don't you come on up and we'll talk about putting some money in your company?"

Driven as much by curiosity as by an interest in acquiring capital, O'Donnell rode the elevator to First Marathon where Holoday, looking more prosperous and confident than during his days at Midland Walwyn, took pride in showing his suite of offices to the older man. Holoday was obviously doing well. So well, in fact, that he was prepared to invest $3 million, US funds, in O'Donnell's company. The cash was available. Was O'Donnell interested? Of course O'Donnell was interested.

There was one condition, Holoday said. In exchange for the $3 million, Holoday was to be made a director of O'Donnell Financial Management, and assigned to manage one of the company's fund portfolios.

O'Donnell wanted an influx of capital, but not badly enough to agree to those conditions. It was not unusual to obtain a directorship in return for a substantial infusion of capital into an existing company — O'Donnell himself had acquired a similar position with Midland Walwyn four years earlier — but Holoday's demand to manage a fund portfolio was out of the question. The skills employed to earn a million dollars in broker commissions are not related at all to those involved in managing investments for a mutual fund. O'Donnell declined the offer, which Holoday accepted with something between good grace and distraction.[15]

Roger and Penny Campbell couldn't help feeling uneasy. Together, they had almost $1.5 million invested with Michael Holoday, but it was difficult to prove it. First Marathon's statements never seemed to match Holoday's effusive assurances, and his scribbled summaries of trades and profits were even less discernible. Whenever they expressed unease over their investments, Holoday would rush over from his First Marathon suite, sometimes stepping out of a chauffeured limousine while babbling on his cell phone, or invite the Campbells to his office for a meeting.

Holoday would assure the Campbells they were making money, using terms like *naked strangles*, *inverted yield curves*, and *leveraged bond plays.* If the meeting took place in Holoday's office, he would make a show of calling to Tracy Ellis, seated at her computer. "Tracy, show the Campbells the computer, would you?" and Tracy would tap a few keys before swinging the computer screen around to display annual earnings of 20 percent or better, although the Campbells were never invited to examine the account records closely.

Holoday's problems kept mounting. A long distance telephone call in mid-April 1994 from Holoday's crusty client Roy O'Hearn, the ex–law book salesman, provided some unintended black humour. It was also the first in a long wave of tremors that would eventually shatter Holoday's ruse.

O'Hearn was growing dubious about Holoday. Whenever O'Hearn tried to get a straight answer from him, some excuse popped out of Holoday's mouth. The responsibility for errors in O'Hearn's statements always rested with "the damned computers," "those stupid accountants," or Tracy Ellis forgetting to do what Holoday had instructed her to do.

"He always told me to call him collect," O'Hearn recalls, "even if he was in Hong Kong or somewhere. He'd say 'Call me collect, anytime. Twice a day if you want.' His long distance bill must have been horrendous! But it never made any difference. I'd call him and say, 'Where's that money you promised to send me?' and he'd respond, 'The stupid mail clerk, I'm gonna get him fired!' or he'd say the courier sent the damn cheque to Singapore. Singapore! Can you believe it?'"

O'Hearn couldn't access his own money, but Holoday never seemed to have a problem getting his hands on cash to buy new and elaborate toys for himself and Maureen. "I saw him with a Jaguar, and then he bought one for his wife," Roy O'Hearn says. "He added a Porsche later, and then a Ferrari for God's sake, and a four-wheel-drive vehicle. I remember saying to somebody, 'That guy's not spending his own money. Nobody spends his own money like that.'"

One summer weekend, Holoday invited Roy O'Hearn to his rented Lake Simcoe cottage. Holoday was personally sponsoring a "poker run," an excuse for owners of high-powered racing craft to tear across the water making stops at five destinations. At each brief stopover, the boat owner drew from a deck of cards, and at the end of the day the owner with the best poker hand was declared the winner.

Holoday had rented a helicopter for the day and he persuaded O'Hearn to ride in it, shooting movies of Michael and Maureen skimming over the lake in *Bad Company,* a high rooster-tail of water soaring in their wake, along with similar craft. "They came across the water like bats out of hell," O'Hearn recalled years later. O'Hearn obviously enjoyed the experience, but he recognized the extravagance of the exercise. "He paid almost fifteen hundred dollars for that helicopter," O'Hearn said, "just to get a few minutes of him and Maureen in that damn boat."[16]

"Michael loved speed," Jacques Soucie remembered. "He could hardly wait to get behind the wheel of that cigarette boat and tear along the water. The wind would be whipping through his hair, the motors would be roaring like thunder, the water would be splashing in, the wake would be spreading behind him, and he'd be grinning and laughing. He loved it!"

More than the cars and the boats Holoday was accumulating, O'Hearn was appalled at Holoday's indulgence of Maureen's family. It was Maureen and her parents, John and Carole Boczan, who O'Hearn believed were reaping the richest benefits from the Bay Street Whiz Kid. "I hear the Boczans, her parents, are complaining that Holoday took fifty or sixty thousand dollars of their money," O'Hearn grumbled. "Hell, if that's true they've got nothing to complain about. They got their money's worth out of him."

O'Hearn's misgivings concerning his broker's activities grew. During a conversation in Holoday's office, after O'Hearn complained to his broker about taxes, Holoday advised his client to hide his money offshore, in the Bahamas or the Caymans, "Like he was doing," O'Hearn said. Later, Holoday convinced O'Hearn to invest $100,000 in a short-term bond play that proved profitable — but not for O'Hearn. The investment earned $11,000; Holoday took $7,000 in commissions, leaving O'Hearn with a net of $4,000. O'Hearn had risked his entire investment for a paltry 4 percent profit.

"That's enough for me," O'Hearn said. The constant lies, the wild spending, and the hints of illegal activities were too much for O'Hearn. He and other clients were being asked to trust Holoday's word, but Roy O'Hearn had heard too many of Holoday's transparent lies to trust him with anything.

Demanding to withdraw his entire investment at once, O'Hearn suspected, would launch another litany of Holoday's lies. Better to take the money out in dribs and drabs. Roy O'Hearn began asking Holoday for $5,000 or $10,000 withdrawals from his account. Holoday always had a reason for stalling, reasons O'Hearn recognized as more lies. "You should leave it in, there's a real market opportunity coming up," Holoday might plead, but when O'Hearn grew adamant, Holoday would give in and promise a cheque "in a few days, a week at the most." The funds wouldn't appear until O'Hearn made it clear that he wanted his money *now, damn it,* and a cheque would finally show up in O'Hearn's mail, or be handed to him by Holoday across the oversized desk in Holoday's First Marathon office.

O'Hearn managed to complete three or four withdrawals this way, each as difficult as pulling teeth, until March 1994 when he hit a brick wall. Holoday just wasn't sending O'Hearn any more money. Promises, lies, and excuses galore, but not a penny from O'Hearn's account.

By mid-April O'Hearn had reached his wit's end. Along with his frustration at not being able to access his money, Holoday's statements to O'Hearn over the past several months were indicating that he owned 110,000 shares of Century Technologies. Really? O'Hearn didn't recall investing in them. Nor was it the first time he had discovered some shares purchased for his account without his permission or instructions. A year earlier, O'Hearn returned from an extended trip in the Far East to learn that Holoday had purchased 25,000 shares of SDI Virtual Reality with O'Hearn's money, adding them to his client's portfolio. O'Hearn had hit the roof and told Holoday to get rid of those shares and put the money back in his account, right now, damn it!

Holoday did, warning O'Hearn he was missing out on a once-in-a-lifetime deal, that SDI was a comer, a sure thing, a solid growth stock. O'Hearn told him to forget about that, just put the cash back in the account and never do it again. Well, Holoday had done it again, and now he claimed the Century Technologies shares were worth $650,000. "Then sell some and get me the money, ten thousand dollars' worth," O'Hearn kept imploring Holoday.[17]

Spending much of April 1994 with friends in Maryland, O'Hearn tried yet again to withdraw $10,000 from his account, this time to cover travel expenses, but Holoday refused to accept O'Hearn's telephone calls. Tracy Ellis would claim Holoday was in a meeting, or in transit between meetings, or on a long distance call, and he would call O'Hearn back as soon as possible, which seemed to be never. O'Hearn gave up and tried asking someone at First Marathon, anyone at all, to send him a cheque. No one seemed able to. In fact, everyone in Toronto kept telling him that he had no Century Technologies shares, no money, no assets at all in his account. He was, as far as First Marathon could tell, broke.

By the third time O'Hearn heard this nonsense, he lost it and demanded to speak to someone at the top, "the highest-level executive you can get me. You get hold of them and have them call me right away, or there's going to be hell to pay!" He barked his telephone number and slammed down the receiver.

When the telephone rang a few moments later, O'Hearn found himself speaking with Senior Vice-President David Wood, who announced that First Marathon would not be able to transfer $10,000 or even ten cents from O'Hearn's account, because it was essentially empty. While O'Hearn's shares of Century Technologies had indeed been valued at $650,000 when transferred, the stock was now virtually worthless.

O'Hearn tried to control his emotions, telling Wood he was mistaken, this problem had existed for months, the funds had been in O'Hearn's account since he transferred it from Midland Walwyn the previous year. What's more, Century Technologies was still being traded at its original market value, Holoday had assured him of that, and First Marathon had better shape up and put its accounting procedures in order, or damn it . . .

Wood's calm and cultured voice interrupted O'Hearn's outburst. "Just a moment," Wood said. "I'll let you discuss this with Michael." O'Hearn heard Wood switch on his speaker phone and Michael Holoday's voice utter an uncertain: "Uh, hi Roy . . ."

Roy O'Hearn launched into a tirade, telling Holoday that he had better ensure that those clowns at First Marathon get their act together, they were still making errors on the statements, and O'Hearn was finding it plenty frustrating.

Holoday, stumbling and gasping, tried to remind O'Hearn that he had been withdrawing funds to place with other brokers, which explained why O'Hearn's account at First Marathon was depleted.

This had the effect of propelling O'Hearn into an even angrier response, the older man's voice suggesting he was about to leap bodily through the telephone receiver into David Wood's office and throttle the two men, one listening with astonishment and confusion, the other stuttering and perspiring. Holoday's statement that O'Hearn had transferred funds from his account to another broker was total hogwash, O'Hearn bellowed. He had not transferred any funds and he, O'Hearn, wanted his money *now,* damn it!

Instead of a reply, Holoday managed to gurgle something through a constricted throat. In Maryland, O'Hearn heard cries of distress and concern on the other end of the line before Wood's voice announced that perhaps O'Hearn should call back later because they had a problem at First Marathon Securities in Toronto.

Michael Holoday had just fainted.[18]

THIRTEEN

It's all coming out tickety-boo.
— MICHAEL HOLODAY, MAY 26, 1994

L ess than an hour later, Roy O'Hearn's telephone in Maryland rang, and a weak voice identified the caller as Holoday. "Roy, you shouldn't have done that," Holoday began repeating in O'Hearn's ear. "You shouldn't have done that. Don't ever do that again."

O'Hearn wanted to know what the hell was going on. Holoday said he would explain later. Right now he was sick, and he was going home to bed.

That evening, Holoday indeed called O'Hearn, his voice calm, his attitude changed. He sounded confident again, soothing. "Roy, your money's fine," Holoday assured the older man. "It's earning a profit and I'll get whatever funds you need. Just be sure to talk to me. I'm the guy who knows what's going on down there. I'm the only guy you should talk to."

O'Hearn asked what had happened earlier. Why had Holoday fainted?

"Just a virus or something," Holoday explained. "I'm home in bed now. I'll get a night's rest and be as good as new." He promised to wire O'Hearn his money the very next day. "You're making money, Roy," he said before hanging up. "You're doing just fine."

The wire never arrived, but later that month Holoday sent O'Hearn a bank draft for $299,000 in US funds, drawn on Holoday's personal account at the Chase Manhattan Bank in Syracuse, New York. "That covers your losses," Holoday said. "Okay?"

O'Hearn wasn't totally satisfied. From that point on, he too began recording his conversations with Michael Holoday.

Michael Holoday's fainting spell in David Wood's office, whether feigned to avoid discussing O'Hearn's account in Wood's presence, or generated by sheer panic, marked the end of Holoday's success at duping most of his clients most of the time. From that point on, he was like a man caught in a high-elevation avalanche, trusting only his instincts to keep his head above the surface, knowing he must ride it to the end.

With genuine irony, the slide began on Friday, May 13.

The entire month of May 1994 was a disaster for Holoday, kicked off by a memo he received from Joe Thurman on May 4. The subject was "Free Riding":

> *It has come to my attention that on certain occasions commodity option positions have been purchased for clients for whom we have no available funds in their stock accounts nor cheques on hand.*
>
> *As you are aware, commodity options contracts are required to be settled on a "same day" basis. Thus, in order to ensure compliance in this area, we must insist that no new positions be initiated for any client who does not have sufficient, readily-accessible funds.*
>
> *Please be advised that future violations will be treated as errors, and that any resulting losses will be charged to your error account.*

Thurman was drawing attention to a basic rule in commodities trading: Transactions can be conducted only when the client has funds on hand to cover the trade. The situation is similar to betting on a horse race. Where legal, bets are placed at the racetrack, or through licensed outlets by purchasing a ticket, entitling the bettor to winnings. Successful or not, the racetrack or agent has the money in hand before the race begins. The alternative is to place a bet with a bookie via telephone. No money is put up unless the bet loses, and bookies have various means, illegal and often violent, of collecting money owned to them.

Investors who trade with no money in their account are known as *Free Riders*. Michael Holoday and many of his clients, unknown to them, had been free riders for some time.

May 7, 1994, marked Michael Holoday's 30th birthday, and a little thing like Thurman's threatening memo wasn't going to prevent the Holodays from celebrating with appropriate hoopla and extravagance. At 30 years of age, most brokers begin to feel confident in their decisions and dealings with clients and start setting their sights on long-term goals. Like a partnership, a home in Forest Hill, a million-dollar annual income.

Michael Holoday had already achieved these objectives (although the partnership was more apparent than real), and Maureen decided his birthday celebration deserved something more than a cake and a romantic retreat. Nothing less than a party to set tongues wagging all over town would be enough, and for several weeks Maureen took charge of orchestrating the event. It had to be at the Four Seasons, of course. For music, strolling musicians; for entertainment, magicians and buskers moving among the guests, and something else, something spectacular. The entire affair would be captured by a full movie crew, and everyone fortunate enough to attend would remember this event for the rest of their lives. They would give thanks for their good fortune at being a friend and a client, and usually both, of Michael Holoday, managing partner, futures division, First Marathon Securities. Maureen's parents, John and Carole Boczan, would be there, of course, and Maureen arranged for them to fly up from Barbados for the weekend, attend Michael's party, and return the following day.

The invitations promised an evening fit for a sultan. Guests rode elevators to the top of the Four Seasons where the entire floor was dedicated to Holoday's birthday celebration. Waiters circulated, discreetly dispensing caviar and vintage champagne, while strolling musicians and belly dancers entertained the guests until, with a flourish, a curtain was pulled back to reveal the dining area. The centrepiece at each round table was a turban, and on cue the turbans rose to reveal fortune tellers whose bodies were concealed beneath the table, and who turned this way and that during the meal, telling fortunes, singing bawdy songs, and reciting jokes.

The meal itself was the finest that the Four Seasons offered, featuring pheasant, scampi, and truffles. The wines were superb, the service impeccable. Michael and Maureen sat at the head table where, one by one, various guests arrived to praise Michael and flatter him. Finally, Carole Boczan took the microphone to read her favoured son-in-law a saccharine poem, leading to its ironic final line: *Michael, Michael, the best is yet to come.*

To Elaine Roberts, who had attended her share of upper-class social events, "It was over the top."[1] She had never seen anything like it in her life. It appeared as though Michael and Maureen Holoday were looking for ways to spend enormous amounts of money as extravagantly as they could. Few families in Canada could exceed the Roberts when it came to measuring net worth, yet even Doc and Elaine Roberts were stunned by the conspicuous expense of Holoday's celebration.

Holoday, Elaine mused, possessed wealth. Whether he had similar quantities of good taste was another matter. Still, she and her father owed Michael Holoday their gratitude for including them in his daily trades, now exceeding $5 million and continuing to generate profits for the family. In appreciation, Doc Roberts gave his apparent protégée a case of vintage Dom Pérignon champagne for a birthday gift. Holoday bragged about the gift, exaggerating its value and implication.

Everyone who attended the birthday speculated at the cost of the affair. It was somewhere, the consensus said, between $50,000 and $100,000.

Around this time, rumours began circulating among Ted Gittings and a few other Holoday clients — and Holoday made no effort to deny them — that Doc Roberts was actually Holoday's biological father, the result of a romantic fling in Roberts' younger days (but not that young — Roberts would have been in his 50s when Holoday was born) and Holoday had inherited Roberts' investment skills in his genes.

Holoday's "over the top" birthday party was the last joyful event he would celebrate as a stockbroker. In an attempt to generate badly needed cash that month, Holoday committed over $2 million to a massive purchase of US bond futures. Convinced that US interest rates were about to rise, which would decrease the value of US bonds, Holoday broke a cardinal rule of his own investment strategy. Abandoning his strangles technique, Holoday put everything on shorting the bonds; in the jargon of the market, he was playing only one "leg," a common approach used by traders who have experienced substantial losses, and who attempt to recoup their investments by overplaying one side several times. Only unsophisticated, foolish, or desperate traders leg in or out of the futures market. Whatever Holoday's motive might have been, the result was predictable — he recorded enormous losses.

Holoday had become an undisciplined gambler, frantic to earn back his losses with spastic decision-making. Yet he remained convinced that he enjoyed access to infinite resources of wealth. How else to explain, in the midst of suffering these staggering trading losses, his offer to purchase 61 Park Lane Circle?

Of all the homes in Toronto, 61 Park Lane Circle was one of the few to compare in size and extravagance with Kenneth Roberts' mansion at 2 Old Forest Hill Road. Both were elaborate in layout and detailing, but 61 Park Lane Circle, in the Bridle Path area several kilometres east of Forest Hill, was even larger and more flamboyant.

Construction of the Park Lane Circle mansion had begun in 1990 when multimillionaire Irving Stern vowed to recreate a home in the style of the grand mansions that dominate the Hamptons on New York's Long Island. The project would be unsurpassed in all of Toronto, a gift to his wife Anne who, at 35, was less than half her husband's age.

Stern's timing could not have been worse. Construction of the 35,000-square-foot house, featuring 2 libraries, 7 bedrooms, 16 bathrooms, 6 fireplaces, an elevator, a ballroom capable of seating 100 guests for dinner, and a 90-foot indoor swimming pool, began just as Ontario's economy collapsed in the early 1990s. The Sterns sank more than $12 million in the property before their finances dried up and, in April 1994, 61 Park Lane Circle was placed on the market for a paltry $5.2 million. The house needed at least another million dollars to finish, categorizing it as something more than a handyman's special. This failed to deter Holoday from placing a serious offer on

the property, boasting to friends and clients that he and
Maureen would soon be residing in a house that would put
Ken Roberts' place in the shadows. On May 10, he submitted the offer, attaching a cheque for $500,000 as a
deposit, and instructed his client Brian Rocks to inspect
the house, promising that Rocks would be retained to complete the interior construction and detailing.

A week later, in response to demands from David Wood
to cover his losses he wrote two cheques, payable in US
funds, to First Marathon — one for $350,000 and the other
for $236,000.

All three cheques were returned NSF.[2]

Holoday's serious cash-flow problems resonated to
Barbados, where John and Carole Boczan's dream of a luxurious and leisurely retirement had become a nightmare. The
couple had wanted to discuss the situation on their brief
return home for Michael's party, but there were too many
distractions. Holoday was paying the Boczans $5,000 a
month for John to supervise the construction of Holoday's
impressive vacation home, within shouting distance of Doc
Roberts' residence. But rent on the villa that Holoday had
leased for them, plus salaries for the maid and groundskeep-
er, ate up most of the money, leaving only enough for the
Boczans to survive on a diet of rice and beans.

This wasn't the worst part. Each morning, when John
Boczan arrived at the construction site, he was confronted
by angry tradesmen and suppliers, demanding to be paid.
Holoday's cheques had bounced, his promises were broken, and contracts ignored. As Holoday's hired man, John
Boczan became the target of their anger, and the disputes
threatened to become violent. John Boczan called Toronto
almost every day, begging his son-in-law to transfer funds
and settle his outstanding bills. Boczan received little
more than promises ("I'll send it out this afternoon") and

excuses ("Damn it, the bank must have fouled things up again"), and after they returned to Barbados following Holoday's birthday party, no communication at all. Michael was busy, Michael was in a meeting, Michael was out of the office, or so John Boczan was informed whenever he called from a pay telephone while outraged Barbadian tradesmen and suppliers glared at him.

The Boczans believed their son-in-law's excuses, at the beginning at least. Ten, twenty, thirty thousand dollars was pocket change for Michael. People must be letting him down. Just hang on, they thought, and everything would be cleared up.

Eventually Holoday confessed to his in-laws that he was having a few financial problems. A dribbling cash flow at the moment, securities tied up, a sideways market. It would pass, but for now, things were a little tight.

The Boczans offered to help in any way they could. They had been with Michael for the good times, they would stick by him during the bad times. What could they do?

Well, perhaps they could assign their Cobourg house to him, Holoday suggested, the one built on the plot of land Carole had purchased, the one John Boczan had built practically with his own hands. It would add to his asset list, and help him over the hump. Of course, the Boczans agreed. Take it, they offered. Send us the papers and we'll sign it over, and they did.

Meanwhile, the Barbadian tradesmen refused to work, and the suppliers stopped delivery of building materials. John Boczan began performing the construction work himself while his wife searched local stores for food bargains and the Roberts family, just across the road, lived as sumptuously as ever.

The value of the daily trades between Holoday and the Roberts now exceeded $5 million, and the Bank of

Montreal was growing antsy at the rapidly rising value of the exchanges.[3]

The wealth of the Roberts family qualified it for special consideration by the Bank of Montreal. But Ron Curry, assigned to manage the Roberts' accounts at Bank of Montreal, became uncomfortable with what he was seeing in the spring of 1994. During a routine review with Elaine Roberts in early April, Curry questioned her about the cheque exchanges between the family and Michael Holoday. At the very least, he noted, Elaine and her father might have to increase the collateral needed to back up the series of bank drafts they kept issuing to this Holoday fellow.

The root of Curry's concern was clear: Should one of Holoday's multimillion-dollar cheques prove worthless, the bank needed a guarantee that its value would be covered by securities pledged by the Roberts. Raising the issue with Elaine Roberts was a gutsy decision, but her assurances that assets existed to cover Holoday's cheques persuaded the account manager that no serious risk existed for the bank. Curry agreed that the bank would continue with the same arrangement that had been in place for over a year and a half, and thanked her for her time.

Curry's superiors didn't see things his way. On May 3, 1994, Curry called Elaine Roberts to say that the Bank of Montreal was not interested in providing any line of credit "for this kind of business."[4]

Elaine and Ken Roberts shrugged off the bank's concern. There was nothing illegal about their actions; they were simply fortunate enough, shrewd enough, and wealthy enough to hook up with an investment wizard who was able to deliver daily returns of about 0.3 percent on their investment. The earnings translated into 80 percent annually, compounding without risk. If the bank didn't want their business, others would be interested.

When Elaine Roberts informed Holoday of the Bank of

Montreal's lack of interest in maintaining the cheque-swapping arrangement, Holoday proposed they bypass the banks and conduct the daily trades through Eastbridge, out of New York. This was clearly a stop-gap measure by Holoday. For almost a week, Holoday looked for a way of maintaining the ruse of cheque kites to convince the Roberts they were making a profit on their day-trade investments, finally conceding that the Eastbridge ploy wouldn't work. Yet, without the two-and-a-half-day clearing time for his cheques to move through Roberts' bank to his own, everything seemed doomed to collapse.

His only hope was to propose the obvious — that the Roberts open an account in his branch of Royal Bank, enabling the cheque exchange to take place instantaneously. This had the advantage of eliminating the bank's float fees, charged to permit the cheque exchanges for such large amounts — fees that were now costing Holoday $40,000 a month.

One way to set the stage, Holoday believed, was to win over the loyalty of a key player within the Royal Bank branch. Who better than Holoday's account manager, Pauline McKitty-Robinson, who had succeeded Glennis MacLean?

Holoday suggested to McKitty-Robinson that she could score a few points with her employer by making a pitch to Kenneth and Elaine Roberts for their personal banking business. Pulling in a personal chequing account with a $100 million monthly cash flow, in US funds no less, would be a coup for the young account manager. It could lead to bigger things in the future. And McKitty-Robinson would always remember who had provided the foot-in-the-door to one of the country's wealthiest families, right?

McKitty-Robinson's sales presentation proved successful; on Thursday, May 12, 1994, Kenneth and Elaine Roberts opened a personal chequing account at the Royal

Bank's branch, 2 Bloor Street West, depositing $5,500,000 in US funds. The move simultaneously boosted the status of Pauline McKitty-Robinson with her superiors, and kicked the foundation out from under Michael Holoday's wealth and career. Holoday lost the two-and-a-half-day cushion he enjoyed between the deposit of the Roberts' bank draft and the time it took for his post-dated cheque to clear through the Bank of Montreal. With both the Roberts and Holoday accounts in the same branch, the transfers would be instantaneous; there would be no more opportunity for cheque kiting.

His solution was to shift the Roberts away from commodities trading to something else. "How about," he proposed on Thursday, May 12, 1994, after pocketing a bank draft worth $5.46 million in US funds representing the current daily trades, "sharing an options trade with me?" Holoday had a "sure thing" options deal. It would roll over on the weekend and return about 5 percent profit. All they needed was $250,000 in US funds, but they had to act today. This was Thursday and the money was coming back Monday. Would it be a problem coming up with the quarter-million in Yankee dollars, like, right now?

No problem at all. Elaine Roberts arranged for a transfer of that amount from an investment account the Roberts maintained with Thomson Kernaghan, a long-established brokerage, and later that day, Holoday walked out of the Roberts' office with $5.71 million in US funds — over $7 million Canadian.

For their May 12 daily trade, Elaine Roberts expected to receive $5.46 million plus another $10,000 to $15,000 in US funds the following day, Friday, May 13. But the funds never arrived. "They're down in New York, still rolling," Holoday informed her. "You're still making money." He promised to provide the repayment after the weekend.

Although Holoday masked it with his usual cool

demeanour, he was desperate; the Royal Bank had just informed him, with an understandable degree of concern, that his joint personal chequing account, the one he and Maureen used to pay household expenses and meet other domestic needs, was overdrawn by $5,142,405.65 in US funds.

Sheldon Fenton couldn't believe his eyes. His First Marathon statement covering options trades revealed that he had been charged $300,000 in trading commissions *in one month!* This was insane. This was wilder than the condo market had ever been. He called Holoday to complain.

"It's a mistake," Holoday assured Fenton. He muttered something about those idiots in the back office, and the crazy computer system. "What can I do to fix things?"

Fenton's response was a simple one: Pay me back the $300,000. And not in a credit to my account, either. Only a cheque would do, made out to Fenton's numbered corporation, the one that appeared on the account statements. Holoday agreed. "It's in the mail," he said.

And later that day it was. Payable to a wrongly numbered company.

Helen Rentis was angry and frustrated. A shrewd, feisty woman, she had grown more and more annoyed over the errors and delays in her accounts at First Marathon, including the ones she opened for her daughter and her aged mother. At one time among the most enthusiastic of Holoday's supporters — just a year earlier, Holoday announced that Rentis' account showed a balance of $282,903.98, a return of 157.6 percent on her original investment— she had encountered nothing but errors and excuses since. Complaints about excessive commissions charged to her account produced promises from Holoday to correct the situation, but nothing more, and investments destined for one of her three accounts seemed to wind up in another. Holoday blamed the computer system, the back-office employees, his assistant Tracy Ellis, the TSE, and anyone or anything that came in contact with her account — except, of course, himself.

She had given up trying to decipher her First Marathon statements, but she would be damned if she would give up her attempts to withdraw money from her account. "No more trades," she instructed Holoday. "I want out."

Holoday kept finding reasons why Helen couldn't access her own money: The trades were closing, the pooled account was frozen, Tracy Ellis forgot to process the cheque, on and on, over and over again.

That was maddening enough, but when Helen Rentis reviewed her April 1994 account statement from First Marathon — she still couldn't tell whether she was making money or not, but at least she recognized trading activity when she saw it — the statement revealed that Holoday was *still* buying and selling options for her. What's more, Holoday had made a risky options trade in the account opened for Rentis' 80-year-old mother. Who makes high-risk trades in an account for someone that age? What the hell was going on?

What Helen Rentis did not know was that her account had been wiped out almost two years earlier while still at Midland Walwyn, and only Holoday's infusion of $77,000, drawn from the $420,000 loan made by the Roberts for "capital funding" when Holoday moved to First Marathon, had kept the fact secret. She was also not aware of a letter, in Midland Walwyn's files, acknowledging the loss in her account and committing her to risk another $75,000 in US funds. She was unaware of it because she had not written the letter, and she certainly had never signed it, although it bore a signature similar to hers.

On Friday, May 13, Rentis was about to leave on a business trip when she telephoned Holoday at his office. "I want my money, Michael," she said, keeping her cool. "No more excuses. Just close out the accounts and send me my money."

Holoday chuckled at the suggestion. He was making money for her, her daughter, and her mother, he reminded Rentis. "Hey, Chuck," he called. "What's the balance in the Rentis account?"

Helen Rentis could hear Holoday in conversation with his trader, Chuck Oliver.

"Wow," Holoday said into the receiver to her. "We've just doubled your money . . ."

"So sell the goddamn thing!" Helen Rentis shouted at him.

Holoday said okay, okay, he would do it. But she was making a mistake.

The only mistake I made, Helen Rentis thought when she hung up, was trusting you with my money.[5]

Compared with her financial advisor, she was lucky. Holoday had lost substantial assets in his own First Marathon trading account by shorting US bonds, believing their value was about to fall. That morning he switched strategies and became bullish on US bonds just as they indeed did collapse. He had lost betting that the prices would drop. Now he lost betting that the prices would rise. The industry term for this calamity is *whipsaw,* and when the markets closed that Friday the 13, the trading account managed by the Bay Street Whiz Kid who trumpeted his "controlled risk strategy" had been whipsawed to the tune of more than one million dollars in US funds in a single day.

The following Monday, May 16, Holoday arrived at the Fahnestock Viner office with good news . . . and not so good news.

The good news was the profit earned on the $250,000 options deal. Holoday handed Elaine Roberts a cheque for $261,718.75 in US funds, an overnight return of almost $12,000 on a quarter-million-dollar investment. Elaine Roberts didn't need a calculator to confirm that options investing was a better profit-maker than the commodity deals. It took almost six million dollars to earn that same kind of profit on the daily trades.

And speaking of the daily trades . . .

"There was a screw-up down in New York," Holoday explained. "The money's stuck there in an account at Eastbridge, and I'm flying down day after tomorrow, Wednesday. I'll bring the money back with me or maybe wire it from there myself, if I have to."

All right, Elaine Roberts replied. But that $5.5 million in US funds belonged to her and her father, and they had nothing to prove it. "We had a cheque in the past," she pointed out. "Now we don't have an account at a bank or a brokerage firm that's holding the funds, that has our name on it, and yet half the funds" — the Roberts' half — "are down there."

Elaine Roberts wanted proof that the five and a half million in Michael Holoday's special trading account was theirs. Not his, not Eastbridge's, not anyone else's, but theirs.

Ken Roberts revealed no suspicions about the location of their money or the status of Holoday's account at Eastbridge. These things happen with money transfers, he said. What's a delay of a day or two?

Holoday agreed with the older man's sanguinity. He understood Elaine Roberts' concern, and he was annoyed that something like this could happen. When he got to New York, the day after tomorrow, he'd rattle somebody's cage down there, get things straightened out, make sure nothing like this happened again.

Meanwhile, they needed to keep up the daily trades, they needed to keep the cash flowing. The $5.46 million would be coming back, along with two days' profits, but if they didn't take a position for the next day's trades, they could lose out big-time.

Ken Roberts agreed with his protégé. The other money was coming back. To keep things rolling, they would have the bank transfer another $5.46 million to Mike Holoday's personal chequing account so he can put the Roberts in the next day's trades.

"And we've still got these option trades going," Holoday reminded them. There was more money, he pointed out, to be made from the options than from the bond commodities. Why not, Holoday proposed, increase their options trade for the next day to about $350,000? He was confident, the way the market was moving, that they could realize better than a 10 percent gain overnight. In fact, he would guarantee it.

Elaine and Kenneth Roberts looked at each other. Ken Roberts nodded, and Elaine faxed a note to Pauline McKitty-Robinson at 2:45 p.m. that afternoon, instructing the Royal Bank to transfer $5.46 million in US funds from their account to Michael Holoday's personal chequing account in the same branch, and issue a cheque for $350,000 in US funds payable to First Marathon Securities. Holoday now had over $13 million Canadian without providing a scrap of paper to justify or secure it. More important to Holoday, his bank account was back in the black, if only by a paltry few thousand dollars.

Bank drafts for $350,000 in US funds are not unheard of in Toronto banking circles, although they remain large enough to draw attention when presented for deposit. Whether the face value of a draft is $350 or $350,000, banking rules forbid the instrument to be credited to any-one, or any entity, except the payee indicated on its face.

Holoday went directly from Roberts' office to the Main
Branch of Royal Bank, presented the draft to teller Joan
Liu, and asked her to credit the draft to his Royal Bank
account, uptown at 2 Bloor Street West. Liu, puzzled,
pointed out that the draft was payable to First Marathon
Securities and not to him.

"It's all right, everything's been looked after," he
explained. He was, Holoday pointed out, the managing
partner, futures division, of First Marathon, the payee.
"Call Marsha Neill, she's my private banking manager
there." Holoday pushed a slip of paper, bearing a telephone number, across the counter.

Liu returned a few minutes later. Things were okay.
The money, almost half a million dollars in Canadian funds,
was deposited in the personal chequing account of Michael
and Maureen Holoday at the Bloor Street branch. Joan Liu
wrote Holoday's name and account number on the back of
the draft, adding the notation "Ph. Marsha, ok to deposit."

No one knows what was said during the telephone conversation between Joan Liu and "Marsha." Whatever was
said (Liu could not recall the conversation six years later),
it persuaded Liu to break one of the cardinal rules of banking: Do not credit funds destined for one payee to a second
entity without having the original payee at least endorse
the instrument. Marsha Neill declared under oath that
she never received such a telephone call. Nor did she have
the authority to approve that breach of banking rules,
especially for such a large amount of money.[6]

The next day, Tuesday, May 17, Holoday paid another
"good news, not so good news" visit to the Roberts office.
The good news: a fat profit — $50,000! — from the previous
day's options trade. Let's keep this going, he suggested. He
had two more options trades to share in the next day. The
Roberts' half would be $415,000 for one and $325,000 for
the other, in US funds. Unfortunately, the screw-up at

Eastbridge was continuing, and just to make things worse, Holoday had to postpone his trip to New York.

Two days later, Holoday returned profits of $10,000 and $12,968.75 to the Roberts on their latest options trade, plus good news from Eastbridge. New York, he explained, would be paying back the Roberts' $5.46 million in five instalments of $1.136 million, totalling $5.68 million, yielding a $220,000 profit. "Makes it worth the wait, doesn't it?" he smiled, and handed Elaine Roberts a personal cheque for the first payment.

When, Elaine Roberts wanted to know, would they see the rest? She and her father, she reminded Holoday, were growing concerned. We're talking millions of dollars here, she reminded Holoday. We want some assurance that we'll see that money.

"Tomorrow," Holoday assured her. "Should be two payments arriving tomorrow."

And there were. The first arrived in the morning, the second after lunch. But just as Elaine Roberts had dispatched the $2.272 million to the account she shared with her father, Holoday called with exciting news: He had another options play, a big one that would take advantage of the coming Victoria Day long weekend, while the Canadian markets were closed and Wall Street continued to operate. Did the Roberts want in? If so, he needed $2.886 million for their side of the deal.

Ken and Elaine Roberts agreed. Holoday's options trades were yielding even bigger profits than the Eastbridge strategy. Elaine Roberts instructed Royal Bank to issue a bank draft for that amount to Holoday, who promptly deposited it to his and his wife's joint account.

Holoday, in one day, had paid the Roberts $2.272 million with a personal cheque and pocketed $2.886 million in a negotiable bank draft, yielding him a net gain of $614,000.

The Victoria Day weekend of 1994 was the last period in Holoday's career when he could enjoy at least some degree of relaxation, and perhaps even harbour a belief that his charade would avoid detection. Upon his return to work on Tuesday, May 24, he faced a barrage of demands, crises, and tantrums, commencing with an appalling tragedy that Holoday managed to make even more terrible as a result of his insensitivity and hubris.

For anyone who feels guilty about missing a credit card payment and chagrined at the idea of writing an NSF cheque, the next four months of Holoday's life would have been a dreadful nightmare.

On the morning of Tuesday, May 24, David Wood called Holoday to his office for a meeting with Wood and Joe Thurman. "Bring Chuck Oliver with you," Wood instructed. Holoday corralled his nervous trader, and the two set off for Wood's office.

The meeting began with Thurman and Wood expressing concern about Holoday's activities at First Marathon. Why were so many of Holoday's clients losing such large amounts of money? Wood wanted to know. Several clients, including Paul Simpkin and Helen Rentis, had suffered losses well in excess of their stated risk capital levels. "I'll be sending them letters informing them that no new trading positions can be taken until they give us something in writing with a new Risk Capital Figure," Thurman said.

Holoday gulped and agreed this was a good idea.

Wood wanted to know about the trading losses in Holoday's client accounts. Couldn't any of these people make any money at all?

"A lot of them are hedging against their cash bond positions," Holoday explained, "so the losses aren't as bad as they seem."

If that's what they're doing, Thurman commented,

they needed to open a second account and identify it as a hedge account with a risk capital separate and distinct from their speculative trading account.

Wood looked across at Holoday. "What about your own trades?" he asked. Holoday had lost over US$2 million so far in May, a stunning loss, even for a Bay Street high-flyer. He had also bounced two cheques to his employer, payment for option positions purchased in his name, totalling US$541,000.

Holoday shrugged. He had learned a lot, he explained. "From now on, I'll concentrate on strangles," he said, "maybe taking an outright speculative position when the market's going my way."

Wood ordered Holoday to limit his outstanding risk to US$250,000. Give us bank drafts to cover all your futures options positions from now on. No more cheques. No more risk of NSF payments. And by the way, Wood instructed, don't carry your option positions up to expiry when they're worthless. Dump them when you can still get something for them, anything at all, and at least cut your losses.

Holoday nodded in agreement. "See that he does it," Wood and Thurman told Chuck Oliver, who agreed as well.[7]

Being dressed down in front of Oliver was humiliating to Holoday, but when he got back to his office, he had little time to dwell on it. Everything was imploding. Everyone was screaming. Every scheme was used to hide a previous lie, and Holoday knew he would have to concoct new lies tomorrow to hide today's stories.

It is not essential to trace each daily event over the last four months of Holoday's career to grasp Holoday's plight, and understand the ways he compounded his troubles by imposing them upon others. In fact, it may be impossible. Like observing a flock of migrating birds, it is only necessary to see the movement of the whole and not the chaos within. In Holoday's case, one need only imagine the panic and conceit that could drive an intelligent individual to continue maintaining the deception.

First things first. Holoday fairly ran from the First Marathon building to Ken and Elaine Roberts' office, where he gave Elaine a cheque for US$1.75 million, representing the fourth payment on the US$5.46 million he claimed was still with Eastbridge in New York. Holoday also handed her a letter. "What's this?" she asked, and Holoday said it was something to ease her mind about the security of their investments.

This agreement, Elaine Roberts read, *is written to acknowledge a lien by you of* (sic) *the following financial market assets of the Futures Division of First Marathon Securities Ltd. and Holoday Investments Inc.* The latter was a shell company created by Holoday to hold profits earned from his personal trading activity. Conveniently, the assets of both entities totalled more than $10 million in US dollars, including $3.5 million in option capital, $1.2 million represented by 300,000 shares of SDI Virtual Reality valued at $4 per share, almost half a million dollars in shares of Consolidated Madison and, most reassuring of all, $5 million in cash. Holoday overestimated his cash position by about $6 million, since his account was overdrawn by $1 million in US funds. "That's what I own," Holoday said. "That's your security."

Elaine Roberts wanted to know what SDI was all about, and Holoday explained the company was a leader in computerization and visual replication, a future Northern Telecom or Intel. Holoday also informed her that he was a principal in the firm, an outright lie. "I'm off to New York in a few days, looking for a market maker for the company," he said. "Somebody to get the stock price up where it should be."[8]

True to his word, Joe Thurman drafted letters to Paul

Simpkin and Helen Rentis that day, noting that losses in both clients' accounts had exceeded their claimed risk capital. Thurman asked each to complete an enclosed Customer Account Update, "and indicate a new risk capital level if you desire to continue trading in the commodity markets." Rentis had set US$75,000 as her risk capital limit; she was down by almost twice that amount. Paul Simpkin, according to First Marathon records, had set a loss limit of US$112,000, but by the end of May he had lost $325,000 of his original $500,000 investment.

The clients were to return the update within five days of receiving the letter. "If you wish," Thurman added, "you may advise your financial advisor by telephone of your new risk capital level prior to returning the Customer Account Update." Copies of the letters were provided to Holoday.

Holoday was too distracted to notice his copies of Thurman's letters until Thursday, May 26, when he arrived at his office that morning, read the correspondence, and almost fainted again. Thurman was telling Simpkin, Rentis, and who knew who else, that they had lost most of their original investments when both believed they had doubled their money. Holoday had to act and, willing himself to remain calm, he dialled Paul Simpkin's home.

"Did you, uh, get anything up there yet, Paul?" Holoday asked, meaning the mail from First Marathon.

Simpkin said, "Not yet."

Holoday breathed a sigh of relief, and then asked if he could make a deposit to Simpkin's bank account that same day. Holoday had tried, he went on, to courier funds to Simpkin, but screw-ups occurred and it would be better if Holoday just did a direct deposit — Holoday was stuttering, nervous, and out of breath — just did a direct deposit to Simpkin's bank. "It'll show up in the morning in your account," Holoday explained. "All you have to do is give the information to Tracy." Then he went on: "I gotta . . . I gotta fax you on your commodity account, your bon, your cash account . . . this morning. Uh, I did some very fancy manoeuvring . . . on your commodity account last Thursday and Friday . . . to, uh, protect your capital. . . . Because we had the market going against us last week . . . so it's come out okay today, but in doing the method I traded, I used two accounts. I used the division account to hedge your personal account. . . . So I've got a gain on one side and I've got a loss on the other side, and I've gotta keep this confidential because I'm not really supposed to do that."

During this outrageous explanation, Paul Simpkin offered appreciative expressions of thanks and understanding.

"But it was either a case of Paul Simpkin taking a thirty percent loss," Holoday said, "or me using my own, my division account with a naked write strategy to hedge your long options, which I'm not really supposed to do for a client, but I . . . sometimes ethics take over rules." Simpkin had no idea what "naked write strategy" meant, but it sounded as though Holoday were riding to the rescue of Simpkin's assets. The outlaw financial advisor plays Lone Ranger.

"Thank you, Michael," Paul Simpkin said. "Thank you."

According to Holoday, he would have to move funds from the division account to Simpkin's bank, and eventually into Simpkin's personal account. He expected it would be about a hundred thousand dollars. Joe Thurman in compliance would be sending Simpkin a letter, because all First Marathon saw was Simpkin's personal account. "They don't know that you're involved in a hedge on the other side," Holoday went on, "so it looks to them like there's a large loss, and then we need an increase in risk capital."

Holoday couldn't resist adding some sweetener to his tale.

"What I've actually done," he said, "the whole good thing out of here is, I've created a tax shelter for you." By hedging Simpkin's money, Holoday claimed, he created a $50,000 capital gains break for his client. "So, I mean," Holoday said, relaxing a little, "on your side it's all coming out tickety-boo. You've actually, potentially, made fifty grand, provided I make you a hundred thousand dollars between now and the end of the year . . . so it's, you're going to get some letters, and you'd be confused if I don't explain them to you today."

With news like that, from a financial advisor so concerned about his clients' well-being, all Paul Simpkin could say was, "I'm a hundred percent behind you, Mike."[9]

Holoday promised to start faxing documents for Simpkin to sign. The documents, Holoday hoped, would be enough to divert Thurman for a while.

Paul Simpkin smiled as he hung up the phone and checked to ensure that his taping device had recorded the entire conversation. Yes, it had. He would keep this tape in a safe place, along with the others.

Next, Holoday had to pacify Helen Rentis, a more challenging task than dealing with the trusting and compliant Paul Simpkin. Rentis was travelling on business, and Thurman's letter would be waiting for her when she returned home. Holoday left a message on her answering machine, assuring her that her account was okay. Everything was fine. She should call him as soon as she returned home Friday night or anytime on the weekend. Meanwhile, he was faxing a very important document to her.

When Holoday hung up, he learned that Suzie Desmond had been rushed to hospital and that the twin boys she had been expecting were delivered by emergency Caesarean section. Complications developed and one of the babies had died. The other was clinging to life. Michael drove to the hospital that evening and, at Suzie's bedside while she held the surviving baby, Holoday played the family hero again — or attempted to.

He would charter a plane, Holoday said, and fly Suzie and Howard and their family, if they wanted to come, to the US, where they could save the baby. Maybe the Mayo Clinic, or some other hospital that specialized in surgery on premature babies.

No, Suzie replied. She was under too much stress already. The doctors held out little hope for the remaining child. "Love him while you can," they had told her, and that's what she was doing — cradling the baby in her arms. She wouldn't go.

All right then, Holoday said. If Suzie and Howard wouldn't let him try for a medical miracle at his expense, he would do all he could to make things right, leave everything to him. He called the Humphrey Funeral Home and ordered their most elaborate service for the deceased baby, the invoice to be sent directly to him. What's more, the baby was to be buried in an expensive plot Michael owned in Mount Pleasant Cemetery, the one originally destined for Michael and Maureen themselves.

Helen Rentis arrived home from her business trip that weekend, listened to Holoday's telephone message, and checked her fax machine. Sure enough, in Holoday's strange, angular scribble, she found a fax from her broker. Holoday's message was a variation to the one he had supplied Paul Simpkin. *I used the Division short account to hedge your long position,* Holoday wrote. He included details of various trades made on Rentis' accounts, including several curious trades made on May 22, 1994 — curious because May 22 was a Sunday.

Compliance has sent you a letter showing

losses, but this is wrong because it doesn't show the profit you earned in the hedge account, which is $145,608 plus tax credits. Disregard the letter from Compliance and I'll give you proper statements on Monday or Tuesday. Please call me at home on the weekend. Thought I would fax this to you to avoid panic.

Holoday may have avoided panic, but he failed to avoid Rentis' wrath. She called Holoday and demanded all the money from her accounts. No excuses, no screw-ups, no stalling. Holoday promised to look after things. On Monday morning, still seething, she called Joe Thurman. "How," she demanded, "can you tell me I lost over a hundred and forty-eight thousand dollars US when my broker says I doubled my money?"

Thurman's response to Rentis was: "I suggest you speak to your broker."

"I certainly will!" Rentis said before hanging up.[10]

Rentis had done exactly what James O'Donnell had advised other Holoday clients two years earlier at Midland Walwyn, and followed the same route the Toronto Stock Exchange was advising in informative brochures distributed to novice investors: *If discrepancies in the account cannot be rationalized with the broker, raise the matter with the compliance officer.* Thurman, however, turned the question back to the individual whose actions would appear most responsible for these same discrepancies.

Sheldon Fenton didn't shout. Hey, mistakes happen. But the cheque that had just arrived, paying him the $300,000 in excess commissions, was made out to the wrong company.

"Aw, hell," Holoday said, and he blamed Tracy Ellis for ignoring his instructions. "Give me the correct number and I'll issue a new cheque."

Fenton provided the information. This time, he ordered Holoday, forget the mail. Send it up by courier.

Holoday said that was a good idea. Fenton gave Holoday the address of his office, noting that it was Suite #300. Holoday copied the address down, carefully writing "Suite #350," made out the cheque, and handed it to Tracy, instructing her to send it by courier, right away.

On June 1, 1994, with a $3.5 million overdraft in his personal bank account, no funds of his own to invest, and a million dollars or so in cheques and promises floating among his clients, Holoday needed another injection of cash, so he visited his personal source of liquid assets, Kenneth and Elaine Roberts. He had a new options trade, he told the Roberts in their Fahnestock Viner office. All locked up. Three million total, two hundred thousand guaranteed overnight profit. Did they want half? It would take a bank draft for a million and a half dollars to get in; Holoday would write his cheque out right now for a million six.

Elaine Roberts ordered the money transferred to Holoday's account, and Holoday scribbled out a personal cheque.

Now he needed cash to cover the $1.6 million. Already scrambling to find the US$10 million that Kenneth and Elaine Roberts believed was invested in Eastbridge, Holoday couldn't afford to bounce a cheque to them. It would cut off his cash supply, doom the cheque-kiting and, perhaps most critically, disrupt Holoday's father-son relationship with Doc Roberts.

This was the point where Michael Holoday, whose entire career had been built on complex lies and fictitious investments, made perhaps his cruellest decision. To maintain the relationship with the Roberts family, to whom the $10 million represented only a portion of their total assets, Holoday would embezzle from his smaller

clients — a hundred thousand here, two hundred thousand there — wiping out their life savings in a doomed
effort to stave off discovery and remain in the warm, affectionate bosom of the Roberts.[11]

FOURTEEN

Never trust the advice of a man in difficulties.
– AESOP

Investment frauds are hardly unheard-of in Canada. Over the years they have ranged from doubtful iron mine prospects north of Lake Superior in the eighteenth century to the infamous Bre-X blunder, fuelled by the claims of unscrupulous stock promoters and the greed of high-pressure investment advisors.

Michael Holoday was not the first Canadian stockbroker to misappropriate his client's funds, nor did he set a record for the largest fraud involving banks and investments. During the early 1990s Julius Melnitzer, a lawyer in London, Ontario, defrauded banks and business partners of $40 million, using phoney stock certificates as security to gain personal loans. A few years earlier the infamous Brian Molony gambled away almost $10 million, lifted from the accounts of the CIBC branch where he was employed as assistant manager. The differences between both the motives and victims of these two fraud artists are striking. Melnitzer managed to spend his way through the funds in a wildly extravagant lifestyle, coincidentally bringing financial ruin to friends and business partners. Brian Molony enjoyed none of the fruits of his illegal labour, carried out solely to appease his insatiable gambling addiction.[1]

In both instances the majority of losses were suffered by chartered banks. While this does not make the crimes any less serious, the impact was at least dissipated among a hundred thousand or so shareholders, rather than a few dozen of Holoday's relatives and acquaintances.[2]

Michael Holoday managed to ruin the lives of many people who trusted him with their life savings. Nor was Holoday's financial assault the end of the abuse; in almost every case, the trusting investors found themselves being pummelled on all sides by Holoday's former employers, the court system, and even the legal counsel they hired to recover their losses.

Substantial losses to individual investors through stockbroker fraud are devastating to the victims, who often lack either the secure protection of the financial corporation or, as the Holoday case proved, access to the firm's reserves. Independent brokers or financial advisors provide no safety net once the clients' assets — and their own — have vanished. Even large independent investment firms, whose assets and staff roster rival those of the banks' themselves, may not protect their clients from the criminal actions of their financial consultants, as Holoday's clients discovered.

Larger bank-backed brokerages may take a more active role in defending and recouping the assets of their customers, depending upon the conditions of the fraud and the firm's policy toward the conduct of its staff. Consider Christopher Horne, whose escapades at RBC Dominion Securities cost his clients and firm more than $7 million over a period of almost 15 years.

During his career, Christopher Horne was among the brightest lights and most colourful figures on Bay Street. He and his partner filled their country retreat with art treasures — Toronto gallery owners began salivating the moment Horne entered their premises — and pursued a

wide range of hedonistic pleasures. Some of his acquisitions bordered on the bizarre, including a prepaid burial
plot for himself and his partner in Toronto's Mount
Pleasant Cemetery, featuring a pre-carved black marble
grave marker, and the purchase of a foppish British title
("Lord of Llandewy Green").

In other aspects, however, Horne's lifestyle was not sufficiently extravagant to draw attention from suspicious
eyes. Few, if any, of his colleagues were sophisticated
enough to realize that some of Horne's beloved art treasures
represented the better part of his entire year's salary. He
had no fleet of vintage or ultra-luxurious automobiles, no
fancy yacht and, while a legendary host among his circle of
friends and associates, no specific activity drew attention to
the possibility that he was living far beyond his means.

"Christopher Horne was a highly interesting individual with a group of clients who trusted him greatly,"
recalled Greg Clark, former senior vice-president, member
regulation, of the Investment Dealers Association. He was
speaking a year after Horne's conviction and sentencing to
five years' imprisonment. "When Horne's clients were told
Horne had stolen money from their accounts, none of them
could believe it."

Horne had been so smooth, so elegant in his deceits,
and so widely trusted that his activities came to light only
when a client, in response to a routine inquiry by RBC
Dominion Securities' auditors, noted that his account balance was lower than he had expected. His immediate
response was to speculate that someone at Royal Bank —
up to that point a cornerstone of trust and stability in
Canada's financial services industry — was misappropriating his funds. The last person he suspected was his
trusted financial advisor, Christopher Horne!

Horne's technique was devious but hardly original. It
depended, however, on the high degree of trust and

prestige that a man with his position and title — Horne
was a vice-president of RBC Dominion Securities — brings
to his relationship with clients.

After creating a Panamanian firm called International
Haven Services, or IHS, in 1980 while based in the
Bahamas, Horne named an innocent trust company official
president and listed the official's wife as a director. Then,
after requesting the president to open accounts at several
Royal Bank branches in the name of IHS, Horne obtained
a series of blank signed cheques, which Horne could use for
his personal needs. He also arranged for IHS statements to
be sent to another innocent official employed at a branch of
the CIBC on Grand Cayman Island.

The complicated arrangement enabled Horne to transfer stolen funds to IHS in Panama and move money from
there to various Royal Bank branches in Canada and the
Cayman Islands. All Royal Bank statements were forwarded to a CIBC branch in Grand Cayman where Horne
would visit from time to time to review and destroy the
statements. These complex manoeuvres were designed to
muddy any paper trail of suspicion and evidence.

"Horne was a fish out of water," Greg Clark suggested.
"He never should have been handling personal discretionary accounts, especially with so much offshore activity. He should have been in the institutional department
where financial controls are strictly exercised. Instead, he
wound up in the international department, and the financial controls that normally apply didn't work in his case."[3]

The realization arrived too late to prevent severe losses in client assets and public trust for RBC Dominion
Securities. To their credit, when RBC Dominion investigators discovered the role of IHS in receiving funds, they
refused to accept Horne's explanation at face value. Who
was behind this company? they demanded. Horne claimed
not to know. Who had access to its funds? Horne shrugged.

The questions continued until RBC investigators uncovered the scheme. Then the firm acted swiftly to recompense the clients. In addition to replacing over $7 million taken from client accounts by Horne, including lost interest on the money from the day of its theft and even lawyer fees incurred by clients to check their legal rights, Royal Bank paid a $250,000 fine to the Investment Dealers Association as a penalty for not controlling their star employee's actions.

Representatives from the Canadian securities industry scoff at suggestions that Horne, Holoday, and others like them are anything but aberrations, rare wanderers from the straight-and-narrow (and mainly self-regulated) path. They are, in some ways, correct. Billions of dollars flow through the Canadian securities and investment industry each week, the vast majority of it shepherded by men and women neither more nor less honest than employees of any other industry.

But everyone on Bay Street also acknowledges that the investment industry is driven by two engines of equal power. One is Greed; the other is Fear. To continue the analogy, both engines are lubricated by the same grease, and it is called Trust.

Only with sufficient levels of trust could Christopher Horne have managed to extend his illegal activities over ten years, without a ripple of suspicion disturbing the calm surface of his relationship with clients. Nor is the trust lubricant confined to easing friction between salesperson and client. Nick Leeson, the ill-fated trader whose Singapore capers destroyed Barings Bank, successfully requisitioned daily transfers of $50 million from London Head Office time and time again. A high school drop-out, Leeson was in his mid-20s and holding a minor post in a distant branch. Yet no one seriously questioned the young man's glib explanations until it was far too late, for two reasons: Leeson

appeared to be wildly successful at his dealings; and every
action taken was armoured with a layer of trust.[4] When
hundreds of millions of dollars must be moved instantly to
take advantage of situations in flux — often the case with
money transfers and futures options — standard procedures don't have time to bridge concerns regarding security.
The gap is filled by faith and familiarity.

One way or another, every investment firm nurtures
similar arrangements between themselves as an organization, personified by salespeople (or registered representatives), and their clients. The ability to construct solid,
long-term relationships with clients is a valued skill for
registered representatives or RRs, who may also be called
account executives, financial advisors, investment consultants, or even managing partners. They are trained,
assessed, and coached to present themselves, their parent
firms, and their services in a highly professional manner.
Every successful investment advisor or licensed sales representative instinctively understands the value of projecting an aura of confidence and achievement toward clients.
Only vast quantities of trust permitted Horne to cover his
actions for so long, and enabled Leeson to succeed to such
a devastating degree.

Here is the knife-edge that rips apart the fabric of the
industry's assurances regarding "aberrations" such as
Horne, Holoday, and others. Trust, the key to unlocking
client vaults and misappropriating whatever is within
them, is the same bait used by investment firms to entice
clients through their doors in the first place. Trust us to
help you achieve wealth. Trust our Blue-Chip Thinking.
Trust our prudent advice. Trust our people to assist you in
making the right decisions.

When individual investors transfer their trust and
their assets based on these promises, they are congratulated by the brokerage for their prescience. But later, if their

trust in the company's sales staff results in the loss of their life savings, they risk being accused of equal measures of greed and gullibility. And that was the salt poured into the wounds suffered by dozens of Michael Holoday's clients.

Many were far from wealthy, and some were more than clients, including close family members and childhood friends. Holoday's willingness to toss aside personal relationships in exchange for the opportunity to line his own pockets knew literally no bounds of time or distance. One example: He managed to dissipate almost a million dollars belonging to Kurt Schleith, the father of his oldest friend — a man whose son had stood next to Michael as his Best Man on Michael's wedding day. Kurt Schleith's nest egg hadn't been inherited or accumulated through some fortunate circumstance. It had been earned through the older man's years of hard work, first as a lumber mill hand, then as the owner and operator of his own mill in Holoday's hometown of Revelstoke, BC. When Kurt Schleith sold the mill, he earned a substantial capital gain, reward for his years of hard work and denial. When he trusted the closest friend of his own son, he saw much of it vanish within months.

Nor were Holoday's victims all financial neophytes. Holoday managed to nab almost half a million dollars earned over Ted Gittings' working career as a prominent publishing executive, even while Gittings was associated with an organization of professionals engaged in managing the treasuries of large corporations. Finally, no one has an accurate count of the number of clients Holoday defrauded, or the total amount of money he pocketed during his five-year career as a licensed broker. The total is far greater than the 14 counts eventually brought against him by the Crown, and certainly exceeds the 30 or so listed in the indictment. It may approach 60 or more. At least a dozen of the people who admitted losing money to

Holoday through his fictitious investments, usually in sums of $20,000 to $40,000, declined to participate in either civil or criminal charges against him, due to the high legal costs, the low prospects of recovering their money, the embarrassment of appearing foolish or greedy, or all three.

Faced with the task of digging himself out from beneath a mountain of debt while simultaneously concealing dozens of frauds extending back three years or more, Holoday went to work. He began by drafting a prospectus for a new mutual fund to be administered by First Marathon Securities where, of course, Michael Holoday was listed as managing partner, futures division. The fund would require bridging capital during its launch period, and First Marathon was offering the opportunity for a select group of clients to participate in the financial package with the prospect of substantial returns. An investment of $200,000, for example, would return a profit of $25,000 within 60 days.

Astute investors might question the massive return in such a short period of time, but mutual funds were the darlings of the Canadian investment community in the mid-90s, thanks to wealthy boomers looking to maximize growth of their RRSPs. To make it more plausible, Holoday linked the prospectus with both First Marathon and one of the country's most prestigious law firms.

Holoday instructed the law firm to send the first of the investment proposals to his client Chester Hooper, now retired and living in his Vancouver dream-house.

With the letter on its way to Hooper, Holoday called Sheldon Fenton, who complained he still hadn't received his $300,000 cheque for excess commissions. Holoday was aghast. "I sent it by courier that same day," he said, shuffling some papers so they could be heard through the telephone. "Here it is. To your office at suite three-fifty."

"It's suite three hundred," Fenton said, and Holoday swore and again blamed Tracy Ellis, then made Fenton an offer. Holoday would personally deliver the cheque to Fenton and give him a chance on a new deal, a good one. Holoday had a three-million-dollar put-and-call strangle that would close in a week and make just under 7 percent. How'd Fenton like to take half of it? Otherwise, Holoday would be forced to liquidate some other deals, and he'd rather not. If Fenton came in for a million and a half, he'd get a million six back in a week, guaranteed.

Let's do it, Fenton agreed. But Fenton wanted something to prove the deal had actually taken place, that Holoday wasn't working some kind of scam here. Sure, Holoday responded. How about the actual trade tickets, showing Buy and Sell amounts? Let's see 'em, Fenton said, and Holoday sent over authentic First Marathon trading tickets placed through Refco Canada. Attached to them, on the First Marathon letterhead bearing Holoday's name as managing partner, futures division, was a list of the trades Holoday claimed he had completed:

Date	Net Transaction	Net Cost/Proceeds (US$)
June 1/94	*Bought 1,255 104 calls @ :36*	*$705,937.50 dr*
	Bought 1,255 99 puts @ :15	*$294,140.63 dr*
June 1/94	*Sold 1,255 104 calls @ :44*	*$862,812.50 cr*
	Sold 1,255 99 puts @ :12	*$235,312.50 cr*
NET PROFIT: $98,046.87 cr		

Holoday included an acknowledgement that First Marathon Securities Limited would "do all things necessary" to cause the first $1.05 million of Fenton's investment to be repaid, with Holoday signing as managing partner on behalf of the firm.

It all looked genuine and convincing. Even if Holoday

screwed up, Fenton assumed, First Marathon would be around to pay. So Fenton released $1.5 million in US funds through three companies he and his wife controlled.

Hooper and Fenton were pussycats compared with Helen Rentis. Holoday had to calm her down and get her onside again, but forget about doing it over the telephone. He invited Rentis to his office "to clear things up," promising that she would be pleased with the money he had for her.

The Michael Holoday who greeted Rentis at his office that Friday was not the confident, cocky financial genius who practically defined the term "Whiz Kid." He was subdued, serious, and thoroughly businesslike. With the door closed, and his voice lowered, Holoday told Rentis he had become so wrapped up in his trading, so busy trying to make money for his clients, jumping on opportunities here, hedging against losses there, that he had . . . well, there were some irregularities in two or three of his accounts. Nothing serious, but he had to tell First Marathon and the guys down at the Toronto Stock Exchange about them. Everything was fine, things would work themselves out, but Holoday wanted Helen Rentis to feel good about her investments in the meantime. So. Why didn't Helen Rentis come with him right now, down to his bank at 20 King Street East, and he would cut her a cheque there, drawn on his personal account, his own money, for US$106,000. "It's for your own comfort level," he said.

Helen Rentis said sure. A hundred thousand Yankee dollars bought a lot of comfort. Let's go. They walked the two blocks to the Royal Bank. Ten minutes later, with certified cheque in hand, Helen Rentis practically ran to deposit the money in her account at Scotiabank.

But Holoday's life had become a carnival barker's game; each time he silenced one pop-up mole with a whack, another showed up to harass him. When he returned from the bank, the next pop-up mole to greet him was an exasperated Joe Thurman.

Four of Holoday's clients — Elaine Roberts, Roger Gordon, Lee Cowie, and Jan Miller — were free riders on their trading accounts, Thurman charged, making trades without putting up the money. Holoday had been warned over and over about these free riders. Thurman reminded Holoday of the memo dated May 4 that said free riding would be charged to Holoday's error account, which meant Holoday himself would have to cough up the cash.

Okay, okay, Holoday said. He hated this kind of dressing down by Thurman, as though Holoday were some kid being scolded by the school principal. And David Wood wanted to see Holoday too, Thurman added. Right away.

Holoday entered Wood's office to find Wood waving a cheque written to First Marathon by its managing partner, futures division, for $120,000 in US funds. It had been returned NSF, the third one in less than a month. What was going on?

My banking records are screwed up, Holoday admitted. He apologized, he was sorry, he would make the cheque good, and it would never happen again. By the way, Holoday asked, that US T-bill for $108,000, the one he had assigned to First Marathon as a comfort deposit to cover Holoday's personal trades? Could he have it back?

Not a chance, David Wood told him. Not a chance in hell.[5]

With things closing in around him — Ken and Elaine Roberts demanding their $10 million plus profits, NSF cheques bouncing back to his employer, the Royal Bank expecting a settlement on his overdraft, no access to the US$108,000 T-bill — Holoday scrambled for money from anywhere and everywhere. Had he the honesty to admit it,

Holoday would have realized he was in the last convulsive throes of a classic Ponzi scheme that eventually topples under its own weight and instability.[6]

Holoday's only remaining source of money rested with clients to whom he had lied over the past three years, assuring them of his success in managing their accounts while disguising the fact that most of their assets were already, or close to, wiped out. They had other assets, however, and Holoday began snatching at them like a cherry-picker, grabbing the ripest ones first.

On Sunday, June 5, he persuaded Martin Karp to invest US$45,000 with him for five days in "a tax-driven investment." Holoday would pay interest at the rate of 1 percent per day, and it was a sure thing — he and Karp would simply exchange cheques.

The next day, from his office, Holoday talked Roger Campbell into withdrawing $239,000 from his First Marathon account and transferring it to a special short-term investment opportunity related to a new mutual fund being launched by First Marathon. "Basically, we'll exchange cheques," Holoday explained. "I bring you a cheque from your trading account, and you give me a cheque for the First Marathon investment." It was another one-week deal paying 5 percent over the term of the loan. He also proposed a $100,000 investment by Penny Campbell in an "international mutual fund" to be guaranteed by First Marathon, using the same cheque exchange — a First Marathon cheque for the amount payable to Penny Campbell, and a cheque from Campbell for the same amount, payable to Holoday "to expedite the trade."

The Campbells agreed. They never suspected Holoday was short of cash, especially when he arrived in a chauffeur-driven stretch limo to deliver the First Marathon cheques and pick up the Campbells' funds. Making small talk with Penny Campbell, he complained in a serio-comic

Dagwood Bumstead manner that wife Maureen was spending $20,000 each month on clothing. Then he clambered back into the rear seat of the limousine and sped away.

Together with Sheldon Fenton's certified cheque for $1.5 million, Holoday was temporarily flush again. He needed to be; Randy Lang called later to complain that a cheque Holoday had given Lang for $194,000 had bounced. Lang wanted his money, pronto. He had also decided to start taping Holoday's conversations.

After talking to Randy Lang, Holoday scurried up the street to deliver a cheque for $1.6 million in US funds to Doc and Elaine Roberts, representing their $1.5 million options trading investment, plus $100,000 profit.

There was not nearly enough in Holoday's bank account, even with Sheldon Fenton's $1.5 million, and the almost $300,000 he had cobbled together from Karp and the Campbells, to cover the cheque to Roberts. Not enough, even, to provide Paul Simpkin, who had been calling each day for a week, with the $10,000 cheque representing investment profits that Holoday had been promising Simpkin for a month. "Come down to my office tomorrow," Holoday suggested to Simpkin. They agreed on a 10:45 meeting. Then he called Helen Rentis and suggested she visit Holoday's office the next day to hear about "a terrific investment opportunity," backed by cash, securities, and First Marathon itself. It would give her a chance to make big money on $100,000 of the $106,000 he had given her the previous Friday. Just a temporary loan, one week actually, no risk and a fat interest rate. Rentis agreed to arrive after lunch.

Wednesday, June 8, started off badly. When Holoday arrived at his office, Tracy Ellis told him Elaine Roberts was on the phone. "It bounced," Elaine Roberts said to Holoday. She meant the $1.6 million cheque.

"I know," Holoday said. He was prepared for it. He knew

what to do. "I'll be right over to explain." Before he left, he sent Tracy Ellis, in another chauffeured stretch limo, to Martin Karp's residence, instructing her to take the client to his bank, obtain a $45,000 bank draft, return Karp home again, and place the draft on Holoday's desk. Holoday had some business to take care of with Doc and Elaine Roberts.

"I'm having some problems," Holoday said to Doc and Elaine Roberts a few minutes later. The problems, he explained, were related to $2 million he lost in his options account. Fortunately, he was generating enough cash flow from his commissions to make up the loss, but not right away.

How about the $10 million that's in Eastbridge? Elaine Roberts asked. Where does that stand?

That, Holoday said, was another problem, and he withdrew a letter from his briefcase and handed it to Elaine and her father.

The letter, dated August 10, 1993, almost a year earlier, was on First Marathon letterhead, and addressed to Paul DeRosa and Walter Kirkland, Eastbridge principals. Signed by Holoday, it represented one of Holoday's more outrageous subterfuges.

This letter, Doc and Elaine Roberts read, *is written to acknowledge that funds in the daily repo trading account will be increased by 1994 to approximately US $10 million. It is also understood that failure to reach this goal will result in the closing of the account. Further to this level of achievement, the account will be subject to the one-year lock-up agreement of the Southbridge Limited Partnership.*

Furthermore, failure to achieve this criteria will result in the forgoing (sic) of the proprietary rights agreement for distribution of the Northbridge Unit Trust to be completed in 1994 as well as any other services Eastbridge has provided to the Canadian market.[7]

The Roberts were stunned. Does this mean, they said, that we can't touch the money for one year?

That's what it meant, Holoday confirmed. He was sorry, very very sorry, that he hadn't mentioned it before, but they had to understand that it was ironclad, his hands were tied.

Being sorry didn't amount to much in the face of more than $10 million of the Roberts' money they couldn't touch for a year, plus a US$1.6 million rubber cheque. The only security the Roberts had for their $12 million in US funds was Holoday's word . . . and, come to think of it, his personal assets. Elaine Roberts demanded a list of Holoday's assets, plus an official statement covering their total investment in Eastbridge.

"Sure," Holoday said. "No problem. Have it for you tomorrow." It was past 11:00. He practically ran back to his office.

Paul Simpkin had arrived on time for his meeting with Holoday, and he was seated near Tracy Ellis's empty desk when Holoday returned from his meeting with Doc and Elaine Roberts, looking pale and dishevelled. "In a minute," Holoday said, waving off the polite older man who had stood up, ready to start their scheduled meeting and, Simpkin hoped, pick up his long-promised cheque for $10,000. "I've got a financial crisis to handle," Holoday said, and he entered the office, swinging the door closed behind him.

Simpkin sat down again. Holoday had not closed the door completely, and Paul Simpkin sat, fascinated, listening to one side of a series of conversations Holoday had with people he telephoned, his voice alternating between cajoling — *This is a can't miss deal, if you don't get on board now, I don't know when I can get you another one —* to pacifying — *I'll have the cheque there today, tomorrow at the latest, Tracy's out or I'd have it for you right now.* Simpkin overheard perhaps half a dozen such calls over the next hour, but the most disturbing was the one Holoday made to his wife Maureen. "We have to tough it out for three or four months," Holoday said, and when Maureen responded with an apparent objection, Holoday grew more insistent. *"I won't be here any longer if I don't do something!"* he almost shouted.[8]

When Holoday invited Simpkin into his office, he was calm again — the smile was there, the pinkie ring flashed, the trouser crease was honed. Simpkin asked if this was a bad day for Holoday. The younger man laughed it off. It was no big deal, things needed handling, that's all. Then Holoday spent 20 minutes explaining that Simpkin was better off leaving the $10,000 in his First Marathon account for a little while longer, maybe until the end of the month. "You're in Northbridge," Holoday explained, "with two-hundred and fifty thousand dollars in bonds and one-hundred thousand dollars in commodities." Normally, it took $500,000 minimum to participate in the fund, but Holoday had pulled some strings, called in some favours, just to look after Paul Simpkin and his wife.

Ten minutes later, Simpkin left empty-handed and Holoday was back on the phone, persuading his client Robert Gray to exchange cheques for US$35,000, using the same ploy he applied to the Campbells.

Helen Rentis arrived at Holoday's office while he was on the telephone in animated discussion with Gray. She took a seat near Tracy Ellis' desk, glanced down, and saw a cheque for US$46,000 drawn from her own account at First Marathon. "What the hell is this?" she demanded from Holoday when he greeted her. She had never author-ized a withdrawal from her account. How dare he do such a thing?

Inside his office with the door closed, Holoday explained that he needed US$150,000 "to straighten out some financial deals, a temporary cash-flow problem." She would receive all her money back, plus a healthy profit, in a week. It had to do with that TSE and First Marathon screw-up he mentioned last week. "Do it as a friend," Holoday said. "Help me out here."

"He was still working in his office," Rentis recalled. "I thought the TSE and First Marathon knew what was going on. He hadn't been turfed out on the street, so the problem couldn't have been very big." She agreed to help Holoday.[9]

Her $146,000 vanished in the crevasse that had become Holoday's personal bank account, but it wasn't enough. Not nearly enough. Holoday called David Wood and asked if they could hold a meeting. Holoday had something to ask of the vice-president, operations.

"What's up?" Wood asked when Holoday entered his office, and Holoday came right to the point: Would First Marathon lend him two million dollars?

No, Wood snapped, it would not. Seeing the desperation on the younger man's face, Wood assumed his problem was the result of Holoday living beyond his means. Wood had seen this before. Holoday wasn't the first hot-shot broker to blow up. Guys like Holoday start making big dollars, and they think they've reached the golden end of the rainbow. Holoday had to pull his lifestyle down a few notches. Wood would help him, if Holoday wanted him to, just as he had helped other high-flying traders come to grips with reality. Sell your property in Barbados and forget about the villa, Wood advised. Sell your house in Forest Hill, and rent an apartment for a while. Cut your spending, get rid of some of the toys, cut up your credit cards, improve your cash position. Holoday could do it. Others had. Just don't try borrowing your way out of trouble, okay?

Holoday nodded, thanked Wood for the advice, and slouched back to his office.

Before leaving for home that night, Holoday prepared a statement indicating that the Roberts' Eastbridge investment totalled $10,160,012.19, and faxed it to the Fahnestock Viner office. Then he typed a list of personal unencumbered assets, headed *Bank Report: Michael Holoday June 8, 1994.* The list was a remarkable work of financial fiction.

The balance in Holoday's cash account at First Marathon, he claimed, was $1,072,000. He owned $1.6 million in shares of SDI Virtual Reality, another $600,000 in shares of Consolidated Madison, and $175,000 in shares of Wye Resources. His real estate holdings were equally impressive: $300,000 for the Cobourg house, $1.2 million equity in his Forest Hill Road mansion, and another $1.2 million for his Barbados property. From there he added boats, cars, motorcycles, snowmobiles, wife Maureen's jewellery (valued at $300,000), $50,000 cash surrender value of a life insurance policy, $48,000 in an RRSP, and $47,000 in personal loans owed him, for a total in personal assets of $7,404,718.75 — in US funds, of course. This news would have elated the Royal Bank, where Holoday's personal chequing account happened to be overdrawn that day by $1,627,538.72.

The next morning, he presented copies of his "assets" to Kenneth and Elaine Roberts in their office. Is this it? they asked. Is there anything else you owe or own?

Oh yeah, Holoday remembered. There's a US$500,000 T-bill on deposit at First Marathon, representing the futures division capital.

Elaine Roberts handed Holoday the fax he sent the previous day, listing the value of the Roberts' investment at $10,160,012.19. Read this, she told him. Then sign it.

Elaine Roberts had added some words, in her tight handwriting, at the bottom of the statement:

> *I, Michael Holoday, hereby acknowledge that E. K. Roberts is the beneficial owner of the ten million, one hundred sixty thousand, twelve dollars 19/100 ($10,160,012.19) United States of America currency. I covenant that the above funds are free of liens or encumbrances.*
>
> *DATED at Toronto, Canada, this 9th day of June, 1994.*

Holoday nodded, shrugged, and withdrew his Mont Blanc pen from a jacket pocket.

We want a mortgage on your house as security, Ken Roberts told Holoday.

And you have to inform Eastbridge about our lien on the assets they have, Elaine Roberts ordered. She was leaving the next day for a vacation in Europe with her two young children. They were renting a car and driving through Austria, France, and Switzerland. She wanted this settled now.

Holoday agreed to everything. He understood their concern. He would make it all good. And he wished Elaine Roberts bon voyage.

He could hardly wait to get out of there. Had he known what awaited him back at his First Marathon office, he might have dallied a little longer.

David Wood couldn't believe it. The brokerage business was as rife with gossip and rumours as any business, but Michael Holoday appeared to be winning some sort of contest for outrageous innuendoes.

That morning, a compliance officer at RBC Dominion Securities had alerted David Burnes of First Marathon about something he heard from an RBC Dominion broker.

The broker said that her client, Roy O'Hearn, complained that Dominion should make up his losses the same way that his other brokerage firm, First Marathon, did. No broker makes up losses, O'Hearn was told, and O'Hearn said that his did. To prove it, he flashed a cheque from Chase Manhattan's Syracuse, NY branch for US$299,000, drawn on the account of Michael Holoday. Burnes told David Wood about it. Brokers making up losses for their clients? What the hell was going on?

Which is what Wood asked Holoday when his managing partner, futures division, returned from the meeting with Ken and Elaine Roberts. What was going on between Holoday and his client O'Hearn?

Wood expected a denial, a moment of panic, perhaps anger. But Holoday remained cool. "I know exactly what you're talking about," Holoday said. "There's a rumour over at RBC Dominion that I'm paying money to Roy O'Hearn."

Holoday never made good on O'Hearn's losses?

Never, Holoday assured Wood.

Wood asked Holoday about the personal cheque to O'Hearn for $299,000. What was that all about?

"We did a real estate deal a few years ago," Holoday said. "I paid Roy what I owed him, that's all. Should I have told you about that?"

Damn right, Wood replied, he should have told First Marathon about any personal financial dealings with his clients. That was a no-no in the business. He should know that.

Holoday said he was sorry.

"Any other financial dealings with clients?" Wood asked.

"One," Holoday said. He owed Kenneth Roberts US$250,000 for the purchase of the Barbados property, but Ken Roberts wasn't actually a client of Holoday's. Roberts' daughter Elaine was the client. So that made it an arm's-length deal, right?

Wood agreed that it seemed to qualify. Then he asked
if Holoday were sure these were the only two deals he had
with clients. "They better be," Wood warned, "because if
there's one more, you're out of this company and right out
of this industry."[10]

Holoday shook his head. Nope, that was all. And he
was really sorry he never got around to disclosing that old
real estate deal with Roy O'Hearn.

Holoday returned to his office, called Mona O'Hearn,
and told her he had a great opportunity for her plans to
bequeath money to the Jesuits. If she would lend First
Marathon $95,000 in US funds from her account for just
ten days, she could earn 10 percent interest. When she
agreed to the terms, he withdrew the funds.

Then he went home to spend a nervous weekend.

Monday launched another week spent calming nervous
clients, cajoling others to advance him funds, and spinning
a new web of lies.

The biggest lie was to Ken Roberts. Before leaving for
a European vacation with her children, Elaine Roberts left
instructions for her father. Ken was to finalize the mortgage on Holoday's Forest Hill home, and see that the $10
million was sent up from Eastbridge. It was a role rever-
sal, the daughter leaving a list of chores for her father to
complete in her absence, but it was necessary in Elaine's
view. The old man was more forgiving to his protégé than
she was, and she feared Holoday would perform some
fancy footwork to avoid meeting his promises. Which is
exactly what Holoday did on Monday morning.

The Roberts' money, Holoday informed Ken Roberts,
wasn't in Eastbridge after all. It was in the company's offshore fund Southbridge, held by State Street Trust in the
Cayman Islands. How it got there, Holoday didn't know,
but the cash could only be withdrawn from the fund at the

end of each month after 30 days' notice. "I might be able to pull some strings and get three million of your money out in a week or so," Holoday suggested, and Ken Roberts said, "Try."

The balance of the week consisted of Holoday's endless efforts to cobble together cash for the Roberts, plus more money for clients demanding withdrawals and, of course, enough dollars for him and Maureen to enjoy the summer. Dozens of guests, including Boczan and Soucie family members, were arriving at the cottage every weekend. There were boats to fill with fuel, and food to buy for barbecues and dinners, and it all took money. Other people's money.

Helen Rentis was expecting to receive back her $146,000 with interest that week. Holoday called to promise he would pay her, using a $1 million refund cheque due from Revenue Canada. It was late. Should be here any day now.

Roger Campbell's loan of $240,000 was also due, along with 5 percent interest. Holoday assured the Campbells their investment was doing well. "Why not leave it for a few days and earn a little more profit?" he suggested. They agreed. But Ray Kundinger had been demanding $35,000 from his pooled account for some time, and he was insistent. Holoday called Campbell back with another idea. Let's build the investment up a little, he suggested. Hey, 5 percent a week is a lot better than they could earn dealing in commodities, and it was a sure thing, backed by First Marathon and all that. Holoday suggested adding another US$85,000 from Campbell's account. They would do the usual cheque exchange thing, and Holoday would provide a legal promissory note.

Campbell went along with the idea, and a few hours later Holoday arrived with a First Marathon cheque for $85,000. But instead of a cheque for an equal amount from Campbell, he asked for two cheques: one to himself for

$50,000, and another for $35,000 payable to Ray
Kundinger who, Holoday explained, wanted out of the
pooled investment. "You're buying his share," Holoday
explained. Just to add to Campbell's comfort, Holoday provided a promissory note on First Marathon letterhead,
pledging as collateral the US T-bill for $108,000 held in
Holoday's deposit account at the investment firm. "You
can't find any collateral more secure than that," Holoday
assured Campbell, which was true except that the T-bill
had already been pledged to First Marathon, and would be
pledged over the next several weeks to at least half a
dozen other clients of Holoday.

Kundinger received the $35,000 he had been demand-
ing, and Holoday had another $50,000 cash in his account.
He also had a new unwitting cheque-kiting partner.
Through the balance of the summer, Holoday talked to
Roger Campbell almost daily, often calling in a panic
around three o'clock in the afternoon with a hot deal, but
they had to act before the market closed, get a cheque
ready, Tracy would be right over, and minutes later Tracy
Ellis would arrive in a chauffeured limousine with a personal cheque from Michael Holoday, managing partner,
futures division, First Marathon Securities Limited. She
would hand Campbell a personal cheque from Michael
Holoday, and take Campbell's cheque across the street to
the Scotiabank branch, where Campbell maintained his
accounts. There she would have the cheque certified before
leaping into the limousine again and vanishing along
Queen Street, back to First Marathon.

Holoday's pyramid continued to crumble. When Elaine
Roberts called her father from Europe to enquire about the
situation with Holoday, and discovered Holoday's newest
revelation — that the money wasn't in New York after all,
but locked up in the Cayman Islands — she exploded. She
wanted Power of Attorney over all the assets Holoday con-

trolled at Southbridge, she wanted confirmation that any
money wired to Holoday's Royal Bank account was deposited in the Roberts' account at that branch, she wanted
Holoday to instruct Southbridge to move as much money as
they could, as fast as they could, out of the account, and she
wanted a mortgage on Holoday's Forest Hill home.

Ken Roberts passed her wishes on to Holoday.

"Sure," Holoday agreed. "No problem."

But a major problem arose on Monday morning, when
Holoday arrived at his office to find a message that Roy
O'Hearn wanted to see him as quickly as possible. Holoday
called O'Hearn. It was going to be a busy day, it was hot
as hell out, the first day of summer. Couldn't it wait?

No, O'Hearn said. They had to meet now. At O'Hearn's
house.

Holoday said he would be there by lunch.

O'Hearn insisted on meeting Holoday at his home in
northwest Toronto in order to record their conversation.
The letter that had arrived from First Marathon that
morning was more than enough to raise O'Hearn's suspicions higher than ever, and prompted him to cue his tape
recorder, hidden in his living room for Holoday's arrival.

The letter was from Joseph Thurman. *Our
Representative Michael Holoday,* Thurman wrote, *has
indicated that he has recently issued a personal cheque to
you in the amount of US$299,000 which represented pay-
ment of a personal loan which was established in 1989. We
request that you confirm this transaction by signing and
returning a copy of this letter.*[11]

O'Hearn waved the letter at Holoday the minute the
younger man walked through the front door, asking if
O'Hearn wanted to go somewhere for lunch. No, O'Hearn
said, he didn't want to go for lunch. "What kind of games
are you playing, Mike?" O'Hearn asked. "What the hell's
going on?"

Holoday took Thurman's letter from his hand, read it for the first time, and sat down. He began rambling through an intricate explanation, saying that O'Hearn's other brokerage firm, RBC Dominion Securities, had wanted assurance from Holoday that the bank draft was good, and Holoday provided it because he didn't want any more hassles for his good friend and client O'Hearn, and somebody from Dominion happened to mention it to Marathon. The transcript from O'Hearn's tape recording reveals Holoday's nervous skating:

> *What happened was, uh, because funds were exchanged involving, uh, you and me, without no one having any knowledge of, you know, why. Um, the street basically is not that big and, uh, their guys called Marathon . . . you know, just to check, you know, just to, to check, you know, just to, uh, look into this and they called my guys and my guys said, Why did you exchange this amount of money with Mister O'Hearn? I said it was related to settling an old real estate loan that I had with him since 1989. Um, you know, that's what I had to say.*

O'Hearn said he would have to consult with a lawyer before signing the letter and sending it back to First Marathon. Then he started demanding answers. "What the hell is the money doing out of the country?" O'Hearn said.

"The money wasn't out of the country," Holoday replied.

"In the Chase Manhattan Bank?"

"That's the, that's the bank, the Royal Bank, that's the Royal Bank of Canada's US affair. Every time you get an account there, if you had an account at the Royal Bank . . ."

"Yeah?"

"It'd be written on the Chase Manhattan."

"It would?"

"Always . . ."

O'Hearn raised a crucial point. "I didn't even *know* you in nineteen eighty-nine."

"Yes, you did," Holoday said.

"I met you in nineteen-ninety."

"Eighty-nine, ninety. That's not important."

It was important to O'Hearn. So were various deals Holoday had made in O'Hearn's account without his knowledge, such as selling O'Hearn $25,000 of SDI Virtual Reality stock that Holoday owned, placing the shares in O'Hearn's account the day after his client left for an extended cruise through the Far East.

Holoday performed some footwork to calm his client down but grew concerned when O'Hearn said he couldn't sign the First Marathon letter without consulting his lawyer. Holoday objected. O'Hearn didn't need to talk to his lawyer. This was just a personal loan Holoday had paid off, that's all. That's the way it should be treated. There was nothing wrong with a personal loan. What's wrong with paying off a debt? Just sign the letter back. It's just a formality. Besides, Holoday had a special refinancing deal for O'Hearn, and O'Hearn's hidden tape recorder captured Holoday's pitch:

> *I've left open enough room between Monday and Friday of this week, today and Friday, for those funds if you wish, uh, to make you about fifteen thousand dollars on a short-term basis. Not because I'm in a, uh, panic situation or anything like that, but in an effort to, hey, make you some return in US funds, and I've always kept you in on any special deals that I've ever done in my life. This is a non, this is a non-brokerage item . . .*

What I've done is, I've taken securities, um, and I've collateralized a bridge loan up to a million and a half bucks against it, securities which I own, and I've taken the funds, uh, and the funds are in my division at First Marathon. So I've made up, I freed up my cash flow, my liquidity, and what I have is a group that is taking out three-hundred thousand dollars by Friday this week. . . . And I have a group which I'm paying off today, three-hundred thousand dollars, period, against a loan which they made, uh, just before you left. Part of the original one-point-five (million), because they have earmarked those funds for some other deal. They're a real estate corporation, Tanalon Investment Management Inc.[12] It's a good corporation. . . . They've done okay. They made it through the recession. So I'm in a period of, uh, five days, we're, you know, you wonder why, I don't really have to pay out one percent a day interest, but the multiples of returns that I make over and above, it's like one of your real estate bonuses, basically. I try to price it off with one of your real estate bonuses, which make you twelve grand or something right up front. And, uh, that's what I've done is, I've written an agreement from the Royal Bank with the safekeeping accounts and security numbers and the whole thing, which collateralizes the five day bridge financing, uh, pays out as a certified form on Friday of this week, with interest of fifteen thousand dollars.

To earn his $15,000, O'Hearn would have to put up $300,000 for one week. Why $300,000? Holoday was remarkably candid:

Well, that's what I thought you had as available funds. So I used one percent on three hundred thousand US and it came to fifteen grand, obviously, in interest. And I thought, uh, like basically what it does is, it allows me to free up cash, and I'm making an investment. I'll tell you right now because you're gonna hear about it in the future. I'm making an investment in ownership of, uh, Toronto Investment Management.

Jim O'Donnell, the former head of Mackenzie Financial, was the individual behind the deal, Holoday explained.

He's already set up six more mutual funds, but again I always knew, the only way to get money in that game is to go in from the inside, not to buy all at once. . . .So the deal closes at the end of the month and what I've done is, I've had to put aside funds until my month-end income comes in, basically.

Holoday would do his friend and client a favour and let O'Hearn in early.

It's O'Donnell Investment Management Inc. It closes the end of June. I mean, you can come in if you want. But you'd have to see all the financials first, and see how feasible it is. It's not gonna be something that's gonna make you money overnight. But on a six-year pull it'll probably make you some money. . . . This is a non-brokers, this is a personal finance situation, non brokers related, it's related to a bridge financing, which Marathon is aware of.[13]

Holoday walked out of O'Hearn's house with US$300,000 of his client's money and O'Hearn's signature at the bottom of the First Marathon letter, confirming that the $299,000 Holoday had paid him two months earlier was part of a real estate deal carried out before O'Hearn became a client.

The balance of the week unfolded according to the pattern Holoday would follow for the next three months — five consecutive days of cajoling money from wary clients to pacify other "investors," followed by weekends at his cottage entertaining Maureen's family. He borrowed $35,000 from Tony Noxon, $105,000 from Dianne Sone (pledging the same US$108,000 T-bill as security each time and promising to pay interest as high as 1 percent per day), and $60,000 from Brian Rocks, who wanted to consult a lawyer first. "We don't have time," Holoday replied. "It's guaranteed safe, backed by First Marathon and me. Lawyers talk, you know, and we don't want this all over the street." Here was a chance to make money, with no risk.

Rocks agreed but he still wanted answers, and later that day he arrived at Holoday's office with a cheque for $60,000 drawn on his business account, plus a handful of First Marathon account statements.

Rocks is an intense and intimidating man, with the hard, lean physique of a construction worker ("On my worst day," Rocks barked during Holoday's trial, "I'm twice the man he is"), and when he leaned across Holoday's desk and jabbed at the balance indicated on his statements, Holoday drew back. "Look," Rocks said, "this statement says I've got a hundred and forty-four thousand with you, but I gave you a hundred and fifty to invest in something safe, bonds and such. You told me I couldn't lose money, but I have. What's going on?"

Holoday swung around to his computer, adjusted the

monitor so Rocks couldn't see the screen, and tapped a few keys. "You've got over a hundred and eighty-six thousand in your account," he assured Rocks. "I made you nearly forty thousand dollars, and that's in slow trading." Rocks said his statement didn't show that amount, and Holoday told Rocks not to believe the statements, that they were always behind, and that "the back office" was always screwing up.

Rocks demanded details on this "can't miss" deal, the one Holoday wanted him to invest in with his $60,000.

The deal, Holoday said, lowering his voice in case someone was eavesdropping, would put Rocks "in the O'Donnell clan," meaning Rocks would join an inner circle of investors providing start-up funds for a new fund to be managed by Jim O'Donnell, former president of giant Mackenzie Financial. The fund would be called Northbridge, and it was important that the deal be kept "off the street," which is why Holoday didn't want Rocks consulting a lawyer. Then, almost as a "by the way," Holoday mentioned that Rocks actually needed another $95,000 to participate.

"I don't have that kind of money," Rocks said.

"Yes, you do," Holoday replied. "Tracy is downstairs getting it right now."

While Rocks was absorbing this surprising news, Tracy Ellis returned with a First Marathon cheque made out to him for $95,000, drawn not from any profit earned in Rocks' account, but from his original investment. Holoday also had two letters prepared, assuring Rocks of the security of his investment, and signed by Michael Holoday, managing partner, futures division, First Marathon Securities.

There was one more thing. Holoday needed a bank draft from Rocks for the total $155,000, made out to Holoday personally. "This way," Holoday explained, "we

can keep the street from learning about it a little longer."
If the draft were in Holoday's name, First Marathon's
involvement would not be revealed. "I'll send you up to
your bank with Tracy in a limousine," Holoday said.

Rocks wasn't a limo kind of guy. He would give Tracy
a ride to his bank in suburban Don Mills in Rocks' own
pickup truck. At the bank, Tracy handled all the paperwork, and on the way back, Rocks began asking questions.
"My statement says I have a hundred and forty-four thousand in my account," Rocks said, "but Mike says it's more
like a hundred and eighty-six thousand. How come the difference?"

The difference, Tracy assured him, was accrued interest, which wasn't showing up in Rocks' First Marathon
statements.

Tracy instructed Rocks to stop at Michael Holoday's
Royal Bank branch at Yonge and Bloor Streets, where she
deposited the bank draft in Holoday's personal chequing
account. Then Rocks drove her back to First Marathon and
returned to work, believing he had made a good investment.

Dianne Sone's "loan" proved daring, even for Holoday, who
assured her that the $100,000 she had earmarked for con-
servative bonds was doing well and "between investments." He called her to say he had another "conservative
investment" that would use the reported $105,000 in her
First Marathon account to earn 7 percent interest over 13
days, backed by securities held at First Marathon. She discussed the proposal with her husband and both agreed
that it appeared safe and profitable. The next day in his
office, Holoday provided Dianne Sone with a promissory
note covering the details, then instructed Tracy Ellis to
accompany her to First Marathon's bank. At the bank,
Ellis sent Sone to wait in a corner, like a child being punished, while she handled the paperwork in discussions

with the teller, calling Sone over to endorse the bank draft. "That's it," Ellis said. "You can go home now."

Sone's original $100,000 had vanished months earlier. So where did the money come from? Without her knowledge, Holoday had opened a margin account in her name and withdrawn the $105,000 from it, creating a debit of $106,410.67 in an account Sone didn't even know she had.

Later that week, Holoday managed to surpass the Sone incident with even more *chutzpah* when 78-year-old Mona O'Hearn called and asked to withdraw money from her account at First Marathon. Her $95,000 loan from ten days earlier was now due, and she needed cash. Holoday invited her to come over "right away," and Mona ventured the several blocks to First Marathon's offices alone. When she arrived, she encountered "some sort of hullabaloo" going on. Holoday, Tracy Ellis, and "some other young man" (probably Chuck Oliver) were engaged in frantic discussions, scurrying here and there for documents, and shouting back and forth to each other in anger and panic.

Holoday calmed everyone down long enough to persuade Mona that, if she could extend her $95,000 loan for a few more days, she would make even more money. Not only that, but if she could hold off needing cash for two weeks, he could make her another few thousand dollars. It worked like this: She would withdraw $65,000 in US funds from her account at First Marathon which, Holoday assured her, was doing very well, and invest it in a bridge financing deal at First Marathon for two weeks, earning 7 percent interest or about $5,000. And there would be absolutely no risk, because Holoday and First Marathon would back up the investment with a US$108,000 T-bill, plus revenues from the futures division of First Marathon of which, Holoday reminded her, he was managing partner.

Almost before she knew it, Mona O'Hearn was having papers thrust in front of her with instructions to sign here,

and here, and here, before Holoday and Tracy Ellis walked
her back to her bank at Front and Church Streets. There,
Mona was shunted to one side while Holoday and Ellis
dealt with the bank staff, returning to have Mona sign
three more documents before sending the elderly woman
on her way home again with a promissory note from
Holoday on First Marathon letterhead, and a debit of over
$80,000 in Mona's First Marathon account, the one she
was using to generate a substantial bequest to her beloved
Jesuits.

The three documents Mona O'Hearn signed at her
bank were bank drafts. Two were payable to companies
owned by Sheldon Fenton, who was becoming especially
difficult about that little matter of the $1.6 million
Holoday owed him. The third draft, for a paltry $8,000,
was payable to Holoday himself.

Between scribbling promissory notes and IOUs in
exchange for certified cheques and bank drafts, the rest of
Holoday's time was filled with spinning tales and writing
assurances to various clients. Roy O'Hearn was sent a
promissory note for $165,000, and when Roger Gordon
asked Holoday to confirm in writing Gordon's account balance, which he needed to begin construction on a dream
house for his family, Holoday more than obliged. *Roger
Gordon,* Holoday wrote on the First Marathon letterhead
listing him as managing partner, futures division, and
addressed to Gordon's lawyer, *has been a value (*sic*) client of
mine for the last 3 years. His trading accounts are 2M0086E,
and 2M5029B. Roger currently has investment capital of
US$150,000.* He added: *Personally I have found Roger to be
a wonderful client and a model citizen in the community.
Should you require any further questions answered regarding Roger's account do not hesitate to contact me.*

Gordon's lawyer made copies of the letter for his client
to distribute to the bank, various tradesmen, and con-

struction materials suppliers. It was a fine letter, one that Holoday's employers, in defending themselves later against civil actions by Roger Gordon, would turn against Gordon, claiming it proved Gordon had been conspiring with Holoday to defraud Gordon's suppliers.

Meanwhile, Randy Lang wanted $385,000 from his account. Holoday explained that Lang's money was "intertwined with my capital right now," and Holoday would be releasing it "in hundred thousand dollar chunks" any day. It was enough to hold Lang off for a while, but almost as soon as Holoday hung up, a furious Martin Karp called him. Karp had just discovered that the cheque for $45,000 Holoday gave Karp a month earlier had been withdrawn from Karp's own account. Not only that, but one of Holoday's "can't miss" bond plays had cost Karp $156,000. *What the hell is going on here, Mike?*

Holoday spent more time assuring Karp that his bond losses "were covered," it was just that certain people were slow to pay Holoday. With apologies, Holoday offered to extend Karp's investment to the middle of August, paying 10 percent over the term. When Holoday was off the phone with Karp, he provided Joe Thurman with a promissory note covering the $299,000 "loan" from Roy O'Hearn, and issued a letter giving Power of Attorney over his assets to Ken Roberts, "just in case I get hit by a truck or something."

On June 20, the second of the Desmond twins, died. "We'll look after it," Michael insisted, and he instructed the baby to be buried in his and Maureen's burial plot in Mount Pleasant Cemetery with the same lavish service as the first.

John and Carole Boczan were relieved to be back in Toronto, away from disgruntled Barbadian contractors always demanding to be paid. When they arrived, after receiving news of the baby's death, Michael suggested they not return to Barbados right away. "Wait until fall," he advised them. "It's the rainy season down there now."

The Boczans remained, partially because Howard and Suzie were heartbroken over the deaths of their babies, and Suzie's parents provided all the emotional support they could.

Something had changed at the Holodays' home, and it was Michael and Maureen's attitude. Michael seemed pre-occupied and edgy during the week, although he appeared relaxed enough at the cottage on Lake Simcoe, roaring up and down the water in *Bad Company*. He and Maureen shared secrets in hoarse, whispered conversations, and one evening the Boczans noticed their daughter and son-in-law packing furnishings into the Jeep Grand Cherokee — a stereo system, some crystal and silverware, paintings and sculpture — and carting them away. "What's going on?" Carole Boczan asked, and Maureen explained that Michael had a few cash-flow problems, a temporary thing.

The Boczans asked if they could help. Maybe Michael could borrow from the Boczans' account at First Marathon, the one with a balance well over $50,000 according to Michael's estimate, which was all they had to go on because they never could figure out those confusing First Marathon statements. Michael just smiled and walked away. How about the Roberts family? Carole Boczan asked later. Won't Elaine Roberts loan him money? Holoday's response was to shake his head and call Elaine Roberts a bitch. She was blackmailing him, Holoday claimed. "She has something over us," Holoday told his mother-in-law. "We have to give her whatever she asks for."

Later that night, standing on the balcony overlooking the ravine behind the house, Holoday relaxed a little with Carole Boczan. This stuff, the cars and Maureen's jewellery and all of that, he told his mother-in-law, they were nothing to him. "When this is all over," he said, "I'll have ten million dollars out of it." Things would get better, he assured her. He just needed a little time. Carole Boczan asked if $10 million would be enough to pay Michael's debts.

"Who cares?" Holoday said. "I've got a lot of tin cans I can bury."

The Boczans understood the implication immediately: Holoday would squirrel away cash, out of reach of clients, creditors, anybody who wanted to get their hands on it.

Through the rest of June, tension continued to build within the house. One night, Carole and John Boczan began asking questions, demanding answers. What was really going on? Why hadn't the contractors in Barbados been paid? Why had Michael and Maureen left them down there to fend off those people alone? What was behind the telephone calls Michael was handling at night, calls that set off angry shouts or clouds of gloom and depression thick enough to carve with a knife? Howard and Suzie Desmond were there as well. They had watched Michael and Maureen's ascendancy to favoured status within the Boczan family over the past three years, and now their concerns and suspicions were as deep as John and Carole's.

Michael replied that he had problems, okay? Problems too big for the Boczans to solve, too big even for them to understand. When Carole and John asked about the status of their account at First Marathon, Michael told them to forget about it, which was enough for Carole to ask for their money back.

Michael told them they wouldn't get it, it was gone.

Gone? Carole Boczan said. Gone where?

"You spent it," Holoday said, and he recited the multiple vacations the Boczans had enjoyed, the gifts of furs

and jewellery, the lavish dinners, and all the other perks
he provided them.

Carole and John Boczan demanded their money. That
was their retirement nest egg. They had signed ownership
of their Cobourg house to him. They would sue to get back
their investment, if that's what it took.

"*I don't owe you any money,*" Holoday exploded. The
Boczans, in fact, owed *him* money, Holoday said, and he
had proof. "I could sue *you!*" he claimed. The Boczans had
nothing to complain about. "If I hadn't spent your money,
you would have anyway," Holoday snapped.

Howard Desmond was appalled. "How can you say
that?" he demanded, and Holoday's response was to point
a finger and tell Desmond to mind his own business.

His life, Holoday went on, had become the stuff movies
were made of. He would come out of this better than ever.
First Marathon, he said, had put up a wall to protect him,
he could do no wrong, he couldn't lose. The TSE? Forget
about them, they couldn't touch him, he was buddy-buddy
with the head of security down there, old Charlie
McDermott. "I've had cases of cappuccino with McDermott
over the years," Holoday boasted. It was vintage Michael
Holoday, all unbridled confidence and outrageous lies. The
Desmonds left, angry at Holoday's attitude; the Boczans
went to bed that evening feeling more uneasy than ever.

The next day, John and Carole Boczan avoided their
daughter and son-in-law as much as they could and decided to go out for dinner. When they returned to 265 Forest
Hill that evening, it was raining, hard and steady. Near
the front door they saw their luggage stacked and waiting.
When they tried their key, they discovered the lock had
been changed. When they rang the bell, then pounded on
the front door to be let inside, no one answered.

FIFTEEN

Still grabbing at that golden ring?
The ride's the thing!
– RAYMOND SOUSTER

une 1994 ended with a maelstrom of telephone calls, cheque kiting, confrontations, and reckless lies for Holoday, sprinkled with laughable errors.

Unable to repay clients for the high-interest, short-term "investments," he could only attempt to pacify them. One method was to offer the US$108,000 T-bill as security; by July, eight of Holoday's clients believed their investment was backed by this same T-bill, already pledged to First Marathon Securities to fund Holoday's personal trading losses. He gave his beloved Jaguar XJS convertible to Roy O'Hearn as additional collateral; O'Hearn disliked driving the car, and eventually discovered it was leased anyway. Holoday held off Sheldon Fenton with elaborate excuses, told Gary Davidson that Davidson's investments had grown so large he needed to sign an agreement raising his risk level to US$85,000 (providing Holoday with additional withdrawal limits) and instructed the law firm Fogler Rubinoff to finalize the mortgage on his Forest Hill home in favour of Ken and Elaine Roberts. Monthly interest payments on the Roberts' mortgage would be $16,000; missing a payment automatically entitled the Roberts to seize Holoday's Barbados property. The

Roberts believed their investment in 265 Forest Hill Road
was a second mortgage, but in reality it was a third. And,
just to make the web of lies even more complex, Holoday
informed the Royal Bank, holder of mortgages numbers 1
and 2, that Ken and Elaine Roberts would be making the
monthly payments on the Royal's mortgages from that
point on, not him.

Holoday was unable either to understand or admit he
was on a treadmill, burning massive amounts of energy
and other people's money while attempting to stave off the
inevitable. Had he seen a memo sent to David Wood by
Compliance Officer Joe Thurman on the last day of June
1994 he might have thrown in the towel and saved whatever remained in the accounts of many of his smaller
clients. Or perhaps not.

In his memo, Thurman noted six ways in which
Holoday had become "increasingly problematic in the
areas of credit and compliance" in recent weeks:

1. *Several commodity option positions have been
   purchased for clients who have no funds on
   deposit with FMSL. These positions are often
   sizeable ($100,000+ value). In several instances
   it has taken five to ten business days to collect
   from these clients, obviously well past the next-
   day settlement we require for commodity option
   trades. We have even had to consider legal action
   on at least one occasion.*
2. *Several clients have had stock account debit balances written off against Holoday's Bad Debt
   Account. That account currently carries a debit
   balance of $60,151.60. As well, there are several
   stock accounts which are either undermargined
   or carrying an unsecured debt.*
3. *Holoday's personal trading has resulted in size-*

able losses (over US$2.155 million in commodity trading). His stock account is currently under-margined by US$94,497. On several occasions, he has purchased commodity option positions in his own account and not paid for the trade until several days past settlement.

4. *Prior to joining FMSL, Holoday indicated that his principal trading strategy involved purchasing straddle positions for his clients. In the past several weeks, he has mostly abandoned that strategy. Most of his accounts have become outright speculators, gambling on which way the bond market will move in the short term. As a result, some of his clients have suffered substantial losses. In fact, over ninety percent of his clients have net trading losses since opening their commodity accounts.*

5. *Holoday has admitted to having at least one outstanding loan from a client (Roy O'Hearn). There may be some question as to whether Holoday's current debt (approximately $165,000) relates to a mortgage he took out several years ago with O'Hearn, or a recent separate loan, as Holoday claims. As well, this client has indicated to outside sources that Holoday has reimbursed him for trading losses in the past, although this claim appears to be unsubstantiated. In discussions with Mr. O'Hearn, I have found his complaints to be general in nature and have some doubts regarding his credibility. Holoday has agreed to provide us with a copy of the loan agreement with O'Hearn, but so far has not done so.*

6. *We know that before he came to FMSL, Holoday was the subject of at least one client complaint.*

*We have received one complaint from a former
employee of his (Glennis MacLean). Upon the
sale of investments which Holoday recommended to her, she appears to have dropped her complaint.*

*In conclusion, it is evident that if FMSL is
going to have a beneficial relationship with
Michael Holoday, we must insist that ALL of his
commodity option trades be paid for in advance
by certified cheque or bank draft unless sufficient
funds are in the client's account. As well, we must
take firm steps to ensure that all of his clients'
stock accounts are properly margined and in
good standing. Holoday's personal trading must
be kept within reasonable limits and all of his
own commodity option trades must be paid for in
advance.*

*If Michael Holoday does not agree to operate
under these terms, or if, upon agreement, he fails
to comply with these terms, I recommend that we
take action to terminate our business relationship with him.*[1]

Elaine Roberts returned from her European vacation on
July 3. She and her father had been in regular telephone
contact during the trip, her father passing on Holoday's
efforts to calm the Roberts' concerns — the mortgage on
265 Forest Hill Road; a real estate listing for the Cobourg
house; copies of letters indicating that negotiations were
still ongoing between Eastbridge and First Marathon; and
a proposal that the Roberts' $10 million Southbridge
investment be declared an asset of Holoday's company,
Holoday Investments Ltd., which would then be transferred to Ken and Elaine Roberts' numbered company.
That one really infuriated her, since it could be construed

to mean the Roberts were assuming Holoday's debts as their own. "No way!" she almost shouted across the Atlantic from Austria.

So nothing had happened during Elaine Roberts' vacation, except more stalling and new reams of paperwork from Holoday. The 30 days needed to withdraw money from Southbridge were up, Elaine Roberts reminded Holoday in the Fahnestock Viner office on her first day back from vacation. She brushed off his enquiries about her trip, she didn't want to discuss it with him, she wasn't interested in showing him snapshots or souvenirs. She wanted straight answers, for a change.

Holoday promised the money was on its way. He expected it any day now. When he returned to his office at First Marathon, he was told David Wood wanted to speak to him.

Wood's message was disturbing. First Marathon, he told Holoday, was no longer interested in maintaining the relationship with their managing partner, futures division. Holoday may have a future in the industry, Wood suggested, but it wasn't there. Maybe with Refco Canada. The idea of transferring his accounts from First Marathon to Refco, which would mean he would first have to raise their value out of a debit position, was chilling to Holoday. He would need at least US$10 million for the Roberts, and half again as much to balance his client accounts. It couldn't be done, and Holoday knew it.

He spent the balance of the week writing cheques on his overdrawn account — US$165,000 to Roy O'Hearn was the largest — and spinning lies to anxious clients. He convinced Brian Rocks to wait another week for his $95,000 plus interest, told Dianne Sone her $105,000 investment had been extended for two weeks with interest, and claimed that Randy Lang's $385,000 was being held at State Street Trust in the Cayman Islands. "They wire funds from New York to State Street Trust in the Caymans, okay?" Holoday explained, the tension in his voice captured on Lang's tape recorder. "Then they wire the money from State Street Trust in Caymans back to New York and then they wire, ah, at a different New York bank account, an account from my name, and then the money gets wired from New York to Toronto."[2]

The convoluted route held suggestions of tax evasion or perhaps even money laundering, but Lang simply made grunts of understanding. In any case, Holoday assured Lang, the funds should be in Toronto by Monday.

There were no funds on Monday, July 11, of course. Only demands from Gary Davidson, Brian Rocks, Roger Campbell, Randy Lang and others, all seeking return of their money. Holoday's personal cheque for $25,000 to Gary Davidson bounced, but Brian Rocks managed to pocket $70,000 of the $95,000 he expected to receive, and Roger Campbell received $19,860. Randy Lang kept calling, but Holoday avoided talking to him. Lang was looking for $650,000 cash, expected from New York that day. How could Holoday talk to him? What could Holoday say this time? When would one of Holoday's clients call David Wood and start demanding answers, the way Roy O'Hearn had? Holoday was getting headaches, he couldn't sleep, he couldn't eat, he didn't even want to go north to his boat and cottage anymore.

He could think of nothing else to do except walk over to Fahnestock Viner and tell them the truth. Well, a version of the truth anyway.

Through Holoday's tearful confession in the Fahnestock Viner office, Ken and Elaine Roberts sat listening to his tale of the vanished millions while various emotions swept through them. "On the most obvious level, we were horrified," Elaine Roberts recalled later. "On another level, we were looking at this kid that we trusted for all these years in such a close way, who is sitting there crying, and we're feeling sorry for him somehow, as crazy as that sounds . . ."[3] How was Holoday going to make things right? they wondered, still believing he could.

When Holoday regained his composure, dried his tears, and slipped back into his jacket after confessing that it had all been a fairy tale — the daily trades, Eastbridge, Southbridge, Northbridge, all of it — he returned to his office feeling relieved. Confession was indeed good for the soul. He still had to find the money he had promised the Roberts, still had to fend off other clients and, truth be told, tap them for more money. But at least he had one less secret to conceal.

Later, the realization hit Elaine. Michael Holoday, the Bay Street Whiz Kid, the young man whom both Midland Walwyn and First Marathon had trumpeted as a commodities trading genius with a unique controlled-risk investment strategy and a future as bright as the midsummer sun, had not been wailing and thrashing in guilt and sorrow for the Roberts and their losses. He had been crying for himself, and his fall from grace and wealth.

That night, Randy Lang reached Holoday at his home. Instead of the $650,000 he had expected, Lang had to settle for another complex lie, this one claiming that Lang's money was tied up with Holoday's in the First Marathon "division" account, except for a portion in Northbridge that required ninety days to close out. Lang accepted the explanation.

Doc and Elaine Roberts wanted Michael Holoday's assets, everything he could carry, drive, and transfer to them. Those were the instructions Elaine Roberts passed to him the next day, July 12. No hesitation, no excuses. Start paying us back the money *now*. Holoday begged for a day to organize things, and got it.

"I've got a lot of demands on my cash flow," he told Ken and Elaine Roberts the next day in their office. He was under control now, the same cool unflappable broker who had managed to access $13 million in US funds from the head of one of Toronto's wealthiest families, the shrewd and tough Doc Roberts. Holoday went through the list for them. He was leasing a villa in Barbados for his in-laws, costing him $5,000 a month (but it wasn't; the Boczans were back in Toronto, the villa's rent unpaid, and the Boczans' personal property, including most of Carole's jewellery, seized on the island for Holoday's debts). He had a long-term lease on the Orillia cottage, payments on the house in Cobourg, life insurance, bank interest, it all added up to $25,000 a month. Chuck Oliver was drawing a salary plus 5 percent of the gross commissions, and there was a drain to First Marathon, and Trace Ellis's salary . . .

How could he have gotten himself into this mess? Ken Roberts asked.

It all started with the Bush-Clinton election in November 1992, Holoday said. He was trading in US bond futures and doing really well, nobody could touch him, but Clinton defeated Bush and the market reacted the wrong way, his clients lost money, who knew Bush would lose? His clients blamed Holoday. Midland Walwyn agreed with the clients and ordered Holoday to make good on the losses.

Elaine Roberts asked for confirmation of Holoday's expenses. Where were his personal bank statements? When Holoday said they were at home, she instructed him to bring them to the Fahnestock Viner office before the day was out.

By the way, Holoday stuttered, there were some bad debts he hadn't mentioned. He owed about $500,000 from his days at Midland Walwyn, plus start-up costs of $420,000 for the futures division at First Marathon. There were bills to pay for the Barbados villa, the architects, the contractors, the building materials. He owed $300,000 on some SDI Virtual Reality shares, $225,000 on shares of Consolidated Madison, $15,000 on his Jaguar, $36,000 on his American Express card, the list went on and on.

Elaine Roberts began claiming the most liquidable assets. Forget the Porsche 911 Turbo; it was worth $60,000 but Holoday owed more than $50,000 on it. His Ferrari 328 GTS was owned outright, however, and Holoday valued it at $85,000.[4] She would take that, along with all of Maureen's jewellery, every earring and bracelet, valued at $300,000. Holoday promised to bring the ownership to the Ferrari and Maureen's jewellery to her before the day was out. Don't forget the bank statements, he was reminded.

Later that day, Holoday handed a box to Elaine Roberts. Inside were his wife's Cartier watch, her Tiffany engagement ring, her diamond earrings, even her gold wedding band. The next day, after Holoday explained that Maureen had been devastated at losing her wedding band, he asked for it back, and Elaine Roberts consented. By that time, she had noticed something strange and revealing: Of all the bank statements Holoday delivered to her, including the personal chequing account in US dollars that he and Maureen maintained, the one with a total cash flow of over US$100 million in the month of June 1994 alone, most had never been opened. The statements, cancelled cheques, debit memos, all the paraphernalia associated with tracking cash flow and balances, remained as they where when mailed to Michael and Maureen months earlier. No one had bothered to read them. Holoday, except for frantic telephone calls from his branch requesting him to cover multimillion-dollar overdrafts, had no idea of his true financial situation, and didn't appear to care.

Over the next ten days, Holoday's to-ing and fro-ing between clients, handing off cheques here, picking up bank drafts there ("Tracy, gotta call another limo!"), continued to gain momentum. He sold 5,000 of his shares in SDI Virtual Reality to Paul Simpkin for $3.625 per share, pocketing the money, and assured Simpkin that a $335,000 loss in Simpkin's account would be replaced, with interest. ("Let's call it a loan," Holoday suggested.) Holoday repaid Brian Rocks $25,000, promising to have the final payment soon. Next, he converted $172,485 owed to Martin Karp into another "loan," this one not due until January 1995, paying 21 percent interest over the term; later, he issued a cheque for $65,000 to Mona O'Hearn. He exchanged $32,000 cheques with Roger Campbell — Campbell's, of course, was certified, Holoday's was not — borrowed $38,000 from Martin Karp for five days, paid the Campbells back $34,500 of their June 16th loan to him, and handed Martin Karp a cheque for $40,000 as payment for the $38,000 (plus interest) he borrowed five days earlier. Karp's cheque bounced. "I told you not to cash it right away," Holoday lectured Karp. He appeared to lose control and screamed, *"Not until I told you to!"* When he calmed down, Holoday said he would issue a new cheque as soon as he was able.

"In sixty days, I'll probably be the wealthiest guy in Canada."

Michael Holoday made this boast in Randy Lang's Mississauga dentistry office on July 18, one week after confessing to Ken and Elaine Roberts that he had lost over $10 million and had no funds to repay them.

"Just recently, two months ago," Holoday added while Lang's tape machine recorded their conversation, "I was the wealthiest young guy in Canada."

"Good for you," Lang said.

"I have to tell you these things," Holoday claimed,

"cause you'll lose confidence, 'cause I owe you money. Unless you know another thirty-year-old that brings in over five million a year in income."

Holoday feared Lang might lose confidence because Holoday had just spun a series of outrageous lies to the dentist — "Is anybody else here?" Holoday had asked, looking around when he arrived — to explain why he was unable to repay Lang the half million Holoday owed him. Holoday claimed he had a $3-million stock deal closing later that week, a $4-million bid in US funds on his Barbados property, and a $2.2-million income tax rebate due from the federal government. It all added up to about $10 million coming in over the next month or so, but damned if the brokerage firms didn't raise the margin as high as 50 percent on government bonds, up from a piddling 10 percent earlier, which meant that Holoday had to cover a big chunk of a $20-million bond position. Since the $400,000 or so that he owed Lang was commingled with Holoday's position . . . well, Lang got the picture, right?

Lang got the picture, but he still wanted collateral, or proof that Lang owned part of Holoday's assets. Money had been removed from Lang's account and the account of his sister, who lived in St. Louis, Missouri, with nothing to show for it. Holoday agreed to have his lawyer draw up an agreement the next day. Then he hopped back into the Porsche 911 Turbo for his return downtown, promising to drive slowly.

Lang said that was a good idea. "People in Porches get killed, and if you died right now, I'm toast!" he called out while Holoday grinned back from behind the wheel.[5]

Two days later, Holoday called Lang with a great idea. He would give Randy Lang a series of $50,000 cheques, 12 of them, totalling $600,000. Wasn't that better than a lawyer's letter?

Roger Campbell had to admit it: Michael Holoday was not only brilliant at making investments for his clients, he was also considerate, and he looked out for his clients' interests in a way no other financial advisor seemed to do.

Take the day in mid-July 1994 when Holoday called Campbell to suggest a meeting with Campbell's accountant. "We're making you so much money, Roger," Holoday said, "that we should be looking at a way for you to meet all your income tax obligations. Better still, we should be exploring ways to cut your tax bite to the bone. Legally, of course."

On July 21, Campbell and his accountant met with Holoday in Campbell's Queen Street office. Holoday claimed he knew a man in Barbados who was an offshore tax expert. This man, Holoday said, had ways to defer Roger Campbell's income tax for 1994, legally spread it across a few years, and reduce the hit. "Because you're making so much money in Northbridge and in these short-term deals I'm doing for you," Holoday told Campbell, "you'll want to defer as much as you can."

Roger Campbell was impressed. So was his accountant, who dutifully recorded the name of the "offshore tax expert" provided by Holoday. Campbell's accountant began trying to reach the man in Barbados, but was never able to locate him.

The next day Elaine Roberts called Holoday and told him — *told* him — to come by the Fahnestock Viner offices. She had something for him to sign.

When Holoday arrived, Elaine slid a letter across her desk to him. She had composed the letter, based on Holoday's confession 11 days earlier and on details he had provided since. The letter read:

> *I, Michael Holoday, of 265 Forest Hill Road, Toronto, Ontario, Canada acknowledge my*

indebtedness to E.K. Roberts and K.A. Roberts (sometimes operating as 1079644 Ontario Inc. or Elka Estates Limited) in the amount of not less than 13 million United States dollars.

Furthermore, I acknowledge that this indebtedness consists of amounts obtained for the purposes of financing certain investment activities which were to be managed by Eastbridge Asset Management Inc. of 135 East 57th Street, New York, New York, 10022 in the name of Michael Holoday and was to consist of activities in the following strategies: Cash-futures arbitrage, and yield curve arbitrage, and from time to time foreign currency trading, covered option writing, and purchase and sale of fixed income securities. I stated to E.K. Roberts and K.A. Roberts that the principal and return were being reinvested on a daily basis. I remitted to E.K. Roberts and/or K.A. Roberts a cheque on a daily basis which purported to represent the settlement of the principal amount of the financing and the daily interest return thereon. The interest on the funds borrowed from E.K. Roberts and K.A. Roberts was calculated to be equal to the return on the investments strategy. I received a cheque or bank draft from E.K. Roberts or K.A. Roberts in the amount of the current day's financing which equalled the current day's investment.

In addition, this indebtedness consists of certain amounts which were obtained in the month of May 1994 for the purpose of financing an investment in option strategies through a commodities account at First Marathon Securities Inc. and which were not used for the stated purpose.

With respect to the investment funds which

*were to be directed by Eastbridge, I did not invest
these funds as directed. I reported a return/inter-
est on a daily basis to E.K. Roberts and then proceeded to reinvest the inflated amount after
exchanging cheques. This continued from
November 1992 through June 1994. The funds
advanced originally and from time to time by E.K.
Roberts were used by me for personal expenditures.*

*I hereby acknowledge that the third mortgage
to 1079644 Ontario Inc. in the amount of one million, six hundred thousand, against the property
known as 265 Forest Hill Road, Toronto, Canada
and registered on July 8, 1994, in the Land
Registry Office for Metropolitan Toronto Registry
Division (number 64), as Instrument Number CA
292636 is a charge with respect to funds previously received.*

*I commit to make regular repayments on
the10th business day following each month-end
in the total amount of my net division earnings
from First Marathon Securities Inc. and from
time to time in additional amounts when feasible.*

*Dated at Toronto, Canada this 22nd day of
July, 1994.*[6]

The letter represented an indictment of all of Holoday's
illegal activities relating to the Roberts over the previous
two years. In the hands of a lawyer, it might have led to
hard-nosed civil action. In the hands of a Fraud Squad
investigator, it would have launched a serious criminal
investigation.

Holoday read and signed the letter, after pointing out
and correcting a minor typographical error, then left, apol-
ogizing for his brief visit by explaining that he had an
important meeting in half an hour. Ken and Elaine

Roberts did nothing with the letter, except file it away.

Why didn't they take civil or criminal action, or at least obtain an opinion on its legal implications, criminal or civil? Perhaps Doc Roberts, at 84 years of age, wished to avoid facing the fact that Michael Holoday, his protégée and near-surrogate son, could be capable of such outrageous criminal activity. He may also have believed that public exposure of Holoday's blatant long-term fraud would make him look foolish, the Grey Fox of Canadian business taken for over $10 million by a smooth-talking kid in an Armani suit. Whatever the reason, Holoday was left to scrounge whatever funds he could find, from anyone.

Leaving the Fahnestock Viner office, Holoday launched a merry-go-round of cheques and tall tales in an attempt to keep the cash flowing, prevent his clients from contacting the police, and meet his promises to Ken and Elaine Roberts. Each day was spent fielding demands for money, creating excuses for NSF or misplaced cheques, scribbling handwritten statements to clients listing fictitious trades and impressive asset gains, pitching new financial schemes, and ducking queries from David Wood and Joe Thurman before fleeing First Marathon for his overmortgaged Forest Hill home where, in the midst of that summer's frenzy, Maureen Holoday announced she was pregnant.

Unable to pay Helen Rentis the $146,000 he owed her, Holoday pledged 200,000 shares of Consolidated Madison as security, and issued a series of post-dated cheques totalling $326,178 to Ted Gittings. Next, he called Brian Rocks, telling him that $50,000 was ready for Rocks, but Rocks first needed to open a commodity account at First Marathon "to move the money around," depositing $50,000 in the commodity account and receiving a cheque from Holoday for an equal amount.

The storm of promises and paper kept whirling

through the balance of July and all of August. Holoday confirmed in a letter to Sheldon Fenton that First Marathon owed Fenton $403,500 in "excess commissions"; Holoday agreed to pay Ken and Elaine Roberts US$3 million for the sale of his Barbados property, issued Randy Lang a letter confirming that Lang's sister held US$385,000 in her option account, and repaid Tony Noxon the US$35,000 Holoday had borrowed back on June 23. "Tell your bank to hold the cheque for ten days," Holoday instructed Noxon. When Noxon's bank refused to comply, Holoday asked for the cheque back. "I'll get it certified for you," he promised, but Noxon never saw the cheque again.

Randy Lang was persistent. Holoday confirmed in a letter dated July 20 that he owed the orthodontist $650,000 in US funds, to be paid a week later with the addition of 12 percent interest, and he sent Lang's sister in Missouri a similar letter stating that the value of her First Marathon account exceeded US$385,000. Letters were comforting but cash was better, and that's what Lang kept demanding.

"The best way to get your cash out of Northbridge," Holoday suggested to Lang on July 28, "is to open a commodities trading account." Then let's do it, Lang agreed, and that day Holoday completed a New Account Application form. On it, Lang had stated his net worth at US$2 million and his risk capital at $400,000. Back at his First Marathon office, Holoday elevated the amounts to $3.3 million and $700,000 respectively, initialling the changes.

In early August, the Campbells received cheques for $31,500, and then were persuaded by Holoday to "reinvest" $28,000 within a week, when Holoday handed across almost US$130,000 in "profits." Holoday also deposited a cheque for US$40,000 into Helen Rentis' trading account, which pacified her somewhat.

Sheldon Fenton continued to be demanding. The letter acknowledging "excess commissions" wasn't sufficient; Fenton insisted on a schedule of repayments to cover his loss, and Holoday provided one to Fenton's lawyers.

Holoday needed still more money, an endless stream of recirculating cash. He could barely accommodate the August $16,000 mortgage interest payment (the first and last he would ever make) to Ken and Elaine Roberts, and most of his local clients were maxed out by now — all he could do was keep money moving in a circle, like a hamster in a wheel, motion without progress. He would have to look farther afield, as far back as Revelstoke and beyond, to the family of his boyhood chum Ervin Schleith and, specifically, Ervin's father Kurt.

Kurt Schleith had fulfilled a dream of sorts. From his hilltop Tudor cottage, he could look beyond his apple orchard to a million-dollar view of the Okanagan Valley. His son Ervin was piloting jetliners back and forth across the continent, and Kurt's investments were doing well. Or so it seemed.

That spring, Kurt and his wife arrived home from a Saturday morning shopping trip to hear the telephone ringing. It was Michael, who sounded elated. "Kurt, I just made you another sixty-eight thousand dollars US," Holoday crowed. "Things are really moving down here. I'll be working all weekend to make you more."

All weekend? Kurt inquired. Even on a Sunday?

"Hey, you can trade anytime," Holoday explained. "I'm making money for you!"

A few weeks later, Holoday called with more good news: Kurt's account at First Marathon was doing so well that Kurt needed to raise his risk asset level from US$500,000 to US$700,000. At first blush, it seemed strange to increase your risk level because your asset value had risen. "It's just a formality," Holoday assured him over the telephone. Holoday even offered to draft a letter and fax it for Kurt to sign, and he did, putting Kurt's own address at the top as though it were Kurt's personal letterhead, a thoughtful thing to do.[7]

When Holoday called Kurt Schleith from Toronto on the morning of August 4, 1994, to chat about a few things, and gradually eased into a deal, by the way, that Kurt might be interested in hearing about, Kurt listened. Holoday had a short-term investment, he explained, for a few select clients only. It was some in-house trading, done for the firm's account — the firm, of course, being First Marathon. There was no risk, and the deal couldn't miss, but it would take a minimum of US$200,000 to participate. In return, Kurt would make $24,000 in four days, which was a hell of a profit, you had to admit, especially for a deal backed by First Marathon itself. "You interested?" Holoday said, "because I've got other people to call if you're not."

Sure, Kurt was interested. Who wouldn't be? A chance to make 12 percent profit in four days, backed by First Marathon? Kurt sent Holoday the US$200,000 and, true to Holoday's word, US$224,000 was wired directly into Kurt's bank account in Kelowna.

Kurt Schleith was hooked.

Less than a week later, on August 15, Holoday called Schleith from Toronto. It was happening again — an in-house trade where special First Marathon clients like Kurt were being offered a chance to make big bucks, maybe more than last time. Same deal as before — $200,000 now and $220,000, $230,000, maybe more, in two or three days, four at the most, but the longer it took, the more profit would be earned. Did Kurt want in?

Schleith wired the money. A week later, he received $240,000 from Holoday. No wonder Michael Holoday was managing partner, futures division, of First Marathon

Securities, a kid the same age as Kurt's son Ervin. The boy was a genius.

Kurt Schleith didn't know, had no way of knowing, that he was Holoday's unwitting dance partner. There were no in-house trades, and no profits to be made. Holoday was simply moving money from one of Schleith's First Marathon accounts to another, and back again. The "profits" consisted of funds withdrawn from Schleith's own account.

Meanwhile, the Boy Genius was scrambling faster than ever, the hamster wheel spinning so fast it threatened to fly off its bearings.

On August 10, Holoday called Chester Hooper, who was relaxing with his wife at their mortgage-free home in BC, about the proposal he had sent the Hoopers a few weeks earlier. Drafted by a prestigious law firm, the proposal stated that Holoday and First Marathon were jointly contemplating a mutual fund based on commodities trading, and outlined the proposed fund in a dozen pages of reassuring legalese. The deal needed bridge financing, Holoday explained in a follow-up telephone call, and a few selected clients were being invited aboard. If the Hoopers invested $200,000 in the nascent fund, Holoday explained, they would receive a $25,000 bonus within a month or two, plus substantial returns.

Hooper explained to Holoday, in a long distance telephone call, that he and his wife didn't have $200,000 in cash.

"Hey, no problem, Ches," Holoday replied. "Just mortgage your house for the two hundred grand."

Holoday was convincing. First Marathon, where Holoday was managing partner, futures division, was a participant along with a big Toronto law firm. It looked like a good deal. Hooper agreed, and called his lawyer, directing him to take $200,000 out of the retirement home that he and his wife had planned for years. When the paperwork was completed two weeks later, Hooper did as Holoday instructed: He wired the money directly into Holoday's personal chequing account in Toronto.

On August 15, Dianne Sone began demanding the $105,000 lent to Holoday for two weeks back in early July. "It's coming," he assured her. "It'll be in your account, you'll see it in next month's statement."

The following day, Holoday asked First Marathon to no longer withhold income taxes from his commission cheques, explaining that he expected to be in a loss position for 1994 and thus would pay no tax. Next, he called Helen Rentis. "You know that $40,000 I paid you last week?" Holoday said. "I need to borrow it back." It was an emergency, Holoday explained, he wouldn't be bothering her otherwise, and he was good for it, wasn't he? Hadn't he paid most of his loan back already? Naturally, he would pay interest, but he really needed a $40,000 certified cheque today.

Helen Rentis still trusted him, still believed that anybody who qualified as a managing partner, futures division, of First Marathon Securities, had to be on the level. So she issued the cheque.

Holoday had become a financial version of a crack cocaine addict, doing and saying whatever it took to get his hands on other people's money. That week, he borrowed US$350,000 from Paul Simpkin, pledging (again) his US$108,000 T-bill as collateral, and added another $35,000 from Roger Campbell. He transferred US$60,000 to the account of Helen Rentis, which made her feel better even if he still owed her $86,000; he gave Roger Campbell a cheque for $114,400; and he talked Martin Karp into exchanging $25,000 cheques "as a favour."

Marlena Titian, a friend of Maureen Holoday's, had

been persuaded like other friends and in-laws to entrust her retirement savings to Michael Holoday when Holoday joined First Marathon. On August 19, Holoday proposed that Marlena make a five-day loan to First Marathon of $61,000 in US funds. She would earn 4 percent interest on the loan, about 300 percent on an annual basis. Marlena Titian agreed when Holoday submitted details of the loan to her on a First Marathon letterhead, and Holoday added almost $100,000 in Canadian funds to his dwindling cash.[8]

He looked around for more. Sitting in Dianne Sone's account was her $50,000 Canada Savings Bond, the one she had insisted he was never to cash, under any circumstances. Holoday had once blurted to Dianne that, thanks to her association with John and Carole Boczan, she was like family to him. Well, hell — what are families for anyway? And he cashed the bond.

Sometime in mid-August, Joe Thurman received a telephone call from a man who refused to identify himself, but who insisted on passing important information to the compliance officer. "Watch out for Michael Holoday and Roy O'Hearn," the caller told Thurman. "There's a raw deal going on between them. They're looking to put a lot of money offshore." When Thurman again asked who was calling, the man replied, "Just look at those two guys," and hung up.

It sounded like a scene from a Sam Spade movie, but Thurman dutifully examined Roy O'Hearn's account statements for any sign of . . . what? What would indicate that O'Hearn was illegally transferring funds outside of Canada, presumably to avoid taxation? Whatever it was, Thurman couldn't locate it. Next, Thurman stopped by Holoday's office. Did Holoday have any explanation for such a call?

Holoday shrugged. Awhile back, he told Thurman,

O'Hearn had wanted some money withdrawn from his account and sent to him immediately, so Holoday used a courier service. "Maybe it was the courier," Holoday suggested. It sounded like a far-fetched guess to Thurman, but he decided not to pursue the matter any further.[9]

Helen Rentis didn't know how Holoday tracked her down at the convention she was attending in Metro Toronto Convention Centre but he did, leaving an urgent message. Tracy Ellis was on her way there, the message read, to escort Rentis to the bank and obtain a certified cheque for $60,000, payable to Michael Holoday. Rentis wanted to know what was going on, how Holoday could be so presumptuous. Who the hell was he to assume he could take $60,000 out of her account whenever he felt like it, and dispatch Tracy Ellis to get the amount certified?

It's a chance to make money, she was told. It's backed by First Marathon Securities, she was assured. Not good enough, Rentis said. She wanted more. Okay, Holoday said. He would do something. She met Tracy Ellis, seated in the back of the ubiquitous stretch limo, and rode to First Marathon. There, Holoday handed her three undated personal cheques for $20,000 each. "I'll tell you when you can cash them," he said. The profits, he promised, would go directly into her account.

Rentis agreed, with reluctance, and returned to her convention.

Ed Fleming[10] had never liked Michael Holoday, never trusted him. There was something too slick, too smooth about the guy, and it wasn't just the expensive suits and the V-12 Jaguar, and the way he sent his assistant in a chauffeured stretch limo to pick up cheques. The guy had "phoney" written all over him. Fleming was branch manager of Roger Campbell's bank. He liked Roger and Penny

Campbell, they were nice people and fine clients, but he didn't like what he saw in the exchange of cheques between Holoday and the Campbells. To his eye, it had all the earmarks of a classic kiting scheme, something he knew the Campbells would never engage in. Not knowingly anyway.

Roger and Penny Campbell were preparing to leave to visit Penny's family in the UK on August 25, 1994, when Fleming called. The Campbells had better get hold of Michael Holoday, Fleming suggested, because a bunch of cheques he had written the Campbells were apparently made of rubber.

The Campbells said they had a late afternoon flight to London. Couldn't it wait? Not with the amount of money involved here, Fleming suggested. Roger Campbell called Holoday and explained the situation while Penny Campbell managed to get them booked on a flight leaving the next day. Holoday agreed to come over for a meeting.

In the branch manager's office that afternoon, Fleming's disdain for Holoday, who sat stone-faced in a corner chair, was strong enough to lower the temperature of the room. Fleming displayed two cheques for Roger Campbell and Holoday himself to inspect, more than $50,000 worth. Fleming had checked; there was not nearly enough in Holoday's account to cover them. Holoday, Fleming said, had better make good on these cheques right away or Holoday's superiors at First Marathon would hear about it.

Holoday laughed and tried to wave off the branch manager's concern. Simple banking errors, he said. A lot of transactions took place around closing time, that's when the money was made, which just happens to be the time a lot of banks close, or delay transfers until the following day. It would be settled easily, what's the big deal? All it would have taken was a telephone call to Holoday at First

Marathon. There was no need for this panic meeting at the bank, no need for the Campbells to delay their trip to England. Fleming was just overreacting . . .

Today is Thursday, Fleming interrupted. Holoday had until Monday, Tuesday at the very latest, to make good on the cheques Holoday had written to Roger Campbell. If he didn't, all hell would break loose.

Holoday assured Fleming that the cheques would clear.

Outside the branch, standing at the curb with Roger Campbell, Holoday's fury erupted. Who the hell was Fleming to talk to him like that, and in front of a client too? Hell, the banks are the ones who screwed up, not Holoday. You know what the problem with that guy is? Holoday said, pointing toward the bank branch. His problem is that he's a bank branch manager making fifty grand a year if he's lucky, and I'm making a million or more a year, and making you rich at the same time, and the guy's jealous, *he's jealous, that's all!*

Campbell said Fleming wasn't such a bad guy, he was just looking after his clients.

"Yeah?" Holoday said. "Well, get him off my back!"

Roger and Penny Campbell left for the UK a day late, and Roger called Fleming from England on Monday. Yes, the branch manager confirmed, Holoday had made good on the cheques, just as he promised.

Campbell felt better. Perhaps Holoday had been right all along. It had just been a banking error.

Kurt Schleith no longer had any doubts about Michael Holoday. How could he? The young man had made Kurt $64,000 profit on Kurt's $200,000 investment in just a few days, and those were American dollars too. These weren't paper profits either; Kurt had the money in his bank account. So when Michael called Kurt on August 26, the

same day the Campbells left for the UK and Holoday finally listed his Forest Hill home for sale at an asking price of
$1.68 million, Kurt was all ears. Another $200,000 in-
house trade? Sure. Kurt wired the money, just as he had
ten days earlier.

Three days later, Holoday again called Schleith, this
time to borrow $90,000 with half of it paid back by
September 1 and the other by September 6, to get Holoday
over a cash-flow hump while a $600,000 deal was being
finalized. Well, Kurt thought, why not?

Orthodontist Randy Lang was being more forgiving to
Holoday than might be expected. Lang was Michael's good
buddy, the guy who joked about driving Porsches at high
speed and the prospects of Holoday being "run over by a
truck," leaving Lang with nothing to prove his investments in Northbridge were hovering around a million
dollars in value.

But, damn it, where was Lang's money?

Commingled with other investments in Holoday's
account, Lang was assured. It would take time to sort
everything out, there was nothing to worry about. As a
matter of fact, Holoday suggested in late August, he would
provide Lang's lawyers with a total list of his assets, and
sign any document the lawyers prepared to ensure payment of the nearly US$1 million that Holoday owed Lang
and Lang's sister. Lang's lawyers could draft an ironclad
agreement for Lang, and Holoday would pay their fees
himself. Hey, it was the least he could do. It seemed to be
more than a good-faith gesture by Holoday, so Randy Lang
agreed.

Using the same list of assets he had provided Ken and
Elaine Roberts back on June 9, Holoday submitted the figures to Osler, Hoskin & Harcourt, Lang's law firm, adding
a modification here and there. He no longer had $235,000

in cash, and the value of his SDI shares had dropped from $1,618,718.75 to $275,000. The Ferrari had been removed from his fleet of automobiles, and the $1,072,000 in trading account funds was now labelled *Revenue Canada Refund*. But Holoday continued to claim $1.4 million equity in the Forest Hill house, $300,000 in jewellery, $49,000 in a non-existent RRSP and, most appealing of all, the Barbados property valued at $1,206,000.

Lang's lawyers fastened on Holoday's real estate holdings. They would draft a promissory note confirming Holoday's indebtedness to Lang for $807,000 in US funds, to be repaid to their client at the rate of $25,000 each week, by certified cheque or bank draft, to Osler, Hoskins & Harcourt. The payments were to be delivered to the law firm each Friday by 5 p.m. beginning October 7 and continuing until the debt was paid back. Along with Holoday's agreement to the deal, Osler Hoskins insisted on holding the mortgage to Michael and Maureen's Cobourg house and Barbados property, and demanded confirmation of Holoday's earned income to date.

Holoday agreed to every condition. What choice did he have? Besides, he couldn't afford to waste time arm-wrestling with a bunch of lawyers. Now he had to start bringing in $25,000 in American money each week just to meet his obligation to Lang.

It was Labour Day weekend, and Holoday enjoyed one last vacation at his Lake Simcoe cottage, racing his cigarette boat, living the good life.

Holoday didn't believe things could grow more desperate. But they did, from the moment he entered his office Tuesday morning.

Helen Rentis' $20,000 cheque had been returned NSF. What, she wanted to know in a voice that could fast-freeze a side of beef, even over the telephone, was Holoday going to do about it? It must be a mistake, he said. He would look into it.

Roger and Penny Campbell called, having arrived home from the UK. Holoday had promised to have up-to-date statements on their account when they returned. Where the hell were they? "Didn't Tracy send them to you?" Holoday said. Things got worse for Tracy that afternoon when Kurt Schleith called, looking for returns on his third $200,000 investment. "Tracy goofed up," he told Schleith. "I'm this close to firing her."

Tracy couldn't help Holoday deal with the other crises that began popping up during the balance of the week. Another $20,000 cheque to Rentis bounced; Holoday's brother-in-law Paul Legere wanted $9,000 from his account to buy a new front-loader ("I'll write you a personal cheque," Holoday said, "It'll be faster"); and Holoday scribbled and mailed a cheque for $25,000 to Chester Hooper in Vancouver (it was returned NSF).

Brian Rocks had been pestering Holoday for his money for weeks. Based on Holoday's assurances of Rocks' new wealth through his Northbridge investments, Rocks and his expectant wife had purchased a new, larger home, making a much smaller down payment than planned because Holoday had been unable to free up funds. Now Rocks' personal debt load was too high for his comfort, he was carrying a massive mortgage, and Holoday was still stalling about the $75,000 he owed Rocks. The day after Labour Day 1994, Holoday handed Rocks three cheques for $25,000 in US funds, each dated on successive days, and Rocks left them with his bank, depositing the first and instructing the bank to process the next two as they came due.

Two days later, Rocks was about to leave for an afternoon game of golf when he received a call from his bank manager. The first of Holoday's cheques had not cleared,

Rocks was told. The next one wouldn't either. "Don't even bother trying the third," Rocks said. What the hell was Holoday up to now? Rocks wondered.

An hour later, Rocks was on the golf course with his buddy John Keen, the man who had persuaded Rocks to invest with Holoday in the first place. Keen answered a call on his cell phone while they walked toward the third hole. He folded the cell phone, tucked it back into his pocket and tossed Brian Rocks a strange look. "That was about Mike Holoday," Keen replied, and Rocks said "What about him?"

Keen explained that somebody had called to say that Holoday had been trying to borrow money, lots of it, from people in the city, and he had been turned down. Nobody was willing to float him a loan. Holoday couldn't borrow a cent.

That was enough for Rocks. He dropped his putter in his golf bag, strode off the golf course, got into his car, and raced downtown to confront Holoday, who knew as soon as Rocks entered his office that he was about to face another crisis.

Rocks waved off Holoday's attempt at a warm greeting. "I need money right now, today, from my account," Rocks said.

Holoday closed his office door and lowered his voice. "Brian, I'll be honest with you," the broker said. "Don't worry about your money. I'll show you what I've got." He left Rocks sitting there while he had Tracy Ellis print a list of his assets, the same list he had originally prepared for Doc and Elaine Roberts three months earlier. "Take a look at this," he said, handing it across his desk to Rocks. "There's millions of dollars there, see? More than enough to cover what I owe you. Basically, I've just got some short-term cash flow problems."

Rocks fixed Holoday with his hard stare, and after squirming a little, Holoday had an idea. Why didn't Rocks

help him sell the cigarette boat, *Bad Company?* Then
Rocks would know money was coming in, and could get
some of it for himself. The boat was worth half a million
dollars, which would easily settle Holoday's debt to Rocks.

Rocks had seen evidence of Holoday's wealth. He had
seen the boat, the cars, the Forest Hill house, the office
facility, the managing partner title. He had no reason to
doubt the list of assets (referred to by Tracy Ellis as
"Mike's Garage Sale") he held in his hand. Rocks decided
he could either work with Holoday, or work against him to
recover the money Holoday owed. It would be better to
work with him, Rocks decided.

"I'll help you list the boat," Rocks agreed. "The money
comes to me."

Holoday said that was fine with him. But Rocks' money
was safe anyway. There was really nothing to worry about.

Ted Gittings was a gentleman, always would be. A gentleman respects the concerns of others, never raises his voice,
and maintains a high moral standard in everything he
does. Gittings had behaved like a gentleman with Michael
Holoday for almost five years, forgiving errors from time
to time, and congratulating Holoday on the enormous success the broker seemed to be having with the money
Gittings and his wife had entrusted to him.

For several months, Ted Gittings and his wife had
been trying to withdraw some of the funds invested at
First Marathon, which now amounted, they believed, to at
least US$400,000. Their requests for withdrawals went
unheeded. Tracy Ellis would forget to do the paperwork,
the bank was slow transferring money, the back office was
a mess, the computers had been down. The excuses came
laden with apologies from Holoday, but the bank didn't
cash apologies; they cashed cheques, which Holoday finally provided in early September. Drawn on Michael and

Maureen's personal US dollar account, one cheque was written for $122,749.54 and the other for $203,427.94.

"Don't cash them yet," Holoday told Gittings when he handed the cheques across. "Not until I tell you to."

Don't cash them? Gittings asked. All the money belonged to him and his wife. Why did they have to wait?

Holoday explained he had made some bad trades, he was going through tough times, he had even listed his house for sale. Holoday assured Gittings he would overcome this and be stronger than ever, but for now he just didn't want Ted to cash the cheques, okay?

Always the gentleman, Gittings expressed sympathy and understanding. At home that evening, he wrote a letter to Holoday that demonstrated Gittings' empathy and the esteem Holoday retained in the minds of his clients, almost to the day that the pyramid finally crumbled.

Dear Michael, Gittings wrote:

You're going through some tough times. I'm sorry, and I hope they're soon behind you. I've enjoyed our relationship over the past five years and hope to continue with you for many more.

Unfortunately, however, your current problems are affecting me, causing me stress and sleepless nights that I don't need at this stage of my life. The purpose of this letter is to ask you to set up a meeting early next week with your accountant and to provide me written acknowledgement of what you owe me and a realistic timetable I can count on for the repayment of our loans to you and the correction of my First Marathon account.

Gittings' immediate concern, he explained was the need to cover $13,000 for a vacation he and his wife had booked six months earlier. He went on to list the various investments made by Gittings, and promises broken by Holoday. It wasn't just for the vacation that Gittings needed the money, it was for retirement income, adding:

> *You're young, Mike, with many productive years ahead. At 66, I don't have that luxury. I'll be as cooperative as I can but I must insist on receiving from your accountant a firm commitment to resolve this matter over a specific period of time. Let's do this early next week.*
> *Best regards,*[11]

The following day, Gittings delivered the letter himself, leaving it with Tracy Ellis who explained that Michael was off somewhere at an important meeting.

Kurt Schleith was growing uneasy. It had been almost two weeks since he wired his third $200,000 "investment" to Holoday, and he had yet to see anything of the $90,000. He began calling Holoday daily; this time the bank was blamed. "I went down there to the CIBC, Kurt," Holoday said, "and yours was on the bottom of the pile. She just never got to the damn thing when she was supposed to." Holoday told his client he had torn a strip off her, and told her to get $175,000 to BC by wire right away, if she wanted to keep her job and Holoday's business. Presumably she did, shaken by Holoday's demeanour and threat.

But the next day, morning in Kelowna, high noon on Bay Street, Kurt answered the telephone to hear a different Michael Holoday from the one he had been talking with over the past several months.

"Kurt," Holoday began, "I violated our agreement."
Schleith asked what he meant.
"Well, I invested the whole amount," Holoday said, "all

four hundred thousand, instead of just thirty percent of it, like you told me to. Now the market's gone the other way and I was in danger of losing it all, all your money. So what I had to do, Kurt, was . . . you know that hundred and seventy-five thousand I wired you yesterday? Well, I had to reverse it because I needed it back here to hedge things for you." If Schleith could wire Holoday forty-nine thousand American, Holoday could complete the hedging and start getting Schleith's money out of the fund bit by bit. "It's locked up in capital, that's the problem," Holoday explained.

Kurt Schleith didn't like the sound of this. Holoday had almost $300,000 in US funds of his money, and now Holoday was asking for another $49,000 because Holoday made a mistake? What was going on? And by the way, how do you call back $175,000 once you've sent it over the wire?

Holoday assured the older man everything was all right, things were going to work out and Holoday would provide daily reports, Schleith's account was in good shape at the moment, worth almost US$700,000, the man was making money hand over fist, this was just a glitch.

Kurt Schleith calmed the doubts in his mind and agreed to wire Holoday another $49,000 in US funds. Holoday, in turn, promised to keep Schleith informed with daily telephone calls.

Kurt Schleith's First Marathon account on that date, September 12, 1994, showed a deficit of $31.71.

September unfolded in an accelerating whirlwind of clients demanding their money and Holoday cajoling funds, moving the cash back and forth like a cartoon character trying to stem leaks in the Hoover dam.

Robert Gray, the former stockbroker, needed $200,000 from his account on October 1 to close a real estate deal. Holoday wrote a letter confirming the money was in

Gray's account, and assuring him it would be available when needed.

He convinced Penny Campbell to invest $27,400 from her First Marathon account into a short-term bond play, a "can't miss deal" she should get in on, but they would have to work quickly. The deal involved transferring $27,400 from Penny Campbell's First Marathon account into her personal bank account, then issuing a cheque for the same amount to Holoday personally. "I'm trying to make you some money here," Holoday promised. "We'll put everything back in your trading account, soon as the deal's done. How does that sound?"

The way Holoday described it, the deal sounded fine. After all, $27,400 represented less than 10 percent of the balance Holoday claimed was in her First Marathon account balance, and that was as much as she was prepared to risk on speculative deals. So she agreed: Holoday arrived in a chauffeured limo with a cheque from First Marathon, took Penny Campbells' personal cheque for the same amount, and returned to Bay Street. The next week, he called her again. "The deal went through," he told her. "The money's back in your account, and we've got a chance to do it again. What do you say?"

Everything appeared to be working. The First Marathon cheque for $27,400 had been honoured. Why not? On September 19, the cheque exchange was repeated, and repeated again on September 23 for $27,500. Things seemed to be working smoothly; First Marathon's cheques were honoured, Holoday invested the funds, and the $27,000 or so was being recycled through her trading account.

Except that it wasn't. Each cheque Holoday handed across to Penny Campbell was in fact a fresh withdrawal from her First Marathon account. By the end of September, when Penny Campbell assumed she had realized a profit from the same $27,500 over three investments, Holoday had actually managed to remove $82,300 from her account without her knowledge.

Tony Noxon had been trying to retrieve a cheque from Holoday for almost two months now. He had invested $35,000 in US funds with the broker back in June, and Holoday had finally given Noxon a cheque for $37,000 on July 29. "Tell your bank to hold it for ten days," Holoday instructed Noxon, and when the bank refused Holoday, in a fit of pique, took the cheque from Noxon and said he would have it certified himself, damn it.

Holoday had been ducking Noxon's near-constant requests to have the cheque returned, and on September 15 he finally explained the situation to his client. "I put it in commodities for you," Holoday claimed. It was one of those opportunities where he had to work fast, Holoday said, but everything turned out fine. Holoday had managed to build the original $35,000 to $45,800 in Yankee funds. Now he wanted to make a personal loan. If he could borrow that same $45,800, Holoday would pay it back with a healthy rate of interest. Noxon agreed. His broker, after all, had generated over $10,000 in profit from a $35,000 investment in three months. Why not?

Kurt Schleith was hearing from Holoday on an almost daily basis, the younger man assuring his client that things were going well, that the value of Schleith's account continued to grow. But that was only on paper. He began faxing documents to Schleith, pages with columns of printed figures listing various bought and sold T-bills, and additional trades added in Holoday's characteristic scrawl. One sheet indicated a "Market Position" of $524,039.13 and a "Cash Position" of $185,000, all in US Funds.

"Now we have to start working that down to cash,"

Holoday said in mid-September. "I'll need another fifty thousand, Kurt."

Really? Kurt wondered. Why did it take more money to get back money Kurt already owned?

It was a matter of maximizing returns, Holoday said. The market was moving, and they stood to make money no matter which direction the market went, but they needed to secure their position and that meant expanding their options. Without it, the entire half-million was at risk.

Holoday was as convincing as ever. On September 21, Kurt Schleith wired a further $50,000 in US funds to his account at First Marathon, and called Holoday to confirm the transfer.

When Holoday hung up the telephone, he confronted Roger Gordon, who arrived at Holoday's office doorway wavering between anger and frustration.

Gordon had been leaving messages with Holoday for weeks. The family's dream house on the hill was half-finished, but work couldn't proceed until some outstanding bills were paid. "I need the money by the middle of September," Gordon reminded Holoday on one message. "I'm coming down to pick it up tomorrow," he added, and Holoday advised him against it. "You'll lose money if you take it now," Holoday said. "You'll pay a penalty for early withdrawal. Wait a week."

Things hadn't sounded right to Gordon. He wanted more assurance that he would receive his money someday, so he called First Marathon and asked to speak to someone about Michael Holoday. He was assured that he had nothing to worry about. Roger told himself and his family to be patient.[12]

Roger Gordon pleaded with the bank and various local tradesmen and suppliers, people who knew and respected him, assuring them that the money existed, it was tied up at his broker's, but he would have it all on September 21.

And now here he was.

Holoday stalled Roger Gordon long enough to obtain two cashier's cheques in Gordon's name, one for $11,000 and another for $12,000. "Okay, here's what you have to do," he told Gordon. "Take them downstairs and have them issue one cheque for twenty-three thousand dollars in my name."

"What do you mean, *your* name?" Gordon said. "Just give me my cheque. I've got no time to waste here."

"This is the only way we can get all your money out without penalty," Holoday explained. "Just get the cheque in my name and bring it back."

Roger Gordon had been trusting Michael Holoday for five years. If Holoday said this was the best way to do the deal, that's what he assumed he should do.

Fifteen minutes later, Roger Gordon returned, having exchanged two cheques in his name for one certified cheque in Holoday's name.

"Let's see that," Holoday said, and Gordon handed the $23,000 cheque across to him. Holoday inspected the cheque, thanked Gordon, and said he would issue another cheque for Gordon later.

Gordon couldn't believe his ears. He and his family were living in a half-finished house, they were over their eyeballs in debt, and their creditors were making threats. He had $150,000 in his account at First Marathon. Why couldn't he get his hands on it?

"Everything'll be okay," Holoday assured him. "I'll bring the cheque out to you tomorrow."

Roger Gordon returned home empty-handed and confused. What the heck had just happened? One minute he had money in his hand, the next minute it was in Holoday's hands, and Gordon was left with nothing but a promise.[13]

Paul Simpkin had been sympathizing with his belea-
guered broker for several months. No matter what
Michael Holoday seemed to do, somebody else was always
fouling things up. The back office at First Marathon had
made an error of $19,500 on Simpkin's account earlier in
the year, and it still hadn't been corrected. Tracy Ellis had
screwed up more than once, and now she wasn't in the
office to do things Holoday had instructed her to do. Then
there was all that stuff about hedging activities Holoday
had taken to protect Simpkin's trades, and how compliance never seemed to understand what their Whiz Kid
was doing.

By mid-September, Simpkin knew Holoday was struggling with a lot of things, including the pressures of a market that just never seemed to go his way, and the need to
restructure the capital investment of the futures division.
So when Simpkin telephoned Holoday yet again to clear
up this missing $19,500 and to enquire about more paper-
work Simpkin had been asked to sign and return, the
older man felt a need to play Dutch Uncle to Holoday who
was, after all, less than half Simpkin's age.

"You know, I'm as old as your father and all that stuff,"
Simpkin said from his house in Campbellford, a hundred
miles to the east, "but you're a young man, and a little bad
luck means nothing to a man of your age." He was repeating, in his own manner, the same thoughts expressed by
Ted Gittings a few days earlier.

"Yeah, I know," Holoday agreed. "That's what everybody tells me. They say it'll end, and 'You're only thirty
years old.' But, you know, it's been three and a half
months of solving these problems, this restructuring, and
it feels like thirty years."

"When you're your age," Simpkin sympathized, "it
seems like a mountain has fallen right on your shoulders,
but believe me, you generally work through it, and it

comes out the better and (you're) smiling afterwards."

Holoday said he could feel it "getting toward that last phase." He complained about all the lawyers he had to hire, and boasted about "a chunk of money from the government in six weeks, and a couple of corporate payables coming in, you know, they're large numbers."

"You got too much talent to be thrown by a little thing like that," Simpkin assured him.

"Mind you," Holoday said, "the problems I'm going through at my age are bigger than what most guys your age ever dream of going through." If Holoday were referring to dozens of clients who were constantly demanding the return of their $20 million from him, he had a point. He couldn't resist a little bragging. "I've been used to those numbers on the plus side so, it's just a game of Monopoly, I guess . . ."

When it was all over, Simpkin suggested, maybe Holoday would be a meaner man.

"I think I'll be a hell of a lot meaner," Holoday snapped, and that made Simpkin laugh.[14]

A week later, Holoday was in the Fahnestock Viner office again, assuring Ken and Elaine Roberts that things were coming together, he would recover their money. In fact, he told them, he was off to Kelowna the following week to discuss the sale of his Barbados property with a group of wealthy German investors, who were willing to pay $2.5 million for the land. And Northbridge was still alive, it was going to be licensed any day now. Once it was up and running, Holoday's income would rise, he'd have the cash flow he needed, things were going to work out, he promised.

Ten minutes later he was back in his office, fending off another potential disaster. Helen Rentis was livid. Holoday's cheques to her were bouncing like a box of ping-pong balls dropped from a great height. What the hell was he going to do about it? The best Holoday could offer was a promissory note agreeing to pay her US$385,000 by March 31, 1995, which he faxed to her while she was in Saskatoon on a business trip. Roger Gordon called several times a day. Where the hell was his money? And Margaret Raines was back. First Marathon was claiming a $130,000 loss in her account. How could that happen? Holoday assured her it was an error, she actually made 8 percent profit the previous month, and if she would stop by his office, he would issue a promissory note covering her losses.

Margaret Raines needed such a promise, such evidence of her unrealized wealth. Based on Holoday's assertions of her earnings in his "pooled account" she had moved into a larger, more expensive apartment and begun dispensing her apparent wealth in a generous manner, paying the college tuition for a friend's son, and helping the children of other acquaintances cover their education debts. These actions brought joy and satisfaction to her. Margaret Raines wanted to share the riches she had managed to acquire, she believed, through management of her funds by Michael Holoday.

"Your money's safe," Holoday assured her. "Come by my office and I'll give you a promissory note, good as gold, secured by a US T-bill."

Margaret Raines promised that she would, sometime later in the week.

Roy O'Hearn was more difficult to fend off. After two cheques from Holoday to O'Hearn, for $100,000 and $30,000, were returned NSF, O'Hearn was losing his patience. In response, Holoday assigned his US T-bill for $108,000 to O'Hearn as security, and promised to send O'Hearn $10,000 each day to retire a total debt now approaching $250,000. The cheques arrived on schedule for two weeks, but seven of the ten O'Hearn received were declared NSF.

Each time O'Hearn called Holoday, he received more promises and more outrageous explanations, all recorded on tape. One September morning, it was Holoday's turn to call O'Hearn, this time to complain about the latest in a series of harassing telephone calls from Dr. Oswald John and his wife. John was demanding the $150,000 he claimed had been removed from his account without John's knowledge, a claim dating back to the Deloitte & Touche audit letter almost three years earlier. In that morning's telephone call, both John and his wife demanded that Holoday do something or they were going to the police, along with their former friend Roy O'Hearn.

Holoday's panicky conversation to O'Hearn, seeking to smooth things over, reveals a dark and nasty side of the young broker, as recorded by O'Hearn:

HOLODAY: . . . *and he, ah, basically he assumed that I have to cover that loss plus the opportunity cost of that capital, which has never been allowed me, to pay it down. That's pure and simple outright blackmail, and the (Deloitte & Touche) letter that he signed at Midland Walwyn in 1991* (sic), *signing off on this issue, and he's threatened afterwards to go back. You know the way he is . . .*

O'HEARN: . . . *I never hardly see him anymore. I even forget what he looks like. . .*

HOLODAY: *Now he's fuckin' greedy, just like the rest of these East Indians out there, you know? You know the way they are, Roy. . . . Anyway, I was rolling so hard I figured, instead of having lawyers go at it, (it would) be easier just to pay this guy off, but obviously when you go into a cash-flow crunch you're not in a position to pay him off anymore. And quite frankly I've reviewed my records (and) from what I can see Ozzie has screwed me for about three hundred thousand US bucks. . .*

O'HEARN: *Three hundred thousand. . .*

HOLODAY: *I'm in a position we're. . . according to my lawyer, I can go after everything he's got.*

O'HEARN: *Okay, that's the thing to do then.*

HOLODAY: *I have to. . . . Now he's screaming down my phone line, saying he's going to tell everybody at the firm about this. Well, I've already told him, you know. . . . Give him whatever the fuck he wants, I've had it with the guy.*

O'HEARN: *Well, how did you screw him?*

HOLODAY: *I didn't screw up.*

O'HEARN: *Well, how did. . . how's he blackmailing you then?*

HOLODAY: *How have I let him blackmail me?*

O'HEARN: *Yeah.*

HOLODAY: *Pure stupidity.*

O'HEARN: *. . . I thought you owed him a lot of money. He told me he couldn't get any money out of you, you owed him a lot of money.*

HOLODAY: *Yeah, bullshit. I'll show you everything. I want you to be aware of this.*

O'HEARN: *All right. Show it to me, maybe tomorrow. . . .*

HOLODAY: *Yeah. . . . You added . . . this problem*

> *with him this morning has cost us a fucking trade. It's cost me about fifty thousand in US profit . . . the market's gone up twenty-two thirty-seconds. I was down here, the fucking draft might make me thirty-five US from our, our capital structure here. I was supposed to put into the market and that phone rang, and I should sue him for that.*

O'HEARN: *Well, maybe you can, I don't know. . . . Now, what about the courier that's coming here with ten grand today, where is he?*

HOLODAY: *First of all, I haven't even checked into that.*

O'HEARN: *Check into it.*

HOLODAY: *Let me complete this talk on Ozzie. I told him I'll talk to him at nine o'clock tonight. Let him cool off. I'm gonna tell him what I just told you. . .*

O'HEARN: *Okay. . .*

HOLODAY: *I'm doing the right thing, Roy.*

O'HEARN: *Look. . . . I don't know who's right and who's wrong here. . .*

HOLODAY: *Do you realize his wife got on the phone today and started swearing at me?*

O'HEARN: *She did?*

HOLODAY: *That son of a bitch, you should have heard him, her yelling at him behind the scenes. . . . That's why he got all riled up. . . . He's been milking me, and it's gone on too long. . .*[15]

Every client of Holoday's, it seemed, was calling him. Some complained, others pleaded, and their emotions ranged from confusion and sympathy to outrage and aggression. Holoday scribbled fictitious statements, drafted promissory notes, sold short-term "investments," and scratched out cheques, all in an atmosphere of pandemonium and chaos so frantic that Margaret Raines, arriving on September 27 to pick up the promissory note for $130,000, stood watching the madness — Holoday flitting back and forth between his telephone, Tracy's computer, and Chuck Oliver's trading desk, alternately shouting and pleading — and decided to return some other day, when Holoday was less distraught.

The next day, Wednesday September 28, Michael Holoday made a decision that amounted to career suicide. Perhaps the look on Margaret Raines' face the previous day, or memories of Ted Gittings' and Paul Simpkin's words did it. More likely, it was either an urge to relieve the unending panic, or a wild chance that his story might be believed. Whatever it was, as soon as Holoday arrived at First Marathon in the morning, he called David Wood's office.

When Holoday called Wood that morning and said they needed to talk, Wood assumed it had something to do with Holoday's arrangements to move to Refco. He certainly didn't expect to hear the tale that Holoday spun for him in Holoday's flat delivery, cool and dispassionate as ever.

Over the past few years, Holoday claimed, he had been blackmailed by a group of clients dating back to his days at Midland Walwyn. It had started with the Deloitte & Touche letter nearly three years earlier in January 1992, when he sent misleading account statements to 18 clients, all of whom eventually signed waivers agreeing not to make any claims against Midland Walwyn. Six clients, however, had seen the difficulty Holoday was in, and they used it to squeeze money from him, threatening to charge

him with various things, reporting him to the Ontario
Securities Commission. Some had drained over $100,000
from him, and they wanted still more. It was blackmail,
Holoday claimed, pure and simple. Now that he could no
longer pay them, they were threatening to take him to the
OSC, making up lies about him.

"Who?" David Wood asked. "Who was doing this?"
Clients blackmailing their broker? In all his years in the
business, Wood had never heard of such a thing. "What
are their names?"

"Helen Rentis," Holoday replied. "Dr. Oswald John.
Ray Kundinger. And three others."

Wood asked Holoday to name the three others.
Holoday refused. "I've talked to my lawyer about it and he
says I've got a strong case," Holoday claimed. "I'm going to
stand up to them, David. I'm going to prove they're lying
about me, and get back the money I've already paid them."

If Holoday were expecting Wood to display sympathy
for his cause, or buy his story with an eye to discounting
any claims about to be made by Helen Rentis and the others, he was mistaken. Instead of sympathizing with
Holoday, Wood was outraged. He believed none of
Holoday's story, and he was fed up with the guy, this
young Whiz Kid who thought he was going to bring
Eastbridge and First Marathon together.

"I got a little melodramatic maybe," Wood recalled
later, "but I stood up and said, 'I'm getting your resignation today. I'm sending Joe Thurman in, and you tell him
the same story you just told me. Then get out.'"[16]

Later that day, Thurman submitted a two-page summary of a discussion he had with Holoday. *There is
absolutely no doubt in my mind that he wilfully deceived
us by not making us aware of the agreement he had with
these clients,* Thurman said. *Thus, I believe that we would
be justified in terminating Michael Holoday for cause.*[17]

This, several hours after Wood had already fired the broker.

Fired Holoday might have been, but he continued to occupy his office at First Marathon for another ten days, a decision First Marathon claims was made on the advice of legal counsel.[18] If so, it proved to be bad advice for many of Holoday's clients, who were left to learn on their own about First Marathon's dismissal of their managing partner, futures division. (It was also in sharp contrast with the treatment accorded Albert Robinson two years earlier at Midland Walwyn; Robinson had barely finished reading his termination letter before being escorted to his desk and closely observed while he packed his personal items, then taken directly to the front door — and all Robinson had done was suggest that the brokerage fire Michael Holoday.)

By September 28, 1994, First Marathon possessed evidence of serious misbehaviour on the part of Michael Holoday, the last in a long series of deceptions, half-truths and questionable activities on his part. Just a week earlier, Holoday had requested that yet another substantial amount — $71,390.58 in US funds — be added to his error account on behalf of Elaine Roberts. Two months earlier, he had attempted to borrow $2 million, and given evidence of serious financial difficulties. Yet instead of being frog-marched to the front door by security, he was permitted to remain in his elaborate suite of offices for ten days with a supply of First Marathon letterhead.

Holoday spent those ten days assuring his family and many of his clients that he was indeed moving to Refco. It was another step up the ladder, he said, this time with an actual trading company that maintained a seat at the Chicago Board of Trade, where all the action took place. To other clients, he began making ever more blatant efforts to acquire their money.

The day after Wood announced that he wanted Holoday's resignation, Holoday wrote a "statement" on First Marathon letterhead and faxed it to Kurt Schleith. According to Holoday's scrawled notation, he had just completed two bond deals for Schleith, producing a profit of $70,571.42 in US funds. Schleith's market position was $348,967.71, and his cash position was $360,571.42, again in US funds.

When Kurt Schleith received this note at his Kelowna cottage, it buoyed his spirits somewhat. He was still awaiting the return of almost $300,000 Holoday owed him from trades made in the previous few weeks, but at least he had written documentation in his hand, forwarded by Michael E. Holoday, managing partner, futures division, of First Marathon.

Holoday called perhaps an hour later, and Schleith assumed the young broker would disclose the transfer of Schleith's funds to him. But Holoday had something else to discuss: yet another "deal," and this one was personal.

"I need your help, Kurt," Holoday said. "You can lend me a hand and make yourself some money too, fully secured." Before Schleith could protest, Holoday announced he would be sending Kurt another fax explaining the deal, and they would discuss it later.

Kurt Schleith's fax machine began unfurling the message from Holoday immediately:

> *Dear Kurt.*
>
> *I am writing this letter requesting your financial assistance. Four months ago I committed to closing a $200,000 Canadian real estate deal in northern Ontario. I have 560 thousand Canadian receivable due on October 3rd, Monday next week. If I don't follow through by Friday, September 30th, on my real estate commitment, I will be sued*

by the other party. I have cash of 92 thousand Canadian on hand. I would like to borrow 108 thousand Canadian, $80,000 U.S., from today until Wednesday of next week, October 5th. I will pay the loan back plus the 45 thousand U.S. outstanding to date for a total of 125 thousand U.S. plus any interest you demand.

The second 45 thousand dollars U.S. of the original $90,000 loan by you to me is in your account at First Marathon Securities Limited. As your position is liquidated, I will transfer cash to you shortly from First Marathon to your Royal Bank account. I am prepared to put up a $109,000 (sic) U.S. T-bill I own and maturing December 15, 1994, part of my division capital structure, as collateral. I have also faxed a copy of the $560,000 Canadian receivable document to you.[19]

Nowhere does Holoday mention that he is about to leave First Marathon, nor that the "$109,000 US T-bill" is not only in the possession of First Marathon as security for Holoday's personal trades, but has already been pledged to at least half a dozen other clients of Holoday. The biggest falsehood is Holoday's claim that he is about to close a $200,000 real estate deal. Such a deal was indeed about to close, but it was Robert Gray's deal, and Holoday had assured Gray he would have the $200,000 in hand. When Kurt Schleith, his concerns softened by Holoday's pledge of the US T-bill as security, transferred $110,000 to Holoday later that day, the broker added all the cash he could lay his hands on and came up with $182,000. Still $18,000 short, Holoday simply removed that amount from Gray's own account at First Marathon, placing it in a deficit position, and transferred $200,000 to Gray just in time to close the deal.

Things were growing much too confusing for Holoday to follow and manage. He had no idea where he was in terms of financial obligations to his clients, and he kept stumbling forward, pulling money out of the hands of those who trusted him, and who forgave his obvious confusion. Listen to him lurch through a telephone call to Paul Simpkin on Thursday, October 6, 1994, after he announces that he will be moving to Refco Canada:

> HOLODAY: *Marathon will still clear your stock and bond business with a joint licence. So I've been in a shambles today on restructuring to reduce our costs and increase our profitability. It's been in the works for about a month now, but they always leave things for the last minute.*
>
> SIMPKIN: *Right . . .*
>
> HOLODAY: *That letter I was going to fax you?*
>
> SIMPKIN: *Yep?*
>
> HOLODAY: *Could you just briefly remind me what it was?*
>
> SIMPKIN: *Well you were, you said you had a four-pager put together.*
>
> HOLODAY: *Promissory note?*
>
> SIMPKIN: *Yeah.*
>
> HOLODAY: *Yeah . . . I do, and I would prefer to be able to do that at my house tonight.*
>
> SIMPKIN: *All right.*
>
> HOLODAY: *And send it to you in the mail.*
>
> SIMPKIN: *Hey, I'm not after you!*
>
> HOLODAY: *I got so many Indians around me right now . . .*
>
> SIMPKIN: *. . . I wasn't after you, and you did say you could have a solicitation*

> *agreement for the Northbridge. I*
> *don't know whether that was ready*
> *or not . . .*
>
> HOLODAY: *We got that and we can mail that*
> *stuff too.*
>
> SIMPKIN: *All right.*
>
> HOLODAY: *We're, we're changing right now . . .*
> *it will take a couple of days to get*
> *back to normal. We're not trading*
> *right now.*
>
> SIMPKIN: *Okay.*
>
> HOLODAY: *For two or three days . . .*[20]

Michael Holoday would never execute another trade. Later that day Refco Canada, informed that Holoday had been fired by First Marathon, changed their mind about offering him a position.

Earlier that year, Holoday had opened a margin account for Marlena Titian, a friend of his wife's, an account that Marlena Titian claims she never requested and thus never knew about. According to Titian the account remained inactive until October 5, 1994, when Holoday, fired from First Marathon but apparently permitted to carry out most of his usual activities, tapped Titian's margin account for $35,000 in US funds and transferred them to his own bank account.[21]

In early October, a fax arrived from a marina in Port Rowan, Ontario. Thanks to Brian Rocks' efforts, Holoday had a firm offer to purchase *Bad Company* for $75,000. Holoday's counter-offer, raising the price to $115,000, was turned down, preventing Rocks from recovering his funds.

Before leaving his office, Holoday reached Roger and Penny Campbell, vacationing in Florida. He had another deal, he told Roger Campbell. A good one. Fat profits in a few days. Did the Campbells want in? They would have to wire the money to him directly.

No, Campbell said, he didn't want another deal. He wanted an accurate statement on his account, the one Holoday had been promising for weeks. Where the devil was it?

"You didn't get it yet?" Holoday said.

The next morning, October 7, 1994, Holoday handed David Wood his handwritten resignation "as a correspondent network (*sic*) to First Marathon Securities Ltd. (Title: Managing Partner, Futures Division)." Wood instructed Joe Thurman to escort Holoday from the building. Holoday's entire career in the investment industry, from arriving on the Street on Black Monday 1987 as a rookie, moving from back-office clerk to the youngest-ever member of the Midland Walwyn Chairman's Club and on to managing partner, futures division, First Marathon Securities Ltd., and finally to disgraced ex-broker, had lasted ten days short of exactly seven years.

That afternoon Holoday, wife Maureen, and their two-year-old son flew to BC, where they spent Thanksgiving with Holoday's parents in the home Holoday had grown up in, along the banks of the Columbia River in the shadow of the Rockies. Before leaving, he hired a limousine to deliver his case of vintage Dom Pérignon champagne, the birthday gift from Doc Roberts, to Roy O'Hearn, with Doc Roberts' handwritten note still attached: "Best on your 30th birthday, Ken."

While the Holodays and their son rode to the airport, Ted Gittings entered Holoday's Royal Bank branch with two cheques totalling $342,000 in US funds and asked the bank to honour them. The response was a wry smile and a shake of the head. Gittings went in search of a lawyer.

SIXTEEN

I grew too rich.
I set my house afire without even
looking at the blaze
– JEAN-GUY PILON, "THE BURNING"

In October 1989, newly minted Fraud Squad Detective Constable Gary Logan was assigned to investigate the attempted use of a stolen credit card by a teenager from Burlington, Ontario. The youth had presented the American Express card at a store in Toronto's Eaton Centre, and a suspicious sales clerk kept him occupied until police arrived. Searching the contents of the boy's pockets, Logan discovered a set of car keys and a parking stub, dated the evening before, from the garage of a nearby hotel.

A call to headquarters confirmed that the owner of the credit card, Joseph Fitch, had not returned home the previous evening. Logan and his senior partner obtained a description of Fitch's car and set off for the parking garage, where they located the vehicle.

"Well, we've got the credit card and the car," the senior detective said. "Now we have to find the owner."

"Maybe he's in the trunk," Gary Logan joked.

He was. Joseph Fitch had been the victim of a random, senseless killing by three bored middle-class Burlington teenagers when he stopped at a Petro-Canada gasoline bar four blocks from his home. One boy ambushed him from behind, pulling a garbage bag over his head while the other struck him several times in the head with a fire extinguisher and a third, a 16-year-old girl, watched. They stuffed Fitch's battered body in the trunk of his Buick and drove the 60 kilometres to Toronto, where they checked into a hotel and went shopping the following day.

Logan's unfortunate comment and his frank retelling of the event years later is one measure of the man: unpretentious and quick to smile at his own folly. In spite of being born and bred in Toronto, Logan projects something of a country-boy persona, often saying goodbye with a rural "Take 'er easy, eh?" It's disarming, this casual demeanour. Given sufficient arrogance, a criminal could be forgiven for deciding he could outwit this man who appears encumbered and gangly. In fact, Michael Holoday's response to first encountering Logan, on the doorstep of Holoday's Forest Hill home, was: "He's not very smart. You can see that."

Take time to observe and assess the inner man, and the assessment of Logan changes. Logan carries an air of determination and calm, never attempting to conceal his apparent lack of sophistication, like a man who knows it is often an asset to be underestimated.

Police work hadn't been Logan's first choice for a career. Leaving high school, he worked in a department store before deciding he wasn't suitable for retail work. He joined the Metro Toronto Police Force in 1974, cutting his teeth as a traffic cop for several years before moving to the criminal investigation bureau and eventually to the fraud squad, where he rose to detective sergeant level. Logan's wife is also a police officer and, like Michael and Maureen Holoday, the couple has three active sons.

Years of general police work, topped with a decade of experience on the fraud squad, might engender a cynical outlook on society, a sense that everyone hides a cheating gene in his or her DNA, but not with Logan. Many of those who stumble along the way, the ones Logan encounters during his fraud investigations, earn a measure of his respect for their intelligence at least. "Had they done the honest thing, they would have accomplished something worthwhile," he speculates. "But once they get their hands on the proceeds of their crime, they squander it all away. Had they even taken the next step and invested it, things might have gone better, although they'd still be guilty. Most of the people who commit large frauds live hand to mouth. They take it, and it's gone. And Michael Holoday is a classic case, isn't he?"[1]

The day after Thanksgiving, 1994, while the Holodays were preparing to return to Vancouver and catch their flight to Toronto, Gary Logan found himself with some rare free time, and decided to visit an old friend, Charlie McDermott, at the Toronto Stock Exchange. McDermott, a former police officer himself, was responsible for internal investigation of fraudulent activity at the TSE. Much of the conversation he and Logan exchanged during Logan's visits was general in nature, reviewing current cases and discussing new investigative techniques, spiced here and there with gossip.

On October 11, 1994, Logan and McDermott had just settled into their chat when an obviously distressed man appeared in McDermott's doorway. "I've got a problem," the man said to McDermott.

McDermott asked what kind of problem the man had.

Serious ones, the man replied. Fraud. Embezzlement. Misuse of client funds. Forgery maybe. Millions of dollars, it looked like.

McDermott pointed at Gary Logan and congratulated the man on his timing. "Here's your man right here," McDermott said, and introduced Gary Logan to Joe

Thurman, compliance officer, correspondent network, of First Marathon Securities.

After Michael Holoday had departed First Marathon's offices the previous Friday, Joe Thurman seized the files Holoday left behind and examined them over the Thanksgiving weekend. Page by page, Holoday's four-year-long deception among dozens of clients was laid bare: the fictitious Northbridge fund, the forged letters to and from Eastbridge, the bridge financing investments, the pooled accounts, all of it carried out under the nose of First Marathon.

For the rest of that day at the TSE, Thurman briefed Gary Logan on the scope of Holoday's activities, as evidenced by the documents. Late that afternoon Logan carted letters, agreements, contracts, and statements away in boxes, trying to assess the scope of the fraud, leaving Thurman to deal with inquiries, some outraged, some tearful, from Holoday's clients, many of them unaware that Holoday had left First Marathon.

One by one, Holoday's clients discovered that Bay Street's Youngest Whiz Kid was a scam artist, and the money they had entrusted to him, as managing partner, futures division, of First Marathon Securities, had been seriously depleted or had vanished completely. Thurman's response was a variation on the same theme: You have been cheated. Get yourself a lawyer.

This was the extent of his advice to Margaret Raines when she was the first to call, hoping to clear up yet another discrepancy in her account, and to Brian Rocks when he telephoned later that day. Roger and Penny Campbell returned from Florida and were switched to Thurman when they asked to speak to their broker, Michael Holoday. The Campbells, who had entrusted First Marathon with a total of $1.8 million, were told that First Marathon did not owe them money — as a matter of fact the Campbells now owed First Marathon over $20,000 due to an overdraft in their account, and a high rate of interest would be charged on the deficit until settlement was made.

Robert Gray tried to call Holoday the day after Thanksgiving and was transferred to Joe Thurman. "How much money do you think you have in your account?" Thurman asked, and Gray said he thought it was over $700,000. Well, it wasn't, Thurman informed him. Gray owed First Marathon money, since his account was now in a deficit position. When Gray, shocked to a near-speechless state, asked Thurman what he should do, Thurman's reply was: "I suggest you flatten your debit balances." In other words, pay the money you owe us.

"We're in serious trouble," Gray said to his neighbour, Lee Cowie, and he told Cowie of his discovery and Thurman's response.

"How much do you think you have?" Thurman asked Cowie when he called First Marathon. Cowie said it should be about $123,000 in US funds. Well, it wasn't. There was basically nothing left.

Roger Gordon was living a nightmare. Relying on Holoday's written assurances that Gordon's investment exceeded $150,000, he had sold the family house, expecting to move into a custom-built home by the first of November. But tradesmen walked off the job in September when money failed to arrive from First Marathon, leaving an empty shell and promising court action. The Gordons' credit cards were at their limit and, on November 1, they had to vacate their previous home to make way for new owners.

Roger Gordon's telephone call to First Marathon elicited the familiar mantra: You have been cheated. Get yourself a lawyer.

When November arrived, with nowhere else to go the Gordon family moved into a single room in an inexpensive local motel. "We couldn't afford two rooms," Gordon explained. The family of five remained there until Roger could gain access to his half-constructed house. Working evenings and on weekends, Gordon brought it to a liveable condition, returning to the single motel room each evening to collapse and wonder how it all happened, where he had gone wrong.

Chester Hooper and his wife were driving to their now-mortgaged retirement home in Vancouver when they passed through Revelstoke. The Hoopers had been concerned about their accounts at First Marathon for some time, and Revelstoke seemed to be an appropriate place to call Holoday back in Toronto and enquire about the return on the bridge-financing investment they had made, the one that required them to mortgage their house for $200,000. Holoday, the Hoopers were told, was no longer employed at First Marathon. All calls to him were being directed to Holoday's lawyer.

The Hoopers drove the rest of the way to Vancouver in distress, and upon arriving home Chester Hooper booked himself on an overnight red-eye flight back to Toronto. In First Marathon's offices, Thurman nodded his head as he listened to Hooper's description of Holoday's phoney investment schemes. It fits a similar pattern, Thurman said. Others are in the same boat. You've been cheated. Get a lawyer.

Ray and Mary Kundinger, whom Holoday had assured in a letter a few months earlier on First Marathon letterhead that they had $725,000 in their account, were told that the account was not only empty, it carried a deficit of $23,439. The Kundingers were informed that settlement for the amount was expected quickly; interest would accrue until then and, if necessary, First Marathon would seek legal settlement to collect the overdraft.

Thurman's advice to the Campbells, suggesting they retain a lawyer, triggered another response. Astonished, shocked, furious, Roger Campbell wanted to do more than talk to a lawyer. He wanted to confront Holoday and hear the broker's explanation for himself, so he drove directly to 265 Forest Hill Road. He could see lights inside and a car in the driveway. He knew someone was home, but no one answered the doorbell or Campbell's pounding on the front door, and he returned home angrier and more frustrated than before.

Martin Karp was convinced that First Marathon had made a serious error on their September statement. They were always making mistakes, that's what Holoday kept telling him. This time, his account was short $100,000 in US funds. He called First Marathon and asked for Holoday, but it was Joe Thurman who answered the telephone. Karp explained his problem. He was a client of Michael Holoday's and his account was missing all of this money. What was going on?

"Well," Thurman said, "you can make money on these accounts and you can lose money too, you know." Thurman suggested that Karp had simply suffered a rather large trading loss.

"This money was already made," Karp explained. "It was a done deal."

The money wasn't there, Thurman replied. Never was. Get yourself a lawyer.

Gary Davidson wanted answers, like everyone else, but when Joe Thurman agreed to provide some he proved as curious about Holoday's misdeeds as Davidson. When

Davidson arrived at First Marathon's office, Thurman escorted him into the brokerage's ornate boardroom. "Pretty nice, eh?" Thurman said as Davidson looked around, admiring the furnishings and decor.

"Actually," Davidson replied, "it makes me sick. It was paid for with my money."

The two men began asking questions of each other, Thurman wanting to know more about Holoday's activities, and Davidson asking where his money went, and how First Marathon could allow Holoday to get away with so much and for so long a time. According to Davidson, Thurman said at one point: "We supervised Holoday to the minimum requirements."

Minimum? Davidson thought. More like non-existent.[2]

For Paul Simpkin, who had played Dutch Uncle to Holoday just weeks earlier, the news of Holoday's departure from First Marathon proved doubly shocking, bringing with it a lesson about the priorities of Bay Street brokerages.

Simpkin was confused and concerned. After Michael Holoday announced he would be leaving First Marathon for Refco, nothing was heard from the broker. More distressing, Refco claimed not to know anything about him. By October 20, two weeks after Holoday's announcement, Simpkin still had no idea where his investments were located. When he called First Marathon and asked for Michael Holoday, he was transferred to Chuck Oliver. And when Chuck Oliver heard Simpkin's voice, he transferred Simpkin to Joe Thurman.

Thurman confirmed that Holoday was no longer employed with First Marathon. This was no surprise to Simpkin, who asked if Thurman could confirm the value of Simpkin's accounts at First Marathon. In contrast with the stumbling, marking-time response of Holoday to this simple request in the past, Thurman had the answer in seconds:

Paul Simpkin was overdrawn by $86,000 in his commodity account and had a balance of $183,000 in his bond account. While Simpkin absorbed this news in stunned silence, Thurman announced that First Marathon would pay off the deficit in one account with the proceeds of another, and forward a cheque for the difference to Simpkin.

Simpkin began to protest. Michael Holoday had assured him that Simpkin's assets totalled more than half a million dollars in those accounts. Was First Marathon going to replace those losses? And why were they talking about liquidating his accounts? Wasn't that decision his to make?

First Marathon, Thurman replied, would not replace the money removed from Simpkin's accounts by Michael Holoday. The brokerage was not responsible for the losses. That was Holoday's doing, not theirs.

"But I came to First Marathon expecting the size and strength of the company to protect me from this kind of thing," Simpkins protested.

"If somebody does criminal activities behind my back," the compliance officer said, "I can't be responsible for that, can I?"

Thurman began grilling Simpkin about his dealings with Holoday. "Did you see money coming out of your account that you couldn't account for?" Thurman asked.

Simpkin admitted he had, and he had asked Holoday for an explanation, over and over again.

"Did you ever loan money to Holoday?" Thurman asked.

Simpkin said not really. There had, of course, been the matter of the promissory note Holoday submitted, but which Simpkin had not signed. "I've been wiped out," Simpkin said in a voice that only a man in his 60s, who had worked all his life to accumulate a measure of wealth for his security and learned that it had vanished, could muster.

Thurman repeated that he would use the funds from one account of Paul Simpkin's to eliminate the debt of the other, close both accounts, and send whatever funds remained to Simpkin.

When Simpkin asked why First Marathon was closing the door on him as a client, Thurman replied that Simpkin had been actively trading in commodities and, with the departure of Holoday, First Marathon no longer employed any commodity traders. Simpkin enquired about his RRSP account — would that have to go as well? Thurman said there was no one at First Marathon to service his accounts, either of them.

"You're kicking me out," Simpkin protested.

Thurman disagreed. "The broker who serviced your account has left the firm. Most of our financial advisors do not handle retail accounts such as yours."

Simpkin continued to press for guidance, some route he could follow, and Thurman suggested going to the TSE. At one point, while attempting to explain why he had trusted Michael Holoday in the face of Holoday's failure to confirm earnings and trades, Simpkin reminded Thurman that "Michael was a managing partner."

"That's just a title," Thurman said. "Just as I am an officer of the firm."[3]

While Holoday's stunned clients learned the extent of their losses, and the refusal of First Marathon to honour them or offer assistance beyond advising they retain lawyers, Michael Holoday scrambled for cash in ever more reckless ways.

His immediate target was Kurt Schleith. Living far from Bay Street, Schleith would be among the last to discover Holoday's departure from First Marathon, providing Holoday with a week or two in which to seize funds. But for what? Interest payments on Holoday's Forest Hill home alone demanded $22,000 each month, and Holoday had no income. A more realistic approach might have been to declare bankruptcy then and there, and to seek legal advice on impending civil and criminal charges. Michael Holoday may have been blessed with various assets, but an ability to accept and deal with reality was not one of them. His tearful July 11th confession to Ken and Elaine Roberts proved to be an anomaly, a one-time-only deviation from Holoday's normal behaviour. From this point on, he committed himself to wider, deeper, more outrageous lies and deceits.

On October 12, 1994, the day after Joe Thurman stumbled into Charlie McDermott's office with his tardy discoveries of Michael Holoday's multiple deceptions, Holoday arrived home from BC and placed a long distance call to Kurt Schleith. "We can make some extra money, like we did on the earlier trades," Holoday told Schleith. "Thirty thousand dollars today will make five thousand dollars overnight." Holoday was as persuasive as ever, and Schleith wired $30,000 to Holoday in the younger man's name — "Make it out personally to me, so we can do the trade quicker," Holoday said — and Schleith received a cheque for $35,000 two days later. Reassured again that Holoday was indeed a wizard, though perhaps with cash-flow problems now and then, Schleith had just deposited the cheque in his account when Holoday phoned from Toronto with a similar deal, this time for $50,000. "It'll make you $7,000 overnight," Holoday promised, and once again Schleith wired the funds to Toronto, in Holoday's name.

As promised, a courier delivered a cheque for $57,000 to Schleith's front door on October 16. Thanks to Holoday, Kurt Schleith had made $12,000 profit in less than a week, which lessened his concern about the other deals totalling $200,000, and prepared him for Holoday's third

telephone call in five days. This time Holoday asked for
$60,000 to be wired directly into Holoday's Royal Bank
account in Toronto, and once again Kurt Schleith instructed his bank to do the transfer.

Unlike the previous trades, nothing came back in two
days and no one seemed to be answering Michael
Holoday's telephone. By Friday, October 21, Schleith was
concerned enough to visit his accountant for advice. "Let's
call somebody else at First Marathon, the compliance officer maybe," Schleith's accountant suggested, and Schleith
agreed. The accountant was connected with Joe Thurman,
but Thurman insisted on talking only to Schleith. "Mr.
Schleith," Thurman said from his office in Toronto, "you
have been cheated. You better get yourself a lawyer."[4]

Three days later, Holoday called Schleith from Toronto
with a proposal. Kurt Schleith didn't want a proposal. He
wanted an explanation, and he wanted his money back —
especially the $60,000 Holoday had wheedled out of him
the previous week, after Holoday had left First Marathon,
when he knew there would be no further trades and no
way to invest the money. Kurt Schleith turned on his tape
recorder, the one connected to his telephone.

"Mike, what happened there?" Schleith asked. He was
concerned, angry, shocked, all of those emotions and more.
"You got that money out of me, there's no other way of putting it. I realize now you did not use that for trading, did
you?"

No, Holoday admitted, he hadn't. He was calling from
his cell phone, sitting in his Jeep, in heavy midtown
Toronto traffic.

"Okay, now you admit it. . . . I believed you. I never suspected any wrongdoing whatsoever. I had the highest regard
for you always. But when this happened, I had to wake up.
I just trusted you fully before. Mike, you took advantage
of that. There is no other way of saying that, Mike."

"That's right."

"There is no other way, and this hurts, Mike. It really hurt me . . ."

Holoday claimed he was not trying to run away from the truth. "I want to put the money back into your bank. I'm not trying to avoid that. I did something wrong and I want to pay it back."

What, Schleith wanted to know, had Holoday done with the $60,000?

"I covered my own liabilities," Holoday responded. "I mean, it was not related to a trade that you would have shared profits on. It was related to covering my own liabilities. Part were investment purposes and part were others, but the difference, which I claimed to you would have been profit, was simply interest that I believe should be paid to you for lending the money."

"I insist on that money back, because it was very, very wrong."

"Well, you're going to get your money back," Holoday assured him. He had a way of doing it. The plan would involve duping Holoday's lawyer, who was handling Holoday's financial matters now, but between them they could get their hands on the $60,000, which Holoday promised would be returned to Schleith.[5]

Holoday proposed telling his lawyer that $60,000 of his remaining assets had been committed to Kurt Schleith before his current troubles began. There were other creditors, Holoday admitted, but if Kurt would go along with things, Holoday could move his school chum's father to the head of the line. "That might involve me dating a letter September fifteenth, collateralizing one of these cash flows to you, which we should have done anyway. . . . Before our other creditors are dealt with, he (Schleith) has to be dealt with. I think I have the right to do that."

He had, of course, no right at all to do that.

Holoday's plan was to courier a letter to Kurt Schleith. The letter, dated September 15, 1994, would commit shares held by Holoday in Consolidated Madison to secure the US$60,000 "loan," permitting Holoday's lawyers to liquidate the shares and forward the money to Schleith, bypassing other creditors. In reality, Schleith would never have seen the money; Holoday planned to obtain the funds directly from his law firm.

"We are going to liquidate all our assets," Holoday told Schleith in another telephone call later that day, "including the house, and give the creditors money, and then get back in business with a clean slate."

What about the $60,000? Schleith wanted to know.

"We are going to do the sixty thousand as a first collateral on the cash, which has come in as receivables. So I said to the law firm . . ." Holoday paused and lowered his voice. "This is not being taped, right Kurt?"

"No," Schleith lied.

"Okay, I've said to them that you have a first lien on the Madison money, which is coming in right now . . ." Holoday had handwritten a letter providing Schleith with the lien agreement; when Schleith received it, he was to fax it back to Holoday's law firm (Holoday couldn't fax the original to Schleith because the fax copy would carry the current date), who would arrange to issue a cheque. In effect, Holoday was recruiting both his client and his lawyer into a fraudulent act.

Schleith remained confused. What was going on? What kind of trouble was Holoday in?

Well, Holoday had more liabilities than assets right now, and he had withdrawn from the securities industry for two weeks, but he would soon be back trading again, maybe in a week or so. He had a position at Refco, just as he had told Schleith, but he was also entertaining offers from Nesbitt Burns and from Wood Gundy. Meanwhile, he retained proprietary rights on the trading techniques he developed at First Marathon, and if they dared to jeopardize that "I can sue them for twenty million US dollars, representing five years of income."[6]

Schleith, who had no intention of participating in Holoday's scheme, listened to Holoday spin lies through three days of long distance telephone calls, each taped by Schleith. During a telephone conversation on October 26, 1994, Holoday indicated that one creditor — obviously the Roberts family, although Holoday never mentions their name — is claiming that Holoday owed them $7 million. "Now, there is a discrepancy," Holoday said. "It turns out there is a discrepancy of three-point-four million US dollars, which we are claiming is not owed. And it's called . . . it's under the criteria of illegal interest. There is actually a criteria called illegal interest. So that's what is being disputed and we might have to take them to court."

Holoday was correct. Under Canada's Criminal Code, an annual interest exceeding 60 percent cannot be imposed and collected, even when the borrower understands and agrees to it. This was more than a claim to Kurt Schleith that Holoday's troubles were not entirely of his own making. It would form a cornerstone of his defence through the years of civil proceedings against him, and into his criminal trial six years later.

The ploy was every bit as audacious as it appears: After cajoling clients to advance money for investments, which he promised to repay with returns exceeding 100 percent on a pro-rated annual basis, Holoday claimed these were personal loans, not investments, and the "returns" were interest. Since the interest exceeded the legal limit, the loans were not entirely collectable. What's more, he could assert no criminal activity was involved, because failure to repay a loan is a civil matter.

Holoday remained confident he would avoid serious

penalties, civil or criminal, against him. On his Thanksgiving visit to his parents' Revelstoke home, he had persuaded his father to advance capital to launch Global Funding Inc., which Michael Holoday ran out of a tiny office at Queen and Bay Streets in Toronto. Global Funding would, Holoday declared, provide expert investment advice to major Canadian corporations such as BCE, Nortel, Air Canada, and Bombardier. "We'll assess the performance of the managers handling their pension portfolios," he boasted, "and tell them who to reward, who to fire, and who to hire as replacements for the lousy performers."[7]

To those unfamiliar with the securities industry, the idea may seem impossible. Can a disbarred lawyer handle legal matters? Can an unlicensed doctor perform medical examinations? Hardly. But neither lack of a trading licence nor accreditation by any official body, government or private sector, restricts the dispensing of investment advice. Anyone can declare himself or herself a financial advisor, examining investment portfolios and suggesting securities to sell, to buy, to retain, for a fee. It remains the duty of the individual investor to measure the advisor's qualifications, if any. Christopher Horne, the RBC Dominion Securities broker, was selling investment advice to clients even while on parole from his jail term.

Chester Hooper returned to Vancouver with only bad news for his wife. Nothing could be found of his original investment or of the $200,000 he had given Holoday after the Hoopers mortgaged their retirement home. The sadness and humiliation overwhelmed his anger, and later that month he sat down and pecked out a letter on his typewriter, addressed to Holoday at his Forest Hill home.

I really do not know how to begin this letter, Hooper wrote. *To say I am confused and over-*

*whelmed by the present situation would be a
gross understatement. I trusted you in every
respect and strangely enough at this moment
have difficulty comprehending what has alleged
to have passed. . . . Can you imagine, for just a
moment, the incredible stress we are under, not
being able to access these funds at this critical
time, even in a modest way?*[8]

Holoday apparently could not. He cut off all contact with
the Hoopers and refused to attend a meeting between
Hooper and Holoday's civil lawyer, Steve Sofer. At the
meeting, Sofer's only suggestion was for the Hoopers to
liquidate a small Registered Retirement Income Fund at
50 cents on the dollar and use the funds to tide them over.
Soon after, the Hoopers sold their retirement dream home;
it was the only way to pay off the $200,000 mortgage they
had taken on it, at Holoday's suggestion.

John and Carole Boczan were as astonished by the revelations of Holoday's fraud as anyone. The Boczans' dream of
a small country house near Cobourg had vanished, of
course, replaced by the large country home that John
Boczan built with his own hands, but Holoday had sold it.
The promise of winters in Barbados was gone as well, and
the Boczans had been banished from Forest Hill Road,
forced to live with daughter Suzie Desmond and son-in-
law Howard and their three children in a three-bedroom
high-rise.

In October, the Desmonds learned that Holoday's second cheque to the funeral director, where Holoday had
insisted on having both of Suzie and Howard Desmond's
infant sons buried with elaborate and expensive cere-
monies, had bounced several months earlier. The funeral
home, wishing to deal with the issue as delicately as

possible, had pleaded with Holoday for settlement of its account, exceeding $8,000, for months without response. Holoday made it clear that he had no intention of honouring his debt. Now the funeral home appealed to Howard and Suzie for settlement.

The Desmonds were mortified. Holoday, in his familiar take-charge mode, had dictated the extent and expense of the funerals, and now the parents had to assume responsibility for the debt when he refused to. Struggling with Howard's fledgling company, the Desmonds managed to pay $10,000 to settle the account.

While the Desmonds were dealing with the financial pain of the unpaid funeral, Michael Holoday delivered even more disturbing news. A court order, Holoday claimed in a telephone call to Howard Desmond, was forcing him to sell various assets, including the twin burial plots in Mount Pleasant Cemetery, the ones originally planned for himself and Maureen.

Desmond asked why Holoday was telling him this.

Well, you have to move the twins, Holoday said. Meaning the still-grieving parents had to disinter the two babies in their tiny expensive coffins, and bury them somewhere else. Howard and Suzie Desmond were horrified at the prospect. Hadn't they suffered enough?

Holoday's response was a shrug. It was out of his hands.

Holoday was lying. No record of any court order relating to the Holodays' burial plot exists.

Under a bleak November sky a few weeks later, Howard and Suzie Desmond stood watching while a backhoe unearthed the tiny coffins of the two baby boys they had buried not six months earlier. The couple bore the expense of relocating their sons to another gravesite. They also bore the pain of the tragedy all over again.

The gravesite was refilled and sold. Later that month

$38,152.19 was deposited into Holoday's trust account at Smith Lyons, the law firm retained to defend him against multiple civil litigations. Holoday had evicted the bodies of his two infant nephews for the sole purpose of obtaining less than $40,000 to cover a portion of his legal expenses at a time when he was $20 million in debt.

While many of Holoday's clients sought legal advice, Gary Logan began assembling evidence of criminal wrongdoing against the former Youngest Member of the Midland Walwyn Chairman's Club, and disgraced managing partner, futures division, First Marathon Securities. Each revelation by a distressed and angry former client led to more shocked investors who had believed everything Holoday fed them about the growth and safety of their money. At one point, Logan lugged a computer down to the TSE where he occupied an office for almost four months, working alone to track the convoluted path of Holoday's various frauds.

Not all of Holoday's victims pressed for criminal charges or took civil action. Some believed Holoday was guilty only of making investment errors, a young guy who got in over his head. Others were either too embarrassed at their apparent gullibility to discuss their losses, or recognized the futility of pursuing either Holoday or the two brokerage houses.

When news of Holoday's disgraced exit from First Marathon reached Randy Lang, he took two steps that could be construed as in conflict with each other. One was to link up with six other former clients of Holoday at Carson, Gross & McPherson, a law firm specializing in investment fraud. They launched a civil action against Holoday, Midland Walwyn, and First Marathon Securities. Lang's other action was to execute his mortgage claim on Holoday's Barbados property. Holoday filed an injunction against Lang's claim, contesting the validity of the note Holoday himself had provided. After a few weeks' wrangling, Holoday approached Lang with a proposal: Holoday would drop his opposition to Lang's claim on the Barbados real estate if, in turn, Lang promised to transfer $100,000 in US funds from the sale of the property to Holoday's company, Global Funding Inc.

Lang agreed. Holoday's Sandy Lane property sold for US$869,324. Of this, $82,000 covered legal and transfer fees in Barbados, $17,000 was claimed by Lang to cover trading losses suffered at First Marathon, $100,000 went to Holoday according to their agreement, and Lang took about $535,000. This left $135,000 to be shared by the rest of the Carson, Gross & McPherson clients, after Lang withdrew from the firm's action against Holoday.

"Holoday owes me nothing," Lang said later. "I have no problem with Mister Holoday." Holoday's other investors, of course, had a problem with Randy Lang.[9]

Doc and Elaine Roberts knew Holoday owed them money; they just didn't know how much. To find out, they retained forensic accountant James McAuley from the accountancy firm KPMG to analyze the Roberts' bank records as well as those of Michael and Maureen Holoday, which Holoday had turned over to Elaine Roberts the day following his tearful confession in the Fahnestock Viner office. "The McAuley Report," as it came to be known during Holoday's criminal trial, indicated that the former managing partner, futures division, of First Marathon owed the Roberts $8,379,691 in US funds, about $10.5 million Canadian.

In the end, the figures were unimportant. The amount, a fortune to average Canadians, made little apparent impact on the lifestyle of the Roberts. The emotional effect of Holoday's escapades on Doc Roberts, however, was substantial. Until Holoday's tearful revelations on July 11, 1994, Kenneth Roberts had enjoyed life immensely, and the enjoyment included pleasures derived from the wealth he had amassed over his 80-plus years. "My father was glad to be alive," Elaine Roberts recalled, "enjoying life and all it had to offer." Holoday's betrayal changed all of that, and ruined the few years remaining for Doc Roberts. In addition to trusting Holoday, Doc Roberts held the younger man "in warm affectionate regard," Elaine Roberts continued. "In the summer of nineteen-ninety-four it all came crashing down. He never recovered from the shock of what Holoday had done to him. He was profoundly humiliated, and believed his track record (of good business sense) was swept away. My father sank into a deep depression. His self-confidence was destroyed. He did not participate in the same activities he once enjoyed, and he declined steadily, both mentally and physically."

In January 1999, Doc Roberts died. His daughter described him as "a broken man."[10]

Sheldon Fenton, who had been suspicious of Holoday's actions for months, instructed his lawyers to demand the immediate payment of $200,000 in US funds that Fenton had loaned Holoday. When First Marathon claimed the loan was Holoday's responsibility, not theirs, Fenton called David Wood directly. When, Fenton wanted to know, was First Marathon going to pay him the two hundred thousand bucks? "His reply," Fenton said later, "was an offer to buy me a kite."[11]

In contrast with Randy Lang, who claimed Holoday owed him nothing, and Doc and Elaine Roberts, who reportedly decided not to pursue charges, Roger Gordon and his family were devastated.

The Gordons' credit rating was nil. Roger Gordon was receiving angry threats from tradesmen and suppliers who blamed him for their losses, and their debt load was staggering. The family of five faced Christmas crowded into a single motel room, while the home they had dreamed of occupying stood as an empty shell. Could things possibly get worse? Yes, they could, and they did.

Working as many hours as he could spare, Gordon managed to bring the home into a liveable state for the winter, but the pain endured, and the cost exceeded anything measured in dollar and cents. "Our eldest daughter had met Michael," Roger Gordon explained. "She saw him pull up in his big car, dressed so well, and then she finds out what he got away with."

The daughter, who had an excellent academic record, wanted to become a dentist. "We expected to put her through university with some of the money that Michael said we had," Debbie Gordon said. "That was our plan. She's like any other teenager, she's looking around for some kind of model, and she sees this guy who gets rich without following the rules, so why should she? Our kids saw the stress we were under, and felt the tension in the house. We told them everything about the way Holoday took our money. We had to."

While Debbie Gordon's attitude was resigned sadness, her husband's anger seethed and threatened to explode. "Lately, I've had dreams about him [Holoday]" Gordon said, "and in my dreams I put him and Paul Bernardo together."

Roger Gordon hired a local lawyer to launch a civil suit against First Marathon, but the night before the case came to trial, Gordon's lawyer called to explain that he could not act for them because his insurance had expired. When the trial got underway, First Marathon's lawyers charged Gordon with conspiring with Holoday. Gordon, they argued, must have known that he had no money in his account at First Marathon. That's why he asked Holoday for the letter in mid-June, declaring that the Gordons' account balance was $150,000 when there was no money to be had. With that letter, the lawyers charged, Gordon was able to obtain a line of credit from the bank. The implication was clear: Roger Gordon, in partnership with the disgraced Michael Holoday, had attempted to perpetrate a fraud.

"What about my credit rating?" Gordon said. Why, he asked, would he do such a thing and destroy his credit rating in the process?

"How much is a credit rating worth?" First Marathon's lawyers demanded.

"They attacked me over that," Gordon recalled later. "They said, 'What's the value of a credit rating? Go see how much you can get for it.' They used their power to crush us. I don't think many people are aware that a company can turn on you that way."

Roger Gordon lost his court case, and lost an appeal to the decision. Soon new, even more outrageous losses began to mount. The Gordons were audited by Revenue Canada for five years running, based on a T5 statement issued by Holoday claiming $20,000 in interest income earned by Roger and Debbie Gordon. In a cruel and maddening joust, the Gordons were accused by Ottawa of failing to declare income from their First Marathon investments, and repudiated by First Marathon for asserting they ever had any money invested with the firm at all. The final blow came when First Marathon countersued the Gordons to recover money that the brokerage expended to defend itself against the Gordons' lawsuit.[12]

First Marathon's defence against lawsuits brought by Holoday's clients was to claim the clients were "authors of their own misfortune,"[13] and deny "any vicarious liability for the conduct of Holoday with respect to these private dealings."[14] They refused to accept responsibility for losses even though, when Helen Rentis and others called to complain about their accounts, the clients had been told, "talk to your broker."

Others found themselves under attack, as though they were more perpetrators than victims. The brokerage sued Gary Davidson, who in 1993 had scribbled his name at the bottom of a letter drafted by Holoday, for $10 million, claiming that Davidson's letter — the one presented to him in the driveway of his home while he raked his front lawn — was partially responsible for the firm hiring Holoday. Holoday's actions, First Marathon claimed through their lawyers, had cost it $20 million. Davidson's letter represented 50 percent of the decision to hire Holoday, thus the $10 million assessment. First Marathon added a $10 million lawsuit against Roy O'Hearn, who succumbed to Holoday's plea and signed a letter explaining that Holoday's $299,000 payment had been in settlement of a personal loan. And when Kurt Schleith asked that his claim against First Marathon be heard in BC, the province where he resided, First Marathon insisted it be heard in Ontario, carrying the case all the way to the Provincial Supreme Court, which denied the brokerage's argument.

The impact of Holoday's actions on the Boczan family was massive and painful. Friends, clients, and other family members had entrusted hundreds of thousands of dollars to Maureen's husband on the family's recommendation, and one by one each discovered that Holoday had lied to them. Their money was gone.

Through October and into November, Holoday promised he would repay their losses sometime, somehow. "In a couple of weeks you'll have all your money back," he told Dianne Sone in late October, adding that he and Maureen "are not the type of people who would do this to somebody." It was all a matter of rebuilding trust, Holoday noted.

A clearer picture of Holoday's attitude emerged when Maureen's sister Kathy was married in Trenton, Ontario.

It had long ago been agreed that Maureen would be a bridesmaid at the wedding, but most family members assumed that she would withdraw, given the impact of her husband's actions on family members and on several of the guests who planned to attend. At a minimum, everyone expected Maureen to arrive without Michael.

Family and guests were shocked to near-silence when a visibly pregnant Maureen arrived at the wedding with her husband in their Jeep Grand Cherokee, Michael greeting various family members as though he were still the shining star, the favoured son. Maureen and Michael booked a room at the same Holiday Inn where other overnight guests were staying, and where the large wedding reception was held. Most people avoided eye contact with either him or Maureen, or simply nodded perfunctorily; no one wanted to tarnish the day for the bride and groom.

Dianne Sone, invited as an old family friend, was not so reticent. Amazed to discover Holoday at the church, she and her husband approached him at the reception, where he stood alone in a corner. "You have a lot of explaining to do to a lot of people," Dianne Sone said. Holoday smiled nervously and suggested they retire to his room to talk.

"We must have been there half an hour," Dianne recalled. "I asked Michael point blank if there was any investment left, and he just shook his head to indicate no. I said, 'What did you do with the money, Michael?' And he just shrugged his shoulders and said, 'Well, I did something with it.'" Holoday offered weak promises to make good on everyone's losses, but Dianne Sone and her husband had heard enough. Shortly after, the Sones launched civil charges against First Marathon, Lawrence Bloomberg, Tracy Ellis, and Holoday.[15]

The ripples of Holoday's tumble extended beyond clients, family, and friends to encompass Tanya Sargent,

Holoday's sales assistant at Midland Walwyn. In an action that strikes most people as more than coincidental, Sargent was dismissed from her position at Midland Walwyn within one day of David Wood's demand for Holoday's resignation from First Marathon. Her sudden release, and her inability to obtain employment anywhere else in the industry — Midland Walwyn declined to provide her with any references — were added to a series of personal tragedies. In the midst of these, she sought legal assistance to launch a wrongful dismissal suit, and when her lawyer's fees absorbed most of her severance package without obtaining any settlement, she endured a near-total breakdown. She survived for the next six years on a small disability income with her godmother, eventually moving to a tiny basement apartment in Toronto's east end.[16]

At the end of 1994, several former clients joined forces in a court-imposed *Mareva* injunction, effectively freezing Michael and Maureen Holoday's assets while legal matters proceeded. In response, the Holodays requested that $50,000 of their assets be released to cover three to five months' living expenses, with similar injections of cash to follow as needed by the couple. In support of this figure, Maureen Holoday submitted a projected monthly budget requiring almost $11,000, net of income taxes. The couple demanded the funds to cover their nanny's salary of $1,200, plus taxes; $1,000 for groceries and meals; $500 for clothing; $400 for babysitting (presumably when the nanny was unavailable); $126 for dry cleaning; and $175 for toiletries and grooming. Factoring income taxes into the figure, the Holodays were claiming they required between $150,000 and $175,000 annually.[17]

The Holodays submitted this budget in December 1994, when Roger and Debbie Gordon and their three children were occupying a single motel room.

In the spring of 1995, someone broke into the offices of Fahnestock Viner. Nothing was stolen except several blank forms pre-signed by Doc and Elaine Roberts for use by their secretary. None of the documents ever surfaced, and no one was charged with the burglary.

Around the same time, Michael Holoday claimed to discover a tape cassette in the mailbox of his Forest Hill home. On the cassette, a man's voice threatened Holoday and his family with violence and death. Police investigated but were unable to identify the voice, or the specific motive for the threats.

Art Lumsden[18] wasn't certain how Michael Holoday had heard about him, but he was flattered when Holoday offered him a job in the summer of 1996, a year before criminal charges would be laid against Holoday. With no inkling of Holoday's past, and as impressed with the ex-broker's presentation as anyone, he listened to Holoday's pitch.

Lumsden was an accountant, and a good one at that. He was happy at his current job, but Holoday's offer was difficult to resist: $150,000 annual salary plus a chance to grow with Holoday's hot investment consulting firm, Global Funding. "We deal with international fund managers," Holoday said, explaining Global's operations. There could be some travel involved. A lot of freedom too. Maybe a chance to own a piece of the company as it grew. Lumsden took the offer.

Within a few days, however, Lumsden had serious second thoughts about his employer. Most of Global's income was derived from Navellier and Associates in Reno, Nevada, of all places. Navellier, a legitimate and highly regarded mutual fund manager, appeared to be forwarding money to Holoday for him to invest, but the accountant determined that the money was being used to cover things such as Maureen Holoday's clothing and beauty salon visits, payments on a new Chevy Tahoe SUV, funding for Holoday's hockey team, and the rental of Holoday's vacation property on Lake Simcoe. Holoday scoffed at Lumsden's concerns about misappropriating funds. He would make it up, Holoday explained, with proceeds from the sale of some oceanfront property in Barbados. What Holoday really needed, he told Lumsden, was an official accounting of Global's income and expenses. Things were a mess, he admitted. Could Lumsden have it by tomorrow? Only if he stayed up until midnight, Lumsden explained. Then do it, Holoday said.

The following day, Holoday had his report. Lumsden, however, had yet to receive any part of the $150,000 salary Holoday had promised. Where is it coming from? Lumsden asked.

Holoday's response was to fire the accountant on the spot. Things just weren't working out, Holoday said. Lumsden threatened to sue. Holoday shrugged, and Lumsden was on the street five minutes later, asking himself what happened, and looking for another job.[19]

For six years, while various civil cases stumbled through court proceedings, First Marathon pleaded on the one hand that its former managing partner, futures division, was solely responsible for client losses and that "the nature of the relationship between [First Marathon] and [various clients] was a pure agency relationship."[20] On the other hand, the brokerage also claimed it had "properly supervised Holoday in the operation of the accounts of [various clients]."[21]

Holoday, for his part, claimed innocence as well. First Marathon, he stated in court documents filed in his defence, had failed to properly supervise him, which had led to substantial client losses for which he should not be held responsible. His clients were "sophisticated and experienced investors" who knew, or should have known, the risks they were taking by following Holoday's advice. Moreover several of them, including retired schoolteacher Margaret Raines, had blackmailed Holoday. His clients "threatened Mr. Holoday, that if Mr. Holoday refused to make the opportunity profit payments [they] would take steps to hinder Mr. Holoday's career, including advising Mr. Holoday's superiors about the losses that Mr. Holoday had already promised to cover."[22]

Michael Holoday had presented himself not just as a fully licensed and qualified stockbroker and investment counsellor, but as a high-profile, widely promoted executive of two of Canada's largest and most successful investment firms. When the bubble burst in late 1994, most of these clients became *persona non grata* to the firms. Holoday claimed the brokerages failed to supervise him properly. The brokerages claimed the clients were "authors of their own misfortune."

It was a *Through the Looking Glass* world that none of Holoday's clients could fathom. How could they, as victims, be attacked by both Holoday and his former employers, who themselves were at each other's throats? The arguments flew back and forth, many based more on legal posturing than on reality.

Meanwhile, Gary Logan slogged on, travelling across Canada and into the United States to interview everyone who had a story to tell about the former Bay Street Whiz Kid. Holoday, Logan decided, was cold, calculating, and callous. "Everybody was fair game to him," Logan said. "He destroyed marriages, took people's life-savings, and literally [wrecked] families." Holoday's actions represented not just a crime of finance, or a faceless crime. "It goes much deeper than that. He has a deep-rooted problem."[23]

After more than a year of investigation on his own, Logan was joined by Detective Constable Jeff Thomson. Where Logan tended to maintain his casual Colombo-style manner, the younger Thomson was a solid physical presence, a barrel-chested cop with the attitude and ability to apply strong-arm persuasion if necessary. As time passed, Thomson developed an intense and undisguised personal dislike for Holoday.

The investigation gained momentum over the next two years while the police officers grew stunned at Holoday's outrageous lies. Obtaining a search warrant for Holoday's financial records, they discovered that a statement Holoday provided the Royal Bank in 1995 claimed he was owed $550,000 from Revenue Canada as a tax refund; that Maureen was about to make a term deposit of $200,000; that the Holodays had a net worth of $2.3 million, an annual income of $240,000 and an anticipated annual income for 1997 of $500,000.[24] Holoday, in Gary Logan's opinion, had lied so wildly and for so long that he was now incapable of telling the truth about anything.

In the spring of 1997, Logan and Thomson took their evidence to the Crown Attorney's office. The case was assigned to Brian McNeely, who agreed with the volume of evidence assembled by the two detectives and issued an arrest warrant.

Of all the Crown attorneys on staff at the time, no one was better suited than McNeely to handle the Holoday case. Son of an Ontario Superior Court judge renowned for his abrasive nature, McNeely is a methodical low-key attorney whose courtroom style favours preparation over dramatics. Like Logan, McNeely's intensity is hidden, leaving adversaries to underestimate him.

On June 9, 1997, Logan and Thomson informed Holoday he was about to be arrested. The arrest could take place at his home or, if he preferred, at 52 Division headquarters at 10 o'clock the following morning. Holoday chose the latter, and he and Maureen, now pregnant with their third child, arrived on time. After being formally charged, Holoday spent the balance of his time with the two detectives chatting about hockey. How much longer would Gretzky play? What was wrong with the Maple Leafs? You ever see Bobby Orr in action?

Logan was amazed. Holoday was facing charges that could lead to spending several years in prison, and he was chatting as though sharing a beer in a crowded pub, killing time on a warm June day.

Holoday was transferred to a holding cell in the basement of Toronto's Old City Hall, where for the next ten hours he shared space with a dozen various thugs, assorted suspects, and a few street people. When the evening meal arrived, Holoday offered his sandwich to "the biggest, toughest-looking guy in the place" thus, he claimed, buying himself protection.

Early that evening, Holoday was released on a $250,000 surety placed by Holoday's father, who had arrived on an Air Canada overnight flight. Except for weekly reports to the Bail Office, Holoday remained a free man for the next three and a half years.

SEVENTEEN

Law is not justice and a trial is not
a scientific inquiry into truth.
A trial is a resolution of a dispute.
– MR. JUSTICE EDSON HAINES, SUPREME COURT OF ONTARIO

Holoday continued working out of his office in the
Thomson Building, directly across from Toronto
City Hall. He dined at the neighbouring Sheraton Centre
and various gourmet restaurants around the city, continued to favour finely crafted suits, retained the nanny's
services, and still resided at 265 Forest Hill Road. What he
failed to do was make payments on the three mortgages
carried on the property — two to Royal Bank and one to
Doc and Elaine Roberts — or repay overdrafts on his personal chequing accounts of more than $500,000. In an
effort to collect the overdraft, the Royal Bank converted
the debt to a personal loan, but this proved just as ineffectual. Holoday, his wife Maureen, their nanny, and growing
family — Maureen gave birth to a third boy in early 1998
— resided in Forest Hill for almost six years without paying a penny against either their $2 million in total mort-
gages or the $500,000 personal loan.

Between October 1994 and October 2000, Holoday
retained a series of civil and criminal lawyers from some
of the top law firms in Canada, including Smith Lyons;
Cooper, Sandler & West; and, for a brief and awkward
appearance at his preliminary hearing on criminal

charges, two junior litigators from the legendary Eddie
Greenspan's office. His life during this period was an odd
extension of his brokerage career: constant scrambling for
cash, continued promises of payment to creditors, outrageous lies, and the assignment of blame to others. He was
required to report each Monday to the bail office to confirm
his residency in Canada, and appeared more than a dozen
times in civil court, where he faced claims filed against
him not only by his duped clients but by First Marathon
and Midland Walwyn, both named as co-defendants.
During the last year of his ongoing civil actions, Holoday
was reduced to defending himself in these matters, unable
to retain professional legal advice.

Most cases were settled out of court or through arbitration. In this manner, the securities firms, primarily
First Marathon, were not required to admit any wrongdoing. Both parties in these actions agreed to sign a confidentiality agreement, assigning penalties should either
side publicly reveal any terms of the settlement.

There is no evidence that any of Holoday's clients,
other than Randy Lang, managed to retrieve more than a
small portion of the money they lost. In one rumoured
instance, a former client who claimed losses of $400,000
against First Marathon finally saw her suit brought to
arbitration four years after discovering her loss. In the
arbitration room, her lawyers and First Marathon's legal
advisors argued back and forth throughout the morning.
At 11:45 a.m. the arbitrator announced that both sides
had 15 minutes to reach a decision; failing that, the session would have to be adjourned for as long as a year or
more before the arbitrator would be available again. The
client's lawyer advised her to settle for First Marathon's
best offer, a reported $195,000. It was less than half the
amount she was entitled to, the client protested. Did she
want to wait maybe another year or more? she was asked.

With reluctance, she agreed to the $195,000 settlement. For his guidance and advice, the lawyer's fees were $95,000, rewarding Holoday's former client with 25 percent of her original investment.

How did Holoday earn a living during the six years spent moving among various Toronto law firms, and fending off dozens of civil actions brought against him by former clients, former employers, and a half-dozen creditors such as Price Waterhouse and Mercedes-Benz? Stripped of his securities trading licence in 1996, and facing banishment for life from the entire industry, Holoday apparently managed to acquire clients and maintain business contacts in Canada, primarily Quebec and the US, promoting himself as a fee-for-service advisor, a role that did not require licensing or regulation as long as he was not placed in a position of trust.

Securities firms as large and imposing as Prudential Securities, Daiwa Securities, and UBP Asset Management, all in New York City, plus investment companies in Dallas, Minneapolis, Anchorage, Montreal, and Vancouver maintained contact with Holoday's Global Funding Inc. during the years following his arrest in June, 1997.[1] Given the confidential nature of the securities industry, little is known of Holoday's role in these investment matters, although evidence was later submitted that he had at least one client in the San Francisco area.

In the spring of 1998, Jeffrey Hoffman, a commercial litigator for the Toronto law firm Levitt Beber, received a routine directive from Hongkong Shanghai Bank of Canada, one of the firm's clients. The bank had an outstanding and apparently uncollectable loan for the lawyer to address. The amount was not excessive — about $30,000 — and the individual who refused to repay the debt, one Michael E. Holoday, was unknown to Hoffman.

Hoffman wrote Holoday the usual letter asking for payment, and a few days later received a telephone call in reply. "I want to strike a deal," Holoday told Hoffman.

"The deal," Hoffman recalled later, "was that Holoday would repay his debt to the bank, through us, at three thousand dollars a week. We agreed, and I forwarded documents for him to sign, instructing him to return them along with his first certified cheque." The documents, which included a Consent to Judgement form, were returned along with an uncertified cheque for the first $3,000 payment. The cheque was returned NSF on May 25, 1998.

Holoday's signature on the Consent to Judgement agreement compelled him to attend a meeting, known in legal circles as an *examination in aid of execution,* in Hoffman's law office. The meeting, on August 20, 1998, took about three hours to complete.

"My first impression of the guy was kind of favourable," Hoffman said. "He was polite, co-operative and, I thought, rather unsophisticated. He had asked me what documents he should bring, and seemed surprised when I mentioned certain routine procedures we had to follow." Holoday claimed his firm, Global Funding, was engaged in advising pension fund managers of investment strategies on a fee basis, generating something over $100,000 annual income for him as president. He also admitted he had made no payments on the two Royal Bank mortgages held on his Forest Hill home for over a year. The third mortgage held by Ken and Elaine Roberts, he explained to Hoffman, was not really a mortgage at all but a "collateralization of a loan."

Among the documents Holoday carted into Hoffman's office was an affidavit signed by him attesting to the truthfulness of a list of his assets and liabilities, the same list he had provided four years earlier to Ken and Elaine Roberts, and to Randy Lang's law firm. Hoffman's questions and investigations easily identified the only asset worth pursuing: Holoday's beloved cigarette boat *Bad Company,* still stored in a Gravenhurst marina and valued at $100,000.

In March 1999, *Bad Company* was sold for $50,000. By the time storage and repair costs were deducted, and Revenue Canada received their claim of $21,000, barely $18,000 of the $300,000 originally paid for the craft was available to be divided among Holoday's long list of creditors.[2]

Crown Attorney Brian McNeely not only had to prepare for a massive and complex trial; he also had to deal with Holoday's slippery behaviour, which continued unchanged from his years as a broker. Holoday, it appeared, was incapable of telling the truth. He eventually lost the support of lawyers representing him in civil matters, and on two occasions, criminal lawyers withdrew from defending him, providing the court with compelling reasons for ending their relationship.

None of this appeared to dent Holoday's confidence. He claimed he could hardly wait to see his former clients squirm under cross-examination, and was especially anxious to attack his in-laws. "When John Boczan gets on the stand," he boasted, "my lawyer will crucify him."[3]

The extent and nature of criminal charges against Holoday dictated the need for a preliminary trial. Originally scheduled for the spring of 1998, the preliminary procedure was delayed by Holoday, who used every means available. These included the departure (twice) of retained legal counsel, difficulties in retaining new counsel, claiming a conflict between civil and criminal proceedings, and using a hearing with the Investment Dealers Association, who sought to have Holoday banished for life, as an excuse. During this time, Holoday traded lawyers as though they were hockey cards. Austin Cooper, Peter West, Christopher Sharon, Frank Marrocco, Eddie Greenspan, and other names from the roster of prominent local lawyers were submitted by Holoday as his trial counsel. Only one, Peter West, appeared on Holoday's behalf to argue his innocence.

Preliminary proceedings against Holoday began in front of Justice W. D. August in February 1999, three weeks after the death of Doc Roberts. Holoday was represented by West, a tenacious but respected criminal trial lawyer who cross-examined many of Holoday's clients in detail — so much detail, in fact, that the session extended beyond its scheduled three weeks and was adjourned to October.

In August 1999, Holoday made an appeal to have the fall session postponed, stating that he was without counsel. West had asked to be removed from the proceedings, citing the same reason other lawyers had employed when withdrawing from Holoday's case: "a total loss of confidence" in the client. ("That means," a noted Toronto barrister explained, "that they were tired of being lied to.") Holoday claimed to be negotiating with counsellors Frank Marrocco of Smith Lyons (to whom Holoday already owed $220,000 in unpaid legal fees) and Eddie Greenspan to act on his behalf. Through the next few weeks, Holoday assured McNeely and various judges that he was within days of retaining one or the other, adding that his new counsellors, of course, would require further delays in order to acquaint themselves with the voluminous files of evidence. When neither Marrocco, Greenspan, nor anyone else came forward to confirm that they had indeed assumed Holoday's defence, he was informed that the second half of the preliminary hearing would take place in mid-October 1999, even if Holoday had to defend himself.

And he did.[4]

Holoday's efforts at cross-examining witnesses were perfunctory and awkward. His mother-in-law Carole Boczan collapsed in tears under his sarcastic questioning; Mona O'Hearn demanded to know how Holoday could face "your sweet baby boys" knowing how badly he had behaved; and Roger Gordon fumed from the stand, shooting daggers at the accused with his eyes. Holoday's actions in defending himself were so blatantly distasteful that one court official asked to be removed from the three-week hearing, saying she could not abide remaining in the same courtroom with the man.

To no one's surprise except Holoday's, Justice August declared that the Crown had presented sufficient evidence for the charges against Holoday to go forward, and a trial date was set for May 1, 2000. Holoday announced he wished to be tried by a judge and jury.

The following April, however, Holoday applied a new delaying tactic. The Royal Bank, which had been attempting for years to eject the Holodays from their Forest Hill mansion for failure to make mortgage payments, had begun the process of suing him into bankruptcy. Holoday fought the bankruptcy proceedings with as much fury as he used in civil and criminal proceedings brought by former clients and the Crown. He was not bankrupt, he claimed. He owned substantial assets, including the case of Dom Pérignon champagne he delivered to Roy O'Hearn in October 1994 (valued at $7,200), $150,000 in jewellery and fur coats, and other unspecified assets totalling $3.8 million. What's more, Holoday countered that the Royal Bank had withdrawn substantial amounts of money from his and his wife's personal chequing account without his authorization, referring to the float charges made by the bank to cover funds shifted back and forth by Holoday during his cheque-kiting activities involving the unsuspecting Doc and Elaine

Roberts. Holoday never complained of the charges, which reached as high as $40,000 per month, until 1997.[5]

Holoday's *chutzpah* reached new heights when, while arguing against bankruptcy proceedings by claiming he had more than sufficient assets to cover claimed liabilities of $1.2 million, Holoday simultaneously sought legal aid for his upcoming criminal trial. "I'm wealthy," he informed the bankruptcy court; "I'm insolvent," he pleaded to Legal Aid. It was a comic replay of his strangle strategy of investing, but once again Holoday lost at both ends: he was declared both bankrupt and capable of financing his own defence.

When Legal Aid turned down his request, Holoday refused to give in, announcing he would appeal the decision, effectively postponing proceedings until the autumn. No one had won an appeal against a decision by Legal Aid, and Holoday was no exception. He did, however, succeed in delaying the criminal trial for yet another six months. Finally, after avoiding mortgage payments for six years, the Holodays were evicted from Forest Hill Road at the end of September 2000. They relocated to a suburban tract house in Thornhill, whose $2,500 monthly rent was paid by Ronald Holoday. Michael and his father appeared to have reached some degree of *rapprochement* since the Holoday family had been snubbed at Michael's wedding nine years earlier.

Ronald Holoday seemed both confused and philosophical about his son and their relationship after Michael's arrest. "I don't know what changed Michael," the elder Holoday said, slumped in his Revelstoke office. "He left Revelstoke, and it's a place where money doesn't really count that much. People live here for the lifestyle and the scenery. Money is not such a big deal here. I don't understand Michael's choice of lifestyle."

If Holoday's surviving son had changed, perhaps it was rooted in that long-ago tragedy. "I'll tell you one thing that changes you," Ronald Holoday said, "and that's when you're eleven years old and you watch your five-year-old brother die under the wheels of a truck, right in front of your eyes. That changes you a whole lot."

But that wasn't the answer to Michael's total shift in values. "I just don't understand Michael's emphasis on money. I don't know where that came from, or why he seemed to become so focused on making a lot of money."

Would his son's upcoming criminal trial reveal some answers?

"I don't think there will be any criminal trial," Ronald Holoday said. "I think they'll have everything sorted out before they go to a trial."[6]

"I really want this one," Gary Logan said, referring to the Holoday trial. In Logan's opinion, Holoday was as arrogant as anyone Logan had encountered during his career. Logan and Jeff Thomson would be joined by Detective Constables Julie Burlie and Rick McKinney during the trial, a necessary move because Logan had been elevated to Internal Affairs since collaring Holoday and would miss several court appearances.

With Holoday's criminal trial date fixed, Gary Logan took the month of August 2000 for his annual vacation. Each day for the entire month, Logan withdrew to his suburban garage where he disassembled a classic old Norton 750 Commando motorcycle, right down to individual nuts and bolts. He cleaned and polished every item and reassembled the Norton into a shining, snarling machine that he planned to ride with pleasure someday, when his six-year-old investigation into Michael Holoday's crimes was complete.

By the autumn of 2000, at least three of Holoday's former clients had died, including the broken-hearted Doc Roberts. Of almost 60 clients at First Marathon, all of whom had lost substantial sums of money based on the firm's audit following Holoday's departure, only half were named in the fourteen formal charges brought against him by the Crown. These included 2 charges laid in connection with actions by Holoday that put the assets of Midland Walwyn and First Marathon Securities at risk, and 12 related to specific investors.

Holoday would be defending himself during the three-month proceedings. Wisely, he changed his mind and chose to be tried in front of a judge, instead of a judge and jury. The ensuing trial lasted 41 days.

Holoday's previous employers and the Canadian investment industry in general had changed. In 1998 Midland Walwyn, the last of the independent national brokerages in Canada, became Merrill Lynch Canada when purchased by the vaunted Wall Street firm. Almost exactly one year later, First Marathon was purchased by National Bank of Canada for $712.4 million.

Michael Holoday's criminal trial got underway at Toronto's University Avenue Courthouse on October 2, 2000, in front of Madam Justice Patricia German, a judge familiar with fraud and embezzlement cases. Throughout his trial, Holoday was granted extensive leeway by Madam Justice German, his wishes accommodated in ways that would not have been afforded an experienced trial lawyer. In response to a request by Holoday, the court did not sit on Fridays, providing him with the opportunity of travelling to Quebec, where the ex-broker claimed to have clients for his Global Funding Corporation.

Holoday was also permitted to cross-examine Crown witnesses in a manner that might have earned a barrister a verbal slap from the judge. He rambled on in a convoluted manner, often asking a new question before the witness had an opportunity to respond to a previous one. On several occasions, the judge provided him with the correct syntax to use in obtaining the answer he seemed to be seeking. Even the Crown assisted Holoday from time to time, providing documents, and raising infrequent objections in a gentle manner.

In his cross-examination of often-hostile former clients, Holoday honed their acrimony further by insisting that they refer to him as "Mister Holoday" ostensibly, he suggested, "to make it easier for the court to follow the transcriptions." During cross-examinations he strutted and postured, dressed in the fitted double-breasted suits he favoured with coloured shirts and silk ties, his hair coiffed and shiny, his manicure perfect. For the first two months he carted in multiple copies of thick, plastic-bound exhibit documents, mirroring the appearance of Crown exhibits right down to cover design and tabs.

None of it mattered. Holoday's cross-examinations were feckless and meandering, often dealing with matters more related to civil proceedings than to the charges he was facing. He seemed incapable of asking cogent questions, or tracing a logical line toward a point that might favour his denial of guilt. For the most part, his methods were ludicrous, and in at least one case, while cross-examining brother-in-law Howard Desmond, it was as damaging to his cause as anything the Crown presented.

Holoday could not resist demanding that clients and family members admit they benefited from his apparent generosity. He referred to vacations, Christmas gifts, sports tickets, jewellery, dinners, and other examples of his ongoing largesse, as though he were shaming his victims for complaining of his thefts from their investment accounts.

Cross-examining Desmond, Holoday again painted himself as the family benefactor. Hadn't he offered to give the Desmonds $25,000 to assist them in buying a house? No, Desmond replied, Holoday had said he would take the money from his mother-in-law Carole Boczan's account, and Desmond rejected that idea. Didn't he give the Desmonds $3,000 to help them purchase a van? Yes, Desmond agreed, Holoday had insisted on it, he wouldn't hear any arguments against the idea. And didn't Holoday pay the burial expenses for the Desmonds' twin babies who had died so tragically back in 1994, and donate the burial plot in Mount Pleasant Cemetery as their resting place?

You did, Desmond said, and then you made us remove the babies and bury them elsewhere because you said you had to sell the plot. And at that, Madam Justice Patricia German gasped and said, "Oh, my God."

Holoday stuttered that a court order had dictated the sale. Crown Attorney McNeely declined to point out the lie. He had no need to; the harm had been done.

The trial extended through October and November, and more than 40 witnesses appeared on behalf of the Crown. Margaret Raines proved calm and meticulous, and her recitation of events was utterly credible. Mona O'Hearn appeared flustered and confused, and avoided lecturing Holoday from the witness stand as she had during the preliminary trial. Elaine Roberts, riding the subway down from Eglinton Avenue carrying notes in a backpack like a middle-aged student attending college classes, managed to retain her dignity and poise over three days of testimony followed by long and sarcastic cross-examination by Holoday. Kurt Schleith flew in from a vacation in Austria and spent three days on the witness stand, swinging between dry amusement and quiet outrage when he recalled Holoday's actions.

To his surprise and dismay, Roger Gordon was not named in the charges against Holoday, and was not called

to testify about Holoday's activities while at the two brokerage houses. McNeely suggested this decision was a
matter of expediency, of selecting witnesses who offered
special insight. Perhaps, but the suspicion lingered that
Gordon, who still seethed with hostility over his treatment
first by Holoday and later by First Marathon, might lose
his composure on the witness stand and hinder the
Crown's case more than assist it.

Nor was Tracy Ellis called as a Crown witness. "We
suspect she may prove more beneficial to the defendant
than to us," Brian McNeely explained.

Among the most curious of the Crown's witnesses was
the Mississauga dentist, Randy Lang, who had mistrusted
Holoday to such an extent that he taped their conversations. After Holoday admitted making unauthorized withdrawals from both Lang's and his sister's investment
accounts, Lang and Holoday appeared to remain the best
of friends, lunching together during the noon break in
Holoday's cross-examination of Lang.

More enlightening, and more devastating to both
Holoday's case and the reputation of the two brokerages
that employed him, was testimony by David D. Walters,
president of a firm with the curiously intimidating name
of Ethics Incorporated. It would be difficult to identify
anyone more qualified to assess the antics of Holoday and
their impact on his clients than Walters, whose firm provides expertise in derivatives to dealers and clients
engaged in civil litigation. A former deputy director,
derivatives and commodity futures, of the Ontario
Securities Commission, he boasts degrees in Economics
and Accountancy, and has testified in a number of high-
profile criminal trials related to investment fraud.

In his appearance on behalf of the Crown, Walters was
a ramrod presence, speaking in paragraphs and drawing
upon an impressive reservoir of experience in the industry.

Holoday, he testified, had "blown his brains out" during the month of May 1994 when the broker lost more than $2 million of his own money. He verbally sneered at Holoday's strategies and, when prompted by Crown Attorney McNeely, dismissed any idea of either effective counselling or ethical behaviour on the part of Michael Holoday.

A more perceptive defendant might have chosen not to cross-examine Walters at all. Perception was not among Michael Holoday's most notable characteristics, however, and his joust with Walters proved destructive to both himself and his former employers.

"If clients are advised by registered representatives," Holoday asked Walters during cross-examination in his convoluted style, "that they should not be dealing in commodities and futures, and they (the clients) are of high net worth, and they still want to have a commodities account and do trades, and speculate, and the broker lets them open up an account, and the firm lets them open up an account, and trades are executed, who is responsible for the results of those trades at the end of the day?"

There was no hesitation on the part of Walters: "The broker and the dealer."

"Not the client?" Holoday said.

"No, the client should have been discouraged from opening the account, and should be forbidden to open the account," Walters explained. "'Open with the competition, but not on my books' should have been the position of the broker and the RR."

Neither Midland Walwyn nor First Marathon was on trial, but Walters' comment identified them as potential co-defendants, since Walters was suggesting that the financial well-being of the client should dominate all aspects of the brokerage business.

By early December, as the Crown's case was winding

down, Holoday no longer trucked boxes of bound exhibits into the courtroom in support of his case. Instead, he distributed stapled sheets of paper to the Crown and the court, blaming the printer for failing to prepare the documents on time.

The Crown finished its presentation with Martin Karp's testimony on December 5, 2000.[7] Holoday announced he would be calling 9 witnesses, a dramatic reduction from the 23 he had declared he would call a few days earlier. He gave no reason for the reduction, but the facts emerged later, along with the story behind the sudden change from professionally bound exhibits to hastily copied and stapled sheets of paper: Holoday had been bouncing cheques again. His cheques to the printer, who copied and assembled his elaborate exhibits, had been returned NSF. He had even written bad cheques to the process-server hired to deliver subpoenas to Holoday's first 9 witnesses, and the server refused to serve the remaining 14 on Holoday's list.

It made no difference, really. Holoday's defence witnesses were as ineffectual as his other efforts. His former branch manager Ben Kizemchuk had little to offer beyond Holoday's promising beginning as a broker, nor did representatives from the Royal Bank, a nervous Chuck Oliver, or a former accountant to Gary Davidson and Roy O'Hearn.

Forensic accountant John Douglas, retained by Holoday to counter the findings of James McAuley, whose forensic review on behalf of Kenneth and Elaine Roberts revealed the scope of Holoday's fraud, was equally weak. Douglas's draft report, based on incomplete records supplied by Holoday, indicated that Holoday owed nothing to the Roberts. Indeed, the report concluded, the records showed that the Roberts family owed Holoday $83 million. Douglas disparaged McAuley's report, suggesting it was faulty and incomplete — a curious response from one CA to another, especially in light of McAuley's position as a partner and senior vice-president of KPMG. Crown Attorney Brian McNeely appeared to take great delight, in his quiet methodical way, in shredding Douglas's testimony during cross-examination.

McNeely was also derisive of John Keen, the only former client of Holoday's who agreed to speak in his defence. Keen, the auto body shop employee who had advised Brian Rocks to place his investments with Holoday, and later announced to Rocks while on the third hole of their golf game that Holoday's financial structure was collapsing, provided perhaps the strangest testimony of the trial. On the stand, Keen boasted of his acquaintance with both First Marathon President Lawrence Bloomberg and Bloomberg's son-in-law Stephen Tuckner, whom Keen said assumed Keen's portfolio following Holoday's departure from the brokerage in October 1994. Tuckner's assumption of Keen's portfolio, if true, contradicted Thurman's blunt statement to Paul Simpkin that no one at First Marathon was handling retail accounts after Holoday was fired. Apparently someone was: Lawrence Bloomberg's own son-in-law, on a strangely selective basis.

Keen disagreed with the testimony of other former clients of Holoday's. According to the body shop worker, Holoday not only reported every bond purchase he made on behalf of his client, he also outlined the risk involved. A good thing, too, because Keen lost money on the account. Those other clients of Holoday's who complained about their losses? Just greedy, Keen suggested. Had Michael Holoday not resigned from First Marathon, Keen testified he would have retained his account with the broker and continued to follow his recommendations.

In cross-examination, not only did Brian McNeely

412 John Lawrence Reynolds

shatter any positive spin Keen tried to add to Holoday's defence, but he also made Keen look like a buffoon. Did Keen have other accounts at First Marathon under Michael Holoday's supervision? "Yes." Was one a commodity futures account? "Yes." Did Holoday keep Keen informed of every trade in that commodity account? "Yes." Every one? "Every one."

What, McNeely asked Keen, was a strike price? Keen didn't know. Did Keen know what a strangle was in commodities trading? "No." Was Keen familiar with the term *option decay?* "No." Could he define a put? "No." A call? "No." Did Holoday ever issue Keen a cheque drawn on Keen's account at First Marathon? "Yes." Did the cheque clear Holoday's bank? "No." Why not? "It bounced."[8]

McNeely had every right, but too much class, to sneer at Keen when he completed his cross-examination. Holoday had no further questions, but he and Keen agreed to meet when court was over that day and have a drink, maybe even dinner.

In early January 2001 both sides made their final submissions, in writing, before Madam Justice German. The Crown's was perfunctory and detailed. Holoday's was bizarre.

Michael Holoday, youngest member ever of the Midland Walwyn Chairman's Club, protégé (perhaps even lost biological son . . .) of Doc Roberts, and heir apparent to Lawrence Bloomberg, "was a lousy broker," according to Holoday's defence. "The accused was not intelligent enough to predict that the markets could go sideways long enough to cause the (strangle) strategy to cause (*sic*) significant losses for his clients. In hindsight the risk was higher than the accused anticipated and expected. The request (*sic*) mental criteria for fraud was not met, because the accused believed in the trading strategy's (*sic*) he recommended to his clients."

Incompetence and stupidity, then, were Holoday's twin pillars of defence, bolstered, according to his submission, by the general deceitfulness of his own clients. According to Holoday, he had indeed earned money and issued payment to the accused to cover their losses. "The best evidence of this," Holoday submitted, "is the fact that the clients that received these payments from the accused did not report these payments to Revenue Canada on their income tax returns," which neatly sidestepped proof that the payments had been made at all. "During the course of this trial," Holoday said, "this was 'the dog that did not bark.'"

It was a silly allusion. On February 5, 2001, Madam Justice Patricia German found Holoday guilty on all 14 counts of fraud. Two days later, while Maureen Holoday sat teary-eyed in the front row of the spectator benches — her first appearance at her husband's trial — the judge revoked Holoday's bail and ordered him held in custody for sentencing.

Judge German's reasons for removing the freedom Holoday had enjoyed since being charged more than three years earlier were compelling. Crown Attorney Brian McNeely called a securities specialist from TD Bank to testify that Holoday had been kiting cheques between the TD and HSBC/Hong Kong Bank of Canada, defrauding the banks of over $40,000 in the process. Taking the stand next, Detective Jeffrey Thomson managed to conceal his glee as he testified that Holoday had paid for the documents used in his defence with bad cheques. "That's a really stupid thing to do," one court official said later, referring to Holoday's actions. "You can talk your way around a lot of things, but you don't hand the judge documents you obtained by fraud."

There was much to discuss among the trial's participants during the four weeks separating Holoday's conviction from his sentencing. A prime topic was the press coverage of the trial — or, more correctly, the lack of it. *Toronto Star* business writer Tony Van Alphen, having reported on Holoday's alleged activities since his arrest in June 1997, covered the Holodays' bankruptcy fight and attended each day's proceedings of the criminal trial, filing stories of each day's testimony. The *Toronto Sun,* hardly an investor's must-read paper, carried reports on the trial from time to time filed by Sam Pazzano, and Toronto television stations featured footage of Holoday's first day in court on their major newscasts.

Readers of Canada's two national business-oriented newspapers could be forgiven if they professed ignorance of the story that unfolded in front of Justice German over a four-month period. The *Globe and Mail* had run two background stories on Holoday, one before and one after he was formally charged, and *National Post* writer Katherine Macklem had covered his alleged escapades and appearances in court following the preliminary trial. But once the trial began, the *Globe* lost interest and the *Post* lost Macklem, who was recruited as a leading business writer by *Maclean's* magazine. Neither newspaper covered the proceedings until Holoday's conviction and sentencing, with the exception of the *Post,* who dispatched a junior reporter to court on the day Holoday presented his written defence. The reporter seized a copy of his submission, bolted for the door, and used it as the basis for an almost incomprehensible update of the proceedings, considering the intricacies of the trial to that point.

On Monday, March 12, 2001, Holoday stood in front of Madam Justice German again, this time for sentencing. Greg Tweney, who played a supportive role during Holoday's criminal trial, presented the Crown's submission himself. Holoday, Tweney stated in a superbly delivered appearance, represented a "systematic course of deliberate criminal conduct." Citing the need for deterrence, and restoring public faith in the financial and investment industry, Tweney asked for a sentence of eight to ten years.

Lawyer Frank Marrocco was retained by Ronald Holoday, who flew in from Revelstoke accompanied by Holoday's two sisters, to plead for a lighter sentence. During Marrocco's presentation he sounded like an actor in an unfamiliar play, unsure of either his lines or his motivation. Something between five and seven years, Marrocco suggested in his stumbling plea, would be appropriate.

A pre-sentence report had been prepared on Holoday while he was held in Toronto's squalid Don Jail, and its contents were almost as damaging to him as any evidence submitted at his trial. Holoday claimed he had "done the best he could" over the previous seven years to settle differences with his clients, and had gone bankrupt in the attempt. More than any of his victims, Holoday suggested, he was the biggest loser of all.

Michael's mother, Mary Lou Holoday, shone a weak light on her family's dynamics when she informed the probation officer who drafted the pre-sentence report that her son "doesn't know where reality begins or ends," and suggested Michael may have acquired his habit of lying from a sister "who also lies and also is in a fantasy world." Her son seemed to lack self-confidence and required a lot of praise, she recalled, although he did possess a good memory. Her husband attributed their son's problems to a total shift in values after Michael arrived in Toronto. "That's not the way he was raised," Ronald Holoday said, referring to the frauds and embezzlements. "Something happened. I don't know what, or why . . ."

Mary Lou Holoday at least had a theory about that. After Holoday met Maureen, his mother stated to the probation officer, he always seemed intent on impressing Maureen and her family with money.[9]

Carole Boczan, anxious to bridge the gulf between herself and her daughter, told the author of the pre-sentence report that her son-in-law had been "generous to a fault, and truly believed he had my best interests at heart." Holoday, in his commentary, dismissed any notion of a *rapprochement* with his in-laws. Maureen's mother, he declared, was dishonest and a liar, "and as a person," he added, "she is a social user." His extended criminal trial? It was "a misuse of public funds," Holoday said.

Holoday, the officer noted in her summary, continued to maintain his innocence. Given "his belief that he is the biggest loser in all that has transpired, and his unwillingness to accept responsibility for his behaviour, it would appear that the likelihood of a community-based disposition, serving as a rehabilitative measure, is limited."[10]

Madam Justice German, for her part, called Holoday "a dangerous man" who had shaken the public's faith in the Canadian financial and investment industry, and sentenced him to 7 1/2 years in penitentiary. She also ordered him to repay over $6 million to his various former clients. All four Toronto newspapers and the three major Toronto television channels covered the sentencing.

The dozen or so participants in Holoday's career who had attended the sentencing — Albert Robinson, Helen Rentis, Roger Gordon, Ray and Mary Kundinger, Brian Rocks, Gary Davidson, Anthony Honeywood and others — filed out of the courtroom while Holoday was handcuffed. Maureen sat sobbing between Holoday's two sisters, who appeared indifferent to both Maureen's plight and the sentencing of their brother.

"It's not enough," was the most commonly heard phrase in the courthouse corridor afterwards. "Not nearly enough." Most had expected 10 years. Some speculated as high as 14 years.

"He'll get more," a subdued Gary Logan said, referring to new charges of fraud committed during Holoday's trial period. "Whatever he gets will be added to this."

"Still not enough," most muttered, and wandered out of the courthouse to be interviewed by reporters or just return home and get on with their lives.

Before Holoday was sentenced, Gary Logan had suggested he plead guilty to the new fraud charges Holoday faced, related to cheque-kiting activities between HSBC and TD Bank. "That way," Logan said, "anything you get will run concurrent with the earlier charges, and you won't need to face extra time."

Typically, Holoday waved away Logan's suggestion. Plead guilty? Not a chance.

Two days after receiving the seven-and-a-half year sentence from Madam Justice German, Holoday changed his mind and pled guilty to the new charges after all. This time, in front of a new judge, Holoday received a sentence of 15 months, to run consecutively with the sentence he had already received. His change of heart, 48 hours too late, cost him more than a year in prison. In all, Holoday would serve almost nine years, requiring nearly three years before parole eligibility.

"He's not too smart, is he?" Gary Logan said, echoing the comment Holoday had made about Logan four years earlier. This time, the relative wisdom of each man was there for all to see.

EIGHTEEN

No legacy is so rich as honesty.
– WILLIAM SHAKESPEARE *(ALL'S WELL THAT ENDS WELL)*

ichael Holoday's career as an investment advisor was bracketed by two significant events. He began work on the day of the largest single decline in world stock market values, a plunge whose impact on Canada was as profound as anywhere else in the world. He departed the business in mid-1994 on the cusp of the longest unbroken period of stock market growth in history.

Most of Holoday's clients did not participate in this growth period because many of the funds they invested with him were lost in bad trades or consumed by Holoday's churning of their accounts, generating only commissions for Holoday and the two brokerages that employed him. The few clients of Holoday's who managed to recover at least a small portion of their original investment missed out on most of this growth before it petered out in the spring of 2000.[1]

When the long process of bringing Holoday to justice ended — a process whose duration of six-and-a-half years almost equalled the length of Holoday's entire investment career — the predictable head-scratching and assessment began.

For many investors, the evaluation involved some

degree of self-flagellation. *How could I have been so stupid?* was the common reaction. The victims blamed themselves as much as they blamed Holoday's perfidy. The reaction may have been understandable, but it was also unnecessary and untrue. Holoday's victims were lacking in neither intelligence nor awareness, and only a few could be labelled greedy. The vast majority were both highly intelligent and conservative in their expectations. They were looking for investment returns somewhat higher than those available from bank instruments such as GICs and savings accounts. Neither stupid nor greedy, they were perhaps guilty only of excessive trust, and not merely of Holoday. They trusted and believed that the two institutions that employed Michael Holoday would stand behind the actions of their representative in the same manner that a chartered bank, life insurance company, or other firms in a fiduciary position are expected to accept responsibility for the actions of its employees. They trusted the various regulatory agencies — the Toronto Stock Exchange, the Investment Dealers Association, and the Ontario Securities Commission — to take a stand on their behalf. Finally, they trusted the legal system through civil law to provide a vehicle through which they could recover their lost funds.

None fulfilled that trust. Investors found themselves not only lacking support from but actually combatting the two brokerages, who denied responsibility for their representative's actions. The experience was shocking, frustrating, and eye-opening. The odds, most of Holoday's clients felt, had been against them from the beginning. They simply had not been aware of the fact.

Neil Gross, who represented several of Holoday's former clients in civil litigation, noted that "stockbrokers and their firms actively portray themselves as professional investment advisors, and correspondingly they must shoulder the greater burden of responsibility that comes with professional status. As would-be professionals, it lies ill in their mouths to evade responsibility by downloading it onto the customer."[2]

More than one of Holoday's clients suggested they would have been wiser to trust their money to a roulette wheel than to Holoday, the Bay Street Whiz Kid. They had a point.

Walk into a gambling casino with a fistful of money and you have no doubt of your location, your environment, or the experience you are about to undergo. The decor is garish, the promises are enticing, and the drinks are free. The odds favour the house. The house runs the game. The rules are clearly stated and cannot be broken. You will know immediately if you have won or lost, and you will usually lose. When you do, you will at least receive a smile, an empathetic shake of the head, and an invitation to return.

Walk into a brokerage house and everything exists to reassure and comfort you. You are reminded, in the firm's advertising and information brochures, of its professionalism. You are told that your financial advisor or registered representative or broker meets high professional standards. You are made aware of the extensive support system that the individual assigned to service your account enjoys, including market research and analysis. You are handed pamphlets listing affiliations with organizations peopled by steely-eyed administrators who tolerate no nonsense. You are informed that the activities of your broker are observed and sanctioned by various government and quasi-legal institutions. You are assured that, while no promises can be made of earnings and returns, you have made The Right Choice in securing your financial future.

You are told all of this without being reminded that the investment advice you receive will be only as good as the individual providing it . . . that the advice may involve a risk of loss higher than those associated with roulette . . . that you may not be aware you have lost money until several years after the loss occurs . . . that the rules may be broken at anytime, and you could be held responsible for losses that occur as a result . . . and that getting your money back could prove as elusive as identifying the winning combination in any odds-based game in Las Vegas. Expect to recover only a small percentage of any losses incurred as a result of the brokerage's malfeasance, and then only after several years of effort and several thousand dollars in legal fees.

Nothing experienced by any of the investors associated with Michael Holoday disputes this observation or provides comfort for Canadian investors. In sentencing him, Madam Justice German commented that Holoday had shaken public confidence in this country's investment markets, due to his multiple breaches of trust. She was correct, of course. She could not comment, however, on the actions of the brokerage firms, or of the industry's regulatory organizations.

Industry representatives claim a tripartite system of safeguards and enforcement is in place to help protect investors against fraud. The three elements — the Toronto Stock Exchange, the Investment Dealers Association (both national in scope), and the Ontario Securities Commission — divide the responsibility in Ontario, but their dedication to the concerns of individual investors is minimal. There may be practical reasons for this, considering the large number of Canadians who trade shares and units in stocks, bonds, and mutual funds. Niggling daily concerns about missing assets are best dealt with at the brokerage level. It can only be hoped that the brokerage's response to concerns is more energetic and effective than Midland Walwyn's and First Marathon's.

The primary concern of the TSE, IDA, and OSC troika is *the accreditation and regulation of member brokerages.* Consider the self-stated mission of each:

The IDA's mission is "to foster efficient capital markets by encouraging participation in the savings and investment process, and by ensuring the integrity of the marketplace." It achieves this goal, for the most part, by ensuring that its member firms "are maintaining adequate capital in accordance with the nature and volume of business they conduct," and it retains "the authority to prosecute individuals who are suspected of wrongdoing and to exact penalties in the form of fines or suspensions from the industry."[3]

"The IDA is also slow," the *Globe and Mail's* Rob Carrick reported in one of his columns dedicated to small investor matters. "Bring them a complaint and you would be extremely lucky if it was resolved in a year. You would also have to forget about compensation for your losses, because the IDA is concerned only about punishing breaches of its rules for broker conduct." Its effectiveness even in that role, Carrick suggested, is questionable. "Doubts remain," he reported, "about how aggressively the IDA goes after rogue brokers, and how co-operative the investment industry is in the process."[4]

The Ontario Securities Commission's stated mission sounds like the IDA's, but played in a different key. The OSC exists "To protect investors from unfair, improper or fraudulent practices, and to foster fair and efficient capital markets and confidence in their integrity." Not a self-regulated organization ("SRO") like the IDA, the OSC reports to the provincial Ministry of Finance and possesses teeth to force settlements, ban participants from the industry, freeze broker funds, apply fines, and wield a regulatory club. Its activities usually make news but generate little in the way of recompense for investors whose savings have been effectively stolen by brokers.[5]

Finally, where does the TSE fit into this picture? It was to the TSE that Joe Thurman headed when he discovered the extent of Holoday's escapades, after Holoday left First Marathon. Why there? After all, Holoday's trades were conducted for the most part not at the TSE but at the Chicago Board of Trade, via Refco.

"We have jurisdiction over any participating organization, no matter what they are trading," explained Tom Atkinson, vice-president of regulation services at the TSE. He was uncomfortable discussing specifics of the Holoday case, even several weeks after Holoday had been convicted. He alluded to Holoday's actions by stating: "When someone is working outside the SRO system, so that normal supervisory action won't catch him, it's a criminal matter."[6]

How can small investors feel secure that someone is watching out for their interests, and that information being provided to them by their broker is true? Steve Kee, manager, media/information services with the TSE, feels the investor is becoming capable of doing it himself or herself.

"Investors are a lot more sophisticated than they were four or five years ago," suggested Kee. "The last survey we did (in 2000) showed that fifty percent of Canadians directly or indirectly held shares in Canadian corporations." How does widening the universe improve the ability of investors to protect themselves from fraud? "You have the Internet, you have access to information, so I think you get a far more sophisticated investor," Kee said. "The access to information means that people learn a lot more, they understand a lot more. The questions they ask are more sophisticated." Much of the driving force behind this growth in sophistication, Kee said, was the rise in discount brokerage trades, where investors become their own trader and compliance officer.[7]

Kee's observation was being shattered even while he spoke, at least as far as the influence of the Internet was concerned. That very morning, the OSC held a press conference to reveal that it had operated a fictitious Web site offering monthly returns of up to 30 percent per month on "international debentures" eligible for RRSPs. The OSC wanted to alert investors to the dangers of relying upon Internet sites for data and guidance. Over six weeks, more than a hundred Canadians accessed the site, many offering to send $50,000 or more without further information.[8]

It's difficult to feel sympathy for anyone both greedy and foolish enough to forward a large chunk of cash based on little more than a Web site promise, but the OSC's experiment proved a larger point. The discount brokerages, who Kee suggested are responsible for raising the sophistication level of investors, encourage clients to carry out their own research — much of it on the Web — while US sources, quoted in the *Globe and Mail* story, suggest that half the messages in Internet chat rooms contain false information.

Edward Nelles, a Bay Street veteran with 23 years experience who now lends his experience to the Small Investors Protection Association, has another counterpoint to Kee's suggestion. "Individual investing is much more widespread than it used to be," he told Rob Carrick of *Report On Business Magazine,* "but the financial acumen of the average investor is lower than it was twenty years ago. This means that a lot of people are taking for granted broker activities that more experienced investors would have kept a closer eye on."[9]

In its package of material produced to reassure investors, the Toronto Stock Exchange describes itself as "a regulatory body governing its own members and listed companies which helps to protect you and all investors."[10] The

Exchange generates multiple news releases each year, declaring its role in various regulatory and disciplinary actions against TSE-listed firms and Canadian brokerage houses. When it comes to dealing with bread-and-butter issues affecting individual small investors, however, its actions appear more circumspect.

In February 1998, the TSE refused to acknowledge reports in both the *Toronto Star* and *Maclean's* magazine that its own investigation had concluded that Michael Holoday was "properly supervised" by First Marathon.[11] This decision tended to strengthen the brokerage's defence against various civil actions brought by former clients, and was expressed in a letter to First Marathon president Lawrence Bloomberg. As a result of its findings, the letter stated, the exchange would not pursue disciplinary action against Bloomberg's company.[12]

The letter was signed by Tom Atkinson, who wrote: "Having reviewed the findings of the [Holoday] investigation, TSE staff has determined that First Marathon Securities Limited properly supervised Michael Holoday while he was employed by them."

Not only is the TSE staff's perception circumspect, but so is their efficiency. Atkinson's letter to Bloomberg is dated December 16, 1997, more than three years after Joe Thurman discovered the full extent of Holoday's fraud, and more than six months after Gary Logan and Jeff Thomson arrested Holoday.

Of course, it was not the brokerage houses that suffered losses as a result of Holoday's activities, notwithstanding any out-of-court settlements that must remain confidential; it was individual investors. In fact, the brokerage houses profited significantly. In 1991, Holoday generated $1,117,499 in commissions for Midland Walwyn; the following year he doubled it to $2,038,823. And in just the first nine months of 1994, First Marathon recorded $3.3 million in commissions from Holoday's various deals.[13]

The TSE's finding that First Marathon had properly supervised Michael Holoday was thrown into serious doubt when another governing body, the IDA, concluded that Holoday "misled and obstructed the compliance-monitoring efforts at Midland and First Marathon by back-dating and forging documents."[14]

In a sheet from *Market Matters,* the TSE's guide to novice investors, the text under "How to Choose a Broker" reads:

> *Even after you pick a broker, remember that you are the one in charge. Your broker can make recommendations, but you make the decisions. Also, if you ever have a question or complaint about your broker's actions, call the brokerage firm's sales or branch manager or compliance officer.*[15]

A number of Holoday's clients had in fact contacted First Marathon about their accounts. The response was for the investors to discuss the matter with their broker.

In evaluating First Marathon's failure to detect and respond to Michael Holoday's fraudulent activities, hindsight provides more than clarity — it reveals a surprising degree of myopia where client interests were concerned.

Consider the various promptings that presented themselves during Holoday's 14 months at First Marathon:

Glennis MacLean writes Thurman, claiming that Holoday is engaged in discretionary trading.

Shortly after MacLean's allegation, Greg Weber responds to an auditor's inquiry by noting a shortfall in his account statement. First Marathon leaves it for Holoday to settle.

Roy O'Hearn calls from Maryland saying Holoday

confirmed O'Hearn's account was valued at well over $600,000 in US funds, but First Marathon's records show his account is virtually depleted. First Marathon treats it as a bookkeeping error. Bookkeeping errors occur — but at the US$600,000 level?

Holoday becomes physically ill in Wood's office when trying to explain the above situation to O'Hearn.

Thurman writes Holoday a memo on May 4, warning the broker about "free riding" on several of his accounts.

Holoday bounces two substantial cheques written to First Marathon — US$350,000 and US$236,000.

Sheldon Fenton pays First Marathon monthly commissions exceeding $300,000 in May 1994. At what point does "churning" become a possibility worth investigating?

On May 24, Wood reviews Holoday's massive personal losses in recent weeks. Seen against other facts, this fails to trip any alarms.

Helen Rentis, unable to rationalize the difference between her account statements and her broker's claims, does precisely what the TSE investor's information material instructs her to do: she calls the compliance officer. His response is "Talk to your broker." Rentis' complaint is a clear echo of the "simulations" Holoday conducted at Midland Walwyn.

Holoday bounces a third cheque to First Marathon, this one for US$120,000.

Holoday is warned for a second time in June about "free riding" by his clients.

Later that month, Holoday's financial status is so desperate he asks for the return of his US$108,000 T-bill, held for security by First Marathon.

A few days later, he asks to borrow $2 million from First Marathon.

First Marathon receives news of Holoday's US$299,000 cheque to Roy O'Hearn.

Thurman summarizes six problems with Holoday in a memo to David Wood dated June 30.[16]

Letters from bitter ex-employees, complaints from disgruntled clients, large-scale personal financial problems, and convenient fainting spells do not, in themselves, prove guilt. But any three or four of these, seen against Holoday's murky reputation, should have been sufficient to generate a deeper inquiry into the activities of their managing partner, futures division.[17]

After September 28, 1994, when Holoday claimed he had been paying blackmail to a number of clients and David Wood demanded his resignation, Holoday remained free to raid client assets. He wrote letters, faxed documents, and, according to Marlena Titian at least, was able to obtain funds from First Marathon on the say-so of documents he created and submitted.

Years after Holoday's frauds ended, the brokerages continued to claim innocence. When the *Toronto Star* made inquiries about First Marathon's responsibilities for Holoday's activities, an executive vice-president at National Bank Financial, successor to First Marathon, referred to the TSE's unacknowledged letter from Atkinson to Lawrence Bloomberg to justify its claim of innocence. First Marathon, said Lorie Haber, had no awareness of Holoday's dealings until after Holoday left the firm. "They took place off our books," he claimed. "There were no complaints from clients during that time."[18]

Of course there were. When complaints were made, the clients were referred to their broker, Michael Holoday who, need it be said, failed to record them for future reference. In its defence against civil charges launched by various First Marathon clients, the brokerage claimed (in Marlena Titian's case) that it "was excluded from knowledge of any such disputes and was not afforded the opportunity to resolve such disputes."[19] How could it have knowledge of

disputes when concerned clients were being referred back
to their broker for explanation and settlement?

Caveat emptor carries as much validity in the stock market
as anywhere. Were all of Holoday's clients either fools or
greedy? There is no evidence that they were. Nor did they
rely on Internet chat rooms or washroom walls for their
information. They relied on trust, and on the expectation
that their brokerage's compliance officer would be vigilant in
identifying and investigating evidence of broker misconduct.

Things may be changing. Peter Hanert, director of
communications at Merrill Lynch Canada, concedes that
in the mid-1990s brokerage management avoided making
calls to clients about compliance matters in fear that it
might disrupt the close broker/client relationship. Now,
Hanert claims, it is "reasonably routine" for brokers to
contact clients about their accounts.[20]

The Investment Dealers Association, the self-regulat-
ing organization that disagreed with the TSE's white-
washing of First Marathon's culpability in the Holoday
matter, has hardened its stand in defence of investors.
After dismissing Greg Clark, its senior vice-president,
member regulation, the IDA appointed Paul Bourque, a
former Alberta deputy minister of justice and deputy
attorney general, in his place. Hiring a top-level lawman
for the job was one signal that the IDA may be taking
investor concerns seriously.

A more decisive step took place in June 2001 when the
IDA announced that it would force all its brokerage members to report every complaint, client settlement, arbitration hearing, and civil action. The data would be filed in an
IDA-monitored database, which will be used to monitor
complaint trends and issues, and pinpoint those business
practices (not to mention the brokerages) that appear to be
generating the most problems.

A step in the right direction perhaps. But the reports will be filed quarterly. And where client settlements are bound by confidentiality agreements between brokerage and client, little or no data will be made available. Finally, the system will continue to depend on the competence and veracity of the brokerages and their compliance officers in responding to client complaints.

Michael Holoday was transferred to Millhaven Penitentiary following his sentencing. After processing and assessment, he was moved to Kingston Penitentiary before being settled in Beaver Creek, near Gravenhurst, Ontario, in early July 2001, just in time to enjoy the Muskoka summer. Beaver Creek, a minimum-security facility, provides extensive recreational facilities and affords inmates the opportunity to live in residential-style units.

Assuming Holoday's record is clear, he will be eligible for day parole in August 2002, parole with restrictions in February 2004, and full parole in January 2007. His sentence will be completed December 11, 2009.

So much for the hard facts, the losses, the legal jousts. None would have occurred without the facet of Michael Holoday's personality that compelled him to steal millions of dollars from people who trusted and admired him. Some believe Holoday's self-centred actions — his proposal, for example, that the Hoopers mortgage their retirement home, and his cashing of Dianne Sone's $50,000 Canada Savings Bond without any apparent deliberation — is proof of an evil mind. Or perhaps it is simply an inability of Holoday, and others like him, to perceive reality in a normal fashion. There is some evidence that the latter opinion is as valid as any.

I encountered Michael Holoday on a few occasions between our first meeting in March 1993 and his arrest in

June 1997. My wife Judy's sister, Carole Boczan, took understandable pride in her son-in-law's achievements and her daughter's good fortune to marry him. When Judy and I were wed in early 1993, I was drawn into the extended family of Soucies and Boczans without engaging in any encounters with Holoday himself. I attended the wedding he hosted for his brother-in-law Paul Boczan and his bride; heard Connie Gould attack a bemused George Gunn for daring to question Holoday's integrity; and was present at the wedding in November 1994 where Holoday told Dianne Sone her money was "gone," offering no explanation.

Any attempt on my part to engage Holoday in conversation at these events or other family gatherings proved fruitless because, I discovered later, Holoday knew that much of my writing activity at the time was being performed on behalf of various financial institutions and mutual fund companies. The Whiz Kid, I assume, was concerned that I might ask unsuitable questions, or make a "No, he can't" remark similar to George Gunn's. So when I approached Holoday following one of his court appearances at Toronto's Old City Hall in October 1997 and asked if we could have a chat over coffee, I expected to be rebuffed. Instead, Michael said sure, and we walked across Queen Street to the coffee shop in the Sheraton Centre.

As soon as we sat down, I placed my tape recorder in front of him. "Michael," I said, "I want to be up front from the beginning. I'm doing a book on you and the criminal charges you're facing."

I half-expected him to rise and leave without speaking. Instead, his grin widened. "I think," he said, "it should be a movie."

Was he joking? I suspected he was. "Okay," I said, going along with the gag. "We'll get Tom Cruise to play you."

Holoday's face grew solemn. He gave the idea some consideration, and then nodded. "That would be good," he agreed. "Tom Cruise will be fine."

He was, without doubt, quite serious.

NOTES

CHAPTER TWO

[1] In one of those curious quirks of history that mean nothing but
signify everything, Lord Revelstoke's family-owned banking firm
was Barings Bank. During precisely the same period that
Michael Holoday was liquidating the contents of client accounts
for his own purposes in Toronto — driven for the most part by
disastrous futures trading — Nick Leeson was in Singapore setting off charges that would demolish Barings, the esteemed 230-
year-old financial institution, also as a result of trading futures.

[2] Conversation with the author, November 1997.

[3] Conversation with the author, Revelstoke, November 11, 1997.

[4] Conversation with the author, Toronto, November 21, 1997.

[5] Conversation with the author, Toronto, November 21, 1997.

[6] Conversation with the author, Toronto, November 21, 1997.

[7] Conversation with the author, Kelowna BC, November 12, 1997.

CHAPTER THREE

[1] Three principals of Osler were convicted in November 1995,
more than 7 years after the firm's collapse (the mills of
Canada's fraud investigators grind exceedingly slow) and sentenced to jail terms. The losses to Osler clients and shareholders exceeded $12 million, and while the principals were banned
for life from investment activities in Canada, they quickly
found work on the fringes of the industry to support themselves
while on bail and awaiting appeal. The entire Osler tale is told
in detail by Deborah Thompson in her book *Greed: Investment
Fraud in Canada and Around the Globe* (Viking, 1997).

[2] Like Osler, Davidson brought its own cloud of scandal with its
assets. The brokerage firm was rumoured to have suffered
heavy losses at its Calgary office as a result of lending money
to clients who chose to invest in the volatile Alberta Stock
Exchange.

[3] Dunnery Best, "Canada: A Nation of Market Timers," *Globe and
Mail,* January 31, 1998, p. B25.

[4] "Midland Boasts Most Sales Staff," *Globe and Mail,* June 26, 1988.

[5] Conversation with the author, November 1997.

[6] Midland Walwyn, the last of the large independent Canadian

brokerage houses, was sold to Merrill Lynch Canada in 1998. First Marathon Securities was purchased by National Bank of Canada in mid-1999. Since all of the elements of Michael Holoday's story occurred well before both events, the firms will be referred to as Midland Walwyn and First Marathon throughout the text.

[7] "Midland-Walwyn Head Had Flamboyant Image," *Globe and Mail,* April 2, 1991, p. A6.

[8] *Globe and Mail,* April 2, 1991, p. A6; *Financial Post,* April 2, 1991, p. 23.

[9] *Toronto Star, Globe and Mail,* and *Telegram,* November 12, 1959.

CHAPTER FOUR

[1] Conversation with the author, January 5, 1998.

[2] Conversation with the author, November 21, 1997.

[3] Conversation with the author, November 21, 1997.

[4] Conversation with the author, November 21, 1997.

[5] Jake Bernstein, "How the Futures Markets Work" (New York Institute of Finance, Paramus NJ, 1989) p. vii.

[6] Bernstein, "How the Futures Markets Work," p. viii.

[7] Conversation with the author, November 21, 1997.

[8] Conversation with the author, November 21, 1997.

[9] Bernstein, "How the Futures Markets Work," p. 136.

[10] Conversation with the author, November 21, 1997.

[11] Conversation with the author, November 21, 1997.

[12] A pseudonym.

CHAPTER FIVE

[1] Conversation with the author, January 14, 1998.

[2] Conversation with the author, April 21, 1999.

[3] Weber succeeded in obtaining his MBA in 1995 and, ironically, was serving as vice-president, security operations, for TD Securities at the time of Holoday's trial in October 2000.

[4] Rentis testimony, October 23, 2000.

[5] Lee Belland, "For the Doctor, the Operation Was a Big Success," *Toronto Star,* December 6, 1974.

[6] Roberts testimony, November 15, 2000.

CHAPTER SIX

1 O'Donnell testimony, October 24, 2000.
2 R. O'Hearn testimony, November 23, 2000.
3 Gittings testimony, November 7, 2000.
4 Gittings testimony, November 7, 2000.
5 Raines testimony, October 10, 2000.
6 This makes strip bonds a preferred choice for RRSPs, where all earnings are sheltered from tax until withdrawn.
7 Raines never saw this document until Holoday's trial; the observations are based on her testimony, October 10, 2000.
8 Raines testimony, October 10, 2000.
9 M. O'Hearn testimony, November 29, 2000.
10 Cowie testimony, October 11, 2000.
11 Sones testimony, November 30, 2000.
12 Conversation with the author, November 1997.
13 Conversation with the author, January 2, 2001.
14 E. Roberts testimony, November 15, 2000.
15 E. Roberts preliminary trial testimony, February 26, 1999.

CHAPTER SEVEN

1 Conversation with the author, January 20, 1998.
2 A number of Holoday's clients testified this was an ongoing problem, one that they kept pointing out to Holoday. These include Ted Gittings, Margaret Raines, and Helen Rentis.
3 Conversation with the author, June 1, 2001.
4 Court documents #016681 and #016682.
5 Court documents #016951 and #016952.
6 Raines testimony, October 10, 2000.
7 Raines testimony, October 10, 2000.
8 Sinclair testimony, October 5, 2000.
9 Sinclair testimony, October 5, 2000.
10 Sinclair testimony, October 5, 2000.
11 In addition to Margaret Raines, Ted Gittings, Martin Karp, Mona O'Hearn, and others testified that they had difficulty reading their Midland Walwyn statements. Some testified, as Mona O'Hearn did, that they just gave up and relied exclusively on Holoday's personal statements.
12 This point of view was submitted later by First Marathon Securities, suggesting a standard industrywide approach to client complaints of this type.

[13] Sinclair testimony, October 5, 2000
[14] Doney testimony, October 3, 2000.
[15] Court document #6352.
[16] Court document #6353.
[17] Cowie preliminary trial testimony, October 29, 1999.
[18] In documents submitted as evidence, and in the author's possession, 61 of Holoday's accounts and their financial status as of December 31, 1991, appear on the list. The majority of these clients were not called to give evidence; as a result, I have avoided revealing their assets.
[19] Court document #6486.
[20] O'Donnell testimony, October 24, 2000.
[21] Sinclair testimony, October 5, 2000.
[22] Raines testimony, October 10, 2000.

CHAPTER EIGHT

[1] Interview with the author, December 6, 2000.
[2] Robinson provided a copy of this letter, as well as a letter received by him from a Midland Walwyn colleague in late 1994, while Robinson was living in Ireland. "I have taken the liberty of enclosing an article from the Financial Post," the colleague wrote, "which concerns a former Midland colleague whom you might recall with something less than affection. Bearing in mind that, even as I write, the allegations are far from proven, nevertheless they do serve as further evidence of the validity of your original, instinctive suspicions." The article dealt with police investigations of Holoday's broker activities, leading eventually to criminal charges brought against him.

CHAPTER NINE

[1] Transcript of interview between Tanya Sargent and Detective Gary Logan, November 27, 1995.
[2] R. Lang preliminary trial testimony, February 22, 1999.
[3] *American Banker Inc.* – Bond Buyer 1989 (Dow Jones Publications Library), p. 6.
[4] *American Banker Inc.* – Bond Buyer 1989.
[5] Court document #016698.
[6] Court document #016838.
[7] Court document #016689.
[8] Raines testimony, October 11, 2000.

[9] Transcript of interview between Tanya Sargent and Detective
   Gary Logan, November 27, 1995.
[10] Conversation with Jacques Soucie, January 21, 1998.
[11] Holoday related this tale to the author in November 1997,
   and others claim to have heard about the trip as well.
   No one, however, can confirm the story.
[12] Court document #015598.
[13] Court document #015577.
[14] Court document #015592.
[15] Transcript presented as evidence, October 23, 2000: "Easter
   Monday," p. 5.
[16] "Easter Monday," p. 7.
[17] Meaning Holoday and his assistant Chuck Oliver.
[18] Transcript provided as evidence, October 22, 2000, p. 8.
[19] Transcript provided as evidence, October 22, 2000, p. 14.
[20] Transcript provided as evidence, October 22, 2000, p. 15.
[21] Pseudonyms.
[22] "Roger Campbell" court testimony, October 2000.

CHAPTER TEN
[1] An excellent review of First Marathon's operating philosophy,
   where the "eat what you kill" philosophy is clearly delineated,
   was provided by journalist Jonathon Harris in "Running
   Scared" (*Canadian Business,* January 29, 1999).
[2] The free-wheeling spirit at First Marathon extended right up to
   the point where it was sold to National Bank of Canada in
   June 1999, when the TSE investigated allegations of insider
   trading at FM (*Report On Business,* June 19, 1999).
[3] The concept proved spectacularly successful and profitable for
   First Marathon, and a tribute to David Wood's design and
   administration; within three years, the correspondent network
   alone was handling $25 billion in securities annually on behalf
   of 50 firms and over 2000 registered representatives. SOURCE:
   First Marathon Annual Report, 1997.)
[4] Wood testimony, October 31, 2000.
[5] Wood testimony, October 31 and November 1, 2000.
[6] Court document #6483.
[7] Court document #6481.
[8] Court document #6518.
[9] Doney testimony, October 3, 2000.

¹⁰ Roberts' testimony, November 15, 2000.

¹¹ Holoday's original proposed name for his cigarette boat — he hand-painted it on the vessel's hull before its engines were installed — was *Northbridge,* showing it off to Roy O'Hearn during one of O'Hearn's weekend visits with Holoday at his rented cottage. Somewhere along the way, Holoday reconsidered and chose the less-provocative but no less ironic title of *Bad Company.*

¹² Conversation with the author, January 21, 1998.

¹³ Conversation with the author, February 27, 2000.

CHAPTER ELEVEN

¹ SOURCE: "The McAuley Report," Schedule 2, Court document #015440.

² Court document #023259.

³ SOURCE OF FIGURES: Forensic audit report prepared by James McAuley of KPMG Investigation and Security Inc. ("The McAuley Report") dated May 26, 1995, and submitted as evidence, October 2000.

⁴ Neither Oliver nor Ellis was charged in conjunction with their activities on behalf of Holoday, and only Oliver appeared at Holoday's criminal trial, as a witness for the defence.

⁵ Roberts testimony, November 15, 2000.

⁶ Holoday repaid the amount, plus $7,400 interest, in four payments to Roberts: $100,000 on October 14; $100,000 on January 11; $150,000 on January 24; and a final payment of $77,400 on January 25. SOURCE: "The McAuley Report."

⁷ A copy of Wood's letter, including the schedule of charges and fees, as well as a receipt for Holoday's US$108,000 T-bill filed as a deposit to cover Holoday's personal trades, is in the author's possession.

⁸ TSE Market Matters – Member Brokers…Your Link to the TSE.

⁹ Wood testimony, November 1, 2000.

¹⁰ Wood testimony, November 1, 2000.

¹¹ Wood testimony, November 1, 2000.

¹² Wood testimony, November 1, 2000.

¹³ Davidson testimony, November 2, 2000.

¹⁴ Thurman testimony, November 28, 2000.

¹⁵ Thurman testimony, November 28,2000.

¹⁶ Thurman testimony, November 28,2000.

CHAPTER TWELVE

1 Conversation with the author, November 21, 1997.
2 Court testimony, November 9, 2000.
3 Karp testimony, December 5, 2000.
4 For the record, the author attended both this reception and the Halloween party described later.
5 Conversation with the author, November 1997.
6 A pseudonym.
7 Court document #5217.
8 Conversation with the author, February 2001.
9 He did not, however, look after his suppliers nearly as well — the company providing the gifts claims it was never paid for them.
10 Conversation with the author, November 1997.
11 Conversation with the author, November 1997.
12 Holoday cannot seem to avoid any opportunity to exaggerate his status and boast of his connections; in an interview with the author, he boasted that he had purchased the land "directly from the Rothschild family."
13 Thurman testimony, November 28, 2000.
14 Sone testimony, November 30, 2000.
15 O'Donnell testimony. Ironically, this was one potential investment that might have made Holoday a wealthy man. Had he found $3 million to place with O'Donnell, the investment would have been worth $60 million two years later — a real-life return that matched some of the fictional returns Holoday was promoting to his clients.
16 Conversation with the author, February 2000.
17 Conversation with the author, February 2000.
18 O'Hearn preliminary hearing testimony, February 1999; trial, October 2000.

CHAPTER THIRTEEN

1 Court testimony, October 2000.
2 The house at 61 Park Lane Circle has a tragic history. In 1997 Irving Stern, despondent over losing his dream home, hanged himself. His widow Anne (who described the mansion as "very comfortable . . . but not overkill") was left destitute. The property sat vacant for three years after Stern's death and was finally placed on the market for $20 million in late 2000.

[3] They had several reasons to be concerned. The total flow
     through Michael and Maureen Holoday's personal chequing
     account for May 1994 exceeded $100 million dollars — more
     than $50 million in and over $50 million out within the same
     30-day period.

[4] Roberts testimony, November 16, 2000.

[5] Rentis testimony, October 23, 2000.

[6] SOURCE: Liu and Neill testimony, November 2000.

[7] Wood testimony, October 31, 2000.

[8] Roberts testimony, November 15, 2000.

[9] Tape transcripts submitted at trial.

[10] Rentis testimony, October 23, 2000.

[11] In addition, to service his debt to Doc and Elaine Roberts,
     Holoday also scrambled to settle the $1 million he owed
     Sheldon Fenton. Together, these debts to two wealthy clients
     drove Holoday to raid whatever assets his smaller clients still
     possessed. On page 20 of the Crown's Written Submissions and
     Closing Arguments, Brian McNeely stated: "In order to fund
     the balance due to BBRM (Fenton's company) and still make
     the payments needed to stall the Roberts, the accused,
     commencing on June 6, 1994, turned to his clients."

CHAPTER FOURTEEN

[1] Both stories are presented in books: Melnitzer's in his
     Maximum Minimum Medium (Key Porter Books); and
     Molony's in *Stung,* a record of Brian Molony's crimes
     written by Gary Ross (Stoddard).

[2] In Molony's case, the casualties included a few unfortunate
     CIBC branch employees whose only crime seems to have been
     working in close proximity to Molony and in total ignorance of
     his fraudulent activities. Their penalty was dismissal.

[3] Conversation with the author, January 1998.

[4] For a detailed description of Leeson's activities and the relative
     ease in which he achieved his deception, read *Rogue Trader*
     (Little, Brown and Company, 1996).

[5] Wood testimony, November 2, 2000.

[6] Named for Charles Ponzi, who in 1920 created a Boston-based
     company supposedly dealing in US postal reply coupons.
     Investors in his company, Ponzi promised, could earn 50 per-
     cent profit in 45 days. When early investors discovered this was
     true, word spread throughout the eastern US and within weeks

Ponzi had collected almost $10 million from over 10,000 eager investors. Ponzi was paying mature notes with funds taken from later investors who, of course, expected their 50 percent profits 45 days later. When the scheme inevitably collapsed, Ponzi was sentenced to a prison term, fled to South America, and eventually died there in poverty. His sole legacy was having his name attached to any fraud similar to the one he originally masterminded.

[7] Court document #015246.
[8] Simpkin testimony, October 18, 2000.
[9] Rentis testimony, October 23, 2000.
[10] Wood testimony, November 1, 2000.
[11] Court document #7212.
[12] A corporation owned by Holoday's client Sheldon Fenton.
[13] Court testimony and transcript exhibit, November 27, 2000.

CHAPTER FIFTEEN
[1] Crown documents #7124 and #7125.
[2] Randy Lang Document Brief, Volume III, Tab 5, pp. 3 and 4.
[3] Roberts testimony, November 16, 2000.
[4] Elaine Roberts sold the Ferrari for $72,000 at the end of August 1994.
[5] Randy Lang Document Brief, Volume II, Tab 7.
[6] Crown document #015257.
[7] The real reason for increasing the asset risk level was in response to Joe Thurman's directive to Holoday after the value of Schleith's trading account dropped so steeply.
[8] Titian's civil Statement of Claim.
[9] Thurman court testimony, November 28, 2000.
[10] A pseudonym.
[11] Court documents #019915 and #019916.
[12] Interview with the author, April 21, 1999.
[13] Interview with the Author, April 21, 1999.
[14] Paul Simpkin transcript, Tape D1, Side 1, September 15, 1994.
[15] Transcript submitted as evidence, November 23, 2000.
[16] Wood testimony, November 2, 2000.
[17] Submitted as Crown evidence, document #7120.
[18] "I called our lawyer, got some advice, and decided to choose October 7 as the official end of Holoday's [association with us]" – Wood testimony, November 2, 2000.

[19] Crown exhibit #48A, Tab 8, pp. 3 and 4.
[20] Paul Simpkin transcript, Tape D1, Side 2, October 6, 1994.
[21] Titian's civil Statement of Claim, p. 9.

CHAPTER SIXTEEN
[1] Conversation with the author, October 30, 1998.
[2] Conversation with the author, March 12, 2001.
[3] From Tape E1, Side 2, submitted as evidence at Holoday's trial, October 18, 2000.
[4] Transcript of Schleith interview with Gary Logan, February 8, 1995. Court documents #018844 to #018846.
[5] Transcript from Crown Exhibit 48A, Tab 12.
[6] Schleith transcript submitted as evidence: Bankers pp. #019049 to #019066.
[7] Conversation with the author, November 21, 1997.
[8] Court document #018253.
[9] Lang testimony, November 17, 2000.
[10] Elaine Roberts victim impact statement, read in court February 12, 2001.
[11] Fenton testimony, October 17, 2000.
[12] Interview with Roger and Debbie Gordon, April 21, 1999.
[13] First Marathon statements of defence against Margaret Raines, Martin Karp, and others.
[14] First Marathon statements of defence against Mona O'Hearn and others.
[15] Sones testimony, November 30, 2000.
[16] Conversation with the author, May 31, 2001.
[17] Affidavit filed by McCarthy, Tetrault on behalf of Maureen Holoday.
[18] A pseudonym.
[19] R. v. Michael Holoday, *Respondent's Omnibus Motion Record,* Tab 2, pp. 20 –21.
[20] First Marathon statement of defence against Margaret Raines (and others). Ontario Court of Justice (General Division) File No. 95-CQ-62990CM, p. 12 (and others).
[21] First Marathon statement of defence against Margaret Raines (and others). Ontario Court of Justice (General Division) File No. 95-CQ-62990CM, p. 11 (and others).
[22] Various civil trial submissions.
[23] Holoday pre-sentence report, February 22, 2001, p. 8.
[24] R. v. Holoday, *Respondent's Omnibus Motion Record,* Tab 2, p. 21

CHAPTER SEVENTEEN

1 Private investigation report dated January 27, 1999
   commissioned by J. L. Reynolds.
2 Conversation with J. Hoffman, March 20, 2001.
3 Conversation with the author, October 31, 1997.
4 Court documents dated October 21, 1999.
5 *Toronto Star,* "Court Poised to Rule on Holoday's Mansion,"
   July 28, 2000.
6 Conversation with the author, November 1997.
7 Conspicuous by her absence was Tracy Ellis, Holoday's assistant. According to the Crown, they feared she would at least
   attempt to speak more in defence of Holoday than testify
   against him. Her current residence, and her job status,
   if any, in the investment industry, is unknown.
8 Court testimony, December 6, 2000.
9 Holoday pre-sentence report, February 22, 2001, p. 4.
10 R. v. Michael Holoday, pre-sentence report, February 22, 2001.

CHAPTER EIGHTEEN

1 No one knows precisely how many clients were defrauded by
   Holoday, nor how much of their money he managed to obtain.
   Several of Holoday's clients who realized they had been
   swindled by him chose not to press civil charges for various
   reasons, including a demand for high retainer fees by some
   lawyers, and the clients' embarrassment at their naivety. The
   Crown, for its own reasons, chose not to press criminal charges
   on many of these cases. Their stories, and the losses they
   suffered, must be added to those included here.
2 From Gross's paper "Stockbroker Malpractice – New Issues
   Hitting the Street," November 1995.
3 *Contributing To Canada's Progress,* published by the IDA.
4 "How IDA Fails in Protecting Small Investors," *Globe and Mail,*
   December 3, 1998, p. B12.
5 Ontario Securities Commission, *A Changing Commission for a
   Changing Market,* 1997.
6 Conversation with the author, March 29, 2001.
7 Conversation with the author, March 29, 2001.
8 *Globe and Mail,* March 29, 2001, p. B6; and March 30, 2001, p. B1.
9 *Report On Business* magazine, July 2001, p. 162.
10 TSE pamphlet, "STRAIGHT TALK 1 — THE EXCHANGE."

[11] *Toronto Star,* February 6, 1998, p. B1.

[12] First Marathon was less reticent about the news. It was First Marathon who sent a news release trumpeting the TSE's "Not guilty" verdict to the *Star* in response to the newspaper's critical reports on the Holoday matter. The TSE apparently would have preferred that news of the decision remain confidential between it and the brokerage.

[13] *Toronto Star,* May 13, 2001.

[14] *Globe and Mail,* August 26, 1999, p. B4.

[15] *TSE Market Matters* ("Member Brokers . . . Your Link to the TSE"), September 9, 1997.

[16] Text from the memo appears on pp. 302–3.

[17] Joe Thurman retained his position as compliance officer when First Marathon was acquired by National Bank of Canada and renamed National Bank Financial. As of May 2001, he remained in that position, watching over the activities of financial advisors and working under the supervision of David Burnes, who originally hired Thurman for First Marathon. Chuck Oliver reportedly continues to act as a futures trader within the Canadian investment industry.

[18] *Toronto Star,* May 13, 2001, p. B1.

[19] First Marathon Statement of Defence v. Marlena Titian.

[20] *Toronto Star,* May 13, 2001, p. B1.

INDEX